# An Introduction to Park Management

## Third Edition

**Samuel V. Lankford**

**Jill Knowles -Lankford**

**Daniel A. Wheeler**

SAGAMORE
PUBLISHING

Publishers: Joseph J. Bannon/Peter Bannon
VP of Sales and Marketing: M. Douglas Sanders
Director of Development and Production: Susan M. Davis
Technology Manager: Christopher Thompson

Library of Congress Catalog Card Number: 2010940603
ISBN print edition: 978-157167- 578-1
ISBN ebook: 978-1-57167- 620-7
Printed in the United States.

10 9 8 7 6 5 4 3 2 1

Sagamore Publishing LLC
1807 N. Federal Dr.
Urbana, IL 61801
www.sagamorepub.com

# Contents

# *Acknowledgments*

Many people have influenced how we view parks and the role they play in our society. We would like to acknowledge Dr. Rolly Berger, Dr. Fred Brooks, and Dr. Bill Niepoth of California State University at Chico, who helped form and guide our early thinking about how parks and recreation can define our community through appropriate planning practices. We would also like to thank Dr. David Povey of the University of Oregon, who worked with us on refining our skills and abilities with regard to urban and regional planning practice by providing us with a unique graduate education experience through Community Planning Workshop. David's involvement in recreation and tourism planning in Oregon has provided us with a model for teaching, working with students and our communities in which we have lived. Dr. Larry Neal of the University of Oregon, for his positive encouragement and support over the years and for all the great travel to conduct consulting on parks and recreation. Dr. Chris Edginton has been instrumental in teaching us the role of parks and recreation from an historical and management perspective. Mr. Grey Hyde, for his insights into the planning of district parks, open space and management of these systems in Springfield, Oregon. We must recognize our dear friend, Hanalei Rozen, unending provider of information and inspiration regarding landscape interpretation. Our friends in Hawaii of the Hawaii Recreation and Park Association, specifically Joyce Sphoer and Willy Ching. Joyce and Willy have shaped the park system in Hawaii for future generations. Thanks to Dr. Ariana Cela, Dr. Oksana Grybovych, and Yuka Inui, who provided many interesting and exciting adventures in community research regarding parks and recreation issues. We would also like to thank Hannah Lang for research and photographs. What a great and accomplished group of professionals and visionaries. If only more communities had these leaders. We feel blessed to have had the opportunity to work with all of them.

We would also like to recognize Dr. Joseph Bannon. One of the most influential books that we read and used early in our careers was Joe Bannon's *Leisure Resources: Its Comprehensive Planning*. That book set the stage for planning and development of our parks in this country, and was a model for this book. We are grateful and honored that Joe Bannon asked us to revise this book. Joe's faith in our ability to complete this book, and his patience are greatly appreciated. We would also like to thank Doug Sanders and Susan Davis of Sagamore Publishing. Their guidance and patience are also very much appreciated. I am sure along the way they were wondering if this book would ever be finished! Thank you for your assistance and professionalism!

Sam and Jill Lankford

Thanks to my co-authors for this opportunity, and thanks to the people who have been my leaders and mentors for their enthusiasm and concern for wise use of our natural and scenic resources. I owe my enthusiasm to them.

Dan Wheeler

# *Preface*

The third edition of this book is intended for park professionals who need a reference book and university students who may have an interest in becoming employed in the parks profession. The book explores the responsibilities of staff and the problems and challenges associated with managing parks in the 21st century. Particular attention is paid to the structure of park organizations, planning, decision making, and politics that ultimately influence the way parks are managed.

Part One provides an overview of parks and park management. Historical aspects of the development of parks are reviewed and detailed. Part Two specifically addresses the multitude of park administrative functions, such as organizational structures, park policies, laws and risk management, funding, personnel, and concludes with maintenance and safety concerns. Part Three provides information on resource planning and management of the resources through citizen involvement, planning, facilities, and environmental management issues. Part Four is an overview of visitor use issues and protection of parks. Topics include visitor conflicts, vandalism, law enforcement, fire management, interpretation, and visitor management services. Finally, Part Five provides a broad overview and examples of sustainable practices in park management, including tools such as ROS, LAC, and VERP and possible solutions to the numerous challenges that park managers must address. It is our belief that sustainable management practices and planning practices designed with environmental management and visitor management are the keys to successful park operations.

This edition, based on the practical and sage advice of Grant W. Sharpe, Charles H. Odegaard, and Wenonah Finch Sharpe in the earlier editions of this book, continues to provide basic, clear, and meaningful examples for park managers and students. We have retained the essence of the material, and the broad topics that those authors provided as a framework for park management. Readers will note that some references are older. We retained references that have historical significance and have been overlooked in the current literature. Some of these ideas are currently accepted as common knowledge. We thought readers would benefit from the seeing the origin of ideas that have influenced park management. We have added throughout the book threads of sustainable park management principles and environmental management issues and tools where appropriate.

Samuel V. Lankford
Jill Knowles - Lankford
Daniel A. Wheeler

*Chapter One*

# An Overview of Park Management

The demand on outdoor recreation areas of every kind has been increasing faster than the supply of lands and facilities can accommodate. Budgets are perennially inadequate, and recreation land acquisition probably could not feasibly support all user demands or perceived "needs." As ecosystems within park lands deteriorate and visitor numbers and the types of uses they demand multiply, a fundamental shift in our approach to managing park lands is occurring. This shift requires moving from a perspective of serving diverse demands to one of "tending" a productive landscape within a regional context. How do we define and measure a productive landscape? How do we interpret and understand the regional context?

The last 50 years have provided a foundation for a shift in the interface between parks and society. This shift requires changes in park policy and management practices that recognize principles of sustainability and the benefits of ecosystem functions and services. Looking through this lens assists in defining "productive" landscapes to recognize present and future generations. This perspective, which includes future generations, those without voice, is a fundamental tenet of sustainability. Ecosystem functions are needed to purify air and water and provide the service of clean water and air. They are needed to detoxify and decompose wastes or moderate weather extremes for us and other life forms with which we share the planet and for future generations. This provides a platform to expand park policy to address more than the immediate needs or desires of a population that currently invests in the resource.

Inherent in many park lands is a suite of ecosystem functions and services that provide long-term benefits to society. This suite of services is often referred to as natural capital, capital that is difficult to ascribe economic value to and is typically undervalued. Ecosystem functions and services can be specific to a region and also contribute to global sustainability. The difficulty in ascribing a particular value is inherent in the difficulty in segregating functions and services. It is often the relationships between resources that provide service. The Millennium Ecosystem Assessment (2005 p. 155), a four-year United Nations assessment of the condition and trends of the world's ecosystems, categorizes ecosystem services as:

- **provisioning services,** or the provision of food, fresh water, fuel, fiber, and other goods;
- **regulating services,** such as climate, water, and disease regulation as well as pollination;
- **supporting services,** such as soil formation and nutrient cycling; and
- **cultural services** such as educational, aesthetic, and cultural heritage values as well as recreation and tourism (http://www.fs.fed.us/ecosystemservices/About_ES/index.shtml).

Our public landscape sits within a regional context with physical, social, cultural, and economic dimensions. A regional approach to landscape management is based on a genuine understanding of regional connections. Our public lands are not "island ecosystems," regardless the scale of the area. They are surrounded by a variety of land uses, such as agriculture or urbanized areas, which invariably influence the ecology of the park. Park managers must use an array of strategies to successfully steward the resources of a park and these strategies must reflect regional influences.

Ecotrust, a non-profit organization working with individuals, organizations, businesses, agencies, and tribes within the bioregion of the Pacific Northwest has created a model of "Reliable Prosperity," a term coined by the late Jane Jacobs. Reliable prosperity recognizes that equity, ecology, and economics are all important dimensions to prosperity. The model in Figure 1.1 illustrates the components of each dimension and provides a framework within which to define and measure a productive landscape. Ecotrust's mission is to inspire fresh thinking that creates economic opportunity, social equity, and environmental well-being.

In addition to the changes in stewardship, park management practice and agency responsibilities over the last 20 years, the U.S. has experienced great generational and cultural changes. These generational and cultural differences and preferences suggest changes in the way in which parks should be developed and managed. Table 1.1. demonstrates  recent research in California that suggests generational and cultural tendencies toward the use of parks in California. It is expected these trends will become more pronounced and influence how are parks are developed and managed.

### Figure 1.1. Model of Reliable Prosperity

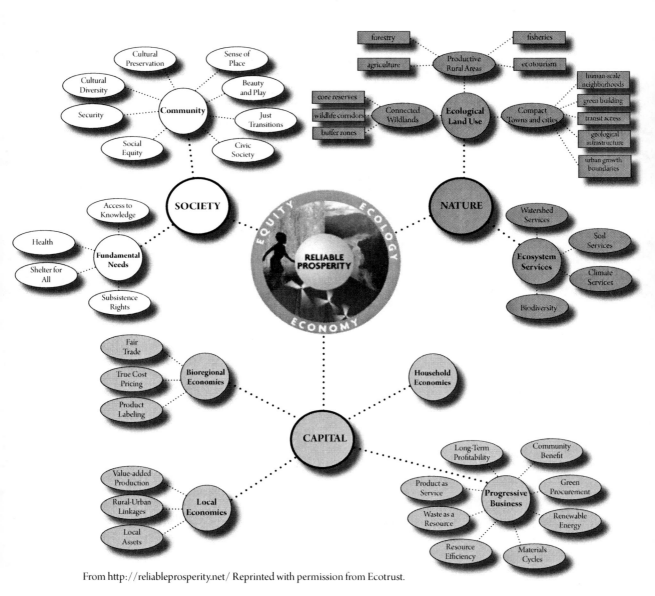

From http://reliableprosperity.net/ Reprinted with permission from Ecotrust.

**Table 1.1. Generational Characteristics of Boomers, GenXers, and Millennials and Park Use**

| Generational characteristic | Millennials | GenXers | Boomers |
|---|---|---|---|
| **Conventional or unconventional?** | Conventional | Unconventional | Unconventional |
| **What they seek outside home** | Entertainment, socializing with friends and family | High-intensity vacations (OHV parks, rock climbing) | Adventure outdoors in nature and unexplored areas |
| **Their ethnic diversity** | More diverse than Boomers, GenXers | More diverse than Boomers | Not very diverse |
| **What they value** | Fast-paced lifestyle with electronic tools; achievements | Spending time efficiently, fast-paced lifestyle; time with people | Spiritual enlightenment, experiences |
| **Where they like to live** | Urban areas | Urban areas | Rural areas |

From California State Parks, Planning Division, March 2010 Newsletter, based on Howe, Neil. (2009). Telephone and e-mail interviews with Recreation Section staff, March 26, 2009 and January 13, 2010. Retrieved from http://www.parks.ca.gov/pages/795/files/millennials%20final_03_08_10.pdf.

Public lands are an important piece in a regional approach to metropolitan design. Phil Lewis, a landscape architect and director of the Marshall Erdmand Academy of Sustainable Design in Madison, exemplifies this approach with the "Circle City" concept surrounding the Driftless Area, the majority of which is located in southwestern Wisconsin. The "Circle City" concept grew out of an analysis of the urban development pattern in the upper Midwest region in relation to the geology of the region. The urban centers of Chicago; Milwaukee and Madison; Minneapolis and St. Paul; and Mason City, Cedar Rapids, Davenport in Iowa, create an urbanized ring around the Driftless Area, the only preglacial landscape in the upper Midwest. Lewis describes how this landscape form, which the glaciers moved around, can serve as a "central park" to a metropolitan ring.

This regional approach is occurring at many scales from the municipal watershed park planning efforts of Woodlands Texas to the efforts of the Peace Park Foundation working toward a network of protected areas that link ecosystems across international borders. There are 32 Peace Parks established on the African continent in an effort to support centuries-old migration routes that support diverse and healthy populations of large mammals—elephants, lions, giraffes, rhinoceros, and the multitude of large game with whom the African people share the continent.

Regional landscape management is not a modern invention. Indigenous people have practiced resource management or actually tended the landscape for millennia. Their practices encouraged productivity of the materials needed to support their lives. Management practices, including burning, pruning and coppicing, sowing, transplanting, tilling, weeding, and selective harvesting created highly productive landscapes in California. As Kat Anderson notes in *Tending the Wild*, this abundance was hard earned; a product of careful observation, experimentation, and a long-term relationship with the plants and animals of a region. This knowledge, relationship, and resulting abundance was not unique to California but was similarly expressed in many landscapes throughout the world.

Park managers must understand the resources being managed and be able to answer fundamental questions about that resource. What is the ecological value of the park within the regional landscape? What is the historic and cultural value of the park within the current social context? What role does the park play to the local economy? Addressing these questions enables managers to address issues of sustainability and formulate policy, partnerships, education and interpretive programs, volunteer programs, and maintenance practices that work toward a coordinated effort to effectively steward park resources. This chapter provides a brief background of the historical context through which parks developed and the development of park management as a discipline.

## WHAT IS A PARK?

Each person carries his or her own image of what the word *park* means based on personal experience. The word *park* eludes precise definition because it has so many uses. Historically, a park has meant such diverse things as a place to bathe, a hunting preserve, a formal garden, places decorated with statuary, a tournament field, an estate of the nobility, an exhibition site for theaters and other entertainment, a common space for tethering livestock prior to bartering, and, in some countries, a place for exercising, walking, and nature viewing. Today we even hear the word used in connection with nonrecreational uses. A cluster of industrial buildings may be called an industrial park, or a cemetery may be referred to as a mortuary park. Park, in the context of this book, is a generic term we used for all recreational lands.

Parks come in all shapes and sizes and have a variety of names. What is known as a park in one location may be known as a recreation area in another. Other names include the more formal designations of parkways, greenways, monuments, and historic sites. There are also designations for parks indicating the governmental level administrating the area, such as neighborhood and community parks, metropolitan parks, county parks, regional parks, state and provincial parks, interstate parks, national-capital parks, national parks, and international parks.

Sometimes names of parks indicate their predominant purpose, feature, or activity, such as wildlife parks, motorcycle parks, tree farm parks, boat parks, ball parks, and museum parks.

Parks commonly accommodate a range of outdoor recreation activities from organized sports to bird watching. Often, recreation professionals categorize parks based on the types of activities supported. Categorizing parks by use narrows the management focus but also minimizes a more holistic approach to park management. Two common categories used to describe recreation areas are activity-oriented structured recreation, or resource-oriented nonstructured recreation. However, one does not necessarily preclude the other. The inclusion of activities in a park is largely a function of size or acreage, proximity to an urban population, and the size of that population. Historical, cultural, and natural features or conditions also determine the way in which a park is developed. The Blueberry Park master plan (Figure 1.2 ) illustrates a range of activity-oriented facilities such as the play area with equipment and play fields while retaining historic features such as the blueberry patch and restoring natural features such as the wetland area. This park also illustrates a number of low impact development features such as the porous paving for parking drained to rain gardens to address storm water run-off.

Activity-oriented, structured recreation relies on specialized facilities that are typically located in urban or suburban parks such as playfields, courts, or swimming pools. These facilities support a mix of indoor and outdoor recreation activities, including various sports, games, arts, and crafts. They generally require the supervisory or instructional services of park personnel. Even when they do not, there is an organized formal structure imposed by the facility and specific rules that characterize this kind of recreation; tennis and horseshoes are two examples. Some spectator sports, such as baseball and soccer at the amateur level, may also be accommodated in these park areas.

## Figure 1.2. Blueberry Park Master Plan

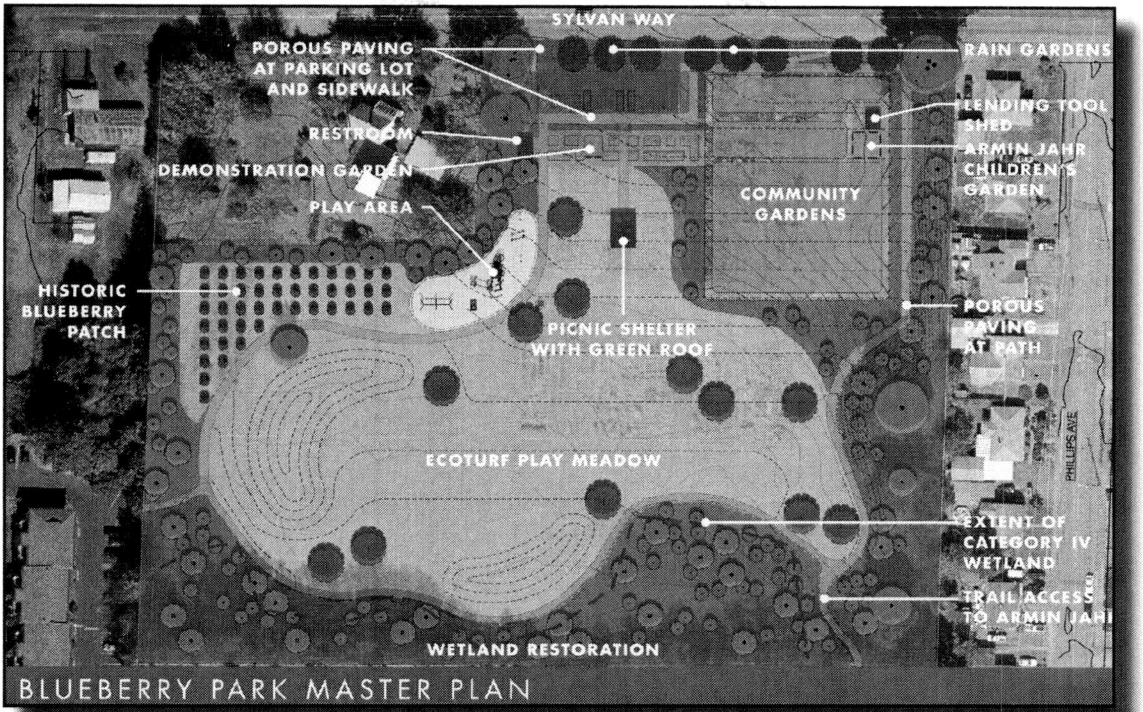

From City of Bremerton Parks and Recreation Department Blueberry Park Masterplan, 2008. Reprinted with permission.

In 1987, the President's Commission on Americans Outdoors inventoried municipal and regional parks. There were approximately 67,700 local or municipal parks containing 3,000,000 acres, 17,000 county parks containing over 5,000,000 acres, and 2,780 regional parks containing 500,000 acres in the United States primarily oriented toward urban recreation (President's Commission on Americans Outdoors, 1987).

Resource-oriented nonstructured recreation typically relies on a particular natural resource or a combination of natural resources that may include lakes, rivers, seashores, meadows, deserts, forests, hills, and mountains. These land or water resources shape the type of activities pursued, and park personnel function primarily as safety-conscious hosts and guardians of the resources. The term outdoor recreation is commonly used to describe this category also. In contrast to the urban or suburban location of game- or activity-oriented recreation, this sort of recreation is most often found at some distance from population concentrations. However, some cities have either historically been endowed or recently acquired large tracts of relatively unmodified areas. These areas are often structured by landscape features such as rivers or streams, ridgelines, buttes, or dunes. Bidwell Park, a 3,618-acre municipal park in Chico, California, was given to the city by the founding family in 1905.

This text addresses resource-oriented outdoor recreation management. The lands that support these pursuits are usually managed by some government agency—metropolitan, county, provincial, state, or federal. The areas dealt with here may be known as beaches, reserves, scenic areas, forests, refuges, natural areas, parks, cultural sites, or recreation areas.

## MISSION OF THE FEDERAL LAND MANAGEMENT AGENCIES IN THE U.S.

**The Mission of the Bureau of Land Management** is to sustain the health, diversity, and productivity of the Nation's public lands for the use and enjoyment of present and future generations.

**The Mission of the Fish and Wildlife Service** is to conserve, protect, and enhance fish and wildlife and their habitats for the continuing benefit of the American people.

**The Mission of the National Park Service** is to preserve, unimpaired, the natural and cultural resources and values of the national park system for the enjoyment, education and inspiration of this and future generations. The NPS cooperates with partners to extend the benefits of natural and cultural resource conservation and outdoor recreation throughout this country and the world.

**The Mission of the Forest Service** is to sustain the health, diversity, and productivity of the Nation's forests and grasslands to meet the needs of present and future generations.

The following three conservation objectives, stemming from the Department of Interior's Strategic Plan (FY 2003-2008), outline the mission responsibilities and ultimate conservation objectives of the various agencies (USFS, BLM, FWS, NPS). These conservation objectives are as follows (DOI-USDA, 2005):

1.  Resource Protection—Protect the Nation's natural, cultural, and heritage resources;
2.  Recreation—Provide recreation opportunities for America; and
3.  Serving Communities—Safeguard lives, property and assets, advance scientific knowledge, and improve the quality of life for communities served.

The **Bureau of Land Management** manages about one-eighth of the total land in the United States. In the Federal Land Policy and Management Act of 1976 (Public Law 94-579), Congress recognized the value of the public lands by declaring that these lands would generally remain in long-term public ownership and recognized the importance of the multiple-use management of these public lands. Acres currently managed by the Bureau of Land Management was 262 million acres in 2009, which is a reduction of 75 million acres since 1987 due to exchanges and sales. The BLM also manages 700 million acres of Federal surface ownerships and privately owned surface for minerals and mining located in special management units.

Figure 1.3 shows a breakdown of percentage of land managed by these agencies in the United States and Table 1.2 shows the details of land managed by the Bureau of Land Management.

## Figure 1.3. Percentage of Land Managed by Agency in the U.S.

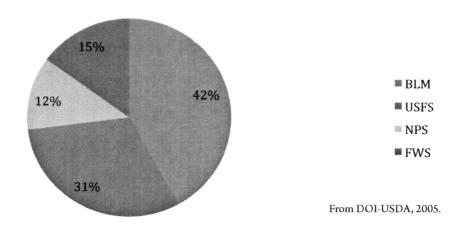

From DOI-USDA, 2005.

### Table 1.2. Type, Number, and Size of Area Managed by BLM

| BLM Special Management Area | No. of Units | Area / Distance |
|---|---|---|
| National Monuments | 15 | 4,806,947 acres |
| National Conservation Areas | 13 | 13,976,146 acres |
| Wilderness Areas | 161 | 6,515,287 acres |
| Wilderness Study Areas | 604 | 15,566,656 acres |
| National Wild & Scenic Rivers | 38 | 1,005,652 acres |
| ACEC Areas | 907 | 12,939,368 acres |
| National Natural Landmarks | 45 | 417,429 acres |
| Research Natural Areas | 184 | 426,566 acres |
| Herd Management Areas | 206 | 29,649,100 acres |
| National Historic Trails | 10 | 4,563 miles |
| National Scenic Trails | 2 | 640 miles |
| National Recreation Trails | 29 | 441 miles |
| National Backcountry Byways | 56 | 3,028 miles |

The **U.S. Fish and Wildlife Service** manages migratory bird populations, restores interjurisdictional fisheries, conserves and restores wildlife habitat, administers the Endangered Species Act (P.L. 93-205), and assists foreign governments with their conservation efforts. Itslands provide essential habitat for numerous wildlife species, recreational opportunities for the public, and a variety of benefits to local communities. FWS manages 96 million acres.

The **National Park Service** manages land in accordance with the individual unit's mission and goals, and provide visitor access where appropriate for education and recreation purposes. Over the past ten years, 25 new units have been established by Congress. These range from the Flight 93 National Memorial to the Cedar Creek and Belle Grove National Historical Park.

The National Park Service manages over 192 million acres of lands, which is an increase of 16 million acres since 1987 (President's Commission on Americans Outdoors, 1987). However, there are a number of ways in which these acres are considered. The DOI-USDA (2005) report to congress on acquisition reports 192 million acres. The 2000-2010 National Park Service Statistical Abstracts (2009) report 79,706,435 million acres under direct management. When adding the non-federal lands to the management system (restrictions, deeds, leases etc.) we see a figure of 84,378,872 million acres under NPS management. Assuming that there are currently 79, 706, 435 million acres under management, that is only an increase of 3 million acres in the last 23 years (since 1987). Table 1.3 shows the details of land managed by the National Park Service.

### Table 1.3. Type, Number, and Size of Area Managed by NPS

| NPS Land Classification | Number | Acres |
|---|---|---|
| National Battlefield National Battlefield Park, National Military Park, and National Battlefield Site | 24 | 71,502.49 |
| National Historical Park National Historic Site, and International Historic Site | 123 | 211,260.60 |

**Table 1.3. cont.**

| NPS Land Classification | Number | Acres |
|---|---|---|
| National Lakeshore | 4 | 228,995.14 |
| National Memorial | 27 | 10,588.45 |
| National Monument | 74 | 2,027,864.58 |
| National Park | 58 | 52,095,045.71 |
| National Parkway | 4 | 177,339.69 |
| **NPS Land Classification** | **Number** | **Acres** |
| National Preserve and Reserve | 20 | 24,191,311.63 |
| National Recreation Area | 18 | 3,700,277.20 |
| National River and National Wild and Scenic River and Riverways | 15 | 746,262.99 |
| National Scenic Trail | 3 | 239,659.27 |
| National Seashore | 10 | 595,013.55 |
| Other Designations (National Mall And others) | 11 | 36,826.96 |
| **TOTALS** | **391** | **44,331,948.26** |

The National Park Service had 285,579,941 million visits in 2009 (National Park Service, 2010) to all of the 17 sites managed by the Park Service. National parks alone accounted for over 62 million of these visitations, which is 22% of the total. National Recreation Areas accounts for 18% of the total visits at over 50 million visits, The National Memorials had 11% of the visits (over 30 million visits), followed by the National Historical Sites with 10% (over 28 million visits). Figure 1.4 presents the use by unit administered (National Park Service, 2009).

**Figure 1.4. Percent Visits to NPS Unit**

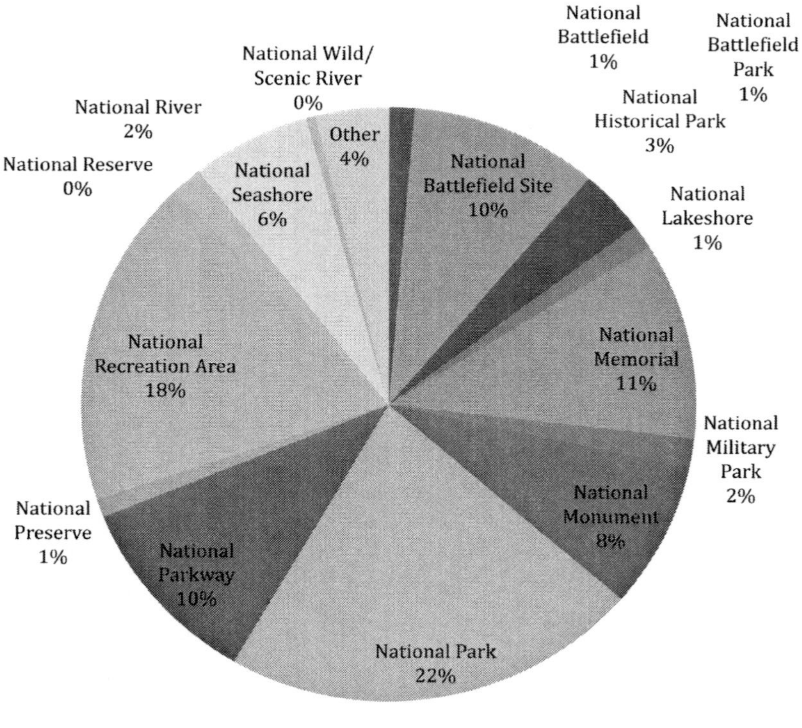

The **U.S. Forest Service** manages over 192.4 million acres of lands (see Tables 1.4 and 1.5). The purposes of National Forests have been set out in various Acts, beginning with the Organic Act of 1898 (P.L. 84-979),which established four basic purposes of Forest Reserves (now called National Forests):

1. Improve and protect the forests;
2. Secure favorable conditions of water flows;
3. Furnish a continuous supply of timber; and
4. Open the Forest Reserves for development and use.

Other legislation broadened the mission for the FS by providing for:

* Acquisition of lands needed for the regulation of water flow of navigable streams or for the production of timber;
* Establishment and administration for outdoor recreation, range, timber, watershed, and wildlife and fish purposes;
* Multiple uses in the combination that will best meet the needs of the American people;
* Control of soil erosion, reforestation, preservation of natural resources, protection of fish and wildlife, development and protection of recreational facilities, mitigation of floods, prevention of impairment of dams and reservoirs, development of energy resources, conservation of surface and subsurface moisture, protection of the watersheds of navigable streams, and protection of the public lands health, safety and welfare. The following presents the type of system, number of units, acres controlled (DOI-UDSA, 2005).

### Table 1.4. Type, Number and Size of Area Managed by NFS

| National Forest System | No. of Units | Area (acres) | Acres not Administered by NFS within boundaries (inholdings) |
|---|---|---|---|
| National Forests* | 155 | 187,811,680 | 37,654,870 |
| Purchase Units | 59 | 361,688 | 1,879,606 |
| National Grasslands | 20 | 3,839,174 | 425,489 |
| Land Utilization Projects | 6 | 1,876 | |
| Research and Experimental Areas | 20 | 64,871 | 8,283 |
| Other Areas | 34 | 295,814 | 592 |
| National Preserves | 1 | 89,716 | |
| **TOTAL** | **295** | **192,464,819** | **39,968,840** |

Note: Included in the National Forest System acreages above are a significant number of Congressionally established Special Designated areas. These areas are identified in Table 1.5.

**Table 1.5. Type, Number, and Size of Special Designated Areas Managed by NFS**

| Special Designated Areas within National Forests | No. of Units | Area (acres) | Acres not Administered by NFS within boundaries (inholdings) |
|---|---|---|---|
| Wilderness Areas | 420 | 34,752,767 | 452,200 |
| National Primitive Area | 1 | 173,762 | 1,350 |
| National Scenic Areas | 4 | 130,435 | 166,600 |
| National Wild, Scenic & Recreation Rivers | 45 | 946,321 | 251,530 |
| TOTAL | 470 | 36,003,285 | 871,680 |

## Other Park and Recreation-Related Federal Agencies

Bureau of Reclamation has 289 areas with recreation facilities, with over 90 million visits annually. These visitors contribute $6 billion a year to the economy and support 27,000 jobs. The Bureau manages 6.5 million acres of land and water. Some Reclamation project areas do not have developed recreation facilities for public use; however, dispersed recreational opportunities such as hiking, photography, wildlife viewing, and hunting may be available. Reclamation is limited by the Federal Water Project Recreation Act of 1965, Public Law 89-72 to providing only "minimum basic" facilities. Only a limited number of Reclamation-managed projects have site-specific authority to fully plan, develop, and manage recreation facilities and improvements on its lands. Eighty-four (84) of the 289 developed recreation areas are managed by another Federal agency under an agreement with Reclamation. This includes agreements that have been entered into with federally recognized Indian Tribes. In many instances, these agreements are accompanied with specific Congressional legislation that authorizes another Federal agency to manage recreation and other land resources at a Reclamation water project using their respective rules and regulations. These areas are managed by the National Park Service (NPS), U.S. Forest Service (USFS), Bureau of Land Management, or the U.S. Fish and Wildlife Service (FWS). Other partners include Bureau of Indian Affairs, local and state governments.

**U.S. Army Corps of Engineers** had over 370 million visitors in 2010 at at 4,300 recreation areas across the nation. The lakes and parks include: over 100,000 campsites, 2,100 miles of trails, and provides 33 percent of all freshwater lake fishing in the United States at 456 lakes in 43 states (U.S. Army Corps of Engineers, 2010). The vision of the Corps' Recreation Program is to plan and manage quality outdoor recreation opportunities in a safe and healthful manner for diverse populations on a sustainable basis resulting in benefits to individuals, communities, the environment and the economy. The mission of the U.S. Army Corps of Engineers is as follows (U.S. Army Corps of Engineers, 2010):

*The Army Corps of Engineers is the steward of the lands and waters at Corps water resources projects. Its Natural Resource Management Mission is to manage and conserve those natural resources, consistent with ecosystem management principles, while providing quality public outdoor recreation experiences to serve the needs of present and future generations.*

*In all aspects of natural and cultural resources management, the Corps promotes aware-ness of environmental values and adheres to sound environmental stewardship, protection, compliance and restoration practices.*

*The Corps manages for long-term public access to, and use of, the natural resources in cooperation with other Federal, State, and local agencies as well as the private sector.*

*The Corps integrates the management of diverse natural resource components such as fish, wildlife, forests, wetlands, grasslands, soil, air, and water with the provision of public recreation opportunities. The Corps conserves natural resources and provides public recreation opportunities that contribute to the quality of American life.*

## America's State Parks

Fifty states have state parks, with over 6,000 units and more than 725 million visits to these parks (see Table 1.6).

### Table 1.6.  Facts About America's State Parks

| | |
|---|---|
| Total Park Visits: | More than 725 million per year |
| Number of state park units: | 6,624 |
| Total economic impact on communities: | More than $20 billion |
| Percent of visitors with children: | 64% |
| Miles of trails: | 41,725 |
| Number of campsites: | 207,063 |
| Number of cabins and lodges: | 7,161 |

From http://www.naspd.org/, retrieved December 14, 2010 National Association of State Park Directors.

In the context of this book, parks are tracts of tax-supported land and water established primarily for the benefit and enjoyment of the public and maintained for the integrity of its natural systems to the benefit of future generations. All lands used for outdoor recreation, whether they are classified as forest, refuge, or in some other way, will be termed parks.

The use of the word *park* can also be a policy matter. The Forest Service, in the U.S. Department of Agriculture, administers almost 193 million acres of land and annually provides over 170 million visitors with recreational opportunities, but it does not use the word *park*. It uses terms such as forest campgrounds and natural areas, but these areas could be classified as parks, and indeed this is what they are frequently called by visitors.

The focus of this text will be on the middle—state (United States) or provincial (Canada) parks—as representatives of the spectrum from national to local. *Visitors* and *users* are the terms we will use for the people who come to parks, those who own them, who love them, and who, if not carefully directed, might well destroy them. Throughout this book, the term *manager* represents the person in charge of the park, thus making it synonymous with superintendent, supervisor, chief, director, ranger, warden, and park attendant.

Parks, especially national parks, may have begun as an effort to prevent private exploitation, as a way of showing our European critics that we in North America had a sense of national identity, or as a lure for tourists. But the rationale behind the creation and maintenance of parks represents more than the sum of these. Parks, especially if the entire spectrum of resource-oriented park lands is considered, have become the focus of even more complicated desires and emotions; however, these are difficult to define with any degree of precision. Again, each person has his or her own perception of a park. Some might say, "Parks are places to play." Others might say, "Parks are everybody's inheritance of intact ecosystems," or "They're a place to get away, a refuge." Playgrounds, historical repositories, sanctuaries, the evolving park idea encompasses and exceeds all of these definitions.

Of course, the definition also depends on the size and location of the park. Local picnicking grounds evoke a different response than do Yellowstone and Banff. On the other hand, if a family lives near a national park, they regard it as a "local park" no matter if it is a place frequented by national and international visitors. Park access, whether local or international, and the uses introduced through that access, will influence park management.

## WHAT IS PARK MANAGEMENT?

Management of a resource-oriented park means, among other things, providing safe access for visitors while protecting the resource. In some parks or areas of parks, access is intentionally denied to limit disturbance. Often, areas of parks are intensively developed to concentrate visitor use to a specific area with a higher capacity for use. Some visitors will occasionally want to use parks in a way that depreciates values, while others will sometimes urge protection to a degree that preempts legitimate use. Policies on use and protection may be formulated at agency headquarters, but the manager is on site and must interpret and enforce the policies to the current investors in the park— the taxpaying public. Just as each person carries a unique perception of a park, each individual also holds a unique perception of how a park should be managed. Accordingly, assumptions regarding appropriate use and appropriate management often lead to problems for park managers. Some of these assumptions are based on "historic" use. Historic use might represent 30 years or it might represent 3,000 years. Invariably there are differences between time frames.

### Origins of Park Management—The Yosemite Grant

Preserving large tracts of land from private exploitation and recognizing the scenic and recreation value for public benefit provides the foundation for national and state parks in North America. This foundation is nearly 150 years old if we equate its genesis with the establishment of the Yosemite Grant in California in 1864. This grant included two separate areas in the Sierra Nevada Mountain Range: Yosemite Valley with its spectacular granite walls and waterfalls, and the nearby Mariposa Grove of Big Trees. The grant contained the first extensive area of "wild" land to be set aside primarily for the nonutilitarian purpose of public recreation and enjoyment of scenery. This land was considered worthless with only three percent of the tract that could be "cultivated." Although the land initially was in federal ownership, the federal government had no policy on outdoor recreation matters, so protection of the land was transferred to the state of California. This land thus became the first state park in the United States.

> ... the said State shall accept this grant upon the express conditions that the premises shall be held for public use, resort, and recreation; shall be inalienable for all time.

Frederick Law Olmsted, who was working at the time near Yosemite Valley, chaired the board of commissioners of the Yosemite Grant. The board asked Olmsted to prepare a report defining the policy that should govern management of the grant and make recommendations for its implementation. This report would be distributed to the California legislature. Olmsted, who had previously collaborated with Calvert Vaux on the design of Central Park, extended the principles applied to Central Park to the designation and management of Yosemite. These principles addressed access, that all classes should be afforded the opportunity to enjoy the scenic beauty of the area in perpetuity. "The establishment by government of great public grounds for the free enjoyment of the people under certain circumstances, is thus justified and enforced as a political duty." Above all, Olmsted underscored the "preservation and maintenance as exactly as is possible of the natural scenery" as the most important asset available to the public. He forewarned of the impacts of visitor use over time.

What many did not realize was that this "natural scenery," imagined as a great wilderness, was largely a tended landscape that had been managed for productive harvests for hundreds of years. Galen Clark, also a member of the board of commissioners for the Yosemite Grant, was appointed the first "guardian" of the grant. He recognized how management practices of the native tribes shaped the landscape and influenced productivity and the scenery. Ten years after his tenure as guardian, Clark wrote to the commissioners of Yosemite Valley:

> My first visit to Yosemite was in the summer of 1855. At that time, there was no undergrowth of young trees to obstruct clear, open views in any part of the Valley from one side of the Merced River across to the base of the opposite wall. The area of clear, open meadow ground, with abundance of luxuriant native grasses and flowering plants was at least four times as large as at the present time. The Valley had then been exclusively under the care and management of the Indians, probably for many centuries. Their policy of management for their own protection and self-interests, as told by some of the survivors who were boys when the Valley was first visited by whites in 1851, was to annually start fires in the dry season of the year and let them spread over the whole valley to kill young trees just sprouted and keep the forest groves open and clear of all underbrush, also as to have no obscure thickets for a hiding place, or an ambush for any invading hostile foes, and to have clear grounds for hunting and gathering acorns. When the fires did not thoroughly burn over the moist meadows, all the young willows and cottonwoods were pulled up by hand. ... Since Yosemite has been under the care of the State of California, it was for many years the policy of its manager to protect the Valley as much as possible from the ravages of fires and to preserve all the young trees from destruction. This constant vigilant care for the preservation of Yosemite has resulted in the whole Valley being overrun with dense thickets of young forest trees, shrubbery and underbrush, and an accumulation of a vast amount of highly combustible material, which in the event of accidental fires, is a fearful menace to the safety of property and the beauty of the landscape scenery...

Galen's letter demonstrates the relatively short period of time for both the memory and the actual appearance of a landscape to change. Galen's letter also exemplifies the lack of understanding between management practice, productivity, and appearance, and yet the scenery was the motivating force behind preservation. Linda Greene, in the historic resource study, *Yosemite: The Park and its Resources,* notes that the boundaries specified to preserve the Mariposa Grove of Giant Sequoia were based on scenic qualities rather than an ecological framework (Green, 1987).

There were some difficulties from the start. The twin problems of inadequate funding and ill-defined policy made intelligent management of the two units impossible. The California state legislature voted little money for facilities and often neglected to appropriate Galen Clark's $500 per year salary. When in 1890, a larger encompassing area was set aside as Yosemite National Park, local communities complained bitterly as many new inholdings were created.

In 1891, the U.S. Cavalry was dispatched to protect the newly established Yosemite National Park lands and the two original units of the Yosemite Grant. Early park management problems included dealing with the ranchers outside the park. Cavalry troopers sought to keep livestock out of the new park. Ranchers had been running cattle and sheep there since pioneer days, and now the park was off limits to them. When the first intruders were taken into custody, it was found there were no penalties for the infraction of park rules, so each herder was escorted to a remote section of the park and released; his sheep at the same time were driven out of the park in the opposite direction. By the time the herder located his animals, the losses were as great or greater than if a fine had been imposed. After several years of this practice, the ranchers learned to keep their stock out of the park (Russell, 1947). The troopers left each year in November and returned in May, being replaced during the winter by civilian rangers, such as Galen Clark. By 1914, with the permanent withdrawal of the cavalry, the park rangers or guardians carried on the work of protection.

## Yellowstone National Park

The first direct federal involvement in the management of a park in the United States started after the establishment of Yellowstone National Park in 1872. Starting around 1800 and continuing over a period of 70 years, fur traders and other parties noted the unusual beauty of the Yellowstone region. Before a bill could be passed, however, Congress had to be convinced that this area of public domain did not have economic potential (mineral wealth) and therefore could be set aside as a "public park or pleasuring ground" because of its geysers, waterfalls, and canyons. There was no state to turn the land over to in this instance, because the area was in Wyoming Territory. The chief proponents of the park were for the most part residents of the territory of Montana who wanted legislation formed along the lines of the Yosemite Grant. Unfortunately for them, the land lay in Wyoming Territory rather than in Montana Territory and was thus politically out of reach. Also, because California was having difficulty administering the Yosemite Grant, Congress was convinced federal ownership was best for Yellowstone. The bill was similar in many ways to the bill establishing the Yosemite Grant. Beyond the fact of setting the land aside, the legislation left much to be desired.

The area was reserved "from settlement, occupancy, or sale under the laws of the United States, and dedicated and set apart as a public park or pleasuring ground for the benefit and enjoyment of the people." The regulations provided "for the preservation from injury or spoilage of all timber, mineral deposits, natural curiosities, or wonders within the said park, and their retention in their natural condition" (S. 392 42nd Congress). The money for management and enforcement needed to protect this area was completely lacking. Unfortunately, in order to get the park established, a promise had to be made not to ask Congress for an appropriation for several years. Thus, the park was established without funds to protect it (a dilemma that was to become familiar in parks throughout all agency levels); but at least a beginning had been made. Despite its shortcomings, the Yellowstone Act would one day become a matter of great pride for Americans and would, in time, bring international acclaim and respect to the United States for its leadership in establishing the world's first national park.

In order for Yellowstone to gain recognition as an area worthy of park status at a time when exploitation was unquestioned on frontier lands, its splendors were well publicized in newspapers and magazines. Consequently, soon after it was established, visitors began to arrive, although there was no official provision made for them. The scenic wonders and chance to bathe in the hot mineral springs (then thought medically effective for a variety of ailments) drew as many as 500 people a year between 1873 and 1877.

Trappers and hunters, who had been using the area for some time, continued their activities because no management restraints were possible. Hide hunters in one spring killed an estimated 4,000 elk in the vicinity of Mammoth Hot Springs (Haines, 1977). Bison heads, selling for $300 each, were being collected in the park. Early park visitors, not able to bring all their supplies with them were living off the land by shooting wildlife. Stagecoaches were held up by robbers. Cattle were driven into the park for grazing. Hostile Native Americans were encountered by visitors. Squatters moved into the park to stake claims and take up residence. Soap was poured into the thermal springs to induce eruptions. Anything loose was thrown into the geysers to see how high it would be ejected during the next eruption. Specimens of encrustations from the hot springs were collected for souvenirs. As the Suttons point out, an entire geyser cone was removed and placed on display at the Smithsonian Institution in Washington, D.C. (Sutton & Sutton, 1972).

The first superintendent of Yellowstone, Nathaniel P. Langford, was expected to work without a salary. Without funds, there was no staff, and without a staff, no law enforcement. Mr. Langford was forced to be an absentee administrator, visiting the park only twice during his five years as superintendent. In any case, what could one person do to oversee and protect a mountainous area three times the size of the state of Rhode Island?

Private enterprise provided rough transportation and spartan quarters, but Langford refused to grant road rights until Congress could be induced to establish concession and entry policies. The vandalism in the hot springs area, as well as the slaughter of the game, drew comment. The publicity thus generated exerted pressure on Congress.

An appropriation of $10,000 was made in 1877, but to do what? Park personnel had no authority to make an arrest, to punish, or to evict anyone from the park (Sutton & Sutton, 1972). The Interior Department eventually asked Wyoming Territory to administer the area, but this arrangement was short lived. Pressures to build a railroad across the park and to open the park to mining increased. Wildlife and timber were still being removed illegally from the park. Later superintendents abused their office by attempting to obtain land within the park for their own use. The funds that were appropriated could not begin to solve the problems of distance, isolation, and established use. In desperation, the Secretary of the Interior turned to the Secretary of War for assistance.

The park was finally placed under the protection of the U.S. Army, whose cavalry and engineers successfully managed it from 1885 to 1918, putting an end to the illegal uses of the park. The soldiers were able to enforce the regulations and alter the habits of those who felt free to take what they wanted. "They removed squatters, captured lawbreakers, hunted down poachers, burned illegal dwellings, and confiscated guns and traps." As noted earlier, Yosemite's problems with illegal grazing and poaching were cured in the same manner. It took "armed intervention" to establish park management in our first national park.

Yellowstone was the first national park, but it is now generally accepted that the Yosemite Grant played a very strong role in the establishment of Yellowstone National Park. Yosemite's publicity and fame helped secure public acceptance for later setting aside large areas of federal land for public recreation. We see this in the following account by Russell. Although Yellowstone became the first national park by name, the ". . .concept that there are places of beauty and of scientific interest which individuals or private interests have no right to appropriate onto themselves, began with the establishment of the Yosemite Grant" (Russell 1964).

Huth echoed these sentiments when he wrote:

Contrary to the usual assumption, it was not the establishment of Yellowstone but rather the setting apart of the Yosemite which was preeminent in the basic conditioning of opinion. Yosemite is the point of departure from which a new idea began to gain momentum (Huth, 1945).

## The Canadian Experience

Following the reservation of Yosemite as a state park and Yellowstone as a national park, the movement spread rapidly. In 1885, Canada established a 10-square-mile reserve around the hot springs at Banff in Alberta and named it Rocky Mountain National Park (later renamed Banff National Park).

The creation of a scenic recreational area and a wildlife sanctuary at Banff was not envisioned by the Canadian government at that time. Parliament and party leaders saw the hot mineral springs at Banff as a source of revenue, a way to bring passengers onto the Canadian Pacific Railway (CPR). The CPR was deeply involved with the Canadian government in attempting to tie the western lands to the rest of Canada, and there was a strong desire to make the mountain section "pay." The prospect of a drawing card rivaling the Hot Springs Reserve in Arkansas was welcome in both quarters. The Banff mineral springs, discovered by railway employees, was envisioned as a national sanitarium of "sanitary advantage" to the public for the treatment of rheumatism and other ailments. Traveling to spas was an occupation of the wealthy in North America and Europe, and this area seemed a good location for a CPR hotel. Canada sought a way to keep Canadian tourist dollars at home and perhaps attract some additional income from the United States and abroad.

Although during the debates some mention was made of the spectacular scenery surrounding Banff townsite, the original reserve was only 10 acres, and even this acreage had to be wrested from the railway employees who had already set up a bath business. The early bathhouse facilities were soon upgraded; hotels were built at several of the hot springs. Unlike the Yellowstone experience, where the concentration of natural wonders and scenery stimulated Congress to set aside a large area to make sure nothing was overlooked, the Banff reserve was originally conceived of as a whistle-stop spa, with the surrounding ranges left out because they might well contain valuable mineral resources. Yellowstone had the advantage of an aura of mystery. Banff was not as remote as Yellowstone; railway survey and construction had already taken place.

In time, as people and governments began to realize what riches the area's scenic and recreational resources represented, most of the Rocky Mountains' upper reaches were designated as Dominion Parks, becoming Jasper, Yoho, Glacier, Mount Revelstoke, Kootenay, and Waterton Lakes. To this day, as in the Rocky Mountain parks of the United States, the absence of supporting lowlands is sorely felt, and the discontinuity of ecological areas presents many management problems, especially with wildlife.

Townsites within the parks were provided for from the start, thus launching the federal government on an endless sea of troubles as it attempted to regulate the activities of the inhabitants.

Hunting, mining, grazing, and logging were accepted uses well into the twentieth century. Canadian officials closely watched the contest in the United States between utilitarian conservationists, represented by Gifford Pinchot, and the aesthetic preservationists, represented by John Muir. Those in power saw Pinchot's ideas as closer to their own. No Canadian equivalent of Muir rose up, and no northern transcendentalism nurtured possessive feelings about wild lands at that juncture. The small numbers of people and the vastness of the land must have seemed protection enough.

## Park Expansion

By the turn of the century, there were five national parks in the United States: Yellowstone, Sequoia, General Grant (later incorporated into Kings Canyon), Yosemite (which surrounded the state-controlled Yosemite Grant), and Mount Rainer. Reserves were also being established throughout the world in South America, Africa, and Australia. Most had problems like those encountered in Yellowstone; indeed, most areas of the world still encounter similar difficulties in park establishment and subsequent management.

In the early years of the 20th century, park expansion continued at the federal level in both the United States and Canada. The areas being set aside were, for the most part, large, nationally significant areas possessing features that held interest for people nationwide and even internationally. The U.S. National Park Service, established in 1916, helped establish federal area standards and began the encoding of park management guidelines.

Certainly, the United States government, supported by several citizens' groups, rapidly developed the concept of parks at a national level. George Hartzog, former director of the National Park Service, ranked the export of this concept very highly:

> Perhaps second only to liberty itself, the national park idea is the finest contribution of the United States to world culture. These parklands are more than physical resources. They are the delicate strands of nature and culture that bond generation to generation. They are, moreover, the benchmarks of our heritage by which we may chart a new course of human and corporate behavior in our nation so essential to the society (Hartzog, 1988).

A few states established parks prior to 1900, such as Adirondack and Catskill in New York in 1885, Itaska in Minnesota in 1893, Palisades in New York and New Jersey in 1895, and Greylock in Massachusetts in 1898, with more states following suit by the early part of the 20th century. However, only the wealthier states could participate, and thus park expansion at the national level continued to be important.

Soon after the establishment of the U.S. National Park Service in 1916, there was a flurry of park proposals. States not represented wanted their potential park lands to receive national recognition. Most did not possess the outstanding attractions required for national park status, and to have included them would have lessened the value of the total system. On the other hand, many of the areas did contain features worthy of protection or suitable for inclusion in a state park system. Unfortunately, only about 19 states had state parks at the time.

To stimulate interest in preserving these state-significant areas, Stephen T. Mather, the first director of the National Park Service, convened a group in 1921 in Des Moines, Iowa, known as the National Conference on State Parks (now the National Society for Park Resources), to discuss state park system expansion. Mather envisioned a creation of state recreation areas within each state comparable in purpose to the National Park Service. The idea was well received, and today all 50 states have state park systems under many kinds of administrative structures.

According to the National Association of Park Directors, there are nearly 5,000 individual state park areas containing approximately 24 million acres. These, too, have a variety of names: parks, monuments, natural areas, recreation areas, beaches, parkways, and historical areas. In the United States, there are also many types of state areas in such categories as state forests and wildlife refuges administered by other state agencies. Over the years, some of these areas have been transferred to the state park agency to manage, and some are transferred to the National Park Service.

Canada was actually the first to set up a government organization devoted solely to the management and development of parks through the institution of its Parks Branch in 1911 (Foster, 1977). However, provincial cooperation with federal authorities in the matter of national parks was not fully achieved until 1930. Provinces were jealous of their considerable powers and did not wish to see mineral and water resources within the national park boundaries denied them. Many of the original national parks were created prior to the western territories being granted provincial status. Until 1930, the federal government retained jurisdiction over the natural resources of the railway belt extending from Manitoba through British Columbia and thus was free to create national parks within this area even after provincial status was established (Nicol, 1968). Just as in the United States, the eastern part of the country, where most of the population was concentrated, lacked proportional national park acreage.

Canadians cannot be accused of being unmindful of the claims of extractive industries, utilities, or business enterprises on their natural resources. Yet lands for provincial parks, admittedly not always well protected from entry for certain national or provincial purposes, were set aside.

Ontario was the first province to develop its own park system with the establishment of Niagara Falls Provincial Park in 1888 and Algonquin Provincial Park in 1893. The rationale for this latter reserve stressed maintenance of the water supply, the desirability of government-regulated logging and wildlife protection, and the potential for hotel and cottage-style vacationing. In 1894, Rondeau Provincial Park was established—a comparatively small area—close to population centers (Morrison, 1979). Until the 1950s, provincial parks were viewed as financial liabilities, and few were established (Nash, 1968). In 1980, Ontario had 127 operational parks, which represented considerable growth over 25 years.

## EARLY PARK MANAGERS

A problem facing early park management was a lack of qualified personnel. There were no college-trained people in the beginning years of park management. The early rangers or wardens were adventurous types, often products of the local mining or logging camp, who could survive in isolated areas. Many of these men continued to work winters in the parks during the years the Army was still in charge, as the troops were not always kept there at that season. From this group, there developed a cadre of very dedicated, capable people who undertook the job of protecting the resources from outside exploitation.

Later rangers, wardens, and managers obtained their positions by various means, including political appointments made by local congressmen and other politicians. "Who do you know?" was sometimes more important than "What do you know?" In some agencies, every time there was a change of political administration, there was a change of park personnel from the director down to the stable boy. In time, park employees were hired from civil service rosters, and this aspect of the political spoils system came to a halt, or was at least alleviated. On the other hand, present civil service standards are such that people with no natural resources background can often qualify for park positions.

In the Canadian parks, the regulations as amended in 1909 made provision for the appointment of game guardians. This was the genesis of the Park Warden Service.

The university graduate entering park work today comes into a system that has gone through many years of adjustment. When the first college-trained people vied for park jobs and were successful in landing them, they were looked on as "babes in the woods" and had to prove themselves capable of handling the challenge.

Persons today attempting to rise within the park organization will find it difficult if not impossible to compete with university-trained park managers. The complexities of the job require a thorough understanding of the principles of managing people having fun. It is no longer enough to simply protect the resource. Today's managers must also provide visitors the opportunity to enjoy themselves without undue hazard and without serious annoyance to other visitors.

## REFERENCES

### References Cited

Anderson, M. K. (2005). *Tending the wild.* Berkeley: The University of California Press.

Brockman, C. Frank, & Merriam, Lawrence C. Jr. (1979). *Recreational use of wild lands* (3rd ed.). New York: McGraw-Hill.

DOI-USDA (2005). Final Department of Interior-USDA Land Acquisition Plan. http://www.fs.fed. us/land/staff/LWCF/Final%20DOI-USDA%20Land%20Acquisition%20Report%20to%20 Congress.pdf

Foster, Janet. (1978). *Working for wildlife: The beginnings of preservation in Canada.* Toronto: University of Toronto Press.

Green, Linda W. (1987). *Yosemite: The park and its resources, volume one.* U. S. Department of the Interior. Washington, D.C.: U.S. Government Printing Office.

Haines, Aubrey L. (1977). *The Yellowstone story: A history of our first national park. Volumes One and Two.* Yellowstone Library and Museum Association in Cooperation with Colorado Associated University Press.

Hartzog, George B., Jr. (1988). *Battling for the national parks.* Mount Kisco, NY: Moyer Bell Limited.

Huth, Hans. (1948). "Yosemite: The Story of an Idea." *Sierra Club Bulletin.* San Fransisco, CA.

Kilbert, Charles J. (1999). Reshaping the built environment: Ecology, ethics, and economics, Washington D.C.: Island Press.

Lothian, W. F. (1977). *A history of Canada's national parks. Volume II.* Parks Canada. Ottawa: Department of Indian and Northern Affairs.

Morrison, Ken. (1979). "The Evolution of the Ontario Provincial Park System," *Park News Toronto*: National and Provincial Park Association of Canada.

Nash, Roderick. (1968). "Wilderness and Man in North America." From J. G. Nelson & R. C. Scace (Eds.), *The Canadian national parks: Today and tomorrow.* Alberta: The University of Calgary Press.

National Association of State Park Directors. (2010). http://www.naspd.org/, retrieved December 14, 2010 National Association of State Park Directors.

National Park Service. (2009). *Statistical Abstracts.* NPS-USDOI, Natural Resources Program Center, Natural Resources Report NPS/NRPC/NRR 2010-039 http://www.nature.nps.gov/ stats/abstracts/abst2009.pdf

Nicol, J. I. (1968). "The National Parks Movement in Canada." From J. G. Nelson, & R. C. Scace (Eds.), *The Canadian national parks: Today and tomorrow.* Alberta: The University of Calgary Press.

Olmsted, Frederick Law. (1952 ). "The Yosemite Valley and the Mariposa Big Trees: A Preliminary Report," 1865, with an introductory note by Laura Wood Roper, repr. from *Landscape Architecture 43*, no. 1 (October).

*President's commission on Americans outdoors: The legacy, the challenge.* (1987). Washington, D.C.: Island Press.

Russell, Carl P. (1964). "Birth of the National Park Idea." From *Yosemite: Saga of a century.* Yosemite Natural History Association.

Russell, Carl Parcher. (1947). *One hundred years in Yosemite.* Berkeley: University of California Press.

Sargent, Shirley. (1964). "Galen Clark-Mr. Yosemite." From *Yosemite: Saga of a century.* Yosemite Natural History Association.

Sutton, Ann, & Sutton, Myron. (1972). *Yellowstone: A century of the wilderness idea.* New York, Macmillan.

*The Yosemite Guide-Book.* (1870). Cambridge, MA: University Press.

U.S. Army Corps of Engineers. (2010). Retrieved December 14, 2010 from http://corpslakes.usace.army.mil/nrm.cfm

U.S. Department of Interior, Bureau of Reclamation. (2010). Retrieved December 15, 2010 from http://www.usbr.gov/.

## General References

Albright, Horace as told to Robert Cahn. (1985). *The birth of the NPS: The founding years 1913-1933.*

Chubb, Michael, & Chubb, Holly R. (1981). *One-third of our time? An introduction to recreation behavior and resources.* New York: Wiley.

*First World Conference on National Parks.* (1962). Washington, D.C.: U.S. Government Printing Office.

Godbey, Geoffrey. (1989). *The future of leisure services: Thriving on change.* State College, PA: Venture.

Ise, John. (1961). *Our national park policy: A critical history.* Baltimore, MD: Johns Hopkins University Press.

Machlis, Gary, & Technell, David L. (1985). *The state of the world's parks.* Boulder, CO: Western Press.

Millennium Ecosystem Assessment (MEA). 2005. *Ecosystems and human well-being: Synthesis.* Washington: Island Press.

National Association of State Park Directors. (1990). *Annual Information Exchange.* Austin TX: Texas Parks and Wildlife Dept.

Nelson, J. G., & Scace, R. C. (Eds.). (1968). *The Canadian national parks: Today and tomorrow.* Proceedings of a conference organized by the National and Provincial Parks Association of Canada and the University of Calgary.

Runte, Alfred. (1979). *National parks: The American experience.* Lincoln: University of Nebraska Press.

Sax, Joseph. (1980). *Mountains without handrails.* Ann Arbor: University of Michigan Press.

Tilden, Freeman. (1962). *The state parks: Their meaning in American life.* New York: Alfred A. Knopf.

U. S. Department of the Interior. (1987). *Restoring American wildlife.* Washington, D.C.: U.S. Government Printing Office.

Wirth, Conrad L. (1980). *Parks, politics, and the people.* Norman: University of Oklahoma Press.

*Chapter Two*

# Organizational Structure

The following chapters deal with the various facets of park management and agency operation as seen from the headquarters. Specific issues addressed include how park agencies set themselves up to deal with visitors and their diverse activities? How do park agencies best organize to provide their traditional public service while staying on top of changes, conflicts, new demands, budget structures, and resource deteriorations? How does the agency organize to serve individual parks? And, perhaps of most importance, how does the agency organize to get the best out of all personnel? This chapter will locate the park agency within other governmental structures.

It is important to understand organizational structure within an agency and know the variety of structural forms agencies can assume. Such knowledge not only enables one to see how an agency relates to other agencies within government, but also gives a clearer picture of how and why government agencies operate the way they do.

Most individual parks within a given agency are too small to have an elaborate organizational hierarchy. They are usually limited to a manager, an assistant manager, and a few seasonal park aids, if even that in some cases. For this reason, they will not have organizational line charts or exhaustive area-of-responsibility lists. Yet at some level of park management, be it state, provincial, or federal, more complex structures are to be found. For clarity, two basic headings will be used to deal with the subject: the park agency among others in government, and the organization of the park agency itself.

## THE PARK DEPARTMENT WITHIN GOVERNMENT

The purposes of most governmental organizations are commonly categorized as service or regulatory. Service denotes an agency that provides assistance to others. For instance, a park department offers many services to the recreating public, such as operating a swimming beach or picnic area or providing interpretation. The term *regulatory* implies that judgments are passed or permits issued, (e.g., in the case of some parks, for the operation of a ski lift). Therefore, all parks come under the category of service agencies, with some having certain regulatory powers also.

Additionally, all levels of government—local, provincial, state, and federal—have legislative, judicial, and executive functions. The executive branch, and the park agency within it, will be regularly and directly affected by the legislative branch, which probably will have a parks committee of elected officials.

The legislator who chairs the parks committee will play a vital role in the consideration of ordinances and legislation affecting the agency and its operations, land holdings, planning, and employees. The chair will also have contact, either directly or indirectly, with the legislative finance committee. Most agencies would have a staff person assigned to work with the parks committee. This liaison is crucial to the success of an agency, so the person must be carefully chosen for depth of knowledge in both parks and legislative matters and for an ability to communicate clearly with both politicians and the public.

The chances are that the judicial aspect at the governmental level will have little relationship to the parks agency. There might be occasional communications concerning the employment of offenders who will have the opportunity to complete some work time in a park, or risk management cases.

## Typical Executive Structure

The executive branch needs much greater discussion, as it is under its aegis that park agencies usually are found. Most park agencies are structured in one of the four following ways. These examples of park agency structure come from the county level. If the municipal level were used, the term "county executive" would be replaced by "mayor;" if state, by "governor;" or provincial, by "premier." The four examples include self-taxing, and a county executive operating under an agency, superagency, or commission form of structure.

**1.   Self-taxing.** A board consisting of three to 11 persons is elected by the voters and possesses the legal authority to tax the property owners of the district. The board will be responsible directly to the voters who elect it. Normally, the board will have some legislative authority and might even have some judicial responsibility. Usually the board will be nonpartisan. This body will engage a chief administrator whose title will be director of parks or something similar.

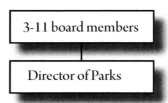

**2.   County executive—agency.** The county executive appoints the director of parks for a specific term or perhaps for an unspecified time, which means this person serves until replaced. This agency administrator reports directly to the county executive. Generally speaking, under this setup, the agency will be more susceptible to partisan politics than any other type of structure.

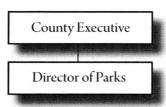

**3.   County executive—superagency.** The county executive appoints the administrator of a superagency who appoints division heads, probably with the approval of the county executive. In such instances, the park organization is a division within a much larger agency and is at the same level as roads, utilities, and similar departments.

**4. County executive—commission.** The county executive appoints a commission of three to 11 members, usually for staggered terms. The commission hires an administrator whose term lasts as long as this person's actions meet with the approval of a majority of the commission members.

There are variations of these four basic structures; however, most county-level park agencies will fit into one of the above four hierarchies. The following charts present some different examples of organizational structure. Note the philosophy in the two state examples of involving the public within the structure of the agency. Figure 2.1 outlines the current structure of the National Park Service. To help refine the roles and responsibilities of the Colorado State Trails Committee, four grant selection subcommittees will be formalized as shown in Figure 2.2. Figure 2.3 lists advisory committees for Wisconsin state parks.

## Figure 2.1. Current Organization of the National Park Service

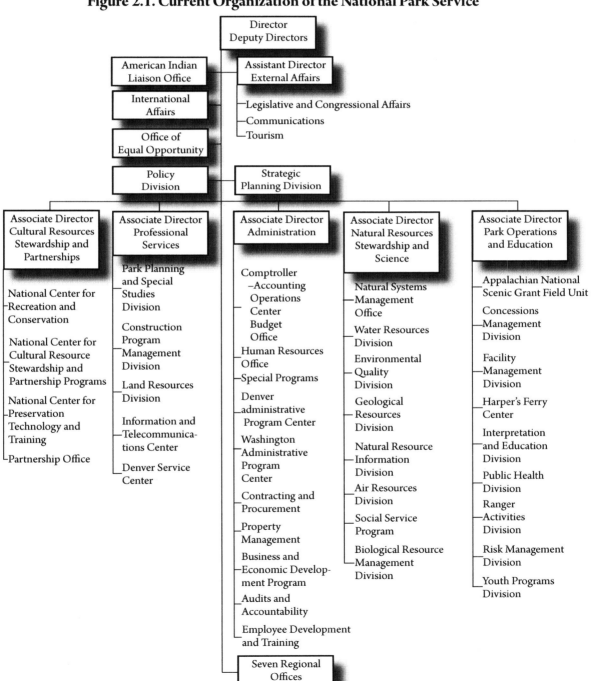

## Figure 2.2. Structure of the Colorado State Parks

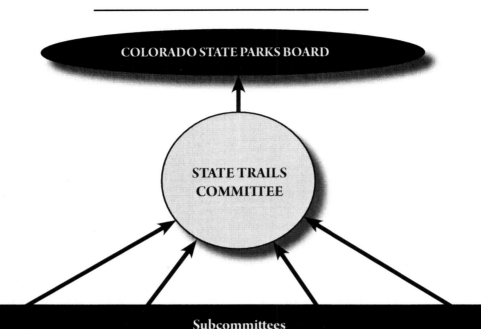

**Subcommittees**

| Recreational Trails Grants | Off-Highway Vehicles Grants | Snowmobile Capital Grants | Planning Grants |
|---|---|---|---|
| **Chair:**<br>State Trails Committee Member | **Chair:**<br>State Trails Committee (OHV Appointment) | **Chair:**<br>State Trails Committee (Snowmobile Appointment) | **Chair:**<br>State Trails Committee (Local Govt. Appointment) |
| **Members:**<br>Public (Up to 10 trails enthusiasts from the general public | **Members:**<br>Public (Up to 10 OHB enthusiasts representing organized OHV) | **Members:**<br>Public (Up to 10 snow-mobile enthusiasts representing organized snowmobiling groups) | **Members:**<br>Public (Up to 10 trails enthusiasts from the genearl public) |
| State Trails Committee (2) | Staff (OHV Coordinator) | Staff member (Snowmobile Coordinator) | GOCO (Ex officio) |
| GOCO (Ex officio) | Staff members (Regional Managers) | Staff Member (Regional Managers) | Staff Member (Trails Coordinator) |
| Staff Member (Trails Coordinator) | | | Staff Members (Regional Managers) |
| Staff Members (Regional Managers) | | | |

---

### Figure 2.3. List of the Advisory Committees for Wisconsin State Parks

All  study committees shall have set responsibilities and goals that consist of addressing citizen concerns; reviewing, studying, and recommending to the Executive Council on assigned resolutions and review of department opinions and positions regarding specific areas directly pertaining to the Study Committee. In order to make the most efficient use of time by delegates, the following advisory committees with specific responsibilities are established. Some committees may be combined into one committee in an effort of efficiency and knowledge. Below is a listing of committees:

Air, Waste, and Water
Awards
Big Game
Endangered Resources and
    Law Enforcement
Fur Harvest
Hunting with Dogs
Migratory
Outdoor Heritage and Education
Rules and Resolution
Trout
Upland Game
Wolf

Alternative Funding
Bear
CWD
Forestry, Parks, and Recreation
Habitat
Legislative
Mississippi River
Public and Private Land
Use
Turkey
Warm Water

---

## Cooperative, Nonstructured Systems

**Integrated system.** From the middle of the century until recently, there were a few isolated instances of combined or integrated systems, even between cities in different states. The 1980s and 1990s saw a marked increase in the variety and number of these systems.

For example, Ebys Landing National Historical Site in Washington State is composed of federal, state, local, and private land and is administered by a board composed of representatives from each of those entities. The board operates under a plan approved by the Secretary of the Interior. The City and County of Honolulu Department of Parks and Recreation manages Hanauma Bay Marine Park Preserve. Yet, the State Department of Natural Resources is charged with lands to high water mark, and the U.S. Fish and Wildlife Department is charged with endangered species. The coordination of the agencies' agendas and missions is one challenge; however, the multiagency effort has saved the bay. See http://www.honolulu.gov/parks/facility/hanaumabay/information.htm for more information.

A different type of integration, or cooperation, is in force at City of Rocks National Historic Site, where the state of Idaho and the National Park Service developed  a master plan that provided for the State of Idaho to operate the area. In the future, we will see more integrated systems as well as a variety of other systems serving the public, as funding gets restricted for parks.

Most recently, due to severe state budget reductions for parks, the State of Arizona has entered into agreements for the operations and management of over 11 state parks. The State Parks Board of Arizona, on the advice of staff, has recommended that these agreements be approved in order to keep the parks open to the public. See http://www.azstateparks.com/board/index.html for details.

**Partnerships.** Doug Eury, former Superintendent of Nez Perce National Historical Park, observed about the park, "If we don't have partnerships, we don't have a park." Increasingly, partnerships are essential and an effective means for the National Park Service to fulfill parts of our mission and foster a shared sense of stewardship that is so crucial for our future. (http://www.nps.gov/partnerships)

## Figure 2.4. Organizational Flowchart for Wisconsin State Parks

### The Public

Wisconsin citizens have a local avenue for input and exchange concerning conservation issues through WCC on a local and statewide level.

### Local County Delegates, County Chairs, and Vice-Chairs

The Conservation Congress shall have representation in each county. Individuals who have the majority vote in their county shall become a delegate from their county. County delegates are elected to serve a two- or three-year term as a county delegate. Delegates of the county at the Annual Spring Rules Hearings and Conservation Congress meeting will elect a Chair and Vice-Chair to represent their county to serve a one-year term.

### District Level and Executive Council

The state is broken down into 12 Districts. The Conservation Congress shall have a 24-person Executive Council that is comprised of two delegates from each District to serve as Executive Councilors. Delegates from within each District on Friday at the annual Conservation Congress convention in May of each calendar year to one-year terms. Executive Councilors shall be elected from all county committee persons and not more than one councilor shall be elected per county, except for Milwaukee County. Current Councilors will actively participate in the Thursday evening Executive Council meeting at the annual Conservation Congress Convention.

### Executive Committee

The Executive Council will elect a Chair, Vice-Chair and Secretary from within the Executive Council on Friday at the annual Conservation Congress convention in May of each calendar year to one-year terms.

### Natural Resources Board

The Wisconsin Natural Resources Board (NR Board) sets policy for the Department of Natural Resources and exercises authority and responsibility in accordance with governing statutory provisions. Chapter 15 of the Wisconsin Statutes delineates the formal duties of the seven-member board. Board members are appointed by the Governor with the advice and consent of the State Senate.

Partnership management has become a core competency to carry out our NPS mission and deliver public service at a higher level. Our challenge is to more effectively grow that competency by building on past partnership successes and develop new capacity service wide. Our management challenge at every level is to effectively align and leverage resources to enable NPS employees and partners to create and sustain more effective partnerships. (http://www.nps.gov/partnerships/about.htm)

The National Park Service and other state park agencies have realized their role needs to shift from trying to do everything themselves to one of empowering others through partnerships. As Brian O'Neill, former Superintendent of Golden Gate National Recreation Area pointed out, "Every time we do it ourselves, we miss out on an opportunity for community engagement." (http://www.nps.gov/partnerships)

## THE ORGANIZATION OF THE PARK AGENCY

There are almost as many varieties of agency structures as there are agencies. Although there is no such thing as "one best system," certain factors are considered vital to proper agency development: separation of the various fiscal functions in order to provide adequate controls, determination of which activities need close daily supervision and which need only general guidelines, and the conjunction of similar functions.

Internally, each agency groups its personnel into administration and operation. Many agencies also have a planning office. Administration (or administrative services) describes those functions that provide for the workings of the agency per se, such as payroll, personnel, or clerical; operations is the name given to those actions necessary to fulfill the purpose of the agency for the park visitors, such as park management or ranger patrol. The planning division is usually placed in resources development, which covers those internal services necessary to chart a course of development, be it in land acquisition, area or facility planning, design and engineering, or determining future needs. There other functions that can fall under the jurisdiction of the local "parks department." These might include urban forestry, cemeteries, greenbelts, arboretums, and botanical gardens. The City of Minneapolis Parks and Recreation's organizational structure is shown in Figure 2.5. Notice the areas of supervision for the operations manager; within each of these areas would be other staff and lines of control.

### Organizational Style

Many park organizations still function on a traditional structured concept of administration. Large business organizations function very efficiently under these rather rigid approaches to administration. However, there has been an increasing trend within governmental organizations, particularly in public service and social agency programs, to adopt a personal, humanistic approach to administration by moving toward more casual superior-subordinate relationships. Within any organization, there needs to be an awareness of the advantage of both the "formal" and "informal" structure.

The formal structure reflects the organization chart and the subsequent policies and procedures, while the informal recognizes that employees are better workers when they don't feel totally confined to small boxes and narrow lines on a chart. Usually there will be elements of both approaches used at different times and modified versions of each used at the same time. Immediate subordinates, at any level of park management, do not want to be bypassed in the chain of command when orders are given, nor do employees further down the line appreciate orders or reprimands from those not listed as their superiors.

### Organizational Structure Development

The sequence of charges illustrated here relates directly to the size of an agency and the complexity of its responsibilities. When an agency is very small or limited in scope, it is highly probable that all of the permanent full-time staff—two to four persons—will report to the chief administrator.

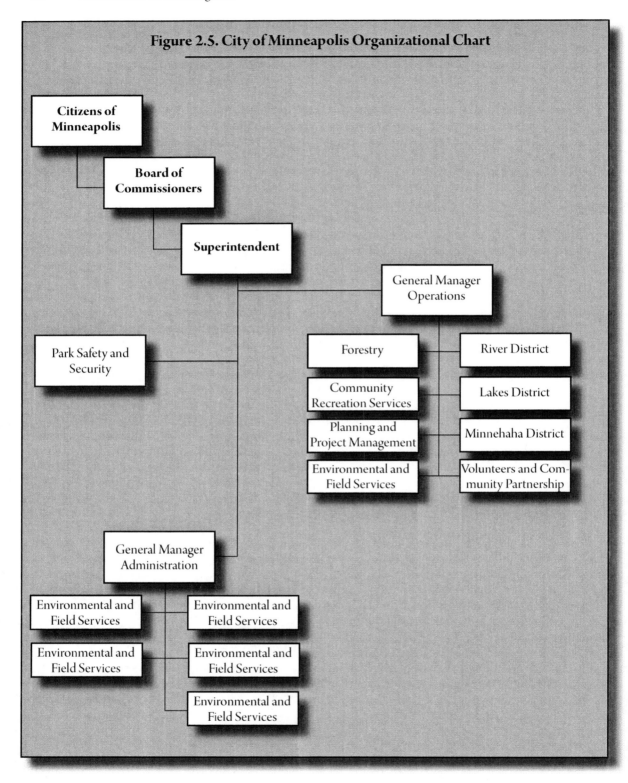

**Figure 2.5. City of Minneapolis Organizational Chart**

As an organization grows, it is probable that the number of persons directly reporting to the administrator will increase until their daily supervision is too time consuming. Administrators will not be able to do a competent job if they have no time for public relations or for creative, holistic thinking. When this point of overload is reached, whether in the whole agency or in one of its larger units, a more complex model is needed, allowing for delegation of authority. This issue is often called span of control.

## Span of Control

This is a term used to gauge the ability of an individual to successfully supervise the work of subordinates. For example, a regional supervisor has several area managers responsible to him or her. These area managers each have several park managers directly responsible to them. As a continuation of this chain, which repeats the inherit relationship at each level, the park managers will exercise control over rangers or wardens, interpreters, aides, lifeguards, and maintenance personnel. If any of these supervisors must personally oversee too many people working at too complex a variety of tasks, control is lost; the span of control has been exceeded.

There is no established number of subordinate positions that a supervisor "should be able to handle." The span of control will depend primarily on the type of functions performed by subordinates. Some programs, by the distribution of the personnel involved or by the nature of the tasks involved, require detailed discussion and supervision, while others need only policy direction and a feedback system. The ability of the supervisor is an issue here. Also, some employees require considerable supervision, while others need almost none, so the individuals concerned play a part in determining the span. It follows that supervisors must have time to give each subordinate the administrative attention necessary for the development of a positive supervisor-subordinate relationship. This translates into time to stop and talk, to answer questions, and perhaps to listen to complaints and suggestions.

**Lines of authority.** It is important that there be clear lines of authority so all employees know not only for whom they work and who works for them, but who has the authority to make decisions and to discipline. An up-to-date organizational chart must be accessible to all, and a copy should be given to new employees during orientation.

Organizational theory makes note of two types of job functions: staff and line. Staff functions imply an advisory position to an executive, while line functions imply that employees have authority of command and carry out the tasks of the organization. Within the organizational structure, staff members usually function in areas related to research, planning, and budgeting, and normally work directly with personnel in line positions. Staff positions customarily branch horizontally on an organizational chart. Line positions are in a direct vertical line below the administrator, and it is from this that the phrase "line employee" comes.

## Delegation of Authority

To choose the right person, and to transfer to that person both the understanding of the task and the sense of responsibility for its execution is a primary function of an administrator. One of the qualities to look for in an administrator is whether he or she knows how to delegate properly and if she or he has the ability to make basic decisions effectively.

As a basic principle, all authority should be delegated to the lowest possible level. What is the lowest possible level? How is it determined? Within the functional areas, the authority level should be at the upward point where two or more functions or geographical areas are involved. For example, the park manager must have the authority to discipline all employees within the park, but the manager should not have the authority to purchase over and beyond the monetary limits set for park managers; someone else has that duty, because it encompasses another control center. The granting person should always seek to delegate the authority as far downward as possible, asking why any particular decision needs to be at a higher level.

Although this sort of independence should be welcomed, supervisory control should be maintained. Feedback from the person to whom you delegated this task, as well as from others concerned with the function, is critical to the supervisory role.

**Responsibility and accountability.** Authority is desired by almost everyone. What is not desired by many is responsibility and accountability. It is crucial to a smooth-running organization that with every authority delegated, there is clearly understood responsibility and accountability.

Within most governments, the law will hold the chief executive responsible and accountable. Logically then, the chief executive retains all authority. In practice, however, this cannot and should not be the case. The chief executive must delegate authority, and a way must be found to place responsibility and accountability along with that delegation of authority.

For example, if the person in charge of fiscal matters is delegated the authority to approve purchases, then responsibility for keeping within the fiscal resources must also be delegated, and this person must be held accountable if the agency spends more than the budgeted amount. Park managers must operate under these same rules, both as delegates of higher authority, and as delegators of authority themselves.

**Areas of responsibility document.** In order to make the responsibility and accountability concepts work, there must be an Areas of Responsibility document. The document, as prepared at the agency headquarters level, should be indexed and contain data concerning all division heads, supervisors, assistants, and others serving in areas of responsibility. Similar documents should be prepared for regional personnel, as well as for all park units, so that required tasks will be handled on a routine basis. Only the agency-level document is discussed here.

The lead section of the document should be an agency organizational chart showing the specific job titles and who fills each position. Normally this would include the head of the agency and subordinates at least three ranks deep on the organizational chart.

The compiling of an Areas of Responsibility document is of limited value if it is not utilized. Ideally, all of the employees of an agency should have a copy for reference. Should the agency not be able to provide sufficient copies, one should go to the receptionist, the mail room, each secretary, and all persons at the executive and supervisory levels. Each region, district, and individual park should have a copy also.

## Coordination

Even with the delegation of responsibility and authority and even with the areas of responsibility documented, there will always be the need for active coordination of employee efforts. Once an organization, be it an agency or a specific park, employs two or more persons, there will always be a tendency for overlap, duplication, and voids. It is normal for people within an agency to talk with each other and to be aware of each other's responsibilities. Or, they bend over backward to avoid potential conflicts, and thus create voids. One of the best methods of averting these situations is to hold regular staff meetings. Brief reports noting actions as they relate to previous goals and actions projected for the future will help employees to keep on course. At these meetings, any overlaps or voids will probably be obvious and thus can be corrected.

## Controls

Just as it is important to delegate authority, it is also vital to provide controls, which are procedures established to preclude improper or illegal acts. The structure of the agency should provide these controls. Two of the more critical areas needing controls are personnel and fiscal.

**Personnel.** Controls are needed to be sure the agency does not exceed its authorized level of employment or fail to act correctly in regard to other regulations affecting personnel, such as the Fair Labor Standards Act, the various acts dealing with equal opportunities, and the Americans with Disabilities Act of 1990. Therefore, the person controlling these actions must be placed in a structure position high enough in the organization to ensure the needed authority.

**Fiscal.** As previously noted, the agency and its units should be administratively structured so as to facilitate fiscal controls. For instance, the person responsible for authorizing the purchasing of goods (supply officer) should be placed under a different supervisor than the person paying the bills (accounts payable).

**Operations evaluation.** This is a process designed to monitor procedural functioning in an agency or in larger park units. A senior ranking employee is usually in charge, with additional staff chosen from various units. This group reports to the director or head of the unit doing the evaluation.

## CONCLUSION

There is no one "best" method of developing agency structure just as there is no one "best" structure. However, the factors mentioned in this chapter should be taken into consideration when developing structure for any level of organization. Park managers should understand the reasoning that shapes their agency's structure and realize the implications of their position within it. Important is the ability to communicate efficiently and effectively with the public and elected officials, and to react quickly to mandates. Therefore, the structure should allow autonomy and authority for employees to address change.

## REFERENCES

Arizona State Parks Board, Intergovernmental Agreements and Agenda Items to keep parks open during budget crisis, http://www.azstateparks.com/board/index.html

Colorado State Parks.http://parks.state.co.us/NR/rdonlyres/4BF640F8-1780-46FE-B81B-3D835F8A8DA9/0/Trailsprogramstrategicplan.pdf)

Flowchart of the organization of the Wisconsin State Parks. http://dnr.wi.gov/org/nrboard/congress/organizational_structure/.pdf

List of the advisory committees for the Wisconsin State Parks. http://dnr.wi.gov/org/nrboard/congress/organizational_structure/organizational_structure.pdf)

National Park Service, (http://www.nps.gov/partnerships)

National Park Service, Organizational Structure http://www.nps.gov/pore/parkmgmt/upload/planning_businessplans_2007_currentoperations.pdf

*Chapter Three*

# Park Management Policies

Policy governs the way an agency shall conduct itself concerning a specific action in a specific situation. Policies emanate from legislative actions, court rulings, and agency self-determination. In some instances, policies are a response to social or political change, reflecting new directions, while in other instances, policy might represent a bold thrust by a single person. In the broadest sense, policies are guidelines for action. As guidelines, policies give a sense of direction, an assurance of consistency. They seek to ensure that an agency carries out its mandate properly.

Most policies stem from the legislative branch of whatever level of government the agency operates within. In recent years, as government has become more complex, the legislative branch has conveyed to the agency more and more rule-making authority within the rather broad policies it has formulated. As a practical matter, this has resulted in a greater amount of policy being set by the agency or governmental executive. An example was the abolition of the Heritage Conservation and Recreation Service (HCRS) by the U.S. Secretary of the Interior, James Watt, with the functions placed within the National Park Service.

The formulation of policy is a matter of critical concern. Policy must be broad enough to provide latitude for responsive decision making, yet be specific enough to enable the decision makers to accurately reflect intent.

"Regulations have to apply to the majority of situations—to anticipate the worse case—they must address the problems they are designed to address. They have to be written in a language and with an intent that is clear" (Hocker, 1988). Unfortunately, regulations sometimes have little effect on budget reductions and political issues that face our parks. As the State of Arizona has experienced, parks are being closed to the public, in light of strong demand and historical preservation issues.

From http://www.azstateparks.com/. Reprinted with permission.

The following notices were posted for the public (http://www.azstateparks.com/). Park advocates and supporters can do little else but attend meetings, give testimony, and encourage government units to keep parks open. Policies in the future must address fiscal issues and sustainability.

The Arizona State Parks Board on January 15 voted to keep nine parks open and close the remaining thirteen State Parks in a phased series of closures starting February 22, 2010, due to six different State Parks funds being swept of $8.6 million. In addition, four parks remain closed due to previous budget reductions. Parks closed on February 22 included Lyman Lake State Park and Homolovi Ruins State Park.

The next park closings will occur on March 29, 2010, and will include Fort Verde State Historic Park in Camp Verde, Roper Lake State Park in Safford, Tombstone Courthouse State Historic Park, Yuma Territorial Prison State Historic Park, Tubac Presidio State Historic Park, and Riordan Mansion State Historic Park in Flagstaff.

The final phased closings will occur on June 3, 2010, and will include Tonto Natural Bridge State Park near Payson, Alamo Lake State Park in Wenden, Lost Dutchman State Park in Apache Junction, Picacho Peak State Park and Red Rock State Park in Sedona.

Not only is funding an issue, but capacity is also an issue that needs to be addressed in policy. As Hass noted in an invitation to a park manager about attending an interagency project on capacity in parks:

He declined the opportunity by saying, "We don't have a capacity problem; we don't want to limit use." This is a dominant perspective among managers of our nation's parks, forests, refuges, rivers, lakes, reservoirs, wildernesses, national monuments and other specially designated areas. That is, we don't need to deal with recreation capacity until we have a problem and want to reduce recreation demand (Haas, 2002).

## RESOURCE POLICY FORMATION

Early North American supporters of parks and open space realized that the natural resources of the new world, while vast, were not endless, and they became concerned with the stewardship of these resources. From Catlin, Olmsted, Muir, the two Roosevelts, Pinchot, Mather, and Albright, to Hewitt, Udall, Laurence Rockefeller, McTaggart-Cowan, Henry M. Jackson, and Leopold, there has grown on this continent a tradition of love and respect for the natural scene and action to conserve its values.

Leadership had been expressed in various ways. In 1988, for example, then-Secretary of the Interior, Cecil Andrews, pointed out that Senator Henry M. Jackson had been either the architect or a key player in the passage of all major environmental legislation over three decades (1950-1983). Senator Jackson and other leaders helped to form basic resource policy on a continent where resources were originally so plentiful that waste of them was the norm.

Decade by decade, the expanding population achieved more leisure time, earned more discretionary income, and found better facilities for travel enjoyment. With newfound leisure, money, and facilities, the public sought more and better opportunities to enjoy the outdoors. But the same public also put more demand on resources for competing uses. In the years following World War II, this process greatly accelerated as the United States and Canada, released from wartime restrictions, designated millions of acres for subdivisions, industrial sites, highways, schools, and airports. Harvesting of timber increased dramatically on both public and industrial lands (Popper, 1988). The resources for outdoor recreation—shoreline, green areas, open space, and unpolluted waters—diminished rapidly in the face of these demands. New policies were needed to mediate demands and control use. Certain policies were tried and found wanting in the face of this pressure. Some of these were modified, and occasionally new policies were instituted.

The attempt to formulate such policies resulted in legislative battles at the federal agencies responsible for providing opportunities for outdoor recreation. Similar problems were faced in many state and provincial capitals across the continent. In some instances, they stemmed from the conflicts among different interests competing for use of the same resources. In others, it was the matter of responsibility—who should do the job and who should pay the bill. Private landowners were faced with the problems caused by the public seeking recreation on their land. Each year the problems increased and resulted in numerous court challenges.

This concern over recreation was not new, only intensified. Several state legislatures had evidenced their interest in the establishment of local recreation lands when they created state park departments in the early 1900s. The National Park Service recognized the need for this level of parks when, in 1921, Director Stephen Mather organized a state park conference. The delegates to that conference formed the National Conference on State Parks, which today is known as the National Society for Park Resources, a branch of the National Recreation and Park Association. Although some state preserves had been established before the turn of the century, this first conference initiated organized review and cooperation on the matter of state parks. In response to the unprecedented demands, state, provincial, county, and local recreation areas of various kinds have also been pressed into service to meet the continent's growing recreational needs and to monitor the level of pressure on recreational resources.

### Laws Setting Major U.S. Resource and Recreation Policy

As previously indicated, policies emanate from several sources, one of which is the legislative process. In the United States, Congress has had much to do with formulating policy. The following is a list of major actions taken since the conservation and use of resources became a recognized issue. Some address land designation, use, and recreation policy, while others are only tangential to these issues. In other instances, these legislative actions set up bodies which in turn formulated policy. It should be noted that there have been revisions to these legislative actions.

*1864*  **Yosemite Valley and the Mariposa Grove of Big Trees** withdrawn from entry as public domain. Granted to state of California for management as a state park.

*1872*  **Yellowstone National Park set aside**. First U.S. National Park, and first instance of federal policy in the matter of outdoor recreation.

*1891*  **Forest reserves (later called national forests) established.** Halted sales of certain public lands.

*1906*  **Act for the Preservation of American Antiquities.** Far-reaching legislation to set aside federal lands of historic or scientific interest. Still used by presidents to preserve public domain.

*1916*  **National Park Service Act.** Mather and Albright's successful efforts to establish a separate parks bureau.

*1932*  **Economy Act of 1932, as amended, Public Law 97-258 and 98-216, 31 USC 1535.** Public Laws 97-258 and 98-216 authorize an agency to place orders for goods and services with another government agency when the head of an agency determines that it is in the best interest of the government and decides ordered goods and services cannot be provided as conveniently or cheaply by contract with a commercial enterprise.

*1933*  **Establishment of Civilian Conservation Corps.** Unemployed men doing conservation work on federal and state lands.

*1934*  **Conservation of Wildlife, Fish and Game Act of 1934, Public Law 73-121, 48 Stat. 401.** Recognized the public's desire to hunt and fish.

*1935*  **National Park System Advisory Board established.**

*1937*  **Pittman-Robertson Act** passed for the enhancement of wildlife.

*1946*  **Bureau of Land Management established**. Consolidated the General Land Office and Grazing Services. Manages large portion of public domain for purposes that include recreation.

*1946*  **Fish and Wildlife Coordination Act of 1946, Public Law 79-732, 60 Stat. 1080.** Authorized agencies of the U.S. Department of the Interior to provide "… … public shooting and fishing areas … … and development and improvement thereof in connection with such resource development."

*1950*    **Dingell-Johnson Act** passed for the enhancement of fisheries.

*1956*    **Colorado River Storage Project (CRSP) of 1956, Public Law 84-485, 70 Stat. 105.** Public Law 84-485, more specifically Section 8, authorizes and directs the Secretary of the Interior to investigate, plan, develop, operate, and maintain public recreation facilities at all CRSP projects and participating projects such as the Central Utah Project.

*1958*    **Outdoor Recreation Resources Review Act (ORRRC).** Created a commission to assess current and future recreation needs and recommend policy. (Their work had such an impact on policy that considerably more about the commission is set forth later in this chapter.)

*1960*    **U.S. Forest Service Multiple Use Sustained Yield Act.** Officially acknowledged outdoor recreation as one of the purposes of national forests.

*1962*    **Fryingpan-Arkansas Act of 1962, Public Law 87-590, 77 Stat. 393.** Public Law 87-90, more specifically Section 4, authorizes the Secretary of the Interior to (1) investigate, plan, construct, operate, and maintain public recreational facilities on lands withdrawn or acquired for the development of said project, (2) to conserve the scenery, the natural, historic and archeologic objects, and the wildlife on said lands, (3) to provide for public use and enjoyment of said land and water areas and, (4) to investigate, plan, construct, operate, and maintain facilities for the conservation and development of fish and wildlife resources.

*1962*    **Recreation Facilities, Elephant Butte and Caballo Reservoirs Act of 1962, Public Law 87-542, 76 Stat. 171.** Provides Reclamation with direct authority to investigate, plan, construct, operate, and maintain basic recreation facilities at Elephant Butte and Caballo Reservoirs as part of the Rio Grande Project, New Mexico. This includes providing access roads and facilities for safety, health, and protection of the visiting public, and provide for the public use and enjoyment of such recreation facilities and water areas.

*1963*    **Bureau of Outdoor Recreation Organic Act.** Created to carry out salient points of ORRRC recommendations.

*1964*    **Wilderness Act.** Set aside certain federal lands capable of affording primitive experiences.

*1964*    **Public Land Law Review Commission Act.** Established to coordinate, where possible, the large body of legislation affecting management of public lands.

*1964*    **Land and Water Conservation Fund Act.** A means of stimulating federal and state outdoor planning, acquisition, and development by use of matching funds. In Congress, these projects go through an Appropriations Committee review process: given the intense competition among projects, funding is generally only provided for those projects with universal support. Initially authorized for a 25-year period, the LWCF has been extended for another 25 years, its current mandate running until January 2015.

*1964*    **Recreation Development, Sanford Reservoir Act of 1964, Public Law 88-536, 78 Stat. 744.** Provides Reclamation with direct authority to investigate, plan, construct, operate, and maintain basic recreation facilities at Sanford Reservoir as part of the Canadian River Project, Texas.

*1965*    **National Park Service Concession Policy Act.** Standardized policy.

*1965*    **Auburn-Folsom South Unit, Central Valley Project of 1965, Public Law 89-161, 79 Stat. 615.** Public Law 89-161, more specifically Section 3, authorizes the Secretary of the Interior to (1) construct, operate, and maintain or provide for public outdoor recreation and fish and wildlife enhancement facilities, (2) to acquire, or otherwise, to include within the unit area such adjacent lands or interests in land as are necessary for present or future public recreation or fish and wildlife use, (3) to allocate water and reservoir capacity to recreation or fish and wildlife enhancement and, (4) to provide for public use and enjoyment of unit lands, facilities, and water areas in a manner coordinated with other unit purposes.

*1965*    **Federal Water Project Recreation Act of 1965, Public Law 89-72, 79 Stat. 213.** Although this legislation also applies to the Corps of Engineers and the Tennessee Valley Authority, it is listed in this section because it is Reclamation's most commonly used recreation-related legislation and it is not considered to be project specific. Public Law 89-72 allows Reclamation to seek qualified non-Federal government partners to manage recreation at its water projects through a management agreement and to cost share in planning, developing, operating, and maintaining the leased areas. Public Law 89-72 also allows Reclamation to transfer recreation and other land management responsibilities to another Federal agency if such lands are included or proposed for inclusion within a national recreation area, or are appropriate for administration by another Federal agency as part of the national forest system, as a part of the public lands classified for retention in Federal ownership, or in connection with an authorized Federal program for the conservation and development of fish and wildlife.

*Note:* Prior to passage of Public Law 89-72, authorization for recreational development at Reclamation projects would have had to be included in the project authorizing legislation or approved by subsequent legislation. In some cases, construction is accomplished under a specific project authorization and management is done under Public Law 89-72. In addition, if a project does not have specific recreation authority, Reclamation is limited to providing only "limited basic" recreation facilities that are required to protect the health and safety of the general public.

*1965*    **Water Resources Planning Act of 1965, Public Law 89-80, 79 Stat. 244.** Established the President's Water Resources Council to guide water resources development and assign benefits on full recreation development for proposed projects.

*1966*    **National Historic Preservation Act.** Established a new program to identify and preserve historical sites and structures

*1967*    **43 CFR part 21, Occupancy of Cabin Sites on Public Conservation and Recreation Areas (1967).** Established when, and by what standards, use of conservation and recreation areas under private cabin permits must be modified or discontinued so as to allow the public use of such areas, and the procedures for renewing, extending, phasing out, or terminating private cabin permits.

*1968*    **Wild and Scenic Rivers Act.** Provided for designation of and safeguards for wild and scenic rivers to preserve these threatened environments.

*1968*    **National Trails System Act.** Designated Appalachian and Pacific Crest National Scenic Trails as initial units of a national system of trails at all levels of government.

*1968*    **Redwood National Park Act.** Preserved significant examples of coastal redwood. Greatly expanded scope and authority of National Park Service.

*1968*    **Architectural Barriers Act.** Directed that buildings' and facilities' design and construction be accessible to the physically handicapped.

*1968*    **Colorado River Basin Project Act of 1968, Public Law 90-537, 82 Stat. 885.** Public Law 90-537, which includes the Central Arizona Project, provides Reclamation with direct authority to, among other things, enhance recreation opportunities on lands covered by the project.

*1968*    **Wild and Scenic Rivers Act of 1968, Public Law 90-542, 82 Stat. 906.** Declared a national policy that selected rivers that possess outstanding scenic, recreational, geologic, fish and wildlife, historic, cultural, or other similar values shall be preserved in a free flowing condition. The law additionally declares that the established national policy of dam and other construction at appropriate sections of the rivers of the United States need to be complemented by a policy that would preserve the free flowing condition of certain selected rivers or sections thereof.

*1969*    **National Environmental Policy Act.** Established policy on environment, created the Council on Environmental Quality, and issued requirement for an environmental impact statement. Although enacted on January 1, 1970, its "short title" is "National Environmental Policy Act of 1969.

*1970*    **Clean Air Act.** Established to protect and enhance the quality of air.

*1970*    **Volunteers in the Parks Program Act (VIP)**. Encouraged citizens to contribute their time and skills.

*1971*    **Alaska Native Claims Settlement Act.** To settle native American and Eskimo claims resulting from Alaska purchase and provide for federal and state public land selections.

*1972*    **Coastal Zone Management Act.** To preserve, protect, develop, and restore the coastal zone.

*1972*    **Marine Mammal Protection Act (MMPA)** of 1972 was the first article of legislation to call specifically for an ecosystem approach to natural resource management and conservation. MMPA prohibits the taking of marine mammals, and enacts a moratorium on the import, export, and sale of any marine mammal, along with any marine mammal part or product within the United States.

*1972*    **Clean Water Act.** To restore and maintain the chemical, physical, and biological integrity of water.

*1973*    **Endangered Species Act.** Conservation, restoration, and propagation of endangered and threatened species of fish, wildlife, and plants.

*1973*    **Rehabilitation Act.** Provided that no person could be denied participation in any activity or opportunity solely by reason of his or her handicaps. Provided also for rehabilitation of facilities and services, and expanded employment opportunities for handicapped individuals.

*1974*    **Water Resources Development Act (WRDA),** is a reference to public laws enacted by Congress to deal with various aspects of water resources: environmental, structural, navigational, flood protection, hydrology, etc. Last revision was in 2007.

*1974*    **Reclamation Development Act of 1974, Public Law 93-493, 88 Stat. 1486, Title VI.** Authorizes Reclamation to investigate, plan, construct, operate, and maintain such short term public outdoor recreation facilities and opportunities that are necessary for the safety, health, protection, and outdoor recreation use of the visiting public at Lake Berryessa as part of the Solano Project, California.

*1974*    **43 CFR part 420, Off-Road Vehicle Use (1974).** Outlined the provisions for establishing off-road vehicle use on Reclamation lands to protect the land resources, to promote the safety of all users, to minimize conflicts among the various users, and to ensure that any permitted use will not result in significant adverse environmental impact or cause irreversible damage to existing ecological balances.

*1975*    **Eastern Wilderness Act.** Designated 16 national forest areas as part of Wilderness System, even though not free of human alteration or not of standard size.

*1975*    **Amended Federal Aid Highway Act.** Authorized lake access and bikeways.

*1976*    **Railroad Revitalization and Regulatory Reform Act.** Authorized 90 percent federal grants to enable state and local governments to plan, acquire, and develop recreation facilities on abandoned railroad rights-of-way.

*1976*    **Coastal Zone Management Act amendments.** Established new program of grants to acquire coastal areas.

*1976*    **Land and Water Conservation Fund and Historic Preservation Act amendments.** Increased amount of funds for federal and state agencies under these two bills.

*1976*    **Tax Reform Act.** Provided tax incentive for preservation of historic structures.

*1976*    **Federal Land Policy Management Act.** Required public outdoor recreation to be considered as a use for public lands.

*1976*    **National Forest Management Act.** Amended the 1974 RPA act to provide for full public participation in Forest Service land management plans.

*1977*    **Surface Mining and Reclamation Act.** Required many changes, giving impetus to recreation in mining areas.

*1977*    **Youth Employment and Demonstration Projects Act.** Established YACC on year-round basis to aid parks, forests, and recreation areas.

*1977*    **Food and Agriculture Act.** Authorized payments to private land owners who allow certain recreational uses by the public.

*1978*    **The Redwood Act** (also Redwood amendment) is a 1978 amendment to the National Park Service General Authorities Act of 1970. The amendment is particularly notable for clarifying and supplementing the 1970 act and the National Park Service Organic Act of 1916.

*1978*    **Heritage Conservation and Recreation Service (HCRS).** Created to identify, evaluate, and encourage protection of the nation's natural and historic resources and plan and fund recreation programs. Assumed most of the functions of the former Bureau of Outdoor

Recreation, the Office of Archaeology and Historic Preservation, and the Natural Landmarks program.

*1978* **Endangered American Wilderness Act.** Designated 1.3 million acres in 10 western states as part of National Preservation System.

*1978* **Comprehensive Employment Training Act (CETA) amendments.** Provided funds for employees in recreation and other areas.

*1978* **National Energy Conservation Policy Act.** Included studies of off-highway recreation vehicles and bicycle transportation facilities.

*1979* **Archaeological Resources Protection Act.** Protected archaeological resources on public lands and Native American lands. Includes pottery, basketry, bottles, weapons, weapon projectiles, tools, structures, pit houses, rock painting, rock carving, intaglios, graves, human skeletal remains, or any piece of the foregoing items.

*1980* **National Wild and Scenic River System.** Added 13 wild rivers to system.

*1980* **Alaska National Interest Land Conservation Act (ANILCA).** Provided for the designation and conservation of certain public lands in the state of Alaska.

*1981* **Heritage Conservation and Recreation Service (HCRS) abolished.** Most duties transferred to the National Park Service.

*1982* **National Wild and Scenic Rivers Act.** Set aside and protected special rivers.

*1983* **43 CFR part 24, Department of the Interior Fish and Wildlife Policy (1983).** Stated that Federal agencies of the U.S. Department of the Interior shall provide for public use of Federal lands in accordance with State and Federal laws, and permit public hunting, fishing, and trapping within statutory and budgetary limitations and in a manner compatible with the primary objectives for which the lands are administered.

*1984* **Forest and Rangeland Renewable Resources Act.** Provided for an updated assessment of rangelands.

*1984* **Wilderness Act amendment.** Effectively banned bicycles from all Federal Wilderness areas.

*1984* **The California Wilderness Act of 1984** is a federal law (Public Law 98-425), passed by the United States Congress on September 28, 1984, that authorized the addition of over three million acres (12,000 km$^2$) within the state of California to the National Wilderness Preservation System.

*1984* **An Act to Authorize Acquisition or Use of Public Lands by States, Counties, or Municipalities for Recreational Purposes of 1984, Public Law 98-552, 98 Stat. 2823.** Authorized the Secretary of the Interior to cooperate with State regulatory or enforcement officials to enforce State resource protection laws on Federal lands, including reimbursement of State expenditures for resource protection and administration, if necessary.

*1985* **Presidential Commission on Outdoor Recreation Resource Review Commission** (ORRRC) called for an update on the previous recreation findings.

*1986* **Congress initiated challenge grants** to the USDA Forest Service and to Fish and Wildlife programs.

*1986* **Emergency Wetlands Resource Act.** Promoted conservation of migratory waterfowl, including acquisition of wetlands and other essential habitat.

*1986* **The National Marine Parks Policy was approved**, which committed Canada to protecting important examples of its marine environment. In 1987, Fathom Five National Marine Park was established in Georgian Bay, by federal-provincial agreement with Ontario, as Canada's first national marine park.

*1988* **National Parks Act** states that "the National Parks of Canada are hereby dedicated to the people of Canada for their benefit, education and enjoyment … and shall be maintained and made use of so as to leave them unimpaired for the enjoyment of future generations."

*1990* **Americans with Disabilities Act.** Provided a clear and comprehensive mandate for the elimination of discrimination against individuals with disabilities in areas of employment, housing, public accommodations, transportation, communication, recreation, institutionalization, health services, voting, and access to public services.

*1990*   **Food, Agriculture, Conservation, and Trade Act.** Provided for wetland reserves, tree planting, watershed protection, and control of weeds and pests.

*1990*   **Amendment to the Clean Air Act.** Provided for attainment and maintenance of national ambient air-quality standards.

*1990*   **Native American Graves Protection and Repatriation Act.** Provides for the protection of Native American graves.

*1990*   **The Green Plan** sets out the Canadian federal government's goal of completing the Canadian National Park system by the year 2000 by having a national park in each of the 39 regions.

*1991*   **Intermodal Surface Transportation Efficiency Act (ISTEA).** Provides for greater use of the National System of Scenic Byways.

*1992*   **Energy Policy Act.** Prohibits the licensing by the Federal Regulatory Energy Commission of any new hydroelectrical power project located within units of the National Park System that would have an adverse effect on federal lands within any such unit.

*1992*   **Authorization and Adjustment Act of 1992, Public Law 102-575, 106 Stat. 4690, Title XXVIII (Reclamation Recreation Management Act).** Due to the increases in the public demand for outdoor recreation and the changes in the economic climate for Reclamation's non-Federal managing partners, Public Law 89-72 was amended by Title XXVIII of Public Law 102-575. Title XXVIII, among other things, updated the old provisions and changed some of the cost share requirements of Public Law 89-72 to allow the Federal Government to share a greater financial burden for recreation development and management.

*1994*   **The Northwest Forest Plan (NWFP)** is a series of federal policies and guidelines governing land use on federal lands in the Pacific Northwest region of the United States. It covers areas ranging from Northern California to western Washington. The NWFP was adopted in 1994 by the Clinton administration as the outcome of a series of studies and hearings that began in 1993.

*1996*   **Omnibus Parks and Public Land Management Act of 1996, Public Law 104-333, 110 Stat. 4093.** Established a commission to consider, review, evaluate, and recommend legislative opportunities for enhanced water-based recreation for public use.

*1998*   **Omnibus Consolidated Appropriations Act of 1998, Public Law 105-277, 112 Stat. 2681, Title X (Canyon Ferry Reservoir, Montana).** As part of the Canyon Ferry Unit of the Pick-Sloan Missouri Basin Program, Public Law 105-277 provides Reclamation with direct authority to investigate, plan, develop, operate, and maintain recreation facilities on land withdrawn or acquired for development of the project; to conserve the scenery, the natural historic, paleontologic and archaeologic objects, and the wildlife on the land; to provide for public use and enjoyment of the land and water areas of the project; and to investigate, plan, construct, operate, and maintain facilities for the conservation of fish and wildlife resources.

*1999*   **The Water Resources Development Act of 1999 (WRDA 1999)**, Pub.L. 106-53, was enacted by Congress of the United States on August 17, 1999. Most of the provisions of WRDA 1999 are administered by the United States Army Corps of Engineers.

*2001*   **Law Enforcement Authority at Bureau of Reclamation of 2001, Public Law 107-69, 115 Stat. 593.** Amended the Reclamation Recreation Management Act of 1992 in order to provide for the security of dams, facilities, and resources under the jurisdiction of Reclamation.

*2004*   **Federal Lands Recreation Enhancement Act of 2004, Public Law 108-447, 118 Stat. 3378.** Authorized the U.S. Forest Service, National Park Service, Bureau of Land Management, U.S. Fish and Wildlife Service, and Reclamation to charge fees at Federal recreation sites that meet certain criteria and to reinvest a majority of the collected revenues into enhancing the site where the fees were collected.

*2005*   **The Caribbean National Forest Act of 2005** is a United States federal law that designates certain United States National Forest land in Puerto Rico as components of the National Wilderness Preservation System.

*2006*    **The Northern California Coastal Wild Heritage Wilderness Act** is a U.S. federal law enacted in 2006 that enlarged existing wilderness boundaries and created new wilderness areas for protection under the National Wilderness Preservation System. These newly designated protected wilderness areas help safeguard habitat for more than 250 endangered species including the California Condor, bald eagle, and the bristlecone pine, the oldest living trees on earth. It also added Wild and Scenic status to sections of the Black Butte River, created the Cow Mountain Recreation Area and designated the Elkhorn Ridge Potential Wilderness Area.

*2006*    **National Historic Preservation Act of 1966** was amended. The Secretary of the Interior is authorized to expand and maintain a National Register of Historic Places composed of districts, sites, buildings, structures, and objects significant in American history, architecture, archaeology, engineering, and culture.

*2008*    **The Consolidated Natural Resources Act of 2008** (Pub.L. 110-229, 122 Stat. 754-876, enacted May 8, 2008; CNRA) was an act passed in the 110th United States Congress and enacted on May 8, 2008.

*2009*    **The Pacific Remote Islands National Marine Monument** was proclaimed a national monument on January 6, 2009 by U.S. President George W. Bush. The monument covers 86,607 square miles (55,428,480 acres, spanning areas to the far south and west of Hawaii: Kingman Reef, Palmyra Atoll, Howland Island, Baker Island, Jarvis Islands, Johnston Atoll, and Wake Island.

*2009*    **43 CFR part 423, Public Conduct on Bureau of Reclamation Facilities, Lands and Waterbodies (2009).** The purpose of 43 CFR part 423 is to maintain law and order and protect persons and property within Reclamation projects and on Reclamation lands and waterbodies. The CFR deals with Reclamation areas that are open and closed to public use, rules of conduct, authorization of otherwise prohibited activities, special use areas, and violations and sanctions.

*2009*    **43 CFR part 429, Use of Bureau of Reclamation Land, Facilities, and Waterbodies (2009).** Set forth the procedures for Reclamation to recover the value of rights-of-use interests granted to applicants and for collection of the administrative costs associated with issuing rights-of-use over lands under administration of Reclamation.

*2009*    **The Omnibus Public Land Management Act of 2009** (Pub.L. 111-11, H.R. 146) is a law passed in the 111th United States Congress and signed into law by President Barack Obama on March 30, 2009. Title I of the bill designates two million acres (8,000 km²) of wilderness in nine states (California, Colorado, Idaho, Michigan, New Mexico, Oregon, Utah, Virginia, and West Virginia) for protection through addition to the National Wilderness Preservation System.

## Executive Orders

*1972*    **Executive Order 11644, Use of Off-Road Vehicles on Public Lands.** Established policy and procedures that will ensure that the use of off-road vehicles on public lands will be controlled and directed so as to protect the resources of those lands, to promote the safety of all users of those lands, and to minimize conflicts among the various uses of those lands.

*1977*    **Executive Order 11989, Off-Road Vehicles on Public Lands.** Amended portions of EO 11644 to, among other things, clarify the definition of an off-road vehicle to include fire, military, emergency, or law enforcement vehicles and provide further direction on the closure of previous designated off-road vehicle use areas.

*1977*    **Executive Order 11988, Floodplain Management.** Directed the leadership of each agency to initiate actions to reduce the risk of flood loss; to minimize the impact of floods on human safety, health, and welfare; and to restore and preserve the natural and beneficial values served by floodplains.

*1977*    **Executive Order 11990, Protection of Wetlands.** Directed agency leadership to preserve and enhance the natural and beneficial values of wetlands in carrying out the agency's responsibilities for (1) acquiring, managing, and disposing of Federal lands and facilities; (2) providing Federally undertaken, financed, or assisted construction and improvements; and (3) conducting Federal activities and programs affecting land use including, but not limited to, water and related land resources planning, regulating, and licensing.

*1995*   **Executive Order 12962, Recreational Fisheries.** Directed federal agencies to the extent permitted by law, where practicable, and in cooperation with states and Indian Tribes to improve the quantity, function, sustainable productivity, and distribution of U.S. aquatic resources for increased recreational fishing opportunities.

*2007*   **Executive Order 13444, Facilitation of Hunting Heritage and Wildlife Conservation.** Directed federal agencies that have programs and activities that have a measurable effect on public land management, outdoor recreation, and wildlife management to facilitate the expansion and enhancement of hunting opportunities and the management of game species and their habitat.

### Other Policy Sources

Policy also emanates from executive actions other than those taken by a president to generate or veto legislation. From time to time, presidents have appointed committees to study recreation issues. Sometimes policy decisions emerged from these sessions and were expressed through legislation and agency action. In other instances, the political climate was not right and findings of such bodies went largely unheeded.

Another source of influence on policy is professional groups such as the National Society of State Foresters (http://www.stateforesters.org/), Society of American Foresters (http://www.safnet.org/), National Association of State Park Directors (http://www.naspd.org/), and National Parks and Recreation Association (http://www.nrpa.org/) that have committees on policy and public legislation. Some of the citizen environmental groups, such as the Sierra Club (http://www.sierraclub.org/), the Audubon Society (http://www.audubon.org/), or the Izaak Walton League (http://www.iwla.org/), also affect policy by support or rejection of certain measures. Many of these groups have combined to block proposed actions through litigation.

**The Outdoor Recreation Resources Review Commission**. By 1958, Congress had decided that an intensive nationwide study of outdoor recreation should be made. The authorizing act, Public Law 85-470, set forth the mission for the Outdoor Recreation Resources Review Commission (ORRRC). It had essentially three purposes: to determine the outdoor recreation wants and needs of the American people then, to project what they would be in the years 1976 and 2000, and to determine what policies or programs should be recommended to ensure that the needs of the present and the future are adequately and sufficiently met (U.S. Department of the Interior, 1962).

This study was made by the ORRRC, a group composed of members of Congress, citizens, and government employees who produced a report containing 27 documents, which are summarized in a single report entitled "Outdoor Recreation for America."

Some of the findings were as follows:

- The simple activities are the most popular.
- Outdoor opportunities are most urgently needed near metropolitan areas.
- Although across the country, considerable land is now available for outdoor recreation, it does not effectively meet the need.
- Money is needed.
- Outdoor recreation is often compatible with other resource uses.
- Water is a focal point of outdoor recreation.
- Outdoor recreation brings about economic benefits.
- Outdoor recreation is a major leisure-time activity, and it is growing in importance.
- More needs to be known about the values of outdoor recreation.

The national outdoor recreation policy that evolved from the ORRRC study stated: *It shall be the national policy through the conservation and wise use of resources to preserve, develop, and make accessible to all American people such quantity and quality of outdoor recreation as will be necessary and desirable for the individual enjoyment and to assure the physical, cultural, and spiritual benefits of outdoor recreation.*

**Implementation.** This policy has required the cooperative participation of all levels of government and private enterprise. In some aspects of the program, government action was required; in others, the private sector has been better equipped to do the job.

**Federal.** Generally speaking, it seems that the federal government is best equipped to (1) preserve scenic areas, natural wonders, primitive areas, and historic sites of national significance, (2) manage federal lands for the broadest possible recreation benefit consistent with other essential issues, (3) cooperate with the states through technical and financial assistance, (4) promote interstate arrangements, including federal participation where necessary, and (5) assume vigorous cooperative leadership in a nationwide recreation effort.

It is difficult, given the widely divergent entities involved, to fix areas of responsibility for states, counties, and municipalities. However, most park practitioners would concur with the following statements as to which level of government was best equipped to handle certain areas of responsibility.

**Provincial and state.** This level of government is most effective in (1) preserving scenic areas, natural wonders, primitive areas, and historic sites of provincial and state significance or regional significance if that region covers two or more governmental authorities, (2) managing provincial or state lands for the broadest possible recreation benefit consistent with the other essential uses, (3) cooperating with the federal government for technical and financial assistance and in comprehensive provincial or state and national planning, (4) promoting intergovernmental arrangements, (5) providing consolation services, and (6) providing strong cooperative leadership.

**County and municipal.** These entities can (1) acquire and develop areas strategically located to best serve the citizens of the governmental jurisdiction involved, (2) provide program leadership to aid area citizens in learning recreation skills, and (3) cooperate with the other agencies and other levels of government.

**Presidential Commission on Outdoor Recreation Resources Review.** In 1985, President Reagan ordered an update of the ORRRC findings. Their goals were to examine the following:

1) The existing outdoor recreation lands and resources and the land and resource base necessary for future outdoor recreation.
2) The roles of the federal, state, county, and municipal governments in providing outdoor recreation opportunities, protecting outdoor recreation resources, and meeting anticipated outdoor recreation conditions.
3) The role of the private sector in meeting present and future outdoor recreation needs, including an assessment of the potential for cooperation between the private sector and government in providing outdoor recreation opportunities and protecting outdoor recreation resources.
4) The relationship between outdoor recreation and personal and public health, the economy, and the environment.
5) The future needs of outdoor recreation management systems, including qualified personnel, technical information, and anticipated financial needs.
6) The relationship of outdoor recreation to the broader range of recreational pursuits, including implications for the supply of and demand for outdoor recreation resources and opportunities.
7) The underlying social, economic, and technological factors that are likely to affect the supply of and demand for outdoor recreation resources, including trends in disposable income and demographic characteristics of the United States.

**Presidential Executive Order No. 12503**
**The White House**

Rockefeller noted in 2002 that:

> The fortieth anniversary of the report, Outdoor Recreation for America, describing the work and recommendations of the Outdoor Recreation Resources Review Commission (ORRRC), is an occasion to commemorate the programs the commission helped to bring about—the Land and Water Conservation Fund, a Bureau of Outdoor Recreation, a national system of rivers and trails, and many others. These programs play an important role in making outdoor recreation opportunities available to the American people. Perhaps even more significant than the specific programs ORRRC helped to create are the changes in national direction that it fostered (U.S. Department of the Interior, 1962).

## POLICY DEVELOPMENT AND CHANGE

Only the head of an agency should have the authority to issue policies. This does not imply that only the head should suggest or be involved in the development of policies. Far from it. Policies should be the result of much coordinated thinking. This should involve all agency personnel. All relevant data should be made available to the policy maker along with pertinent observations. The wise policy maker will solicit input.

One of the most difficult aspects of policy formulation is trying to predict the future. There are multiple variables affecting the implementation of policy. Outcomes may be quite different than what was intended. Wengert (1967) stated it this way:

> The decision-maker is, in short, acting under conditions of uncertainty, created in part by limitations of knowledge, in part by limitations in time, and in part by limitations of technique. Problem identification and problem solution in the area of resource policy can obviously be improved by use of planning techniques—by logical analysis and rational calculation. But planning should never be confused with certitude. Rational techniques for identifying resource problems and preparing proposed solutions cannot assure correct answers, but must deal in terms of approximation and probability. The technique used may represent the highest level of rationality; it may be mathematically precise. But the nonrational and irrational aspects of human behavior must also be included as part of the matrix from which policy decisions will flow.

New developments arise both from the public with its new vehicles and outdoor recreation needs and from government itself as legislation is passed that either centrally or peripherally affects recreation areas. These events will require the adaptations of existing policies or the development of new ones. It is important that policy adherence be one of the checkpoints in supervision, not only to assure compliance with guidelines, but also in order to recognize the discrepancies that indicate the need for revision or new policy.

### A Case in Point—Beach Driving in Washington State

Note that politics is very much a part of the formulation of policy. The following case history shows how changing use of a resource called for political decisions as well as policy formulation, and it outlines the part played in this formulation by agencies, executives, legislators, the public, and the courts.

The State of Washington has 2,337 miles (3,470 km) of marine shoreline, of which 157 miles (250 km) front directly on the Pacific Ocean. This frontage has varied topography, consisting of both low-bank sandy beaches and high-bluff outcroppings. The beach itself varies in width from zero to approximately one mile (1.6 km) of sand resource. Washington's beach is different from similar areas in the United States in at least one respect. There are no major population centers on this beach and, therefore, there is neither the intense push for commercial and high-density living accommodation nor the pressure of hordes of people living "right next door." This relative isolation has also meant that local citizens have developed their own use of the beach and have very strong proprietary feelings about it and their use of it.

Prior to 1966, the beach was administered by the State Department of Natural Resources (DNR), which operated under laws requiring it to receive the highest economic values from lands that it administered. Such uses included mining and oil exploration and, on the beaches, nonrestricted sand removal and unlimited driving. It must also be noted that established, or "historical," policy plays an important role in this case. In the territorial days of Washington, the only easy north-south route near the coast was along the beach. As a result, the state had declared the beach a public highway.

In the early 1960s, many Washington citizens became increasingly interested in preserving all state-owned ocean beach lands for conservation and recreation purposes. Several special interest groups began to express concern about the way in which the ocean beaches of Washington State were being administered.

Local and out-of-state beach users were on the beach in increasing numbers; local governmental authorities were becoming concerned about the rapidly escalating costs of beach maintenance; health officials were alarmed at the sanitary conditions; families, especially those with children, were concerned about safety. As one father, holding his bruised daughter who had been hit by a car on the beach, painfully put it, "Doesn't my daughter have a right to use these beaches, too?"

There was no beach policy, per se, only policies that had been formulated for other land resources, but they were being applied to the beach situation. The time was ripe to develop a beach policy and decide who would administer the policy. This also meant changing the historical beach-use policy.

During the 1967 legislative session, a conservation-minded governor responded to all of these factors and groups by submitting an executive request calling for the administration of the beaches to be transferred from DNR to the Washington State Parks and Recreation Commission (WSPRC). This bill, containing legislative policy as suggested by the governor, became one of the most controversial bills of the decade as an elected body (the legislature) was asked to consider a request from the elected governor to transfer jurisdiction from yet another elected official (head of DNR) to an appointed body and its director (WSPRC). The controversy becomes more easily understood when one understands that the head of DNR and the legislative majority were of one party, and the governor was of another.

It might well have been that the bill would never have passed had not the legislators agreed that an important issue was at stake, and that policy, not politics, needed their attention. It was decided that the beach administration would stay with DNR if the legislature determined that the best use of the beach was for revenue purposes. Conversely, the administration would be transferred to WSPRC if the best use was for conservation and recreation. The latter use was deemed the better by the legislature. Within the statute that transferred jurisdiction, several policies were set forth; one dealt with the thorny issue of driving on the beach.

The legislature decreed that all automobile use could not be banned from the beach, but use could be regulated by WSPRC. This legislative policy seemed too vague to WSPRC, which asked the state's attorney general for a ruling of legislative intent. That response indicated, in essence, that WSPRC could ban some of the automobiles from some of the beach some of the time, but not all of the automobiles from all of the beach all of the time. This preservation action received considerable public and political support, including legislative action requiring that a minimum of 40 percent of the beaches be closed.

The following is a brief summary of the steps then taken in the process of formulating a policy for the beach driving issue. Note that a standard planning format was followed.

1.  Research of other areas. In this instance, in-depth consultation was held with state government officials in Oregon, California, Hawaii, and Florida.
2.  Data gathering. Information and statistics concerning laws governing the beaches and automobiles, accident/death reports from the beach, location and cost of constructing and maintaining beach access roads, and data on need and cost of patrolling were compiled. Drivable sand areas were located and noted on maps.
3.  Data analysis was conducted.
4.  Preliminary driving regulations were developed based on data analysis and assumptions.

5. A preliminary plan of action was developed leading from preliminary regulations to final rules.
6. A cross-section of staff reviwed the plan to locate the flaws in the prepared regulations and the plan of action. (All of the steps above were handled by the director after conceptual approval by the WSPRC.)
7. The proposal was presented to the WSPRC, the formal policy maker. (This body approved the proposed policy.)
8. The proposed policy was discussed with legislators from the directly affected area as well as those on the legislative parks committees.
9. The proposed policy was discussed with local officials, including county commissioners, mayors, and sheriffs.
10. Briefing meetings were held with key individuals from groups sympathetic to the proposed policy (held while steps 8 and 9 were in progress).
11. The proposal was discussed with the individuals opposed to the policy.
12. A carefully laid-out media campaign was initiated by WSPRC prior to the holding of public meetings.
13. Public meetings to receive input were held both in beach communities and in population centers from which most of the beach users originated.
14. The staff assembled and analyzed all data received from the meetings and developed a final proposal.
15. The regulatory plan was published by the Commission. Final hearings were held prior to legally adopting rules that it believed were consistent with the policy.

Adoption of this plan was not an easy task. The local user population voiced strong opposition to banning automobiles from even small stretches of beach as suggested by the Commission. These local users, as well as some others, wanted to cut up logs for firewood, remove sand, advertise the beach as the longest drivable beach in the United States, have easy access to razor clam beds, and continue their own unrestricted driving.

Those who did not want any restrictions on where automobiles could drive took one last approach to the issue—that of questioning who had policy authority. In late 1980, the Washington State Supreme Court, in a split decision, ruled that the legislature had not conveyed this particular policy authority on the WSPRC, even though this had been its intent. The determination of this policy went back to where it had started in 1967—in the state legislature. It was up to that body to clarify the language of the statute in order for WSPRC to have undisputed policy authority.

In 1989, the state legislature transferred the obligation of selecting the 40 percent pedestrian-only areas to five local coastal jurisdictions. The WSPRC served as a consultant only, leaving the major choice of closed areas up to the local people. After some refinement of the resultant plan, the commission adopted it in February 1990. The policy now provides for 40 percent of the beach to be closed to driving between April 15 and the day after Labor Day. Recent surveys show public support for the new policy.

The beaches remain a place of wild beauty. For approximately 220 days a year, auto driving is permitted on the entire beach, and during the spring and summer, approximately 145 days, 40 percent of the beach is now reserved for pedestrian-only use. It has taken many years and much compromise to frame a policy acceptable to both the local population and the agency administering the policy.

## A Case in Point – Alcohol Consumption in Park

Policy on the drinking issue is invariably subject to vacillation, yet few policy decisions have as much impact on the park manager as does this one. There are those who favor a comparatively open policy, stating reasons such as the following:

- Ethnic background—"We always have wine (or beer) with our meals."
- Honesty—"It is being done now undercover, so let's be honest about our actions."
- Family rights—"We do it at home, and this is our home away from home."

- Consistency—"Beer and wine are sold and can be consumed in other public places, why not here?"

Those who wish a more restrictive policy state the following reasons:
- Expense—"Law enforcement must be stepped up when people are under the influence of alcohol, so costs increase."
- Litter—"More cans and bottles are strewn over the park. This increases maintenance costs and looks ugly."
- Disturbance—"There is more boisterous noise when liquor is allowed."
- Mores—"Liquor use is offensive anywhere, but particularly in a family campground."

In between these two policy extremes is the park manager who must administer the written policy when facing those users who insist on established historical use or ethnic right. And in many instances, the actions of the manager, ranger, or park aid representing the manager will bring about a change in policy. The following situation is typical.

The agency policy is clear: "No alcohol." After a very brief period of practical experience, the new park manager changes his or her phrase from "Sorry, alcohol is not allowed" to "Please put it in a paper cup—it's not allowed, you know, but you're OK."

As more "OKs" visit the park, wine, and beer bottles appear on the picnic tables and only the "hard stuff" is in the paper cup. Before long, visitors and managers are asking, "Why can't the law be changed? After all, the rowdy ones can still be arrested under other laws." And so the policy is softened, and alcohol is allowed under certain conditions in certain places in the park.

The chances are that one of two patterns will evolve out of the "alcohol situations": 1) A new manager will take over this park whose actions will depend on his or her background and past park experience (i.e., the enforcement could become more lax or more stringent), or 2) The legislative body will receive so many complaints—from both directions—that it will pass new legislation. In either event, the chances are that some alcohol will be consumed and not everyone will be pleased. Of course, such violations of the law as consumption of alcohol by a minor or driving while under the influence must always be promptly dealt with.

Over the course of time, any given park manager will find his or her day brushed (if not deeply affected) by such "policy hassles." The chances are that each manager of significant tenure will also encounter one or more of the following policy dilemmas.

## Case In Point—Leash Policy

Dogs initially will be forbidden entirely. Then they may be allowed if on a leash. Then they are allowed on a leash, but only in certain areas. Then they are forbidden again, but agency- or concessionaire-provided kennels are available in some tucked-away place. And so it goes, until the whole cycle starts again. See the end of the chapter for dog-related policies and controversies. An example of dog leash law policies follows (http://www.threeriversparks.org/activities/dog-off-leash-policies.aspx):

### Dog Off-leash Area Policies—Three Rivers in Plymouth, Minnesota

Three Rivers has specific policies for dogs in off-leash areas. For the safety of all park users, please adhere to these policies. Violation of any of these rules and conditions can lead to a citation and/or revocation of your pass. The Park District reserves the right to reject or cancel passes for any reason and will restrict days or times of use as necessary.
- Users of the dog off-lease areas must carry or display a daily or annual pass.
- Dogs must be under control at all times. No exceptions. A dog is considered under control if it will come when called. Dogs must not be permitted to interfere with other people or dogs, unless permission is granted by each handler for dogs to play together.
- Handlers must remain in the area with their dogs at all times.

- Each handler must clean up and dispose of dog feces in a sanitary manner. A trash barrel is provided at each site.
- Aggressive behavior is not acceptable.
- Permit holders must have certification of current rabies vaccination for each pet readily available when using the dog off-leash area. Puppies under the age of four months are not allowed in the off-leash areas.
- No more than two pets per dog handler are allowed in the area at any given time.
- Children must be closely supervised by adults and should be instructed about proper behavior around dogs.
- Off-leash area use is only allowed during park hours (5:00 a.m. to sunset daily, or as posted by the Park District).

## Case In Point—Noise in the Parks

Many people take the city with them—T.V., radios, tape decks, souped-up hot rods, motor bikes, and their boisterous voices. There are decibel laws, but these are rarely enforced. And after bedtime, then what? Most policies state all is to be quiet after 10:00 or 11:00 p.m.  Other noise-related problems such as motor bikes have been addressed in noise ordinances. The Australian Government has released a report, "Motor Sport Noise," and how to regulate the problem (http://www.tams.act.gov.au/__data/assets/pdf_file/0005/45734/motorsportsnoise_envprotpol.pdf).

As an example of the magnitude of the noise problem and other issues that require park policies, U.S. Senator Dianne Feinstein (D-Calif.) was concerned that proposed revisions (in 2006)  to National Park Service Management policies could seriously weaken protections currently enjoyed by our nation's national parks. In a letter to National Park Service Director Fran Mainella, Senator Feinstein expressed concern that these revisions would harm the air quality, pristine quietness, and interim protection for wilderness areas awaiting official designation.

> *"Our national parks are America's cathedrals,"* Senator Feinstein wrote. *"I am seriously concerned that your proposed revisions to the National Park Service Management policies will erode the protections that make our parks such remarkable places."*

Senator Feinstein wrote that revisions to the policies would severely impact:
- Air quality—Proposed revisions would include demoting "clear skies" from an essential component of the parks to an "associated characteristic," appearing to allow for some accommodation of air pollution. Air quality is a critical problem for Joshua Tree, Yosemite, and Sequoia-Kings Canyon, where between 2000 and 2004 there were more than 315 unhealthy ozone pollution days.
- Wilderness stewardship—Proposed revisions would weaken interim protection for lands deemed suitable for wilderness designation, but not yet recommended to Congress by the President, which could take years.
- Noise pollution—Proposed revisions would remove important language about preserving, within the parks, the natural quiet of areas undisturbed by human-caused sound. (SOURCE: http://feinstein.senate.gov/06releases/r-nps-mngt.htm).

The copy of the letter to the National Park Service Director is in the appendix of this chapter.

## Case In Point—Mountain Bikes

Mountain bikes are in conflict with several trail user groups, and have created some challenges for park managers.  As early as 1988, the California Department of Parks and Recreation developed a mountain bike policy that included the following.

Generally, paved and unpaved park roads, unless otherwise posted, are open, and trails are closed, to bicyclists. Unpaved roads may be closed and trails opened upon a written order by the District

Superintendent, approved by the Regional Director, that specifically considers criteria which reflect the safety of all users and potential impacts to park resources and values.

Also in 1988, the Washington State Parks and Recreation Commission adopted a policy giving local park managers discretion in all trail closures, the exceptions being interpretive trails, exercise trails in natural areas, and nature preserves that are declared closed to mountain bikes. A public hearing must precede any discretionary closure.

During that same year, many closures were occurring in other parts of the country. For example, Pennsylvania State Parks reaffirmed a regulation prohibiting bicycles from any trails not designated closed.

The greatest difficulty may be with consistency, as these last few examples have shown. Policies are generally restrictive, and the public manages to slowly loosen them up until the restrictions have to be tightened again. This, too, is part of being a park manager: knowing how to live with these inevitable modulations. However difficult it may be to work with "hard and soft" policies under "flexible" direction, it is probably easier than coping with unwritten policy.

Presently, there are about 30 properties managed by the National Park Service that include trails approved for mountain bikes now, according to Mark Eller, communications director for the International Mountain Biking Association. Longsdorf and Kucharewski (2006) found in a study on mountain biking at state parks and park districts that:

> Eighty-six percent of state parks participating in the study allowed on-road or off-road mountain bike activity, compared to only 31 percent of participating park districts. Out of the 26 state parks or park districts allowing mountain biking, 65 percent reported experiencing increased mountain bike activity, while 38 percent considered mountain biking either a resource management or recreation-management concern. Of the 21 state parks or park districts not allowing mountain biking activity, 57 percent indicated mountain bike users illegally trespassing on park grounds, and 52 percent indicated having discussed opening areas to mountain biking or including mountain biking in future management plans.

Mountain biking is currently taking place at ski areas during the summer. The ski areas are holding events, and also using this as a means to gain off-season revenues.

## Case In Point—Environmental Policy

### Wheaton Park District Goes Green!

The Board of Park Commissioners voted to adopt an environmental policy recommended by staff at the January 21, 2009 board meeting. The Wheaton Park District's commitment to environmental stewardship and appreciation of increasing public awareness and concern about environmental issues led to the creation of an Environmental Policy Committee and development of a park district policy. The policy will assist the Wheaton Park District to achieve environmental excellence in all park district programming and operations and will further promote the district's role model status of sound environmental practices. By educating the staff and community, it will lead to changes in practices, which will result in positive environmental changes overall. As a park district, we are committed to setting an example and adopting a leadership position in establishing and maintaining sound environmental policies, practices and educational opportunities for the employees and patrons of the Wheaton Park District.

### Environmental Committee Mission

To establish and maintain sound environmental policies, practices and educational opportunities for the employees and patrons of the Wheaton Park District.

**Environmental Policy Summary:**

*Policy 1.0 Purchase and Use Environmentally Safe and Sensitive Products*
Purchase products for use in facility and park operations which minimize negative environmental impacts, taking into consideration the effects of product production, use, safety, storage, disposal and cost.

*Policy 2.0 Wise Use and Protection of Air, Water, Soil and Wildlife*
Actively seek and implement ways to conserve and protect water and soil, enhance air quality, limit the production and release of damaging pollutants, and protect wildlife.

*Policy 3.0 Wise Use of Energy Resources*
Actively seek and implement ways to conserve energy resources and investigate methods of applying alternative energy technologies.

*Policy 4.0 Reduction and Handling of Waste*
Reduce waste production, reuse and recycle materials from facility and park operations, and handle hazardous and all other wastes according to lawful and safe procedures.

*Policy 5.0 Open Space Planning and Preservation*
Protect and restore indigenous natural communities such as prairies, woodlands and wetlands, and promote the reclamation, acquisition, preservation and management of other open space areas.

*Policy 6.0 Environmental Education and Interpretation*
Provide education and interpretation opportunities for staff and the public which increase appreciation for the natural world and promote environmentally conscious lifestyles, emphasizing selective consumption and low-impact resource use.

To read more, visit (http://www.wheatonparkdistrict.com/pgs/parks/green_policy.html).

## Implementing Policy

Because policies are usually developed and adopted only after considerable involvement by many people, it is reasonable to assume that the employees who administer the policies will need some time and assistance in understanding them. They should be informed as to why the policy was needed in the first place, how it is to be implemented, and under what circumstances it is in effect.

Once the policy is adopted, copies of it are reproduced in sufficient quantity to assure its availability at each park area, as well as at headquarters, and also on web pages. It is equally important that time be given to policy matters during the regular in-service training programs so that all are aware of policies and know that they apply to everyone, from the top administration down. When new employees are hired, policies should be discussed with them as a regular part of introductory training.

## CONCLUSION

Some policies are matters of routine, and administering them is no great problem. Others, as this chapter has pointed out, are hard to formulate, and may be even harder to enforce. Painful as the administration of policies might be to the manager at times, they are a necessity and a reality that those aspiring to managerial positions must face. Meeting the needs of the public is a most complex task.

To protect the rights of the recreationist, to protect our fragile and beautiful parks, and to give the manager half a chance to succeed, we need policies. And, imperfect as they may be, they do guide and validate our actions in a civilized society.

# REFERENCES

## References Cited

Australian Capital Territory Government, 2002, Motor Sports Noise, http://www.tams.act.gov. au/__data/assets/pdf_file/0005/45734/motorsportsnoise_envprotpol.pdf

Cappiello, D. (2008). *Bush to help open national parks to mountain bikes.* Associated Press. Tuesday, October 13, 2008.

Chicago, County MN, Parks and Trails Policy Manual, http://www.co.chisago.mn.us/file. aspx?Id=8f78d24d-1fe3-42ea-b3c9-082f402e6a86

City of Toronto Parks and Recreation. (2009). Dogs and Parks Controversies, http://www.toronto. ca/parks/dogs.htm

Hass, G. (2002). ORRRC at 40. Parks and Recreation, May 2002, retrieved from http://findarticles. com/p/articles/mi_m1145/is_5_37/ai_86505437/?tag=content;col1

Hocker, J. (1988). *"The Uses of Our Land."* Proceedings of Henry M. Jackson Foundation Symposium, Seattle, WA.

Longsdorf, E., & Kucharewski, R. (2006). *Mountain bikes and metropolitan park districts: Issues and trends in trail management identified by state parks and park districts in Ohio*, Proceedings of the 2006 Northeastern Recreation Research Symposium. http://americantrails.org/resources/ ManageMaintain/OhioMtnbike.html

Montana Fish, Wildlife and Parks Policies, http://fwp.mt.gov/parks/permits/default.html

Office of the Auditor General of Canada, Parks Canada, http://www.oag-bvg.gc.ca/internet/English/ parl_oag_199611_31_e_5062.html

Popper, F., (1988). *"The Uses of Our Land."* Proceedings of Henry M. Jackson Foundation Symposium, Seattle, WA.

Resources for the Future, Outdoor Resources Review Group, http://www.rff.org/News/Features/ Pages/OutdoorResourcesReviewGroup-BackgroundStudy.aspx

Rockefeller, L. S. (2002) "From the ORRRC chairman—Outdoor Recreation Resources Review Commission - Brief Article". Parks & Recreation. FindArticles.com. 16 Mar, 2010. http:// findarticles.com/p/articles/mi_m1145/is_1_37/ai_82743101/

Tennessee State Park Policies, http://www.state.tn.us/environment/parks/policies.shtml

Three Rivers, MN Parks Department, 2009, Dog Policies, http://www.threeriversparks.org/ activities/dog-off-leash-policies.aspx

U.S. Department of the Interior. (1962). *Outdoor Recreation for America. A report of the President and to the Congress by the Outdoor Recreation Resources Review Commission.* Washington, D.C.

Wengert, N. (1967). *Natural Resources and the Political Struggle.* New York: Random House.

## General References

Albright, Horace M. (as told to Robert Cahn). *The birth of the National Park Service.* Salt Lake City: Howe Brothers, 1985.

Albright, Horace M., & Albright Schenck, Marian. (1999). *Creating the National Park Service: The missing years.* Norman: University of Oklahoma Press.

Alexander, Glen. (1988). *Mission and product perceptions of the NPS by members of the U.S. House of Representatives and NPS executives.* Chicago: University of Chicago Press.

American Academy for Park and Recreation Administration. (1980). *Proceedings for Symposium VI: The Americans outdoors. The legacy; the challenge.* Champaign, IL.

Bastic, Marie, & Bradley, John. (1991). "SCORPS after 25 Years, A New Beginning." *Trends.* Park Practice Program.

Clawson, Marion. (1988). *Two generations of history of outdoor recreation resources for the future.* Washington, D.C.: National Park Service.

Dana, Samual Trask, & Fairfax, Sally K. (1980). *Forest and range policy: Its development in the United States* (2nd ed.). New York: McGraw-Hill.

Everhart, William C. (1972). *The National Park Service.* New York: Praeger.

Hartzog, George B. Jr. (1988). *Battling for the national parks.* Mt. Kisco, New York: Moyer Bell Limited.

Ise, John. (1961). *Our national park policy: A critical history.* Baltimore: Johns Hopkins.

Lee, Ronald F. (1972). *Family tree of the National Park System.* Philadelphia, Pennsylvania: Eastern National Parks.

Mackintosh, Barry. (1991). *The national parks: Shaping the system.* Washington: National Park Service.

Rettie, Dwight F. (1995). *Our national park system.* Urbana, Illinois: University of Illinois Press.

Ridenour, James M. (1994). *The national parks compromised: Pork barrel politics and America's treasures.* Merrillville, IN: ICS Books.

Wirth, Conrad L. (1980). *Parks, politics, and the people.* Norman, Oklahoma: University of Oklahoma Press.

Shankland, Robert. (1970.) *Steve Mather of the national parks.* New York: Knopf,

Godbey, Geoffrey C. (1989). *The future of leisure services: Thriving for a change.* State College, PA: Venture.

Hendee, John C., George H. Stankey, & Robert C. Lucas. (1990). *Wilderness Management* (2nd ed.). Golden, CO: North American Press.

Hummel, Don. (1987). *Stealing the national parks: The destruction of concessions and park access.* Bellevue, WA: The Free Enterprise Press.

Machlis, Gary E., & Tichnell, David. (1985). *The state of the world's parks.* Boulder, CO: Westview Press.

McClosky, Michael. (1986). "The Wilderness Act of 1964; Its Background and Meaning." *Oregon Law Review*, Vol. 45, June, 1986.

Meyers, Phyllis, & Reid, Ann Christine. (1986). *State parks in a new era: A survey of issues and innovations.* Washington, D.C.: The Conservation Foundation.

Parks Canada. (1979). *Parks Canada Policy.* Ottawa, Canada.

# Appendix

**Letter sent by Senator Feinstein to Director Mainella**

February 16, 2006

Dear Director Mainella:

Our national parks are America's cathedrals. Their pristine air quality, the quiet of their rugged beauty, and the wild character of their land are just a few of their extraordinary qualities. I am seriously concerned that your proposed revisions to the National Park Service Management policies will erode the protections that make our parks such remarkable places.

One area of particular concern is park air quality. Proposed changes to the management policies include demoting "clear skies" from an essential component of the parks to an "associated characteristic". The definition of "natural condition" has also been altered to include man-made impacts. These changes appear to allow for some accommodation of air pollution.

Air quality is a critical problem for several California parks, including Joshua Tree, Yosemite, and Sequoia-Kings Canyon. For example, from 2000-2004, there were more than 315 unhealthy ozone pollution days in Sequoia-Kings Canyon, and the Environmental Protection Agency formally designated these parks as ozone non-attainment areas. Most pollution affecting national parks comes from sources outside park boundaries, and park officials must retain oversight over, and the authority to object against, permits for major air pollution sources.

Another area of concern is wilderness stewardship. The proposed changes to the park management policies weaken the obligation of the National Park Service to inventory its lands to determine those that have wilderness character. Among the lands likely affected by this change is Redwood National Park.

The proposed revisions would also weaken interim protection for lands deemed suitable for wilderness designation, but not yet recommended to Congress by the president. The president's review can take years, and protection during this interim period is important to preserve the wilderness character of these lands.

A final area of concern involves the natural quiet of the landscape. The proposed revisions would remove important language about preserving, within the parks, still areas undisturbed by human-caused sound. Encroaching noise from off-road, recreational vehicles and motor traffic may all impact visitor enjoyment. Airports have been proposed in the vicinity of several California parks, including Joshua Tree and Mojave, and noise from airplanes can also disturb natural quiet.

Noise may be especially problematic for parks in rapidly growing areas like Joshua Tree, or in heavily visited parks like Yosemite. Quiet contemplation of pristine environments is, for many people, an integral part of the experience of visiting National Parks, and the National Park Service's policies should be geared toward minimizing noise.

In the past, National Park Service Management Policies have been revised only once every ten years or more. Yet the most recent revision of these policies was completed in 2001. I am unclear why new revisions of the policies are needed now, or why many of the proposed changes are considered necessary to enhance the Park Service's ability to fulfill its mission.

To ensure that revisions are only accepted after careful consideration and with adequate public involvement, I respectfully request that any proposal you put together as a result of this public comment period be subject to another comment period of 90 days.

Sincerely,

*Dianne Feinstein*

United States Senator

# Chapter Four

# Recreation Law and Risk Management

Recreation law refers to the laws by which park agencies must operate. Liabilities are responsibilities the agency and the park manager assume when that operation takes place—in other words, when a park is open or closed to the public. One must also remember that policies carry varying degrees of law and interpretation. California is faced with closures of parks to balance the budget, yet the following memo demonstrates the complexity of the laws and the risk management and liabilities for these closures:

The extraordinary September 14, 2009 memo by the California Department of Parks and Recreation Legal Office analyzes "potential liabilities if units of the State Park System close, partially close, or are operated at reduced service levels." The memo is being distributed as a guide to park managers for "mitigating risks."

- Legal liabilities from "dangerous conditions" in unstaffed parks, deteriorating facilities, and risks to adjoining property from occurrences such as wildfires. The memo concludes, "From a liability standpoint, closing the parks would probably not benefit state parks and could, in fact, increase its liability for dangerous condition of public property";
- Contractual obligations from grants, land donations, concessionaire contracts, and earmarked federal and state funds may leave the parks legally obligated to keep operating despite a claim of funding shortfalls; and
- Public safety dangers and legal claims from nuisance uses and trespass. The memo predicts that state losses from theft, encroachments and other unauthorized uses "will only increase if state parks cannot take immediate and effective action. ..."

"Closing parks may be far more expensive than keeping them open and operating," stated California PEER Coordinator Karen Schambach. "Paradoxically, in order to avoid losses of life and property, California will need to spend its supposed savings to keep families out of beaches, parks and recreation areas." (Source: http://www.peer.org/news/news_id.php?row_id=1242)

## RECREATION LAWS

### Federal Lawmaking Bodies of the United States and Canada

**Federal supreme courts.** The U.S. Supreme Court and the Supreme Court of Canada will sometimes issue decisions that will affect an agency, particularly in the field of human rights and law enforcement. Also under this heading are laws pertaining to visitors, such as the Official Languages Act of Canada, which states that all official publications must be in both French and English. When dealing with these decisions, the concerned agency personnel should be in close contact with their agency's legal counsel.

**Federal legislative bodies.** The U.S. Congress and the Canadian Parliament will frequently pass legislation that will have a definite effect on a park agency. Although the method will vary depending on the size of the agency and the level of government in which it operates, someone in the agency should be assigned to keep abreast of these laws. This can usually be done through the provincial or state association of cities, counties, or municipalities.

The Congress and Parliament pass laws, and the courts rule on the legality and applicability of the laws, but the federal agencies, under the president or prime minister, administer the laws. Within that administration is the ability, authorization, and direction to issue guidelines. It is vital that concerned agencies not only be aware of those guidelines, but also play a role in their development. Unless the agency is large, it probably will not be able to do this on its own.

**Federal agencies.** Federal agencies that have particular relevance for the park and recreation field are as follows:

**Canada**
Minister of Forestry and Rural Development
Minister of Indian Affairs and Northern Development

**United States**
*Department of the Interior*
    Bureau of Indian Affairs
    Bureau of Land Management
    Bureau of Reclamation
    Fish and Wildlife Service
    National Park Service
    Office of Water Research and Technology
*Department of Agriculture*
    Cooperative State Research Service
    Extension Service
    Forest Service
    Soil Conservation Service
*Department of the Army*
    Corps of Engineers
*Department of Transportation*
    U.S. Coast Guard
*Department of Treasury*
    Federal Law Enforcement Training Center

**Provincial and state government.** The governments of the 10 provinces, the Yukon and the Northwest Territories, the 50 states, the Virgin Islands, the Commonwealth of Puerto Rico, and the Territories of the Pacific, have variable organizational structures, but they all have courts, legislatures, and executive agencies. The need for close monitoring that has just been stated regarding the federal government is even more important when the relationships under considerations are closer to home, such as provincial government to provincial agencies or state government to local agencies. These latter sorts of relationships will generate far more decisions that, in turn, will have more direct effects.

**Supreme courts.** The state supreme court will often issue decisions affecting state agencies. These decisions are published in court reports called Supreme Court decisions and are readily accessible through the state association of cities, the state association of counties, and local law libraries. This is also true for provincial courts. For an understanding of those decisions, which can often be confusing to the layperson, one should rely on the agency's legal counsel.

**Legislatures.** These bodies will pass many laws directly affecting their state or provincial agencies. The laws are known as statutes and are normally quoted under revised codes, such as the Revised Codes of Illinois (RCI). These statutes or revised codes supersede all other state rules. In some cases, state and provincial law merely supplements local law, and in others it applies only to state/provincial lands and state/provincial agencies and has no effect on local land or agencies.

State government has its own laws and rules relating to lobbying and participation in legislative working. This might also be true of an agency's particular level of government. These issues and this authority must be clear before an agency can act in the legislative arena. Also, those responsible for such matters must be cognizant of what tasks the state professional associations or societies can perform for them.

As at the federal level, where federal agencies issue rules or regulations that become law, many state-level agencies have legal power. Under what are commonly called administrative procedures (or something similar), these agencies can adopt rules that have an authority in the law just one step below that of statutes. These rules are usually called administrative codes and have the name of the state preceding it, such as the Pennsylvania Administrative Codes (PAC).

At the state level, there are fewer agencies to be concerned with, but they must be dealt with more frequently, and there is a deeper involvement than there is with federal agencies. These agencies will include, by whatever title they might have, parks and recreation, labor and industries, human rights, environment, and natural resources. These formulations are generally applicable to the Canadian federal-provincial relationship also.

**Local governments and agencies.** In almost any given province or state, there are more local agencies concerned with parks than the combined total of all the provincial, state, and federal agencies in the parks field. These local agencies possess certain similarities from state to state and province to province.

**Courts.** One similarity among all local levels of government is that there is no city supreme court. Also, most lower court rulings that affect two or more jurisdictions will be appealed to higher courts, Therefore, from a local agency's point of view, lower courts are not nearly as important as the provincial court, state supreme court, or appellate court.

**Legislative bodies**. A local legislative body might be a county council, a city council, a special policy or taxing board, a municipal council, or some other entity. These bodies have the same basic authority over their jurisdiction as does the provincial or state legislature over the entire province or state. However, they are subject not only to constitutional limitations, but also to the preemptory authority of the state or provincial legislatures. What they enact becomes an ordinance and it is the law in the geographical area.

**Agencies.** Normally the local parks agency does have the power to make enforceable rules. At the same time, there must be an awareness of what power does exist, and the agency officials must become acquainted with the corporation counsel or other persons providing legal advice to local agencies.

## Types of Law

Park managers and administrators must be aware of the following facts, opinions, and rulings concerning laws that affect park personnel.

**Common law.** The common law consists essentially of several centuries of American and British law and is applicable today where there is no specific statute or constitutional provision controlling an issue. The common law determines the liability of a landowner for injuries occurring upon the owner's land by categorizing the land users and analyzing whether the landowner has met the standard of care owed to that particular class of users. The common law recognizes three categories of land users.

*Trespasser.* A trespasser is a person who enters the landowner's property without permission. For the park manager, a trespasser on public land is anyone who passes into an unauthorized area that is clearly marked as such. The common law imposes the minimal standard of care upon the landowner with respect to the trespasser—the duty of not intentionally injuring the trespasser. In most provinces and states, the landowner owes no duty to the trespasser to maintain the land in a safe condition for the trespasser's use.

*Licensee.* A licensee is a person allowed or permitted by landowner to enter upon the land for the licensee's pleasure or benefit. People entering upon the public land outside planned and marked recreational areas to hunt, fish, trap, remove wood, camp, or hike are probably licensees. They are on the land primarily for their own benefit, and the state is making no representations as to the condition of the land. The common law does not require the landowner to constantly inspect the land to make it safe for the licensee. If the landowner does become aware of a dangerous condition on the land that the landowner can reasonably expect the licensee to encounter, common law does require the landowner either to remove the dangerous condition or warn the licensee. The landowner does not, however, have a duty to remove or warn of a hazard that is open and obvious—especially if it is reasonable to expect that the licensee will observe the hazard and recognize the risk involved.

*Invitee.* Three kinds of invitees exist. First, a person who is invited by the landowner to enter the landowner's land for some purpose of advantage to the landowner, is an invitee. Examples are the business representative, police officer, firefighter, or doctor invited by the landowner for a purpose benefiting the landowner. Second, a person who pays a fee to enter upon another's land, such as a skier or a golfer, is an invitee. Third, a person invited as a member of the public to enter upon land that is held open to the public is regarded as a "public invitee." Typical examples would include persons attending a church or users of public recreational facilities. The duty the landowner owes to these invitees is the highest legal standard imposed upon landowners. The landowner must regularly inspect the premises for any unreasonable dangerous conditions and must either cure such conditions or warn the invitee of their existence.

One additional category of land users should be mentioned: the small child. Under one doctrine, a landowner who maintains a condition upon his or her land that is dangerous to children because of a child's inability to appreciate the danger, and that the landowner can reasonably expect a young child will be attracted to, must exercise reasonable care to protect children. This attractive nuisance doctrine has been applied to railroad turntables, abandoned refrigerators, construction projects, and other similar situations. Generally speaking, the doctrine applies to artificial conditions on land, not natural conditions, and applies to children from the ages of approximately four to 12 years.

In the past, public agencies have enjoyed immunity from liability for natural conditions on public land through the doctrine of sovereign immunity. Today, however, sovereign immunity has largely been abolished by the federal government and most states. In most states, standards apply with equal force to public and private landowners. With the abolition of sovereign immunity and with recent court decisions allowing sizable damage awards, many public and private landowners have been reluctant to open their lands for public recreational use in an attempt to limit their liability.

At any rate, the above general rules of law probably apply to any state with respect to obligations owed to persons coming into public land. In many states, these general rules of law have been modified by recent studies.

**Constitutional or statutory law.** These laws are exactly what they purport to be. Constitutional law is that law as set forth either by the United States or an individual state constitution, while statutory law is either as adopted by the United States Congress or a state legislature. In the United States, the federal constitution is a grant of authority, while state constitutions are a limitation on authority. In other words, if the U.S. Constitution does not grant the authority, the federal government does not have it, but if the state constitution does not take it away, the state has the authority.

**Public use laws.** One typical state statute provides that any landowner, public or private, who opens land to the public for outdoor recreational purposes, without charging a fee of any kind, is not liable for unintentional injuries to such users. The statute does not apply to injuries resulting on the land from known, dangerous, artificial, latent conditions for which warning signs have not been conspicuously posted, and the statute does not affect the attractive nuisance doctrine. Thus, with respect to public recreational areas in many states where no fee is charged, the landowner can only be liable for injuries sustained on such land if the injury was caused by (1) an artificial condition, (2) that was hidden, (3) that was dangerous, (4) that was known to the landowner to be hidden and dangerous, (5) and for which no warning sign had been conspicuously posted.

The statute does not affect recreation areas for which an entrance fee is charged, and we must presume that the highest common law standard applied to invitees applies to these areas. Where a fee is charged, the landowner must inspect the premises for unsafe conditions and either cure the defects or warn the public of them.

**Navigable waters laws.** Because states and provinces contain navigable waters, all agencies should obtain legal opinion as to what is navigable water and what is non-navigable water. Stated broadly, navigable waters are those that can be traversed by a small boat. The public has the qualified right to boat, swim, fish, and otherwise use the surface of the navigable water regardless of whether the beds (land under the water) are publicly or privately owned.

**Human rights laws.** There has been a continuing development in federal, state, and provincial laws, as well as court rulings, dealing with human rights, especially for women and minorities. Human rights legislation also means that there should be concern about the qualifications for both entrance-level and upward-mobility employment. A typical statement pertaining to visitor use that presently is required on all publications in most states is this: "No person is denied the benefits of (area's name) facilities because of race, creed, color, sex, age, or national origin."

## LIABILITIES

### Risk and Liability

Some parks have only minimal problems that can usually be handled by planning and signage. Other parks, because of their location and inherent conditions, contain real hazards for the unwary, such as rocky or unstable cliffs, fast-moving streams, ocean currents and surf, unpredictable animals, and weather extremes. Visitors could be acting without full realization of the problems if they miss the warning signs and somehow get past the barriers. These could be considered unaware risk-takers.

There are also visitors who deliberately participate in activities considered to be high-risk recreation such as rock climbing, hang gliding, and river running. These thrill seekers are looking for challenges to match their skills and daring. Obviously, there is a much higher potential for injury and for liability. These people have been considered intentional risk-takers.

A third group also exists: those who could be classified as impromptu thrill-seekers or spontaneous risk-takers. These visitors read the signs and are at least minimally aware of the dangers, but decide on the spur of the moment to climb over the fence, approach the lip of the waterfall, or pet the buffalo.

Whichever category visitors fit into, they must be warned, watched, and in some cases, waylaid because, depending on the circumstances, park managers could be held responsible if visitors meet danger. The best protection lies in proper design, construction, and maintenance of facilities. Fortunately, most agencies will defend the employee who was acting in performance of duty and in a reasonable manner in light of all attendant facts and circumstances. Lawsuits, however, are very expensive and time consuming, regardless of who wins.

Some agencies are self-insured, while others have commercial insurance policies. Some individuals carry a personal liability policy, while others do not. Park managers should make such a determination whether to carry a personal liability policy after consulting with their agency's legal advisor.

Almost all park and recreation agencies today have adopted risk management plans and policies. For example, Asheville, North Carolina has adopted the following policies (http://www.ashevillenc.gov/uploadedFiles/Business/Business_With/Risk%20Management%20Plan.PDF):

#### Policy
1.1.a This policy statement establishes uniform procedures for managing Departmental exposure to loss and minimizing legal liabilities and personal injuries.

1.1.b Refer to the City of Asheville General Administration Policy titled "Risk Management and Insurance Planning Program".

1.2 The City of Asheville Parks and Recreation Department desires to protect itself against losses, per occurrence or in the aggregate during any financial period which may significantly affect Departmental personnel, property, its budget or ability to fulfill its responsibilities.

1.3 The City of Asheville Parks and Recreation Department recognizes that any loss of life or serious personal injury to employees or members of the general public are unacceptable.

1.4 The City of Asheville Parks and Recreation Department will manage its risks of accidental loss by applying a process that includes:

1.4.a. A systematic and continuous identification of loss exposure.

1.4.b. An analysis of these exposures in terms of frequency and severity.

1.4.c. The application of sound loss prevention and loss control procedures.

1.4.d. Ongoing review of available and economically beneficial risk finance alternatives.

As noted in the plan, the "implementation of the City of Asheville Parks and Recreation Department's risk management plan is predicated on establishing clear and concise policy direction. The department, in cooperation with the risk management division and its director, are charged with the responsibility of making and carrying out decisions that will minimize the adverse effects of accidental losses to the City of Asheville. The City of Asheville provides employees who are responsible for monitoring policies and procedures pertaining to risk management. The Park and Recreation Department has a safety committee at the park maintenance division, led by the assistant superintendent of parks. In addition, the human resources department has a training coordinator that performs duties on a city-wide nature."

## Some Representative Cases

The following represents some liability situations that have occurred in recreation settings in the last half-century.

**Natural hazard.** *Smith v. United States,* (383 F. Supp. 1076 1974). In an incident at Yellowstone National Park, the Smith couple entered the park with their 14-year-old son, Cameron. The family paid the entrance fee and received a brochure that warned that the hot natural pools were dangerous, that they should stay on marked trails, and that parents should supervise their children carefully. After viewing several well-marked thermal pools, the family parked at a paved turnout and walked down an unmarked, unposted trail to a boiling pool with steam arising from it. Cameron went to the edge of the pool and leaned over to look. The embankment caved in, tumbling the boy into the water. Cameron was severely burned and received permanent scars over most of his body. The court said that even though the family members may have been invitees when they entered the park, that status was lost when they left the paved parking area and ventured down the unmarked trail. The court said that it would not be practical or reasonable to require the Park Service to post warning signs at every thermal pool and that said bank was not a condition that the park service could reasonably have been expected to find. Further, the court felt that the Smiths were adequately warned of the danger by the brochure and the obvious and apparent dangerous nature of the boiling and steaming pools. The court finally held that the park service met its duty of adequately warning the Smith family of the dangerous condition and that the family itself was negligent by proceeding as they did. (Handy, 1978).

**Lightning strike.** *Schieler v. United States* (642 F. Supp. 1310 1986). The plaintiff was injured when he was struck by lightning while standing on Moro Rock in Sequoia National Park. Schieler's complaint alleged that the National Park Service negligently failed to provide any warning about the dangers of being struck by lightning. He contended that the failure to warn did not fall within the discretionary function exception to the Tort Claims Act.

The National Park Service argued that the presence or absence of any warnings was a policy-level decision. The government presented evidence that the superintendent of Sequoia National Park had established a sign committee and that this committee determined that before they would place a sign there had to be a demonstrated need for it. No need for a sign had been shown for Moro Rock because there was no prior record of lightning striking it. The district court judge wrote the following:

> The conduct here involved required a decision, and that decision calls for the exercise of judgment and discretion by administrators and officers of the Park Service. Any attempt by the court to evaluate such a decision would require it to examine Park Service priorities in its administration of the park and question decisions made for policy reasons ... A review of the decision ... would encroach into the decision-making process of the Park Service. The discretionary function exception is intended to protect this process and the courts are barred from reviewing the same in a tort action. (Rankin, 1989).

**Diving incident.** *Judd v. United States*, (650 F. Supp 1503 1987) A similar action against the USDA Forest Service was barred by the discretionary function exception in this subsequent case. In this case a 38-year-old accomplished diver and his friend hiked a quarter of a mile into the Cleveland National Forest to a pond area. The forest service knew people used the area for swimming and sunbathing, but there was no evidence of any prior diving or jumping injuries at this location. The Service had not "developed" the area; it was a natural pool formed by run-off water from the mountains. The recreation visitor, Steven Judd, tested the pool for depth and found a deep depression. He and his friend dove from rocks about 10 to 15 feet high into the deep area of the pond before Judd decided to try a dive from a shelf that was 35 feet above the pool. He climbed the rock and attempted a swan dive; his head struck the bottom and he suffered severe injuries. He claimed that if the government had posted a warning sign, he would not have attempted his dive.

The court found that the decision not to post warning signs was discretionary. It looked to the Forest Service policy, as embodied in the *Forest Service Manual*, which requires warning signs to be posted only in "developed" areas of national forest. In other areas, the local administrators may use their discretion in deciding whether or post signs warning of dangers. (Rankin, 1989).

**Snowmobiling.** On January 2, 1982, Brian Corey was injured while operating a snowmobile in Farragut State Park. The injury occurred when Corey struck a cable that was strung across a path in the park. The state of Idaho had installed the cable in an area open for snowmobiling; it was not designated as a closed area. When Corey brought an action against the state, the state moved for a summary judgment citing the Idaho landowner liability limitation statute (Idaho Code Section 36-1604 (b) [31]).

The Idaho law defines recreational purposes "…hunting, fishing, swimming, boating, camping, picnicking, hiking, pleasure driving, nature study, water skiing, animal riding, motorcycling, snowmobiling, recreational vehicles, winter sports, and viewing or enjoying historical, archaeological, scenic, or scientific sites when done without charge of the owner."

The trial judge granted the motion to dismiss, holding that the state was immune from the liability. The Idaho Supreme Court upheld the decision and said, "There can be no question that the landowner liability limitation statute is expressly applicable to the factual situation" here. There was a vigorous dissent that called the opinion a "travesty" and suggested that a situation where a cable "picked off" a vehicle rider with no posted notice might fall into the "willful and wanton misconduct" category.

**Recreational swimming areas.**  *Ward v. United States* (208F. Supp. 118 1962). The United States leased a swimming area on Lake Hasty in Colorado to a private recreational association. The United States had developed the recreational area and remained active in administering the site even after the lease. A 16-year-old girl, who paid no fee, drowned while swimming in the pool shortly after several young boys had been playfully ducking her. Her family sued both the association and the United States for negligence. The court awarded a judgment for the family, ruling that the United States, by setting aside the area for swimming, by constructing facilities for that purpose, and by posting signs inviting the public to use the area for swimming, had induced the public to believe that measures were being taken to safeguard activities at the area. The court said the United States therefore had a duty to require reasonable supervision and that it breached that duty in failing to have a lifeguard supervising the area.

**Wild animals.** *Claypool v. United States*, (98 F. Supp 202 1948). A visitor, William Claypool, entered Yellowstone National Park and paid the entry fee. He received a brochure and asked the attendant ranger whether it was safe to camp out because of the presence of bears. The ranger replied that it was safe. The brochure warned against feeding, aggravating, or inciting the bears. Mr. Claypool camped out one night and then moved to another site. Having seen some bears in the interim, he again inquired of a ranger as to the safety of sleeping outside. The ranger responded that hundreds of people sleep outside in Yellowstone every night and that the bears never attack without provocation. Mr. Claypool camped out once again. At 1 a.m., a bear attacked his tent and injured him. Mr. Claypool successfully sued the park service. As it turned out, three days previously, another bear or bears had been involved in an unprovoked night attack, an event unheard of in the park for over 20 years. The day after the first attack, several rangers searched for, found, and killed a grizzly bear believed to be the original assailant. The court held that Mr. Claypool was an invitee and that the park service was aware of a new and extraordinary danger of which it had a duty to warn Mr. Claypool. The court held the Park Service liable for the injuries sustained.

***Ashley v. United States***, (326 F. Supp. 499 1964). Another visitor, Mr. Ashley, paid his fee, received his brochure, and entered Yellowstone National Park. While sleeping in the front seat of his car with his right arm resting on the window sill, a bear bit his elbow, causing serious and permanent injuries. Mr. Ashley sued the Park Service. The court found that the Park Service had no notice whatsoever of the bear's dangerous propensities and that the park service had met its obligation of informing the public regarding bears by issuing the brochure. This opposite result shows that the facts of each case really make a difference in the outcome.

## Hazard Trees

From the preceding description of specific cases, it is apparent that lawsuits can arise from many sources. Fortunately, all parks do not have problem grizzly bears or black bears, but most have trees. For this reason, we will look at the hazard of trees more closely.

The various states' and provinces' immunity statutes might provide the recreational landowner protection from liability for natural hazards because natural catastrophes, such as those caused by wind, cannot be foreseen. On the other hand, attorneys for some agencies have advised that enough loopholes exist in the statutes to justify a hazard tree rating program as one further means of limiting liability. Handy (1978) recommended that such a program be implemented in all areas where a fee is charged, where the site is developed, or where signs are posted inviting the public to use a particular place because, by taking such action, the landowner is indicating the site is safe for public use. If suit is brought, it is usually to the agency's advantage to settle the case out of court so that precedents do not become established in damage awards against the government. This procedure is less costly to the public purse and the plaintiff gets a better settlement with fewer legal fees. Out-of-court settlements also make sense when one understands that damages from natural events differ in many ways from case to case, so that the application of case law to these situations would often result in inadequate comparisons and unusual, if not incorrect, damage awards (Joy 1994).

**What is a hazard tree?** Mills and Russell (1980) describe a hazard tree as one that is defective and, because of its location, may fall (or "fail") and cause personal injury or property damage. For a hazard to exist, there must be a valuable target, such as people, a building, or a car, in close proximity. An example of a hazard tree is one near a place people have been invited, such as in a picnic area or campsite, in a parking overlook, or at an interpretive panel or sign. In the past, there have been millions of dollars' worth of property damage and numerous fatalities and injuries in parks from tree failures. A defective tree deep in the forest and away from people is not a hazard tree, however, because there is no target (Mills & Russell, 1980).

A healthy tree seldom presents a hazard. With so many different tree species, however, and so many conditions under which they grow, all trees should be suspect. Limbs may fall from a perfectly healthy tree through the process of natural pruning. Mistletoe causes a loss of vigor in otherwise healthy trees. Lightning, frost cracks, and fire scars can expose the inner bark to fungus and insect attack, as can axe and knife wounds caused by thoughtless visitors. Shade-tolerant trees, healthy in their natural stands, can become weakened due to sudden exposure to sunlight when adjacent trees are removed during the construction of campgrounds, roads, or parking lots. Shallow-rooted trees may lose their wind firmness when tree removal opens up the stand. Road cuts and trenching for sewer or water pipes often sever roots, and these wounded parts also become entryways for fungus infection. Soil compaction around trees caused by construction equipment, autos, horses, and humans can weaken trees, and even the growth habits of trees, such as leaners, volunteer tops, split crotches, and other deformities can create hazards.

Even healthy-looking trees do not live forever, and at some stage of their life, their viability is lessened and they can no longer ward off attacks from fungus and insects nor stand the strain of a heavy snowload or strong winds. A good inspector can usually locate the telltale evidence of such weakened conditions. As Mills and Russell state, "Failure to carry out periodic inspections and to correct detectable tree hazards could leave recreation site owners open to costly lawsuits in the event of a serious accident" (Mills & Russell, 1980). Managers should acquaint themselves with the details of the liability situation in their particular area and should be well aware of agency policy on this matter.

Systematic inspections for hazard trees should be carried out annually. Any tree within falling distance of a campsite, picnic site, interpretive sign, building, parking lot, or any other place where people linger should be examined. According to Mills and Russell, the best time to conduct a hazard tree inspection is in the spring after trees have been exposed to winter storms and before heavy seasonal use of the area. Inspections may also be needed after hardwoods have leafed out or after the occurrence of a severe summer storm. Inspections should be carried out by at least two people, permitting simultaneous viewing and discussion of the condition of individual trees.

## TORTS

A tort is defined as a civil wrong not arising from a contractual relationship, giving the person who suffers from the wrong a right of action for damages. It is also defined as a breach of legal duty not imposed by contract.

Each state has its own process for handling tort claims. The following description utilizes the federal basis but is applicable for all states in general terms.

### The U.S. Federal Tort Claims Act

The U.S. Federal Tort Claims Act permits damages to be awarded as a result of claims against the United States for damage to or loss of property or on account of personal injury or death caused by the negligent or wrongful act or omission of any government employee who was acting within the scope of his or her office or employment. This applies to circumstances where the United States, if it were a private person, would be liable to the claimant for such damage, loss, injury, or death in accordance with the law of the place where the act or omission occurred. The period within which a claim may be made is limited to two years.

The government has no right to recover a judgment from its employee in cases where a judgment has been paid arising from an incident where the government was held responsible as the principal and the employee (agent) was not sued. However, this does not mean that the government may not require reimbursement from the employee for loss or damage to the government property that was involved in the incident.

## INVESTIGATING ACCIDENTS

Any action taken by legal counsel must be based largely on the reports that comprise the file, and these papers have their origin, in most cases, at the scene of the accident. Accurate reporting of all essential facts is extremely important. In the typical case that a park manager may be called on to investigate, the opportunity to acquire information is fleeting. Full details should be recorded at the time the accident occurs. This aspect cannot be overemphasized in accidents that occur in parks, because the persons involved are likely to be visitors whose homes are many miles away. It is often very difficult to supplement information by correspondence. For this reason, all employees must be instructed in the correct procedure.

Neither the employee, in making the initial report, nor a follow-up investigator for the agency should state conclusions of his or her own concerning responsibility for an accident. The employee must state all facts, whether such facts are favorable or unfavorable to the agency or to an agency employee. Conclusions as to responsibility for an accident are not only out of place, but also, in some instances, may make it difficult to achieve an objective determination of liability. That determination, of course, must be based on facts. When reporting or investigating an accident, it is useful to try to put oneself in the place of people who may have to use the report. Nothing should be left to the imagination. This does not mean a report should be voluminous or long winded, but one should never assume that the person who uses the report will be able to visualize and adequately assess a situation that seems obvious to the recorder. Getting the names and addresses of all witnesses is extremely important. If that proves impossible, the recording of vehicle license numbers will enable investigators to obtain needed information later.

Photographs are especially helpful to a person who must mentally reconstruct the circumstances of an accident. An instant self-developing camera and film serves this purpose best, because it is known immediately whether or not the accident scene has been adequately recorded.

If there are visual indications that should be noted in the report, they should be described with some care. For example, in the instance of motor vehicle accidents, skid marks or open alcohol bottles provide testimony much as a witness would. If there are signs, signal lights, or street or road marks that may have significance, these also should be described. Often weather conditions and visibility are considerably important. The location of the vehicles, if this is a vehicle accident, is especially important, as is the character of the road and the direction of travel of the vehicles. Note that statements made by participants in an accident immediately following the incident can prove to be of considerable importance in the event there is a trial. Further, if there is a law enforcement officer also investigating the accident, the park should endeavor to obtain a copy of this officer's report to be submitted as a part of the file.

Failure to conform to a required standard of care under the particular circumstances constitutes negligence. There should be included in an accident report not only facts that may show negligence on the part of the government driver, but also those that may show negligence on the part of the private driver or some other person, or that may indicate some special condition contributing to the accident and resultant damages. Information of this kind would help to determine whether a claimant was guilty of some contributory negligence, which could bar all or part of his or her claim. Claimant negligence could even become the basis for a claim or counterclaim by the government for damages to government property.

It is also important that persons charged with the responsibility of determining a claim have information with respect to vehicle ownership. It is desirable, therefore, that the report include an investigation into who owns the involved vehicle. If this is not the driver, the investigator should find out by whose authority and for what purpose said vehicle was being operated.

Accidents involving motor vehicles have been emphasized here because today most accidents do seem to arise from their negligent operation; however, the same care should be exercised in filling out a report on any type of accident. In parks, where citizens are regarded as guests and where these guests use facilities that have been constructed for their benefit and enjoyment, injuries can result from what may seem to be very harmless situations. Recreation agencies have responsibility for maintaining the premises in a reasonably safe condition for the benefit of the persons who may be expected to use them, and this includes their own employees. Persons who use park facilities are entitled to expect a reasonable amount of attention will be paid to their safety while on such premises.

Falling is frequently a source of injury and resultant claims against the government. If you are charged with the duty of investigating an injury arising from such an event, be sure that you describe the exact location of the fall and the condition of the premises at the time of the accident. Again, photographs are especially helpful, even though it may be necessary to take pictures some days after the accident occurred.

The following is a sample directive and accident reporting procedure.

Effective immediately, the Accident Form 01 (Appendix at the end of the chapter) is to be completed for all accidents occurring on any agency property. Form 01 should be completed by authorized staff immediately after rendering assistance as necessary to the injured party. The completed Form 01 is to be forwarded through the chain of command to the Assistant Director of Operations within five working days of knowledge of the accident.

The form has two primary functions: (1) to gather facts to assist in adjudicating claims against the agency, and (2) to ensure that the conditions leading to the accident have been changed as much as possible to prevent recurrence. Thus, recording all the facts in as much detail as possible is essential to is usefulness.

Special attention must be paid to accidents occurring on concession-controlled areas of a park. Each manager with a concession must effect an agreement with the concession to report accidents occurring on concession-controlled property to the park manager as soon as they occur.

The manager should review such reports. If a serious accident is reported or the accident may lead to legal action that will cause the agency embarrassment, the manager should complete Form 01 on this accident with the assistance of the concessionaire.

## SUBMITTING CLAIMS

There should be a standard form for claimants who have been injured or whose property has been damaged. When those individuals wish to file a claim against an agency, how helpful should an employee be in furnishing such claim forms? As a purely legal matter, information with respect to the filing of a claim should never be volunteered. If an injured person or that person's representative asks about the matter, it is then the park employee's duty to inform such persons that they are entitled to file such a claim should they desire to do so, and copies of the claim form should be furnished. There should be no voluntary statement with respect to whether or not the person requesting the claim forms is likely to be successful in filing such a claim.

On the other hand, it would not be proper procedure or good agency public relations for an employee to be evasive or non-communicative if it is clear to the employee that the injured person is uninformed and desires to know whether or not there is some way that a claim may be submitted. This is where discretion will be very important. Park agencies want to create a climate for visitors that make them enthusiastic supporters of the goals and objective of the agency. If injured persons find out later that there were available claim forms of which they were not made aware, they could feel that the agency, rather than just the employee, was not cooperative and cordial. Remember, too, that the file of accident reports and other documents may be inspected by the claimant on request.

## CONCLUSION

For park managers, understanding the laws that affect public safety is important. Managers deal with large numbers of people who are out of habitat and trying out new equipment or driving in unfamiliar terrain. Accidents are inevitable. Professional handling of legal details as well as other aspects of these mishaps is the mark of a competent manager.

Vigilance in the matter of hazards in the park is mandatory, as is routine inspection and maintenance of facilities. Not only must the public be kept from harm, but the agency must be protected from litigation.

## REFERENCES

**References Cited**

Handy, N. J. (1978). "Recreational Resource Management from a Legal Perspective." Paper presented at New Perspectives for Outdoor Recreation II. Fort Wordon State Park, WA.

Joy, Kerry. Personal correspondence. British Columbia Parks and Outdoor Recreation Division, Victoria.

Mills, L. J., & Kenelm, R., (1980). *Detection and correction of hazard trees in Washington's recreation areas: A how-to guide for recreation site managers.* Olympia: State of Washington Department of Natural Resources.

Public Employees for Environmental Responsibility, (2010). http://www.peer.org/news/news_id.php?row_id=1242

Rankin, J. S. (1989). "Trends in Liability for Visitor Injuries in Public Parks." Trends. *Park Practice Program, 26*(4):28-33.

U.S. Department of the Interior. (1961). *National Park Service.* San Francisco, CA: Office of the Field Solicitor.

Wisconsin State Park Incident Report. (Courtesy of http://dnr.wi.gov/org/land/parks/trails/pdf/trail_incident_report.pdf

## APPENDIX

### A Sample Accident Form Used by Park Employees Immediately After Rendering Assistance to an Injured Party

1. PARK: _____     DATE: _____

2. Person completing form: _____

3. Injured person's name: _____

   Address: _____ Age: _____

4. Date of accident: _____

5. Location of accident: _____

6. Explain, in detail what injury was sustained: _____

   _____

7. Explain, in detail, how the accident was reported to you as having occurred: _____

   _____

8. Did your investigation verify that this is how the accident occurred?

   Yes _____     No _____

   If the answer to #8 was no, explain what your investigation determined happened.

   _____

   _____

9. If there were witness to the accident, list their names and addresses:

   NAME: _____     NAME: _____

   ADDRESS: _____     ADDRESS: _____

   _____     _____

   PHONE: _____     PHONE: _____

10. What treatment was rendered to the injured party? _____

11. Where photographs taken? Yes _____     No _____     (if yes, please attach)

12. If vehicles were involved, what where the license numbers? _____

    _____

The following is completed only when a park vehicle is involved in an accident with another park-owned vehicle and/or park property, and the accident occurred on park property.

13. Vehicle #1 _____     Driver: _____

    (make, year, license No., tag no.)

    License No.: _____

    Vehicle #2 _____     Driver: _____

    (make, year, license No., tag no.)

    License No.: _____

    Estimated cost of repair: _____

    Vehicle #1          Vehicle #2

Describe park property damaged: _____

14. NOTE: Completing this form does not making a claim for medical or other benefits under the Workman's Compensation law. To file such a claim, your doctor must assist you in filing a Department of Labor and Industries Accident Report Form. This should be done immediately, and in no case later than one year after the injury.

15. What steps should be taken to prevent a reoccurrence of this accident?

    _____

16. Have these steps been taken? Yes _____     No _____

    If no, when and by whom will they be taken?

    _____

    _____

17. _____

    (Signature of person completing form)

# Chapter Five

# Funding and Budgetary Issues

Sound fiscal management happens when qualified personnel are hired to manage the financial operations and budgeting of the organization. The following are key job requirements for the fiscal manager of a park agency. As one can see, the job is complex and requires a background in finance or accounting.

**Fiscal Operations Manager**

- Demonstrate hands-on management style and organization skills in coordinating financial systems
- Provide practical and creative approaches to address challenges and develop opportunities
- Build partnerships and secure resources that benefit program objectives
- Robustly manage resources including the development and control of multiple operating funds
- Create a shared vision/goal and work in a continuous improvement framework
- Support and enjoy a fun, productive, team culture focused on world-class service
- Communicate effectively with city departments, city administration and city council

The ideal business/fiscal operations manager must have a bachelor's degree from an accredited college or university in accounting, finance, business administration or related field coupled with over five (5) years of increasingly responsible accounting/executive/administrative experience and comprehensive background in related government and business disciplines. Experience should demonstrate the ability to effectively manage a complex business operation including budgeting, public relations and business operations. Candidates with prior financial experience with golf, convention, hospitality and/or entertainment venues highly desired. Experience with government financial processing software (Lawson) is desired. (source: http://texas.jobing.com/fiscal-operations-manager-parks-and-rec/job/2236454/nocache)

## FINANCING RECREATION

In all probability, the procurement of sufficient funds will always be a problem in the recreation field. Parks frequently lack a constituent lobby group. In times of tax revolt or budget reductions, this lack of representation is disastrous for park funding. As California and Arizona State Parks can testify, there is also evidence of a lack of awareness and sympathy on the part of decision makers. Effective support for parks takes many years to build and needs politically competent resource people to continue building support. Once again, the call must go out for parks personnel to involve themselves in politics and to encourage other to do so.

### Funding Categories

Some governmental units require that all agency-generated revenues be deposited in the general fund, while others permit the agency to use the revenues. Basically, all revenues are organized in one of the following categories.

**General fund.** Although the title may vary, all levels of government have a fund into which receipts flow. For the purposes of this chapter, consider the general fund as the depository for revenues that are not designated for any specific purpose and that may be expended in any way the legislative body decrees.

**Dedicated funds.** These, as the name implies, are funds that are dedicated to a specific use or a specific agency. For example, the Federal Land and Water Conservation Funds are for a specific use but may be expended by a variety of public agencies. The federal Historic Preservation Funds are also for a specific use but for both public and private entities. The federal Dingell-Johnson (fish) or Puttman-Robertson (wildlife) funds are used for research, and for the purchase and development of game refuge and public hunting grounds, and they are almost always expended by one agency, usually the state fish or wildlife agency. Revolving funds, as noted below, are another type of dedicated funds.

**Revolving funds.** Under certain circumstances, the legislative body will permit the agency to establish an account for revolving funds. These are funds the agency both generates and spends within general legislative authority. This is usually done to provide for the replacement of equipment or for programs if the income generated completely covers the cost of operating a particular activity or service.

Many agencies find it difficult to secure funds for purchasing equipment. To alleviate that problem, they establish a revolving fund for equipment. The equipment revolving fund should be developed at the time the agency budgets funds on the expenditure side of the ledger to pay itself for the use of the equipment. The amount paid is either per hour (machinery, boats) or per mile (automobile). This amount must not only cover the operating expenses (usually gasoline), but also be sufficient to fund replacement of the equipment when necessary.

### Sources of Revenue

All revenues are placed in one or more of three funds: general, dedicated, and revolving. Where and how are these revenues obtained?

**Anticipated and unanticipated revenues.** When an agency prepares its budget, it must estimate and identify planned expenditures and list all anticipated sources and amount of revenue.

Revenues received in excess of the amount anticipated are not usually considered unanticipated and may not be expended by the agency. Only a new source of funds is considered as unanticipated. For example, the agency anticipates $40,000 from camping fees, all of which is deposited in the general fund. The agency has an extraordinarily busy year, increasing the camping fee revenues to $60,000. The $20,000 is not considered unanticipated revenue and may not be available to the agency.

Unanticipated revenues, then, are revenues from a source not contemplated at a budget time. For example, a windstorm fells 70,000 board feet of timber. The revenues from salvaging that timber would be unanticipated. To enable salvage, the governing control agency will usually permit the agency to spend the unanticipated revenues up to the amount necessary to log, clean up, and replant, but this may not entail an amount in excess of the amount to be realized from the log sale.

If the agency is a self-taxing district, it may make its own decision as to whether or not it chooses to spend its unanticipated revenues. Should the agency not be a self-taxing district, and most are not, some higher control authority will make that determination when the occasion arises.

**Additional funding—nongovernmental.** Though agencies normally handle funds only from governmental sources, there is a large and variable source of funds available from nongovernmental sources. An agency can always use additional funds to acquire, develop, and operate areas, facilities, and programs no matter how many dollars it is allotted from the legislative authority. Some of the other ways an agency might raise funds from commercial and noncommercial sources follow.

**Commercial.** A close working relationship with private enterprise has shown to benefit parks agencies. Here are a few examples of such cooperation.

- The production of outdoor recreation guides, park brochures, or agency films could be accomplished as a joint venture whereby the agency provides the text, the commercial firm provides the funds, and both receive credit. For example, the manufacturers or wholesalers of mountain bikes might well finance trail or safety brochures.

- The development and operation of a campground, golf course, or ski area could be managed as a commercial venture under agency rules and regulations. The entrepreneur can make a profit and the public will be served.
- Granting a private developer a utility easement across agency land could result in a needed development on agency land.
- The passage of an ordinance requiring that all new subdivisions set aside park areas, or money in lieu of these areas, can generate lands and funds for an agency.

**Noncommercial.** One of the major sources yet to be fully tapped for financial revenues for park and recreation use is that of the noncommercial, nongovernmental organizations. Within that resource are the foundations.

Canada and the United States have literally thousands of foundations who yearly fund parks and recreation. Some of these foundations are international; others allocate funds to recipients in a localized area only. It is suggested that every park and recreation agency in North America contact the local library for a listing.

A municipality, state, or province might choose to organize its own parks foundation. Some, such as the California State Park Foundation, serve only the sponsoring agency, while others, such as the Washington Parks Foundation, serve all park and recreation agencies in a geographical area. In Canada, contact the local Provincial Community Service Branch. In addition to foundations, there are considerable financial resources in the proceeds from bequests and donations. These are usually within the community foundation system at the local or county level.

**Grants.** As previously indicated, the subject of grants deserves special handling. Grants are available from both governmental and nongovernmental sources. They may be used for capital or operation requirements. They are available to both public and nonpublic agencies as well as to individuals. The art and technique of securing grants is called grantsmanship and is a most important process. However, the grant process is very competitive and often agencies do not have grant writers for assistance.

**Private philanthropy.** As previously indicated, there are vast amounts of monies available through private philanthropy. Success here will also depend on the grantsmanship of the agency. These techniques are becoming so important that intensive training sessions are held weekly at some places in North America. Many municipalities, colleges, universities, and private agencies engage persons whose sole function is to procure grants. The activity is becoming so technical that the subject is being added to many college curricula.

**Government grants.** These might be federal grants to state or local agencies, state grants to state agencies, or state grants to a lower entity. The latter include those grants from a federal source administered through the states. There are two basic types of government grants. The first uses a formula for determining the amount. Grants from the Land and Water Conservation Funds, Historic Preservation Funds, and Boating Funds operate this way. Those that go directly from the federal government to the specific agency, such as the Dingell-Johnson Funds, use a formula as well. In the second type, no formula is used to determine the amount. With the advent of block grants from the federal government, the various lower levels of government have greater freedom of allocation.

**Bonds.** Bonds are interest-bearing certificates of debt issued by a corporation or government by which an agency gains immediate access to funds while committing itself to fulfillment of an obligation. Three categories of bonds are mentioned here, but bonds may have many variations and often bear the name of the issuing authority.

*General obligation bonds.* These bonds pledge full faith and credit of the municipality and are paid for by general taxation. General obligation bonds provide for the early acquisition and completion of development with payment prorated over several years, during which time the site is usable.

*Revenue bonds.* Revenue bonds are not used unless the financed projects return revenues. The revenues produced by specific earning assets are pledged and, as such, the issues are dependent on the governing authority to receive revenues from use of the facility constructed in an amount sufficient to pay the principal and interest. These bonds have the same advantage as general obligation bonds, but the disadvantage is having to make payment on schedule from the revenue received.

***Special assessment bonds.*** These sorts of bonds are used where special benefits to property are equal to or greater than the assessment. These bonds are used and paid for by the residents of the local area, such as a sewer district. They are often called LIDs (local improvement districts), or Tax Increment Finance. Like the general obligation bonds, they pledge full faith and credit of the governing agency.

**Special tax levies.** These are taxes levied against a special source, such as cigarettes or gasoline, for a special purpose, such as park development or boating access. This method supposedly has the advantage of enabling the agency to predict the amount of revenue and ensure the income over a long period of time.

**Fees and charges.** These can be levied for almost everything, depending on the past history and policy of an agency. Effective lobbying, or the lack of it, is the key to instituting a charge or to preventing one. Fees are commonly charged for showers, dog kennels, boat rentals, horseback rides, firewood permits, camping, parking, day-use entrance, guarded beaches, special equipment, special instruction, and activity entrance.

Fees have their own administrative costs; some fees are collected directly by an employee from the user. Fees are also collected by mechanical devices, such as those charged for hot water showers or gas or electric stoves. The original cost of the unit must be considered in addition to the fact there are still personnel costs for the collection of the monies and for the maintenance of these mechanical devices. There also is the cost of vandalism and stolen monies. Sometimes fees are collected by an employee from honor boxes, where users are requested to deposit the amount due. Again, employee costs as well as potential misappropriation must be considered. The possibility of theft or use without payment must also be taken into account.

Additional fees may be charged for out-of-area visitors. This decision will undoubtedly be made by the legislative authority. Similarly, there are many states and provinces where non-residents pay extra charges for hunting and fishing licenses.

## CONCESSIONS

The subject of concessions is of great importance. In North America, the term "concession," as it relates to park use, means a space or privilege within a park for a subsidiary business or service. Examples are overnight accommodations or places to buy food, rent canoes, or obtain rides accompanied by interpretation. These outlets are not only a potential source of income but also a key factor in major development and park operation. For this reason, concessions are being handled as a major unit within fiscal management. These concessions are bid upon by the businesses and awarded the contract for a specified time based on performance.

### Concession Policy

If a concession-type service is contemplated, the agency must determine whether it is already being provided in close proximity to the park. If the answer is yes, then the service should not be provided in the park. Should agency policy require that all services are to be agency provided, standard operation procedures should be followed and no further explanation is needed.

However, should the agency policy provide for concessionaires, there are three possibilities: (a) when it is reasonable to assume a profit can be made, the special service should be granted to private concession operators, (b) when it is not reasonable to assume a profit can be made, the service should be provided by the agency, or (c) the service should be provided as a joint or combined operation. The reason for this approach is that the agency already made the decision that the service was necessary and was not being provided close by. Therefore, it should be provided even if it is not a money maker.

This last point arises from a philosophy of holding the monetary return to the agency secondary to the public service provided by the concessionaire. There will invariably be an outcry from business interests if the agency puts itself in a position of competition with the private sector.

## Manager-Concessionaire Relationships

With the granting of a concession, the agency creates a very delicate twofold relationship between the agency's park manager and the concessionaire.

**Business.** The concession is a private business venture, one that must return a profit in order to provide an incentive for the concessionaire to serve the public. One of the problems lies in the quality of goods handled in gift shops. Part of the public is outraged by imported "junk" being sold in what they perceive as a natural area. On the other hand, people might not buy "expensive" local arts and crafts if they are for sale. The "junk" might sell and help the concessionaire stay in business while handling less lucrative but necessary services. Also, the manager will be concerned that the concessionaire usually charges higher prices than do merchants in nearby towns. However, the manager must remember that the transport and personnel costs are higher, while the season is shorter, for the concessionaire.

## Controls

The park manager is the on-site agency administrator of the concession agreements within the boundaries of the park. To do that job effectively, it is crucial that the manager be fully cognizant of the authority under which he or she operates. Administrative duties usually include, but are not limited to, assuring the following:

- The operation is in basic compliance with the terms of the agreement.
- The hours of operation are adhered to unless otherwise authorized by the manager.
- The facility and premises are maintained in a clean, safe, and sanitary condition.
- Operating personnel are clean, courteous, and qualified to serve the public.
- The inventory is adequate to meet reasonable expected demands.
- The operator is maintaining a daily cash-flow sheet. This does not need to be checked daily, but it must be ready for spot checks.

In addition, it is essential that the park manager be familiar with and subscribe to the agency's policy relating to the public service concessions. The concession operation is an integral public service function under the manager's command, and the concession operator is an extension of the park family. When viewed in this light, it should be obvious to the park manager that assistance and guidance expended on behalf of the concession operation not only is an obligation, but also will reflect managerial competency.

How does the U.S. National Park Service handle its concessions? Congressional policy is "to encourage and enable private persons and corporations to provide and operate facilities and services deemed desirable for the accommodation of visitors." Concessionaires fill a vital role in helping the National Park Service (NPS) carry out its mission. Private companies work with NPS in order to offer services to park visitors, which are not provided directly by the government. Concessionaires specialize in these operations and are thus able to provide quality services at reasonable prices. By welcoming the private sector as a partner in park operations, the National Park Service broadens the economic base of the region and communities surrounding the parks.

In concert with other NPS divisions, the Commercial Services Program administers nearly 600 concession contracts that, in total, gross over $1 billion annually. NPS concessionaires employ more than 25,000 people in a variety of fields during peak seasons, providing services ranging from food service and lodging, to whitewater rafting adventures and motor coach tours. As stated in the Concessions Management Improvement Act of 1998, concession operations "are consistent to the highest practicable degree with the preservation and conservation of resources and values of the park unit." (http://concessions.nps.gov/)

## BUDGETING

A budget is a fiscal road map to aid the agency in getting where it wants to go within the laws governing the agency. It is a tool that forces the agency to realistically review its priorities and place them within the limits of available funds. It is a bookkeeping process that projects income and expenditures. All agencies and units of agencies have a budget and must learn to operate within its restrictions.

Over the course of time, with changes in administration, agencies will sometimes be instructed by a higher authority to bring in a budget request that reflects what the higher authority believes the agency needs. Regardless of which method is used, the agency might also be directed to submit details via the program budgeting system (PBS) or by some other breakdown.

### Types of Budgeting

**Specific amount budgeting.** The advantages of this system are that time will not be spent developing programs that will not be authorized (no matter how badly needed), and that every avenue will be explored in order to do as much as possible within the given resources.

**Current level budgeting.** This implies that the agency will fund the same programs and to the same degree for the next budget period. In addition to the advantages and disadvantages noted for the specific amount budgeting, this type has other disadvantages, such as precluding shifts in programs as needed during the budget period. Also, with cost of living increases and inflation, current level is actually a decrease and will necessitate the reduction or elimination of one or more programs.

Some current level budgets include current level plus cost of living, plus extended programs, plus new programs. These options provide decision makers the opportunity to know how much money it takes to conduct the existing program. The budget should also contain an explanation of what is involved and what benefits are expected by extending existing programs and/or initiating new ones.

**Need budgeting.** Budgeting is a year-round activity. Practically speaking, the budget should be developed on the basis of need no matter what the instructions are, as it is the only way to plan for the future and to continually strive to fulfill that plan. This is the prime advantage to need budgeting. The disadvantage is that the agency might spend considerable time developing programs that will never be funded.

**Zero-based budgeting.** Here the agency assumes that it has no monies and, therefore, no personnel and no program. From that zero base, the agency builds its budget based on priority. Note that few agencies are required to conduct zero-based budgeting even though it is often discussed. The zero-based process is advantageous as it forces the agency to carefully consider its priorities. It is also very time-consuming, as the budget request must be prepared from the ground up each year.

### Budget Preparation

Most agencies divide the agency budget into two main categories: capital and operating. Here, operating will cover recurring activities such as salaries, utilities, goods, and services. Capital budget will deal with items that are not recurring, such as land acquisition, development, and major equipment.

As budgets move up the chain of command, various components should be combined so that when the final budget reaches the decision maker, the needs are classified by category as well as by operating division.

### What Happens Next?

Park managers and park staff give considerable thought, time, and effort to preparing a budget. It is natural that they want to know what happens to the budget after it leaves the park. This information should be given to the park manager at the same time the budget instructions are issued.

The manager needs to understand the different inputs as the budget grows through various levels, and the high probability that many changes will be made. To continue to build staff morale and confidence, the fiscal office should also inform park managers as to the reasons for any changes.

## Operating Impact

Earlier in this chapter, note was made of the differences between capital and operating budgets. There is an additional aspect to the discussion, and it is called operating impact. Most agencies will be directed to present their budgets with at least a major division between those funds necessary to operate what they have (operating budget), and those necessary to effect major improvements and acquisitions (capital budget).

The preparation of the capital budget is similar to preparing the operating budget. However, there is a major difference: The capital budget should contain an operating impact. Operating impact is the name given to the amount of operating funds that need to be added to the operating budget if the agency is successful in receiving appropriation for the capital request. The operating impact must include planning and engineering costs, such as for rangers, utilities, goods, and equipment; all of this will be part of the operation once the proposal becomes a reality.

Furthermore, as more funds are expended for capital and more line staff are added, there will be need for more support staff. Therefore, the addition of support staff in the agency's payroll, fiscal, clerical, and supply sections should be considered.

## Getting It Approved

All of the budget preparation effort will be to no avail if the budget office and the legislative body do not pass the budget. For this reason, the park manager will undoubtedly receive some special instructions from the director.

The manager might be instructed to invite area legislators to the park to view certain needs that are reflected in the budget request. News coverage might also be suggested. The manager might also be instructed to be at a budget hearing or, perhaps, to stay away. It is important that the manager and supervisor understand each other and the reason for the instructions. Figure 5.1 is an example of an ordinance to adopt a budget for Oak Park, Illinois, note the dates the ordinance is in effect.

## ACCOUNTING

Assume now that the legislative body has passed the budget. It is time to set up the books and implement accounting. Accounting is not simply bookkeeping. It is the dynamic process that shows whether one is following the fiscal road map one laid out when budgeting. Accounting includes the following:

- knowing income,
- knowing expenditures,
- knowing cash flow,
- knowing what is committed via a contract (purchases) for which the service or item has not yet been received. These are called encumbrances,
- estimating correctly what services will have been used prior to the actual billing, such as electricity and water. These are called accruals, and
- knowing where you are, compared to where you should be, fiscally.

## Handling of Funds

The chances are that either the agency or the governmental entity in which the agency operates will have very specific rules concerning how park managers will requisition goods and supplies and, subsequently, how the agency will make those purchases and account for the goods. The

**Figure 5.1. Budget Ordinance**

---

**Ordinance #2008-12-01**
**Combined Annual Budget and Appropriation Ordinance**
**of the Park District of Oak Park**
**For Fiscal Year Beginning January 1, 2009 and Ending December 31, 2009**

An ordinance adopting an annual budget and appropriating such sums of money as may be deemed necessary to defray all necesssary expenses and liabilities of the Park District of Oak Park, Cook County, Illinois, for the fiscal year beginning January 1, 2009 and ending December 31, 2009 and specifying the objects and purposes for which such appropriations are made and the amount appropriated for each object of purpose.

BE IT ORDAINED BY THE BOARD OF COMMISSIONERS OF THE PARK DISTRICT OF OAK PARK, COOK COUNTY, ILLINOIS:

Section 1: The following are the Annual Budget and Appropriation items for the park district of Oak Park for the fiscal year beginning January 1, 2009 and ending December 31, 2009:

---

securing of equipment requires at least seven separate actions. First, and perhaps most important, the employee must identify the equipment needed to do the job.

Then the paperwork starts. The first piece is the requisition. The requisition does not give the authority to purchase. It is the document that contains the information needed do to assist the purchasing people in making decisions.

The purchasing people now determine whether sufficient funds are available and in the proper account. Next, the item required either "goes to bid" to select a vendor or a vendor is selected form a predetermined listing.

A purchase order is then sent to the vendor who is to provide the equipment to the park. After the park employee verifies that what was received was the ordered item, the vendor is paid.

**Inventories.** No matter what your level of authority in the park, there is an inventory of the equipment. Managers need to be certain the equipment is all present and in good shape before you become accountable for it. This process should be on paper and signed by at least one other person. New items received at your park need to be recorded by whatever process is used by the agency. Transfer of items to another park or deletion as a result of breakage should also be recorded.

**Handling cash.** Nearly all full-time park employees will handle cash at some time. When you do, remember certain basic facts and rules. Regrettably, some citizens will believe that you are trying to pocket some for yourself. Therefore, you need to be constantly alert about your handling of money.

To assist you, here are two suggestions: Give and receive receipts whenever possible, and never mix your cash with that of the public. Don't "borrow for a day" from the petty cash fund or other such account with the thought that you will repay it tomorrow. Most agencies keep a close watch on these matters, typically through auditing procedures.

**Audits.** Agencies are audited by designated authorities within the states or provinces as well as by the appropriate federal authorities if they expend any federal funds. Regular audits, by their nature, are conducted as late as a year or more after the end of the fiscal period being audited. As a result, any improper procedure by park personnel will continue for that length of time because the involved person(s) will not be aware that it is not acceptable. In the case of illegal procedures, these, too, will continue until brought to light. Also, any irregularities or downright thefts of funds can grow to major non-correctable proportions in such a length of time. These situations can be alleviated, if not completely corrected, by the use of an internal auditor.

This internal auditor service must be on a continuing basis with reports filed regularly. The internal auditor should be responsible to and report to one or two of the top people in the agency. An internal auditor will not prevent misappropriation of funds nor eliminate use of improper fiscal procedures.

The following budget submission letter (abbreviated) for an audit from the PenMet Park District indicates the type of language being used in a budget submission to the public and board.

January 1, 2010
Budget Message

Dear District Commissioners and Citizens:
It is my pleasure to present the 2010 budget for the Peninsula Metropolitan Park District (PenMet Parks). For 2010, the Budget has been balanced in accordance with state statutes and the fiscal policies directed by the District Commission. This budget is balanced upon a foundation that emphasizes the influence of the District's mission statement and its goals. For the first time in the District's history, PenMet Parks received the Government Finance Officers Association's Distinguished Budget Award for its 2009 budget. In addition for the fourth year in a row, Washington State Finance Officers Association awarded the District its Distinguished Budget Award for that same budget. (Source: http://www.penmetparks.org/media/DIR_14401/2010$20Budget$20091116.pdf

## CONCLUSION

The importance of competent fiscal management cannot be overstated. Quite a few park professionals either lose their jobs or are placed in secondary management roles because of a lack of ability in fiscal management. It is hoped that this chapter will stimulate the student as well as the practitioner of park management to gain more knowledge and experience in fiscal matters and to recognize their importance in career development.

## REFERENCES

**References Cited**

Illinois Department of Natural Resources, Becoming a Park Concessionaire, http://dnr.state.il.us/lodges/becoming.htm

Park District of Oak Park, IL, 2010 Annual Financial Audit, http://www.oakparkparks.com/NewsandInformation/OPPD%20Final%20AFR%2012-08.pdf

Park District of Oak Park, IL, Ordinance to adopt budget. http://www.oakparkparks.com/AboutUs/CurrentFinances/B&A%20ORDINANCE%202009.pdf

PenMet Budget 2010, http://www.penmetparks.org/media/DIR_14401/2010$20Budget$20091116.pdf

National Park Service, Commercial Services, 2010, http://concessions.nps.gov/

National Park Service, Doing Business with the Park, 2010, http://www.nps.gov/lame/parkmgmt/businesswithpark.htm

# Chapter Six

# Personnel Management

Gifford Pinchot said, "The first condition of success in any job is not brains, but character. Over and over again, I have seen men of moderate intelligence come to the front because they had the courage, integrity, self-respect, steadiness, perseverance, and confidence in themselves, their cause, and their work."

In most park and recreation agencies, the greatest percent of the total operating costs will be for personnel wages and fringe benefits. Effective personnel management seems to be a blend of two distinct competencies. One involves knowledge of the mechanics of administration, such as hiring, types of positions, and conditions of employment. The other depends on the ability to lead and inspire others. Requirements for the first can be gained through experience; requirements for the second are more elusive.

## HIRING

Persons responsible for hiring must take the time, have the patience, and exercise the skills necessary to recognize the type of person who will succeed on the job. Procedures must be developed that aid the comparison process. The agency must develop certain criteria to use in filling the vacant position and compare applicants to the criteria, not to each other. The National Park Service lists the following job titles (http://www.nps.gov/pais/parkmgmt/jobs.htm). As one can see, each would require specific training and experience.

Groups of occupations are as follows:

- Administrative and clerical
- Information technology
- Concessions management
- Trades and crafts
- Engineering, design and facility management
- Fee collection and dispatch
- Fire management
- Park ranger (law enforcement, interpretation, public affairs, park management)
- Park guide
- Safety management
- Science and resource management

### Defining the Skills

Before starting the process of recruiting personnel, it is crucial to determine what skills are needed to do the job. What is preferred in educational background and experience, especially experience relative to the position in question, and what personal qualities are needed to do the job?

There are many ways to determine what skills are needed. One procedure is to make a list of all the performances each job requires with the estimated emphasis (time requirements) for each of these. This list is often called a CQ (classification questionnaire) or KSA (for knowledge, skills, and abilities). This is usually compiled by human resources with management input.

## Recruitment

Recruitment is the process used to locate the most qualified people and to interest them in applying for the position. After determining the job to be done and the minimum qualifications needed to do it, there are legal constraints to be considered. When these have been taken into account, an application form should be designed to elicit the necessary information from the applicants.

The potential applicants must be located and informed of the opening. At this point, a recruitment bulletin is developed, usually a single sheet of paper containing pertinent data about the job requirements, minimum qualifications, salary, and process for applying. The bulletin should also contain basic information the potential employee needs, such as job title, job location, and some data about the job from the classification questionnaire. At the federal level, the website http://www.usajobs.opm.gov/ is accessible for job recruitment and for applicants to apply for vacancies. Each state and most larger parks agencies have online recruitment systems managed by their respective human resources management office.

Agencies also provide these bulletins to colleges, universities, professional societies, and other agencies, and they often make direct contacts with these organizations to ensure wide dissemination of the job opportunity and qualifications. The guidelines set forth here are basically aimed at recruitment of persons into the agency. However, nearly all of the suggestions also apply to employees seeking a different job within the agency.

There are many ways an agency can obtain information about applicants to enable it to select the best possible person for the job. These include a combination of the following factors:

- The completed application form along with requested materials such as graded course transcripts, letters of reference, a list of past employers, and documentation of work experience
- Telephone or in-person discussion with references, past employers, peers, and subordinates
- Review of college transcripts with particular emphasis on achievement in the courses related to the job to be filled. Where possible, look for subsequent improvement in low grades as a measure of the person's ability to adapt and learn, as well as for consistent high achievement.
- Examination—written or oral
- Personal interview

## Examination

Prior to the formal evaluation of qualifications, the list of applicants is checked to certify that all applicants meet minimum requirements. These might include education level, certain skills and licenses, and specified experience in certain types of jobs. The people who make the certified lists are now further identified by one of two types of evaluations.

1. A review panel evaluates all of the data provided by the applicant, often using this information to rank the applicants on the basis of education and training (called E & T) or knowledge, skills, and abilities (KSA). Sometimes the ranking is affected by a weight system whereby certain characteristics are given more value than others. These values are set by the supervisor in preparation of the original document [the KSA, or classification questionnaire (CQ)].
2. A review panel might also administer a written or oral exam. Because the persons taking the examination have already met minimum qualifications, the examination should be geared to discover and reflect the particular skills and characteristics needed for the job. For example, if law enforcement is an important requirement, then the examination should reflect the applicant's knowledge and experience in this area.

As a general rule, an oral examination should be given in the later stages of the selection process when only top choices are left, as it usually entails the presence of a panel, making this form of examination costly. The oral examination panel might include persons who are qualified in park management but who are not from the agency concerned. For this reason, and to assure uniformity of standards, the hiring agency should provide the examining board with some guidelines. At the same time, the panel must be cautioned against favoring any applicant by its manner of questioning. The following are examples of questions that an examining panel might use in determining the strengths of individuals being considered for entry-level park ranger positions. They will probably supplement these with questions coming out of their own area of expertise.

- Why do you believe you are qualified to work for this agency?
- What do you believe your experiences and education could contribute to this park organization?
- What do you know about this agency, and its objectives, purpose for existence, and structure?
- What are your long-range goals?
- How would you handle the situation if your superior gave you an order you believed to be unethical or illegal?

Members of the examining panel are often asked to make note of their impressions of each individual interviewed. These are confidential and are for the use of the administrator responsible for the final decision.

**Personal interview.** The lists have been certified and the evaluations have taken place. It is now time for the supervisor in question to interview the certified candidates. This might be done in person or by telephone. By talking with the applicants for a few moments, one can observe another dimension of their personalities.

## Selection and Probation

Matters covered would include moving expenses, starting date, starting salary, and any special conditions of employment. The unchosen candidates should also be thanked for applying and should be notified that the vacancy has been filled after the successful applicant has accepted the position. The technical and legal aspects of the selection process will be set forth by agency rules. These should be clearly understood before starting the hiring process and should be followed throughout.

This period of time, usually six months, is an important part of the personnel selection process. During this time, employers should carefully and continually review the new employee's work. Regrettably, few employers utilize this probationary period properly and are faced with employees who underperform.

There are four basic reasons the probationary period is significant:

1. There are some persons who are outstanding in tests, but inadequate on the job, and there are others who do mediocre work on a test, but who function very well in the actual situation. Six months should be sufficient to find this out.
2. In most parts of North America, it takes six months to effectively observe new personnel, particularly field personnel, in both the busy and the slow seasons.
3. The agency can determine whether the employee fits into the agency, and the employee has an opportunity to see whether the agency fits his or her expectations and career plans.
4. The employee has a chance to adjust to the new job and begin to perform up to capability. Should the employee not work out, termination at this time does not involve the legal steps necessary for permanent employees.

## TYPES OF POSITIONS

Those being hired full time usually will be in one of two basic categories: civil service positions or exempt positions. Civil service positions are also referred to as "covered." The titles might differ from place to place, but the concepts are still the same.

## Civil Service

Most agencies will be required to hire one of the top three on the civil service register of names provided by the personnel department. For some jobs, an agency may select from an "open register" any person who has met the minimum qualifications and passed any required examination.

Another variation is the reduction-in-force (RIF) register, which usually takes precedence over all other hiring registers. For instance, should lack of funds necessitate the elimination of a Ranger II position, the person presently filling that position would have the right to take a lateral position from a person who has less seniority or to take a lower position (Ranger I) in the same way.

## Exempt Positions

Basically, an exempt position is one that may be filled by the hiring authority without reference to specific requirements. Standards governing these positions will vary from agency to agency and even from exempt position to exempt position within an agency. What is true for hiring is equally applicable for dismissal, as persons filling these positions can be dismissed without cause. The agency head and staff reporting directly to this person are usually in exempt positions.

## Special Employment Categories

The trend continues for increased employment of other than full-time regular employees. Sometimes the wages of these employees are budgeted, such as for park aides and lifeguards, while at other times, these are non-budgeted additions, such as enrollees in federally funded special programs that usually change, at least in title and often in thrust, with every change of administration. It is important that management personnel, at every level of authority, be aware of these hiring opportunities.

**Part-time employees.** Part-time employees could be engaged on a full-time basis in such positions as lifeguard or park aide and work only part of the year (seasonal), or they could work less than full time each week throughout the year. Other similar combination of days and parts of the year are possible.

Whether seasonal or less than full time, these employees enable the agency to augment its staff with specialists during the busy season without having to employ them when there is little for them to do. These positions also afford the opportunity to engage college students in the summer, thus providing them with needed income and valuable experience while at the same time giving the agency the opportunity to hire qualified individuals and to see them in operation.

College intern programs afford an agency the opportunity to employ a volunteer who is highly motivated to work and learn, as park work is that person's chosen profession. In this way, the intern will be able to consider the agency as a potential place of employment, and the agency can carefully screen the intern as a potential employee. These programs vary in length from a college quarter on a part-time basis, to a given term, staggered over two or more years, on a full-time basis.

**Conservation and work training programs**. The decade of the 1970s saw a great increase in federal government programs and funds for the hiring of special groups. During that period of time, the U.S. government spent over $64 billion on these programs, funded the Comprehensive Employment and Training Act (CETEA). Today, the AmeriCorps (http://www.americorps.gov/), and the Student Conservation Corps (http://www.thesca.org/) are popular ways in which young or underemployed people gain experience with park agencies.

## RULES GOVERNING EMPLOYMENT

Many factors have an impact upon personnel relations. Careful consideration must be given to all standards that affect the work environment.

## Authority

Usually the authority to engage, dismiss, or severely discipline an employee is set forth by the legislative body of the government in which the agency is located. The administration of any agency must be aware of its authority and of the rights of the individual. View the entire human resources system with civil service and hiring practices at http://www.co.solano.ca.us/civica/filebank/blobdload.asp?BlobID=4668.

## Conditions of Employment

Conditions of employment include such matters as pay, sick leave, vacation, hours and places of work, dress code, behavior, and many other factors. Conditions of employment emanate primarily from three sources: statutes, union contracts, and agency policies and rules.

An agency must define the performance requirements and the type of person needed to do the job. It is important that persons being hired know what is expected of them. These expectations constitute the conditions of employment, and the agency must apprise the new employee of them. An orientation session should be held at the main office, covering the "Need to Know" information applicable to all employees. This should be followed by another briefing at the place where the new employee will work.

## Affirmative Action

Affirmative action is the title given to a program developed in recognition of decades of discrimination in hiring and promotional practices with regard to women and minorities. Agencies are required to develop a program that reflects the present status of the agency's affirmative action, the goals it has set to remedy the situations, and the method by which the agency will bring about these goals.

Agencies continually monitor their programs, usually with a specific person assigned to that role. Often this person is called the Equal Employment Officer (EEO), or the person works in the Office of Equity Management.

## Conflict of Interest

Due to the nature of many jobs in the field of outdoor recreation and park management, there will be frequent and varied opportunities for holding a second job outside the agency in consulting, landscaping, or sales, for instance. To be certain that the agency and employees are both above reproach, there is usually a policy providing guidelines for acceptable outside employment.

# TRAINING

Individuals normally come to an agency with at least the standard requirements of formal education and experience indicated by hiring requirements, but as in all major employment situations, they must learn on the job. It is important that the employer and employee discuss possible training opportunities. Personnel management skills that need particular emphasis, both in university courses and during on-the-job training, include the knowledge of how to be a team member and how to lead other employees. The National Park Service has a website for training of personnel with approved courses (http://www.nps.gov/training/policies.htm).

## Pre-training

It would be desirable if every employee could undergo training prior to being placed on the job. Unfortunately, very few agencies can offer this opportunity for full-time year-round personnel. However, seasonal employees are usually hired in such quantity at a given time that a pre-training session can be held, such as summer camp staff or fire fighters. Pre-training should include a thorough orientation to the agency's organizational structure, philosophy, policies, procedures, and benefits.

### On-the-Job Training (OJT)

The supervisor (perhaps the park manager) should spend considerable time with the new employee during the first several weeks. The employee must be made aware that this is common practice and must be introduced to the necessity of establishing checkpoints. As this person shows evidence of understanding a particular part of the job, another supervisor should expose him or her to another facet of the operation.

**Detailing.** Detailing is a special type of OJT that should take place far more often than it does. Here an employee, who would benefit from the experience, fills a temporary vacant position, perhaps for two or three months. This gives both the supervisor and the employee a chance to assess the match of position and employee abilities.

## EVALUATION

The process of evaluation should take place constantly, not only when there is an improvement to suggest, but also at a time when honest compliments can be given. The more formal performance evaluation usually requires a checklist of some sort, in writing, signed by both persons. It is usually done at three specific times: 1) midway in the probationary period to let the new employee know how he or she is doing, 2) just prior to the end of the probationary period, which is the time to decide whether to keep the employee, and 3) every year thereafter.

Performance evaluations are enhanced if they list goals to be accomplished and contain a plan, worked out between the two individuals, to help implement the goals.

Performance standards should be developed as an agreement between employee and supervisor as to what is expected during the evaluation period. Goals should be set for the next evaluation.

## SPECIAL CONSIDERATIONS

Special consideration for employees will continually change. Currently the following are noteworthy.

**Office conditions.** Attitudes, habits, and morale will be substandard where the work environment is sub-standard. Serious consideration must be given to space, temperature, air quality, air circulation, computer radiation, lighting, noise, and the individual work station, including that of the disabled employee.

**Individual wellness.** Every agency, regardless of size, needs to give serious consideration to the wellness of its employees. This includes the opportunity for daily exercise, regular health checks, and health seminars and fairs. It also means assisting employees to avoid or recover from any and all drug-related problems.

**Child care.** Whether a single entity or in cooperation with other entities, the resource agency must address the situation of working parents.

## MOVEMENT

Agency personnel will be moving constantly. Sometimes that movement will be a lateral transfer; at other times, it will be an advancement. Sometimes there will be a reduction in force for various reasons, and sometimes a straight-out dismissal will occur. Let us take a look at the various categories.

## Transfer

Before considering transfers for any reasons, an agency administrator must check with the personnel officer or legal counsel to be certain what authority exists. In some instances, the employee's approval for any type of transfer might be needed, while in other agencies, transfers can be made at the agency's will or for cause.

A transfer should be considered a valuable tool. In some instances, it provides the opportunity for an employee to gain wide-ranging experience in a planned program for career development. In other instances, it might be necessary to separate those who have tried, but are unable, to reconcile personal differences. In still other cases, an employee might not do well in a particular geographical area. Whatever the circumstances, the supervisor and the employee should clearly understand the reason for the transfer and make sure there is agreement on details such as moving expenses and the date of transfer. Before considering the filling of any vacancies within the agency with promotional or open-register competitive candidates, the employer should do the following:

- Encourage any employee, who desires to do so, to apply for the position by filing a written intra-agency transfer request with the agency's personnel officer.
- Consult the intra-agency transfer register composed of names of employees who have requested a transfer.
- Consider all employees filing for transfer to the vacant position.

## Advancement

As previously noted, one of the legitimate desires of employees is the opportunity for growth within the agency. It is the responsibility of each supervisor to be aware of his or her employees' goals as they relate to advancement. Many employees are happy and doing a commendable job right where they are, and that should be respected.

## Reduction in Force

Earlier in this chapter, reduction-in-force (RIF) in relation to employment was discussed. RIF also comes to play in abolishing positions. This might be caused by a cut in the budget or by the reduction of an activity and corresponding abolition of a position. Whatever the cause, occasionally an agency will be obligated to dismiss persons who are doing a good job and who otherwise would not have been dismissed. There are often laws or policies dealing with how such reductions must be implemented. This is usually a major item in union contract negotiations with unions. Since any such reduction will be disruptive, it is critical that the reduction-in-force plan be developed as far in advance as possible.

## Dismissal

Later in this chapter, under Supervision, we will discuss general discipline. For the purpose of this chapter, "Dismissal" will be considered the ultimate in disciplinary action. Because dismissal action is often challenged and sometimes overturned, and because of the amount of time and effort dismissal action takes, those in authority will often not dismiss an unsatisfactory employee, but will place the person in a position where their actions, or inaction, will do the least harm. This method of handling a personnel problem is not recommended. If it has been determined that the employee in question was properly instructed in the first place and was informed of any failings or improper actions; if it has been decided that there is no position in the agency where this person can be of value; and if it clear that this employee cannot improve, then dismissal is in order.

The entire procedure must be carefully coordinated with the agency personnel officer. It should also be noted that an employee should never be asked to resign unless the agency is prepared to dismiss this person if he or she chooses not to resign. Managers need to keep notes and file reports of misconduct of the employee; they must also inform the employee of the noted misconduct.

## Exit Interview

When an employee leaves the agency, there should be an exit interview, whether the employee is leaving as a result of dismissal, resignation, reduction in force, or the end of the season or temporary employment. Through a properly conducted interview, the agency can gain valuable information about supervisory practices, work conditions, employee attitudes, and other matters. Subjects for discussion in the exit interview should include reason for leaving, agency strengths and weaknesses, quality of supervision, suitability of performance evaluations, and adequacy of pay scale in relation to job responsibilities. There should also be a request for suggestions for the improvement of personnel management.

## SUPERVISION

The administration develops policy and provides overall direction for the organization. The employees are engaged in day-to-day operations. The supervisor is the person in between, and for most parks this is the park manager. It is the supervisor's responsibility to plan, organize, lead, control, and staff. The supervisory should do the following:

- Plan the work of the unit. Determine the amount of work per person and assign it, trusting the people to whom it is delegated.
- Determine whether the amount and quality of work is according to plan.
- Put the right people in the right jobs.
- Organize the unit properly in order to carry out the plan.
- Provide leadership in decision making.

The supervisor should be willing to criticize tactfully if criticism is called for. The supervisor is in that position because of knowledge of what needs to be done and how to get it done. The ability to give constructive criticism is an indispensable supervisory skill.

### Job Attitudes and Incentives

For the supervisor to be able to use human skills effectively, there is also a need to understand the employees' job attitudes and incentives. Many studies reflect the fact that supervisors and employees do not view employees' needs in the same light. These studies show supervisors have tended to think in terms of wages, job security, and promotions, while the employees have viewed their needs as appreciation for work accomplished and being made to feel a part of the team.

Employees seek to express creativity, to gain recognition, and to experience achievement. They also seek to be part of a team and help with decision making and problem solving. It will make the role of the supervisor and employee much easier and more effective if each is able to understand and perhaps even help fulfill the needs of the other.

### Communication

An increase in the amount of information flowing through organizational channels does not necessarily mean that the channels of communication are open and being used properly. The information and directions that flow downward through formal channels are only a small part of the total communication operation. No matter how elaborate the system of formal communications established within an organization may be, this system will always be supplemented by informal channels. Every agency has a grapevine. Administrators must learn how it works and use it. Every agency has email and websites; they must learn how to use the system to inform employees.

## Scheduling

In scheduling personnel, it is important to schedule not only for maximum job results, but also for maximum personal satisfaction of the employee, and these may not always be the same. Some tasks are more menial and less challenging than others. Some require technical knowledge, while others do not. Some afford the opportunity to place persons outside of their job classification as a learning opportunity and should be so utilized. When scheduling, a supervisor needs to take monotony, fatigue, and other factors affecting the employee into consideration. One must always be flexible and consider alternate scheduling in case there is a change in the weather or disruption in the schedule.

## Discipline

Discipline is needed for a variety of reasons. The usual one is failure to do the job. Should discipline be oral or written? These are the choices and each needs consideration.

When failure to do the job is the complaint, it should be assumed first that the supervisor has not properly communicated to the employee the information necessary to get the job done. When this possibility has been checked, the next assumption must be that the person did not understand it. It is only after both of these possibilities have been eliminated that one must assume that the person is not able to do the job and must be placed somewhere else or let go.

Unwillingness to do the job is also a matter for disciplinary action. This is a separate consideration from the above and must be dealt with as such. It might be that the person has just reasons, such as an unreasonable supervisor or unpalatable working conditions. If this is the case, the cause should be remedied. On the other hand, if the attitude has no basis in external circumstances, then the person, if not able to be retrained, must be let go.

Disobedience calls for disciplinary action. Again, the supervisor of the person giving the order must first be certain that the order was understood and was just and reasonable. If not, the situation should be corrected. If the order was sound, the disciplinary action might be suspension or dismissal.

Violation of the law is cause for disciplinary action. This might be include theft, falsification of record, or violation of any a number of statutes or rules, such as those against sexual harassment or the use of controlled substances while on duty. When this occurs, your agency's legal advisor should be contacted.

In any of the foregoing situations, there are certain rules to be followed to preserve the dignity of the employee, the supervisor, and the agency itself:

- Never discipline in front of others unless the recipient forces you to do so.
- Meet with the employee personally. Look the person in the eye.
- Assume that this person is innocent of both wrongdoing and intent to do wrong.
- Document the charge against the employee precisely and in unemotional terms.
- Hear the person out.
- Outline the disciplinary action clearly.
- Inform the person of appeal rights and of who within the agency might be of assistance.
- . If action other than dismissal is taken, do not refer to the disciplinary action again, either to the concerned employee or to others. It should be a closed book and noted by the supervisor only as a reminder, if necessary. No discussion of it should take place with anyone else.
- If the action is suspension or dismissal, follow up the meeting with a letter.

## CONCLUSION

As employers and taxpayers, each of us must be concerned with the fact that much of the resource agency's funds will be expended on personnel costs. Any effort to reduce these costs through humane and skillful management will benefit all. Remember what you learn, and practice your skills at every opportunity. Park managers need to learn to control themselves and to direct others when called upon to do so. These abilities will enable managers to stand in good stead in every phase of management and will be of crucial importance in advancing their career. The appendix contains the Miami Dade County Employee Evaluation for Parks Employees.

# REFERENCES

## References Cited

California State Parks Field Training, http://www.parks.ca.gov/default.asp?page_id=22567

IUCN-WCPA Global Task Force on Protected Area Management Training, Bibliography http://www.trentu.ca/org/tfpa/iucn.htm

Miami Dade County Human Resources, Employee Evaluation, http://www.miamidade.gov/hr/labor_relations_evaluations.asp

National Park Service, Training and Development Standards, http://www.nps.gov/training/policies.htm

West Virginia State Parks, Historic and Nature Interpretation Personnel Training, http://mypeoplepc.com/members/chingwe/trailsinc18thcentury/id17.html

# Appendix

## Miami Dade County Employee Evaluation for Parks Employees

**EMPLOYEE INFORMATION**

| Name:   Last | First | M.I. | Employee ID Number |
|---|---|---|---|
| Classification | Status | | Period Covered<br>From:    To: |
| Department | Division | Unit | Prob. End Date (If applicable) |

Reason For Review
    ❑ Merit Raise    ❑ Status Change    ❑ Annual Review    ❑ Other (Explain)

**ATTENDANCE AND OBSERVANCE OF WORKING HOURS**
(Standards listed in this section may be used as guidelines)

| | |
|---|---|
| ❑ Outstanding | No absences, always on time. |
| ❑ Above Satisfactory | One to two occasions absent/late. |
| ❑ Satisfactory | Three to four occasions absent/late. |
| ❑ Needs Improvement | Five to six occasions absent/late. |
| ❑ Unsatisfactory | Seven or more occasions absent/late. |

**QUANTITY OF WORK**

| | |
|---|---|
| ❑ Outstanding | Unusually high output, meets emergency demands. |
| ❑ Above Satisfactory | Consistently turns out more than standard for the job. |
| ❑ Satisfactory | Completes assignments as expected |
| ❑ Needs Improvement | Amount of work is below normal operating standards |
| ❑ Unsatisfactory | Amount of work is substantially below normal operating standards |

**INITIATIVE/ COOPERATION**

| | |
|---|---|
| ❑ Outstanding | Seeks additional responsibilities, suggest ideas to improve efficiency or effectiveness. Goes out of his/her way to cooperate with supervisors, fellow workers, or public. |
| ❑ Above Satisfactory | Accepts all additional responsibilities, shows interest, promotes cooperation with others, and recommends new procedures. |
| ❑ Satisfactory | Accepts responsibility, successful in cooperating with others, responds well to new conditions. |
| ❑ Needs Improvement | Leaves problems/situations as he/she finds them, cooperates reluctantly. |
| ❑ Unsatisfactory | Ignores suggested changes, functions with difficulty in a team situation, treats others in an abrupt or rude manner. |

## SAFETY

| | |
|---|---|
| ❏ Outstanding | No preventable accidents, recognizes and resolves safety problems. |
| ❏ Above Satisfactory | No preventable accidents, always adheres to all safety regulations. |
| ❏ Satisfactory | No preventable accidents, usually adheres to all safety regulations. |
| ❏ Needs Improvement | One preventable accident, disregards some safety regulations. |
| ❏ Unsatisfactory | Two or more preventable accidents, ignores safety regulations. |

## JOB KNOWLEDGE

| | |
|---|---|
| ❏ Outstanding | Performs job independently, handles all assignments well, complete understanding and application of rules and procedures. |
| ❏ Above Satisfactory | Performs job fairly independently, handles most assignments well, knows procedures and rules. |
| ❏ Satisfactory | Performs job with little supervision after instructions, knows most procedures and rules. |
| ❏ Needs Improvement | Occasionally has difficulty understanding job function, disregards some rules or operating procedures. |
| ❏ Unsatisfactory | Follows instructions with difficulty, violates rules and procedures. |

## PERSONAL APPEARANCE

| | |
|---|---|
| ❏ Not Applicable | |
| ❏ Outstanding | Always reports to work dressed appropriately or with clean uniform, exemplary grooming and personal hygiene. |
| ❏ Above Satisfactory | Reports to work with uniform or dressed appropriately, presents well groomed appearance, good personal hygiene. |
| ❏ Satisfactory | Usually reports to work with appropriately dressed or with uniform, acceptable personal hygiene and grooming. |
| ❏ Needs Improvement | Occasionally reports to work without uniform or inappropriately dressed, grooming and personal hygiene sometimes unacceptable. |
| ❏ Unsatisfactory | Frequently reports to work without uniform or inappropriately dressed, poor personal hygiene and grooming. |

## REPORTS AND CORRESPONDENCE

| | |
|---|---|
| ❏ Not Applicable | |
| ❏ Outstanding | Always completes reports promptly in a clear and accurate manner requiring no revision. |
| ❏ Above Satisfactory | Completes all reports promptly in a clear and accurate manner requiring little revision, reports are completed on time. |
| ❏ Satisfactory | Completes reports with few required revisions, reports are usually on time. |
| ❏ Needs Improvement | Reports incomplete and needs constant review to insure accuracy, some reports are late. |
| ❏ Unsatisfactory | Reports and correspondence inaccurate and incomplete, reports are frequently late or not done. |

## RATER'S OVERALL EVALUATION

❏ OUTSTANDING:                 Performance surpasses job requirements, employee displays initiative and creativity enhancing departmental efficiency and/or effectiveness.

❏ ABOVE SATISFACTORY:          Performance surpasses job requirements.

❏ SATISFACTORY:                Employee is performing as required.

❏ NEEDS IMPROVEMENT:           Performance does not fully meet requirements.

❏ NEEDS IMPROVEMENT:           Performance is inadequate and must be corrected.

**RATER'S COMMENTS:**      (In what ways can or must the employee improve performance?)

If an employee is eligible for a merit increase, check the one of the following:
❏Granted        ❏Deferred,      re-evaluate in       months.

If an employee is eligible for permanent status, please check one of the following:
❏Granted        ❏ Denied        ❏Extended for       months with employee's written permission (attached)
(Note: Probationary Period may not extend beyond one year)

This report is based on my observations, knowledge of employee's performance and review of applicable information.  It represents my best judgment of the employee's performance.

**Rater's Signature:**                              **Date:**

**Print Name:**                                     **Title:**

I have reviewed this report and discussed it with the Rater.  It represents an accurate appraisal of the employee's performance in accordance with Administrative Order.  I concur in the recommendation, if any, as to merit raise or permanent status.

**Reviewer's Signature:**                           **Date:**

**Print Name:**                                     **Title:**

I acknowledge that I have received a copy of this evaluation.  I have had an opportunity to discuss it with my supervisor.  In signing this evaluation, I do not agree with the conclusions, I understand that I may write my comments below or on another sheet of paper.

**EMPLOYEE COMMENTS**

**Employee's Signature:**                           **Date:**

*Chapter Seven*

# Maintenance and Safety

## MAINTENANCE MANAGEMENT

Comprehensive and systematic park maintenance is aligned with the principles of sustainability. Though depreciation is inevitable, the life of a facility or piece of equipment may be extended significantly through proper maintenance. As costs rise for both replacement and new construction, it becomes imperative for park managers to better maintain existing facilities. Planned maintenance actually earns money through increased operating efficiency because power and fuel costs are reduced. Money is also saved by avoiding lawsuits that could arise from charges of negligence.

The objectives of a park maintenance program are to keep the park environment clean, healthy, and safe and to conserve public monies by conscientious care of facilities and lands. Maintenance entails care of park buildings and other structures, including energy, water sanitation, and light systems; care of beaches and grounds, including soil, turf, or native grasses and forbes, shrubs, and trees; repair of roads and trails; and care of all park equipment. An effective park maintenance program informs future facility planning decisions.

Maintenance means more than just reacting to emergency situations. It means identifying potential management concerns or issues before they become problematic. Maintenance management therefore encompasses preventive (routine and planned) maintenance, which includes the periodic inspection of equipment. In this way, replacements and minor repairs can be made, perhaps preventing a costly breakdown. Negligence tends to result in a general lack of concern for an area and typically will increase maintenance requirements over time. In effect, maintenance is a deterrent to vandalism.

The following factors affect the park's maintenance operation: type of visitor use, interpretation of areas, seasons of use, original design, latitude, altitude, labor relations, and environmental factors, such as weather, topography, soil type, and vegetative cover.

The title "maintenance manager" can refer to the park manager or assistant or, in the case of larger parks, to a person who deals specifically with the more complex maintenance tasks. The maintenance manager, especially in the latter instance, must be exceedingly versatile and knowledgeable. Experience in budgeting, personnel management, equipment and facility use and repair, and public relations is necessary to meet the demands of the position of maintenance manager in a large park. In a small park the manager will have to meet many, if not all, of these challenges as well. No matter what the size of the park, all personnel should be involved in maintenance that involves matters such as litter pick up or noting equipment in need of repair.

### Maintenance Objectives and Standards

Maintenance objectives must be established that reflect the purpose of the park. Once park maintenance objectives are agreed upon, standards are established to help achieve those objectives. Standards frame the "window" of conditions desired. Once standards are established, conditions must be monitored to ensure conformity. Local conditions of each park will influence the standards set and the schedule of inspections. Sticking to standards requires routine monitoring.

Time schedules and budgets might have to be adjusted as current conditions are measured against the standards. Are standards being met or slighted? Is time being wisely spent? Perhaps standards are not being met between scheduling and supervision as required. Perhaps the maintenance routine is taking too much time and energy because standards are unrealistically high. These possibilities must be kept in mind when monitoring conditions and allotting time.

## Maintenance and the Public Image

Good maintenance procedures are often unappreciated, as they may never be noticed by most park visitors. In fact, visitors usually take for granted the fact that lawns are mowed, restrooms cleaned, garbage cans emptied, and grounds are free from litter. They expect the drinking fountains to work properly. Seldom will they write letters when things are in mint condition. Let something appear run down or out of order, however, and complaints will be forthcoming. Sometimes complaints signal a need for additional visitor education.

Maintenance staff members usually come in contact with park visitors more frequently than any other park personnel. For this reason, maintenance staff should have an accurate general knowledge of park resources, a reasonable conversational ability, a pleasant demeanor, and attend to their personal appearance. These are qualities managers should keep in mind when hiring and training employees. A rude employee or an employee unwilling to answer questions intelligently and cheerfully creates an unfavorable impression for the park agency.

Maintenance employees must be assisted in gaining an understanding of the agency and its objectives and the importance of their role in achieving those objectives. Pride in work is necessary. One way to encourage this pride is to solicit participation in the decision-making process. Maintenance personnel should attend regular staff meetings and have input on education and volunteer programs. In addition, administrative staff should participate in regular maintenance activities.

Maintenance personnel are important members of the team. Since they perform services for the total park management operation, the maintenance staff should not look on their work as merely custodial or menial, but should be encouraged to view it as an integral part of park management. It must be pointed out to them that it is their work that keeps all other programs running.

## Maintenance and Park Design

All too frequently, maintenance problems are, at least in part, the result of poor planning and design. Present recreation pursuits are not always the ones for which the park was originally designed, and this creates unavoidable difficulties. The number of visitors and amount of use may exceed planned expectations. Even in new parks, planners have sometimes been too removed from the day-to-day problems of maintenance staff and consequently have designed areas and facilities that produce unnecessary problems for the maintenance division. Architects and contractors can slight the requirements of good maintenance practices in order to keep the construction costs within available funds.

Checklists are useful to ensure that maintenance considerations are included in the planning and design of facilities. More importantly, including maintenance staff in the planning and design process can help to avoid or minimize costly mistakes. In addition, maintenance staff involvement in the planning and design process assists in ensuring maintenance staff members understand the design intent of the facility. At a minimum, the maintenance manager must study the design to determine whether the plans will result in extra maintenance efforts and costs. Examples of things to look for would be the location and number of electrical outlets, the ease of access to plumbing facilities, the use of inappropriate building materials (requiring early replacement), inadequate surface finishes (making cleaning difficult), or wood in contact with the ground, which may cause deterioration of the wood at an unacceptable rate, the extent of managed areas for mowing and other landscape maintenance.

## Maintenance Personnel Management

Park managers not directly involved in maintenance should not isolate themselves from the maintenance staff, but should be available in order to encourage good communication. When possible, the park manager should involve the maintenance staff in the budget and planning processes as well as other park functions.

The staff must be kept on the alert and positively motivated. The supervisor can promote this by being aware of both successes and deficiencies in employees' performances, by helping to correct any shortcomings, and by being ready to reward employees for improvement. Outstanding performance should be recognized by merit increases or job advancement. Certain staff members should be given an opportunity to expand their horizons through the additional training cited below.

Many maintenance positions are entry-level positions paying minimum wage. The total work force, however, ranges from general laborers to highly skilled mechanics and tradespeople, with salaries much higher at the upper levels. Opportunities should be provided for motivated employees to advance.

In some instances, park personnel do not have the expertise or equipment to accomplish certain projects and the work must be contracted. Repairs on sophisticated sanitation systems, motors, and electronic apparatus are examples. Frequently, the smaller or less complicated construction jobs can be done by park staff (day labor) just as effectively. In most instances, the park staff can do a given job for less than a contractor because no profit is required. Another reason for in-house work is that park maintenance crews usually have greater sensitivity and dedication to the work, resulting in less damage to the area than might be incurred by a contractor crew.

Because the maintenance staff must be able to repair almost anything found in the park, a wide variety of skills is required. Larger parks usually have a separate maintenance division employing mechanics, plumbers, electricians, carpenters, and painters. In some smaller parks, one or two employees do all of these tasks. In even smaller parks, the park manager or assistant manager will have to do most maintenance jobs because there is no one else around. This requires park managers to have or acquire many practical skills and abilities, including knowledge of plumbing, wiring, and repair of small engines. It must be stressed that this test of self-reliance comes to most park management graduates at some point in their careers.

**The maintenance supervisor.** A maintenance supervisor may be necessary in a larger park with considerable maintenance needs. Maintenance supervision requires a wealth of talents. Such persons must have technical knowledge of equipment and an ability to plan and implement a functioning maintenance program. Supervisors must prepare budgets for future programs, supervise human resources, be responsible for safety, assist in the actual work, act effectively in emergencies, supervise construction projects, and even advise the park manager on matters related to chemical control of vegetation, safety problems, pollution abatement, energy conservation, and other environmental issues.

## Maintenance Employee Training

Maintenance personnel must have training consistent with the level of work they are expected to perform. Certain permanent maintenance staff will need additional training in order to keep pace with technological advancement. This can come through on-the-job training, workshops, correspondence courses, or training opportunities made available by equipment manufacturers. Many agencies have provisions for tuition reimbursement for vocational night courses at community colleges. Also, with so many seasonal people entering and leaving the maintenance workforce each year, there is a need for seasonal on-the-job training for new employees.

As park ambassadors, the maintenance staff must be trained in public relations, park cultural and natural history, park policy, rules, regulations, and personal appearance standards as well as the technical and safety skills required for the job. It is the park manager's duty to ensure that staff receives suitable training. In some instances, the training may be left to other experienced employees; however, the manager must monitor the apprenticeship to ensure that the training proceeds in a satisfactory manner. Training can be tracked and displayed on a matrix to facilitate whether staff receives appropriate training. The matrix could include all areas of training needed.

The better informed the employee, the better total park operation. Also, the promise of continuous on-the-job training may attract and help retain good personnel.

## MAINTENANCE MANAGEMENT SYSTEMS (MMS)

A maintenance management system is a creative way to record and analyze information to assist in planning, problem solving, and decision making. It can assist a maintenance manager in allocating human, physical, and financial resources and can be used to evaluate the performance of the department. The Pacific Northwest Maintenance Management School developed a version of this system of planning for park maintenance to include essentially four parts:

1. Asset inventory—identifying and measuring assets,
2. Maintenance activity inventory—identifying the activities necessary to maintain the assets,
3. Maintenance activity time standards—determining length of time to maintain assets, and
4. Frequency of maintenance—times per year maintenance activity should be performed.

A maintenance management system relies on setting performance measures, gathering reliable and consistent performance data, and using performance information for accountability and decision making. Numerous software programs are available to assist in this type of data collection and management. However, this software does not minimize the tasks of initial identification of assets, inventory of maintenance activities, standards of length and frequency of maintenance activities.

Most major cities, many state and provincial park agencies, and several Canadian and U.S. land agencies developed their own MMS in the 1980s, and information can be obtained from any of these agencies. Some of the considerations necessary in developing such a system are described below.

### Job Scheduling and Labor Efficiency

The objectives of programming maintenance work into a schedule are to 1) increase to the highest degree possible the productive utilization of the maintenance staff, 2) coordinate the work to minimize interference between other maintenance groups or individuals, 3) coordinate with other park activities to minimize interference with and from these other programs, and 4) provide the best possible services with the available resources of personnel, equipment, and materials.

Scheduled (routine) maintenance work is done periodically according to a predetermined time schedule. Such schedules should yield the following information:

- *What* needs to be done,
- *Where* it needs to be done,
- *How* it should be done, and
- *When* it should be done.

Types of scheduled maintenance include the following:

- Facilities examination and repair (buildings, signs, trails, bridges, and roadways),
- Grounds keeping (mowing grass and weeding),
- Landscaping (vista clearing, trimming shrubbery, ornamental and barrier plantings),
- Cleaning (garbage hauling, policing grounds, and providing janitorial service),
- Preventive maintenance routines (vehicle lubrication and service, equipment lubrication, heating and ventilating service), and
- Operating routines (pumping plants, swimming pools, and sump pumps).

There are three types of maintenance services: emergency, routine, and planned. Emergency service is required when a facility demands attention (e.g., a broken water pipe or a plugged toilet). Routine service is given on a regular basis to keep equipment and facilities running efficiently (e.g., lubricating equipment and cleaning restrooms). Routine service also includes ground maintenance activities, such as mowing and filling in holes. Planned service is specific maintenance scheduled without waiting for an emergency, but much less frequently than routine services. Examples would be roofing a comfort station every 10 years or replacing truck brake linings every 50,000 miles. The maintenance manager determines which category has priority. Labor, equipment, and supplies must be coordinated for maximum efficiency. A lot of time and effort can be wasted in maintenance work. Haskell (1970) lists the following delays:

- Waiting for orders in the morning and at noon,
- Looking for the crew leader to determine the next job,
- Visiting the site to find out what must be done,
- Taking unnecessary trips to stores,
- Making return trips for tools,
- Searching for the crew leader in order to get a supply-withdrawal authorization,
- Going back to the shop when another job is in the vicinity of one just completed,
- Dispatching three people to a job that two could very easily do,
- Waiting for workers from other crafts to start or finish,
- Looking for the job site,
- Confusion and backtracking because of countermanded orders,
- Waiting for other employees to vacate a site,
- Trying to make up for insufficient information on blueprints, and
- Searching for materials that are on order, but have not yet arrived.

The solution to most of these delays is effective scheduling of work crews, equipment, and materials. Scheduling should occur at least one day in advance, although some projects may need a week or more of lead time. Work schedules should be set up within normal work time, allowing overtime only in emergencies, and then holding it to a minimum. A detailed map of the park in the maintenance office as well as a checkout board listing job site and estimated time of return for each crew or employee might be helpful. New equipment, new techniques, revised procedures, policy changes, and similar matters should be noted on a central bulletin board or through an efficient memorandum system.

**Record keeping.** The work accomplished, materials used, staff required, and time required should be recorded. This provides information for weekly, monthly, and annual reports. Interested parties know what has been done and when. This data provides information for planning future projects as well as cost figures for budget preparation.

**Seasonal workloads**. Most park visitation is seasonal, which results in heavy workloads for a short period. The staff is also expanded seasonally to accommodate these increased maintenance needs. Some parks defer certain types of maintenance work, such as tree trimming and removal, equipment and building repair, and painting until after the busy visitor season has ended. Such a plan keeps experienced personnel on the job throughout the year and provides a base on which to build the temporary maintenance staff the following season. These employees will be needed to train seasonal staff in the following year and contribute their expertise to the job itself. Managers cannot release skilled employees at season's end and expect to rehire them the next year. Their abilities will command steady employment elsewhere if the manager cannot arrange the work schedule to keep them on the payroll year round. Unfortunately, many park agencies cannot afford to keep skilled construction labor on the payroll all year, so major developments and skilled services may have to be contracted out. There are many highly qualified maintenance "retirees" who only want seasonal employment.

The key to successful operations and maintenance is a carefully planned work schedule that is followed. A number of factors should be considered while planning the work schedule:

- Season of year,
- Priority of work items,
- Expected public use,
- Capability of park staff,
- Anticipated work hours available, subtracting time for annual leaves, etc.,
- Restrictions on overtime, and
- Varying weather conditions.

Checklists need to be established based on the location of a park and its specific and regional conditions. The maintenance manager must know the visitor use pattern and the weather and proceed accordingly.

## EQUIPMENT

Most workers want to do the job as quickly as possible while expending the least physical effort. This means using labor-saving machines rather than hand tools. The equipment needed varies with the job to be done. However, the equipment available will vary with the size of the park and its financial resources. All parks need standard cleaning equipment for the daily care of restrooms, but not all parks can afford elaborate aerial tower trucks used for tree trimming and removal. Some equipment may be shared between parks on a scheduled basis or rented if to be used only a few times a year. Shared mobile equipment allows fewer pieces of costly equipment to be used in more area.

Equipment selection is important. High-quality, rugged, industrial-grade equipment with a long life span is usually the most economical. Machines requiring continuous repair are seldom available when needed, and this is annoying, disruptive, and costly. When purchasing, seek the advice of the mechanics who must maintain the machine and of the person who has to operate it. Their experienced counsel will probably save future headaches and pay off financially in the long run.

When selecting equipment, one should ask other questions as well. Will this machine do the necessary job? Can parts be easily obtained? Is it easily serviced? Is it dangerous to operate? Can inexperienced staff help operate it? Will it be a safety hazard to park visitors?

Specialized equipment, such as stump removers, crawler tractors, concrete mixers, power saws, and front-end loaders, should be used only by trained personnel. No employee should be allowed to operate any equipment unless he or she understands its purpose, its operating technique, and its basic care and maintenance. A sign-out system for equipment gives the maintenance supervisor better control.

The manufacturer's manuals that accompany new equipment should be kept on file in the maintenance office. Where practical, a copy should also be available with the equipment. These should be read and understood by the operator before using the equipment. The servicing and storage instructions should be carefully read and observed.

### The Inventory

An inventory record should be kept for all tools and equipment owned by the park. The list should include the name, cost, date of purchase, serial number, model number, specifications, warranty data, and storage location. The data from hour meters should also be received. Equipment should have records kept on dates of routine maintenance and repair costs of parts and labor. Such records are invaluable for purposes of budgeting, determining costs of specific tasks, planning for scheduled maintenance, and reporting thefts. In some instances, the recording of hours of use or miles of service on equipment is utilized for scheduling routine maintenance as well as servicing and repair.

## Service and Repair

All equipment is covered by warranty for a certain length of time, assuming normal servicing. After the warranty has expired, of course, it is still necessary to continue lubrication, oil changes, filter changes, battery tests, antifreeze installation, spot painting, and other minor repairs and adjustments. Some work will have to be done in commercial repair shops by skilled workers if the park staff is not equipped for such work.

## The Maintenance Manual

Each park manager should see that a maintenance manual is prepared as a guide to the step-by-step procedure for working with all equipment and facilities. It should include the manufacturer's service and repair suggestions. This manual serves as a ready reference for new employees as well as those not able to remember the minor details of a particular maintenance activity.

## SUSTAINABILITY AND MAINTENANCE CONSIDERATIONS

Many parks have reviewed their park management and maintenance practices through a sustainability perspective and developed specific sustainability plans. Portland Parks and Recreation Sustainability Plan is accessed at http://www.saferoutesportland.com/parks/index.cfm?a=226587&c=49294. Sustainable practices within park operations must address energy inputs and outputs and "waste" cycles.

Solid waste management should also be addressed through the parks maintenance management system. Solid waste management has become a major concern for park managers, taking more time and costing more money. Solid waste is generated from internal operations or brought in by visitors. This could include anything from packaging and food scraps, scrap metal, to light bulbs and construction materials. Initial efforts to address solid waste management adopted a product life cycle perspective of cradle to grave. Recycling expanded to include efforts to reduce and reuse. Now we have progressed to think in terms of cradle to cradle. Products might be designed so that, after their useful life, they provide nourishment for something new, either as "biological nutrients" that safely re-enter the environment or as "technical nutrients" that circulate within closed-loop industrial cycles, without being "downcycled" into low-grade uses (as most "recyclables" now are) (McDonough, Braungart, 2002).

Reducing and rethinking how solid waste can be managed requires a program of awareness, education, action, and commitment to continual improvement. Parks need to address solid waste management through policy and operations. Effective management may require changes in solid waste contracts, concession agreements, and equipment.

Xanterra, the nation's largest park concessions management company, has adopted waste minimization practices throughout the concessions operations. Zion Lodge composts all of its food wastes, lawn clippings, and shredded paper. Xanterra will soon convert the 11,000 gallons of used cooking oil in Yellowstone to biodiesel to fuel their vehicle fleet. The 2015 environmental vision performance goal is to divert 50% of all solid waste generated from landfill using 2000 as a baseline date. Table 7.1 reflects Xanterra's performance toward solid waste management. The company exceeded its goal by 2006.

The Institute for Local Self-Reliance tracks municipal recycling effectiveness. Many communities have diverted 50%-60% of their total waste from the landfill and some communities have adopted zero waste plans.

Municipal record-setting recycling programs:

- Compost yard trimmings,
- Target a wide range of materials,
- Require resident participation,
- Institute economic incentives, and
- Design programs for convenience.

### Table 7.1. Total Solid Waste Generation and Recycling/Diversion

| | Recycled/Diverted (lbs) | Generated (lbs to landfill) | Recycling/Diversion Rate (percent) | Recycled/Diverted per Room Night (lbs) |
|---|---|---|---|---|
| 2000 | 1,868,118 | 13,451,191 | 12.19 | 1.84 |
| 2001 | 2,052,550 | 13,076,047 | 13.57 | 2.11 |
| 2002 | 2,619,191 | 13,110,093 | 16.65 | 2.7 |
| 2003 | 4,369,103 | 11,110,248 | 28.23 | 4.48 |
| 2004 | 4,291,104 | 10,780,736 | 28.47 | 4.46 |
| 2005 | 5,142,710 | 11,801,975 | 30.35 | 5.4 |
| 2006 | 5,945,037 | 9,257,622 | 39.11 | 6.19 |
| 2000-2004 change | 218% | -31% | 321% | 335% |

From Xanterra Company, 2011, retrieved from http://www.xanterra.com/solid-waste-1-5346.html

These characteristics can be adapted for a park operation. The most successful system should increase the park visitor's role and reduce the crew's involvement in handling solid waste. Many park operations require visitors to carry out what they carry in.

## SAFETY

Safety is an issue that concerns all park personnel. Parks must be secure refuges for visitors and provide a safe work environment for staff. Safety issues and concerns vary widely between parks, depending on the park location and use, both legal and illegal. Management must establish a safety program that is relevant to the location and the tasks that are required of personnel.

### The Park Safety Program

A park safety program should enable park staff to respond to unpredictable situations. It must address injury prevention, occupational hazards, deaths, fires, motor vehicle collisions, property damages, criminal activity and lawsuits against the agency and its employees.

The basic objectives of the park safety program are the reduction of accidents involving agency staff, park visitors, concessionaires, and contract personnel. Each employee must accept responsibility and maintain constant alertness to prevent accidents on the job. Each person should report hazardous conditions or unsafe practices and take steps to eliminate them where indicated. Accident prevention thus becomes a part of that person's job description. The employee must believe in safety, practice safety, and insist on safe working conditions if accidents are to be avoided. Employees should participate in identifying safety issues within an agency. The National Park Service has initiated a safety program where the employee is responsible, in part, for safety assessment called a Job Hazard Analysis.

A job hazard analysis or JHA is a technique that focuses on job tasks as a way to identify hazards before they occur. JHA is a multistep process designed to study and analyze a job. It breaks down a job into steps, which provide a means of identifying and then eliminating or controlling associated hazards. The JHA results in a detailed written procedure for safely completing a particular job. (NPS, 2005)

### Maintenance and Park Safety

A safety study conducted by the National Safety Council revealed that of all the park-related occupational injuries, 66 percent involved maintenance personnel. Yet it is the maintenance division that usually has the responsibility of taking corrective action against unsafe conditions in the park.

There are several reasons for this apparent contradiction. The maintenance staff works more with tools and other high-risk equipment than do other park employees. Much of the maintenance staff includes young seasonal employees who often have no previous work experience and limited safety knowledge. Their work takes them to isolated areas where supervision is often limited. Also, maintenance workers frequently work along roads and are thus exposed to moving vehicles.

Most agencies are covered by some type of industrial insurance. The rates charged to the agency are reflective of the payments made for injury to employees. A safe program saves money in insurance premiums and staff time lost to address medical and legal issues due to injury.

All levels of government require their park systems to have a work safety program. If there is no state-operated safety program, employees may be covered by OSHA (the Occupational Safety and Health Act of 1970) in the United States. In Canada, each province has its own work safety program, usually under a workman's compensation board. Such work safety programs set the standards for the member agencies.

## Inspection

It is difficult, in most instances, to separate safety inspections from maintenance checks. Maintenance checks require a significant amount of time, suggesting the need to combine safety and maintenance inspections. One purpose of inspections is to see whether the park is operating properly. For example, a spring inspection would be for the purpose of ensuring park readiness for the summer season. A summer inspection tour would be a check on maintenance standards and the proper handling of park visitors. This sort of inspection is frequently made by a higher authority than the park manager and might not be announced. Such inspections include grounds, building, facility, and equipment safety monitoring and point out any weaknesses in maintenance performance levels.

The park manager should make his or her own routine inspections. Concern for the park and visitors should be the main reason for in-hours inspections. Reports of inspections and repairs must be kept as a part of the management and maintenance record.

Visitors have a right to assume that all park facilities are routinely checked for safety and that repairs are made when indicated. The responsibility and importance of making prompt and adequate repairs must be impressed on employees. Accidents may not be completely preventable, but there is no excuse for cursory inspections or incomplete repairs. Should the park manager have no financial resources to implement such repairs, the area should be closed or the particular piece of equipment should be withdrawn from public use.

To make sure facilities are inspected on a regular basis, each park should have safety inspection schedules for all facilities, including playground equipment, docks, buildings, grounds, parking areas, roads, and trails. All items should be listed with a space for check-off and comments. An inspection would have (a) the name of park, (b) the facility, (c) the date, (d) the name of the inspector, (e) the condition of the facility or areas, and 6) suggested corrective action as required.

In order to assist the park manager or safety inspector in making the most complete inspection possible, a checklist, adopted from the National Park Service, will be found in the Appendix at the end of this chapter. It offers a reasonably comprehensive hazard review of conditions and facilities. Purely maintenance concerns, such as painting and roof conditions, could also be checked at this time. Individual parks are advised to make deletions or additions as needed. Any unsafe acts by workers or visitors seen during the inspection tour should be noted, and corrective action should be suggested.

## Employee Safety Training

The park manager must see to it that all employees are properly trained for the jobs they are expected to do. This includes pertinent safety information. Necessary first-aid and rescue equipment must also be on hand and periodically inspected. Emergency medical services are considered in chapter 18, Care of Visitors.

Training should include how to recognize potential hazards, what proper safety clothing and equipment to wear (shoes, goggles, gloves, and hard hats), the proper approach for lifting bulky objects, the method of handling volatile fuels, and the care and handling of hand and power tools. There are numerous other aspects, depending on the operation involved. Training methods include pre-employment safety training packets, demonstrations, film and slide programs, bulletin boards, and home study courses. It is extremely important that skillful, dynamic instructors be given this task. Otherwise, the employees may tune out the information although they appear to have had adequate instruction, because they attended the program.

To assist park personnel with the safe use of pesticides, the National Park Service, in cooperation with the Environmental Protection Agency, produced four training videotapes. These can be obtained from the National Park Foundation, 1101 17th Street NW, Suite 1008, Washington D.C. 20036. See also http://www.ipmnet.org/tim/Pesticide_Ed/Pesticide_Education_Audio_Visual_Mat.html for more details.

Safety should be a part of every orientation and training program for new employees. Safety meetings should be held weekly, perhaps at the start of the day, keeping them limited to five or 10 minutes. Any accidents that have occurred since the last meeting should be reviewed. Also, hypothetical situations can be used to solicit responses that identify correct safety procedures. A different safety technique can be demonstrated at each session. Short safety sessions should also be on the agenda of every staff meeting. This way all employees will be kept apprised of the safety program and its effectiveness. Periodic half-day or all-day safety training sessions should be considered.

Fire pre-suppression is an important part of park safety also, because the maintenance staff will probably form the backbone of the fire-fighting crew; the relationship is a close one.

Employment consideration could be given to seasonal applicants who have completed standard first-aid training courses. Also, short courses for park personnel in first aid, emergency medical training, vehicle traffic control, water safety, skiing safety, mountain climbing, rescue work, and other special park needs should be offered. The instructor should spend time and thought preparing these sessions. Help from outside the agency should be used whenever possible. Safety posters should be displayed and changed periodically.

**Environmental Hazards**

Decade after decade, we have increased our dependency upon chemicals. It is now recognized that increased exposure to a variety of chemicals causes illness and threatens the lives of current and future generations. There are many resources by which to become better informed. Nevertheless, we will briefly address hazardous waste and protection for park personnel.

It should be evident that protection of people is the top priority when dealing with hazardous wastes, both known and unknown. Dalton (1986) tells us there are several things to keep in mind when there is a "find" or report on hazardous wastes or materials:

*   Don't charge into an area that is contaminated or where there is visible evidence of a spill or release of toxic or unknown chemicals (odors, gases, fumes, ground or water discoloration, dead animals, and a cloud of colored vapors can all be indications of potential hazards).
*   Unless you have back-up personnel and proper protective clothing or equipment, DO NOT enter the suspected zone of contamination. Notify or report incident, evacuate area immediate to site and downwind, post the area with signs or cordon off.
*   Activate your contingency plan and proceed with the notification section. Call in a professional clean-up contractor and support personnel, call the National Response Center at 800-424-8802 and also the appropriate state agency dealing with spill response.
*   Don't assume anything when dealing with chemicals or hazardous wastes. Report only the facts that you have been told or have seen for yourself. If not certain, have someone investigate (from a distance using field glasses) and report back to you with the facts.

• Make certain that you understand the limitations of the protective clothing and equipment you are wearing. Know your own limits. Use good judgment and care; try to determine exact location, amounts and danger before allowing anyone to enter the contaminated zone.

## CONCLUSION

Maintenance, more than any other park function is needed year round and is needed regardless of park visitation. Even if the park is "mothballed," maintenance is needed. Maintenance—its personnel, equipment, and supplies—consumes a major portion of the park budget and deserves the attention of top management.

The safety record of a park carries a message about management's ability to foresee problems and prevent them, as well as its ability to keep employees at all levels informed and aware regarding safety. Maintaining a good record requires a deep conviction of the importance of this subject along with creative energy intelligently directed.

## REFERENCES

**References Cited**

Barr, James P., & Gierloff, Christi. (1991). "Developing a Solid Waste Plan for State Parks." Trends. *Park Practice Program, 28*(1):8-15.

Dalton, Thomas F. (1986). "Managing Environmental Health Hazards." Trends. *Park Practice Program, 23*(1): 5-10.

Haskell, Theodore J. (1970). "Scheduling Maintenance Functions: Getting the Right Things Done." *Proceedings, Park Maintenance for the Administrator. Park and Recreators Institute.* Davis: University of California.

McDonough, William, & Braungart, Michael. (2002). *Cradle to cradle: Remaking the way we make things.* New York: North Point Press.

Michigan Department of Natural Resources. (nd). Field Manuel. Lansing, MI. http://www.ilsr.org/pubs/pubswtow.html.

National Park Service. (2005). Job hazard analysis: Identifying risks sooner rather than later! Retrieved June 2010 www.nps.gov/training/tel/guides/jha_pguide_010605.pdf.

# Appendix
## Safety Inspection Checklist

DATE:
INSPECTOR:
PARK UNIT:

| | Satisfactory | Inadequate | Comments |
|---|---|---|---|
| **Park Entrance:** | | | |
| Condition of paving | | | |
| Deceleration turnouts | | | |
| Approach markers | | | |
| Entrance sign | | | |
| Checking station maintenance | | | |
| Traffic stripes | | | |
| Lighting | | | |
| Traffic controls | | | |
| Seasonal hazards | | | |
| Rock or tree hazards | | | |
| Reflection markers | | | |
| **Parking Areas and Roads:** | | | |
| Condition of paving | | | |
| Intersection | | | |
| Signs | | | |
| Guardrails | | | |
| Parking turnouts | | | |
| Danger trees | | | |
| Tree or rock falls | | | |
| Emergency phones | | | |
| Seasonal hazards | | | |
| Reflectorized markers | | | |
| Traffic stripes | | | |
| Lighting | | | |
| Garbage cans | | | |
| **Trails:** | | | |
| Drainage | | | |
| Condition of surface | | | |
| Footbridges | | | |
| Guardrails | | | |
| Signs | | | |
| Garbage cans | | | |

|  | Satisfactory | Inadequate | Comments |
|---|---|---|---|

**Piers and Docks:**
    Signs
    Railings
    Pilings
    Lifesaving equipment
    Ladders, ramps, steps
    Decking surface
    Garbage cans
    Cleats secure

**Beaches:**
    Broken glass
    Debris
    Marker buoys
    Lifeguard stand
    Navigation aids

**Utility Centers:**
    Entrance signs
    Electric services
    Water systems
    Fencing, gates
    Wood and metal shops
    Storage areas
    Machinery shielding
    Flammable rags
    Safety maintenance
    First aid supplies/services
    Power and hand tools
    Power mowers
    Fire suppression equipment
    Fire hydrants
    Fuel storage
    Paint storage
    Furnace room
    Roof drainage
    (Maintenance concerns)

|  | Satisfactory | Inadequate | Comments |
|---|---|---|---|
| **Residence Areas:** | | | |
| Signs | | | |
| Roads | | | |
| Walks | | | |
| Lighting | | | |
| Flammables | | | |
| Fire hydrants | | | |
| Electric services | | | |
| Fire escapes | | | |
| Fire suppression equipment | | | |
| Garbage cans | | | |
| (Maintenance concerns) | | | |
| | | | |
| **Administrative Building, Visitor Center:** | | | |
| Entrance signs | | | |
| Interior signs | | | |
| Electric services | | | |
| Water systems | | | |
| Sanitation | | | |
| Emergency shelters | | | |
| First aid supplies/services | | | |
| Slippery floors | | | |
| Steps and ramps | | | |
| Guardrails | | | |
| Drinking fountains | | | |
| Automatic sprinklers | | | |
| Fire hydrants | | | |
| Fire suppression equipment | | | |
| Fuel storage | | | |
| Furnace room | | | |
| Emergency exits | | | |
| (Maintenance concerns) | | | |
| | | | |
| **Concession Units:** | | | |
| Entrance signs | | | |
| Electric services | | | |
| Water systems | | | |
| Sanitation | | | |
| Service area | | | |
| Warehouse | | | |

| | Satisfactory | Inadequate | Comments |
|---|---|---|---|
| Fencing | | | |
| Mobile equipment | | | |
| Ropes and guy wires | | | |
| First aid supplies/services | | | |
| Food handling | | | |
| Flammables | | | |
| Ladders, steps | | | |
| Boat-handling | | | |
| Fire suppression equipment | | | |
| **Contractor Units:** | | | |
| Signing of detours | | | |
| Maintenance of detours | | | |
| Materials hauling and storing | | | |
| Fencing and barricades | | | |
| Shoring trenches and cuts | | | |
| Water | | | |
| Sanitation | | | |
| Scaffolding | | | |
| Mobile equipment | | | |
| Ropes and guy wires | | | |
| Night lighting of hazards | | | |
| First aid equipment | | | |
| Hard hats | | | |
| Fuel storage | | | |
| Flammables | | | |
| Explosives | | | |
| Firearms | | | |
| Ladders | | | |
| Rigging | | | |
| Welding | | | |
| Power tools | | | |
| Hand tools | | | |
| Fire suppression equipment | | | |

|  | Satisfactory | Inadequate | Comments |
|---|---|---|---|
| **Grounds (picnic, camping):** | | | |
| Signs | | | |
| Condition of surfacing | | | |
| Restrooms | | | |
| Water systems | | | |
| Electric services | | | |
| Fences | | | |
| Barricades | | | |
| Stoves and grills | | | |
| Picnic tables | | | |
| Garbage cans | | | |
| Playground equipment | | | |
| Holes ditches | | | |

*Chapter Eight*

# Citizen Participation and Involvement

One of the principles of sustainable park and natural resources management is citizen involvement in a meaningful and collaborative fashion. Citizens can be involved in park management by performing tasks under agency supervision, by participating in decision making through information input, or by belonging to a special interest group. There are differences between the personal assistance offered by individual volunteers and members of special interest groups and the policy-influencing advisory role sought by user groups or those groups whose members express a broad concern for environmental affairs. All of these groups are considered stakeholders who have interest in the management, planning, funding, and maintenance of parks. This chapter recognizes these differences and clarifies them through the framework of volunteers. The individual and various groups are addressed and are followed by a separate discussion of special interest groups.

In some organizations, a few individuals make major decisions without soliciting ideas and input from several sources; however, within a park agency, the person responsible for decision making must obtain advice from stakeholders. This can come from within the agency, from other agencies, and from private citizens or groups of citizens.

Citizens provide assistance in the decision-making process and play an important role in the implementation of decisions. They inform the agency about special needs, generate feedback about facilities and programs planned or provided by the agency, and reflect public opinion concerning the agency itself. Correct handling of public input can assist continued growth of the park agency and its services, help resist infringement by other departments, and aid in avoiding crippling reduction during times of limited financial resources. As one can see in Figure 8.1, the process of citizen involvement informs the plans, the management, and the programming of our parks.

In order to plan and manage parks effectively, the U.S. National Park Service has developed an extensive Internet system for gaining input from stakeholder groups. By visiting http://parkplanning.nps.gov/, any person may comment on a variety of plans, environmental impact reports and scoping documents, and volunteering.

## VOLUNTEERS

Reasons for volunteering include a desire to serve, a need to learn about one's community, a desire for recognition, or a wish to share interest and knowledge with others. Business and industry management frequently encourage employees to volunteer their services in community work, thus providing incentive for citizen involvement. Often these volunteers formalize their efforts into a group called Friends of the Park. For example, the Hanauma Bay Nature Preserve Marine Park in Honolulu, Hawaii, is supported by volunteers aptly named Friends of Hanauma Bay. The Friends of Hanauma Bay volunteer for environmental education programs, parking and visitor services and also support the management team in lobbying for support for policies and funding of the Preserve. See http://www.friendsofhanaumabay.org/index.html for more information and for how they have organized a very effective program.

**Figure 8.1. Citizens and the Park Planning System**

Involvement can be as passive as responding to a questionnaire or as active as offering to help and making a definite commitment. Some citizens who wish to be involved will contact the agency; others need to be sought. However they present themselves, volunteers are needed and should be welcomed, whether by the director of the agency, a park manager, or an employee at some other level within the park agency. Volunteer assistance in various aspects of park management is becoming more important as budget cuts decrease park staffing. Perhaps it might become necessary to have certain sections of linear parks maintained in this way.

How and where should volunteers be found? How should needs be presented so that potential volunteers are attracted? How do we identify the ones who are willing to serve as individuals? How do we identify those who want to serve only within a group? The first thing that should be done in order to answer these four questions is to compile two lists.

1.  List the job/function/service areas in which the park or agency needs help beyond that which can be hired on the official payroll. Needed personnel could include instructors, office workers, research aides, or persons to oversee such special time-consuming projects as the creation of a historical garden or the preparation of a living history costume event.

2.  List individuals and groups who want to aid the park or agency. Where does one secure these names? As a start, contact retirement organizations, conservation organizations, recreation groups, churches, service/fraternal groups, and college outdoor recreation and park management classes. Also consider contacting the National Center for Volunteer Action and the Volunteer Services of the American Association for Retired Persons.

Once these two lists have been prepared, match the first list to the second and contact the volunteers. Perhaps a key volunteer can be found to accomplish this organizational work and assist in running the volunteer program.

## The Individual Volunteer

Individual volunteer involvement presents far greater opportunities and advantages to the agency than do groups. Individual volunteers are able to perform some of the same services as employees and cost the agency comparatively nothing. They can be used on a regular basis from daily to once per week. Such persons can be utilized at the agency headquarters in general services, as a consultant, or for special needs. An example might be a retired business executive aiding in budget preparation. Volunteers can assist at individual parks as well. Most park managers would have no difficulty utilizing volunteers in a variety of functions, such as clerical and organizational work, special interpretive service, or sign preparation and repair.

Individual involvement also presents problems. Individuals may require close supervision and sometimes cause disruptions. Often they are not deeply committed and cause frustration by not showing up where and when scheduled.

## General Interest Groups

These groups are usually broad in scope and purpose, and will offer assistance even if they do not benefit directly. Service clubs fit this category.

Scouts or other youth groups who do benefit directly may build trails for the experience and public service entailed, as well as for individual recognition within their groups. Also, volunteer search and rescue groups have proven extremely helpful to recreation agencies at all levels. The National Park Service has developed an extensive website for organizations like the Boy Scouts to find information, volunteer, and become involved with park management and maintenance. See http://www.nps.gov/gettinginvolved/youthprograms/boyscouts.htm for more details.

## Citizen Boards

A citizen board differs from a special interest group in that it has a much broader base of interest. Many examples exist with regard to function and mission of the these boards. In Westchester County, New York, the following is typical of a county park board:

> The Westchester County Parks, Recreation and Conservation Board comprises nine members who are appointed by the County Executive for a term of one, two, or three years. They are selected to represent the public interest in the area of parks, recreation, and conservation. A representative of the county legislature serves as liaison to the board and the county commissioners of parks, public works and planning serve as non-voting ex-officio members. The legislative liaison to the board has voting powers.

> As required by county charter, the parks board has the responsibility to develop and recommend programs to formulate and approve plans for parks and open space development. In addition, all matters of regulation, use, fees and charges require board approval. (http://parks.westchestergov.com)

In Tennessee, the Department of Environment and Conservation has published an extensive Parks and Recreation Citizen Board Training Manual. See http://www.state.tn.us/environment/recreation/pdf/cbtmanual.pdf for more details.  The importance of the citizen board was summed up nicely in a presentation by Earl T. Groves, Chairman of the Board of Trustees, National Recreation and Parks Association, when he made the following comments:

> There are many advantages to citizen involvement in recreation and park programs. Enumerating just a few of these, we can recognize that citizen participation creates the feeling that we, as citizens, have a voice, whether directly as a board member, or indirectly, through a board member that we may know and feel free to talk to. It is a democratic approach, and one that gives visibility and credibility to recreation and park programs in a community. Board members provide, usually at no charge, advisory and consulting services that are of great value. Many of these citizens are also involved in other community activities and provide communication with other public agencies as well as private and voluntary organizations. The citizen members are involved in the business community and have contacts with private businesses and industries, as well as with wealthy citizens. These contacts can lead to substantial contributions and financial support. With the right approach, contributions of land and facilities for recreation and parks use can often be generated through these contacts (Groves, 1978).

**Policy-making boards.** The policy board is either appointed by the head of the particular level of government such as a governor or minister, or elected by the citizens of a particular geographical area, such as a park and recreation district. As noted in chapter 2, Structure, the policy board usually has the right of hiring and dismissing the park agency director. It is generally accepted that citizens are assured of a broader interest in their park needs through the policy-making board, whose membership provides a wide range of experience as well as representation of the total geographic area. Those citizens who are interested in park matters are able to express their opinions to a board member who lives close to their location. The staggered appointment of park board members usually provides that a majority of the board will survive a change in the appointing authority, thus decreasing the potential for partisan political maneuvering.

The board members should be informed by the appointing authority as to what is expected of them in both time requirements and responsibility. They should be told what authority they have—and do not have.

For the board to be properly involved, the park agency director should regularly communicate with the chairman, and, to a lesser degree, with the total board. The board should be actively involved in the decision-making process even when the director is the one to make the decision. They should be solicited for ideas and should be involved in the pleasurable aspects of decision making as well as the unpleasant.

**Advisory boards.** There are many types of advisory boards or committees. They are operated in various ways and for many purposes. They often give advice to the director or the elected executive. They may be specialists in a particular subject or represent a geographical area. Sometimes a committee for a specific purpose will be appointed by a park manager to function at that park only, but advisory committees are usually appointed by the director. They can provide constructive support to a park agency if used properly and if provided sufficient supportive assistance. With careful selection, such a committee can provide a community-level sounding board for the department and can broaden the basis of public support for the agency's endeavors. Advisory committees can also help alleviate the stigma of insensitivity that is attached to many government agencies that have little or no input from the public they serve. There must be adequate recognition for the services and accomplishments of the group or for outstanding committee members.

There are some problems with advisory committees. The required liaison and other departmental supportive services involve considerable staff time. If the advisory committee is to be an effective group, the projects or programs must have a real purpose and need. The act of establishing such an advisory committee represents a commitment on the part of the department for involvement in that service and in that program.

The committee findings and the recommendations must be carefully considered and used in making decisions if the agency is to establish and maintain an image of integrity and credibility with the public. This does not mean that all recommendations must be accepted and acted on. There are basically two types of advisory boards: terminal and ongoing.

*Terminal.* These committees deal with a specific subject matter or with a definite goal: either a specific problem that needs resolving or a general subject for a stated period of time. It is important that these committees end their term of service cleanly at the appropriate time.

It is normally easier to keep the interest of a terminal committee, as they usually are composed of persons who are interested in the particular subject matter or they would not have been willing to serve in the first place. Also, because they know there is an end of the road, they tend to feel a sense of urgency and a need for accomplishment.

**Ongoing.** In government situations where strong executive control is required or desired, the ongoing or continuing advisory committee provides the necessary public involvement to ensure that the taxpayers' needs are being met or are at least considered. In other words, such a board helps the agency present full service within budgetary and policy limitations. The administrative authority of the agency still rests in the hands of the executive branch of government, but the advisory board can serve as a buffer for repercussions from decisions made by the agency, thus freeing the agency administrator from various outside pressures.

The ongoing advisory committee is one of the more difficult to deal with, and yet it is one of the most rewarding if the agency is able to handle it properly. Ongoing advisory committee members have a tendency to believe they are in management, and when they make decisions and give them to the person who appointed the committee, often they forget their advice will not always be followed. At the same time, their input is useful and should be taken seriously. These individuals reflect their constituents' as well as their own diverse backgrounds. It is important that they be heard.

There are many ways to establish advisory committees. Most state and municipal park and recreation departments have their citizen participant processes online and also list committees and advisory boards in which citizens can become engaged. These also advise citizens on how they should approach the governmental unit should they want to form an advisory committee. For example, the Alaska Division of Parks and Outdoor Recreation, Department of Natural Resources has developed a resource website for advisory boards and management councils that address a range of park management issues. These can be viewed at http://dnr.alaska.gov/parks/misc/boards. htm.

## "Friends" Groups

As noted earlier in the chapter about the Friends of Hanauma Bay, the friends group is one that should be given consideration especially during times of monetary or political difficulties. Friends often start by their own initiative to assist an agency with a particular need. Sometimes they continue in the role of "friends of the park," while at other times the organization may terminate, such as when the promotion of a bond issue is over. Sometimes the organization will actually become a bona fide partner with the government entity, whereby the government provides the area and facility and perhaps the major maintenance while the friends raise funds, provide minor maintenance, and operate the facility. For example, Stone Mountain Park near Atlanta, Georgia, which is a self-supporting park created by the state, and developed and operated by a committee appointed by the state. See http://www.stonemountainpark.org/ for more details.

## Docents

Here, volunteers take a course conducted by the agency to ready them for working with park visitors in a teaching or guiding capacity. The creation of a docent program should be considered for certain types of areas and for certain types of activities, particularly ongoing indoor programs. For example, in certain museums, there are excellent programs where people learn to become tour guides for the museum. An excellent example is the East Bay Regional Park District in Oakland, California. The following is an excerpt from their website: http://www.ebparks.org/getinvolved/ volunteer/docent

**Something truly special happens when you share yourself with others …**

For over 30 years, the East Bay Regional Park District has provided opportunities for members of the public to do just that—share their love of nature or their passion for history by becoming docents.

Remember the first time you positively identified a red-tailed hawk? Or how excited you were when you first saw a butterfly chrysalis? These are life-changing moments for many of us. If you become a docent, you could be the one to share these moments with other park visitors!

If you have a passion for learning and sharing, a love for nature or history, and would like to share your passion with like-minded people who share your enthusiasm for encouraging stewardship in the parks, then you will find a visitor center that can help you become an East Bay Regional Park District docent. New docent training programs will be offered this winter at most of the visitor centers, so call a Visitor Center today and find out how you can get involved.

## Evaluation

Can volunteers be evaluated? Should they be evaluated? Yes, and in the same way that paid employees are, impartially and on an ongoing basis. If workers, volunteer or paid, are informed of desirable and undesirable qualities and performances at set intervals over the duration of the job, they have the chance to eliminate weak points and strengthen good ones. If volunteers undergo a firm, fair evaluation, they feel useful and know they are being taken seriously. If a volunteer fails to improve, thus becoming a detriment of the program, then that person can and should be dismissed as any paid employee would be. It is important to note that volunteers are sometimes working with an agency to gain experience for future paid employment. Therefore, these volunteers need feedback in order to improve their performances.

A report at the time the volunteer leaves the agency is done much in the same way as the evaluation, but with a different goal. Its goal is to provide a record of the volunteer's job experience that can be used as a reference for rehire or for the benefit of future employers.

Evaluations of the supervisor and the staff by the volunteers is in use in some agencies. The intent of such an evaluation is to gain an understanding of the needs and wants of volunteers, to make sure their suggestions are under consideration, and to obtain an outsider's view of operations to which the volunteer has been exposed.

## Recognition

Evaluation will bring light to certain individuals who have done outstanding work and will offer the agency or manager an opportunity to give such persons recognitions and thanks. Recognition can take many forms. Special volunteer banquets can be held annually or more frequently. Volunteers can be provided with certificates of appreciation signed by an important person, such as the head of that level of government or a representative from the legislative branch. British Columbia Provincial Parks provides deserving volunteers with a certificate of appreciation along with volunteer recognition pins. The local newspaper and other news media might do special articles on volunteers. Volunteer workers can also be recognized for their contributions at meetings of the legislative body of the appropriate level of government.

In summary, managing volunteers and support groups takes staff and agency time and supervision. The California State Parks has developed a *Volunteer In Park Program Guidelines*. This guide is designed to recruit, manage and supervise volunteers, and gives advice on how to evaluate and recognize the volunteers. See http://www.parks.ca.gov/pages/735/files/vipp%20 guidelines%202003.pdf for more information. Figure 8.3 demonstrates the detailed application process for volunteers.

## SPECIAL INTEREST GROUPS

Increasingly, citizen involvement through activist groups is affecting land-management decisions. These groups are questioning and shaping policy at the federal, state, provincial, and local levels. Agencies must find ways both to give these activists access to the hard information

## Figure 8.3. Volunteer Application

# PARK VOLUNTEER APPLICATION

Vermont Agency of Natural Resources
Department of Forests, Parks & Recreation
Vermont State Parks

**Note: Please fill out One application Per Person. Thank You!**

| | | |
|---|---|---|
| **Last Name** | **First** | **Middle** |

| **Primary Contact Information** | | **Alternate Address/Contact Information** | |
|---|---|---|---|
| Street | | Street | |
| City | | City | |
| ST | ZIP | ST | ZIP |
| Dates at Address | | Dates at Address | |
| Phone | | Cell/Alt. Phone | |

Email Address:_____

## AVAILABILITY & PREFERENCES

Dates Available (6 wk. min. required)_____

Type of Camping Unit_____ Length _____

Additional Considerations_____

Pets_____ Type & Number_____

*Valid proof of Rabies Vaccination Required*

Please Check any Preferred:

| Hookups | Park Environment | Park Facilities | Environment |
|---|---|---|---|
| ☐ Water | ☐ Busy Park | ☐ Camping | ☐ Lake or Pond |
| ☐ Electric | ☐ Quiet Park | ☐ Swimming/Picnicking | ☐ Lake Champlain |
| ☐ Sewer | | ☐ Boating | ☐ Stream or River |
| ☐ Dump Station | | ☐ Fishing | ☐ Open, Grassy |
| | | ☐ Hiking | ☐ Mountains, Wooded |
| | | ☐ Bicycling | ☐ Remote |

Geographic Location (SE, SW, NE, NW)_____

Park Preferences_____

Other Information/Requirements_____

Please briefly describe the goals of your volunteer service_____

_____

Have you ever volunteered for a state or national park before?_____ If yes, please describe:_____

_____

## SKILLS & INTERESTS

The following list of skills represents many tasks you may be asked to perform as a Vermont State Parks Volunteer. Please rank your familiarity with each item on a rating scale of 1-3 on the line provided (1=no experience, 2=some experience, 3=expert)

| | | | |
|---|---|---|---|
| Cash/check/credit card handling | _____ | Grounds Maintenance/Landscaping | _____ |
| Customer service | _____ | Janitorial/Building Maintenance | _____ |
| Telephone | _____ | Equipment | |
| Computer | _____ | Lawn Mower | _____ |
| Typing | _____ | Garden Tractor | _____ |
| Public Relations | _____ | Power String Trimmer | _____ |
| Visitor Programming | _____ | Golf Cart | _____ |
| Working with Youth/Teenagers | _____ | Other _____ | |

Do you hold a current Drivers License?_____State____#_____Exp_____

Other certifications_____
Are there other experiences, skills, or qualifications that you feel would benefit your Volunteer work in a Vermont

State Park?_____

_____

Is there any type of work you would not perform?_____

Please indicate all work schedules you are willing to work_____

_____

Please Attach on a separate piece of paper a current Resume or brief listing of your work and volunteer history, describing the duties of each profession or job. Also please include at least 2 references, preferably professional, with contact information (name, title, phone, address if available, how you know this person).

Have you ever been convicted, imprisoned, placed on probation, under supervision, fined for violation of any law including motor vehicle violations?_____If yes, explain in full detail on a separate attached sheet, including dates.

*Thank you* for submitting this application for consideration to Vermont State Parks' Volunteer Program. By submitting this application, I agree:
- To give consent to Vermont State Parks for an investigation of employment history
- I understand that a criminal background check may be required prior to starting work
- I understand that consideration for the volunteer position(s) applied for will be based on the information on this application and attachments
- If accepted by Vermont State Parks, I will comply with all rules, regulations, and policies set forth

I certify that statements made on this application and attachments are true and complete and that nothing has been withheld that would affect this application. I understand that any false statement on this application may be considered cause for dismissal, if accepted.

_____

| *Print Name* | *Signature* | *Date* |
|---|---|---|

| Please Return Application to: | Volunteer Coordinator<br>Vermont Dept. of Forests, Parks & Recreation<br>100 Mineral Street, Suite 304<br>Springfield, VT 05156 |
|---|---|

P-55W, 11/06

they require and to incorporate these demands into the decision-making and planning process. If agencies do not keep communications open and practice good relations, they run the risk of having their policies and practices criticized and perhaps distorted in the media, or debated piecemeal at hostile public meetings. In addition, the need for developing and managing our parks and resources in a sustainable manner calls for extensive and meaningful citizen involvement.

As George Hartzog (1988), former director of the National Park Service stated:

> Make no mistake: Citizen involvement and the spotlight of a probing media can bring about significant improvement in government management. It does not take many citizen complaints, exposés, and editorials to turn up the heat on the Congress and administration. This combination can start a tidal wave of corrective action (Hartzog, 1988).

In North America, we have long accepted special interest groups, perhaps first under religious auspices and then in politics. Acceptance, of course, does not imply agreement. Many people feel pressure groups, lobbyists, or special interest groups, are, at best, necessary evils—unless, of course, it is *their* special interest. A special interest group in this context is usually a collection of people who are interested in a specific activity or a specific use of an area. That does not sound too bad, but sometimes they want to exclude other users, and that causes difficulties.

Often, a group will favor the agency position on one issue and oppose it on another. For example, a group interested in the preservation of a natural area might join with a group desiring land for hunting. If successful in securing the area, the two groups might move to opposite sides when the question becomes "Should hunting be allowed?"

These special interest groups may often be found among the ranks of volunteers helping individually or as a group within a park agency. ATV or horseback groups work with backcountry rangers to provide access and facilities and to create goodwill for their groups, both with the agency and with the general public. For other organizations, their main sphere of operations is in policy formulation, and they are usually well represented at public meetings and hearings, often by salaried personnel. Their services and contributions can also be utilized by appointment of individuals from such groups to advisory or citizen boards.

Advisory committees from special interest groups can be very effective. The special interest committees can also create problems when the park agency's concerns do not align with the committee's established priorities. For example, an advisory committee established to give programming direction to the departments concerning use by visitors with disabilities might generate enough enthusiasm, interest, and participation to identify needs far beyond the capabilities and regulatory limitations of the agency. Committee members can become disillusioned rapidly if such a situation is not handled properly. Sometimes an umbrella-type advisory committee functions better for an agency. This would mean an outdoor recreation advisory committee that appoints subcommittees within its own framework; in this example, one would deal with facilities and programs for those with disabilities based on both foreseeable and long-term needs. This subcommittee would seek input from various groups representing such visitors and relay it to the umbrella committee, which would oversee all these matters and keep them in control and proportion as part of its advisory function.

## PUBLIC MEETINGS AND HEARINGS

There is another type of citizen participation somewhat different from volunteering. It is that form of organizational involvement that occurs through public meetings and hearings.

It has not always been so, but today in North America, more and more citizens are attending and participating in public meetings regarding park activities and policies. These meetings are held to seek public input into the decision-making process and to serve as a means of disseminating information. In the United States, The National Environmental Policy Act requires public agencies to seek out and take into consideration all viewpoints on proposed actions involving federal funds.

The typical public meeting is somewhat relaxed in nature and often allows considerable interaction among those present. Usually this sort of gathering is not conducted under rigid rules. An increasingly popular form of public meeting, stressing small size and informality, is the workshop. Here techniques such as sitting close together at tables and facing one another at close quarters are used to promote mutual understanding.

A more structured type of public meeting is the hearing. During the hearing, the citizens have the opportunity to have their names registered and their views, along with the formal presentations, placed on record. The hearing is often prescribed by law and must be conducted under set rules. The agency legal counsel has the duty of deciding when a hearing is required.

Regardless of the level of government in which your agency operates, it is important to be familiar with the laws, rules, and policies governing such hearings. In nearly all instances, these rules will include a requirement for a placement of an official notice. This posting will undoubtedly include everything from a notice on a city hall or post office notice board to the formidable-looking *Federal Register* carrying notices of proposed federal actions. The register is available at any federal agency office.

Stimulating people to come to a public meeting is a difficult task and must be well thought out. One of the best methods is direct contact with the various interest groups discussed earlier. This is particularly true when the subject matter is not very exciting. The usual media channels should be considered, as should the posting of extra notices. For hearings, the agency will probably need to place an official paid notice in one or more newspapers of general circulation.

Conducting a meeting dealing with a highly controversial subject is a difficult task. Sometimes the agency will conduct such a meeting itself, while at other times a competent, objective outsider will be asked to handle it. As the new practitioner often learns all too quickly, the person conducting the meeting will frequently be the park manager or the ranger. Whoever conducts the meeting needs to be aware that the crowd can be unruly. Suggestions 5, 6, and 7 in the following list will help when the atmosphere becomes tense. As a last resort, postpone the meeting until tempers cool.

1.  Notify the appropriate persons, including the news media, in ample time, and state the agenda clearly.
2.  Arrive at the site in plenty of time to take care of basic communication needs. Are the microphones working? Is there water for the speaker or chairperson? Are there chairs for all? Is there directional signing on the access roads, building, hallway, and doors? Are there pencils and paper available? Is a copy of the agenda available for everyone, if appropriate? These preparations set a tone of calm and openness that reflects favorably on the sponsoring agency. Don't depend entirely on others to see to these details. Delegate them, but be there to see that these things have, in fact, been done.
3.  Keep the staff team small. Don't give the impression of intimidation by bringing a whole stable of experts. Too many representatives might also signal apprehension. Often a staff person will play the role of an expert witness, such as a backcountry ranger testifying concerning the establishment of use limits. Whatever the reason for staff involvement, a cardinal rule is "don't speak unless asked."
4.  Use registration cards or attendance lists.
5.  Receive all suggestions without comment; a debate should not be conducted at this sort of meeting.
6.  Allow no cross-examination of speakers by persons in the audience.
7.  Find light moments and capitalize on them. To laugh at ourselves is to gain perspective and release tension.
8.  Try to summarize as seems advisable; at the very least, do so at the end of the meeting or hearing.
9.  Listen to what people are saying not only in words, but also in body language. Also, try to be cognizant of what they are not saying.
10. Make no exception to the rules.
11. Accept written comments, and advise people that these will receive as much consideration as the oral comments.
12. Be sure to state that this hearing is not for voting but rather to gain input, which will assist in the decision-making process.

Generally, new or innovative programs of some magnitude are apt to find better public acceptance if they are preceded by public meetings. The meetings do several things for the program and the department. They offer an excellent way for the agency to receive suggestions and get feedback. They provide an opportunity for public education about departmental benefits of the program itself, promoting greater public understanding and, perhaps, eventual acceptance.

In the context of such meetings, it is essential that the department identify and invite all persons or groups desiring to be heard. Those who are identified as being in opposition to the program should also be invited. Quite often, because of the nature of the program, it is possible to have co-sponsorship or multiple sponsorship of meetings. This is usually desirable, because it broadens the exposure of the meetings to the general public and avoids the appearance of imposing ideas from above. The State of Oregon has a land use system that has as its Goal 1: Citizen Involvement. All land use, park issues, and community development efforts must incorporate extensive public input. The following guide has been developed for that purpose: http://www.oregon.gov/LCD/docs/publications/putting_the_people_in_planning.pdf

The Bend Metro Park District in Oregon provides another illustration of the role of community involvement in park management.

### Community Involvement

BMPRD is committed to involving our residents in the planning and development process by:

- Conducting periodic community interest and opinion surveys that help guide our long-range planning and development efforts. A community survey was last done in the spring of 2004 to inform the Comprehensive Plan project.
- Hosting project meetings to invite residents to share their desires and concerns regarding the development of smaller parks in their neighborhoods.
- Hosting community-wide meetings to gain citizen input concerning the design and development of larger park projects.
- Staying in touch with the community through presentations to neighborhood associations, service clubs, professional and business associations, schools, and various other organizations. If you would like more information concerning these presentations, please contact, Director of Planning and Development.

## PUBLIC RELATIONS

In parks and recreation work, public relations means little more than the ability of people in an organization to express themselves to those they serve to the end that all may profit through understanding.

Through skillful public relations, an agency can ensure that the public is aware of its objectives and operations and that decisions affecting the public are based on the agency's knowledge and understanding of that public. The public makes vital decisions at the ballot box. People get their information in large part from the mass media, which serves as a source for their attitudes and actions, so it behooves the agency to pay attention to its communications with the media. This function is most effectively handled through a public affairs officer.

Park agencies are constantly engaged in public relations for better or for worse. Avoidance of this sort of communication is impossible, as in every contact any agency personnel has with the public–through news releases, speeches, letters, phone calls, on the sidewalk, or on a self-guiding trail–the agency is sending a message. This is true even if not one word is spoken. As citizens deal with agency personnel, they become aware of the agency attitude, and as citizens use their parks, they take note of each park's general appearance and upkeep. These, too, are forms of communication and are thus powerful public relations tools.

There are several ways of communicating with citizens for sound public relations, including the following.

## Letters

Few things show the character and purpose of an organization better than its mail, both incoming and outgoing. The outgoing mail carries the message and the quality of its source. The incoming mail brings the proof of failure or success. It is of utmost importance that letters should be alive. Dry, formal, official letters stamped all over with pallid impersonality are poison.

When sending a letter (hard mail copies or emails and Internet information), whether initiating correspondence or responding to it, one should not only be aware of the audience, but also of the specific purpose for which the letter is being sent. Basic purposes of the communications are: (a) to ensure accuracy, (b) to make transactions binding or demonstrate structure, (c) to furnish complete records, (d) to provide the least expensive communication, (e) to make contacts, (f) to promote goodwill, (g) to talk more effectively, and (h) discuss services. In the case of park agencies, the discussion of services, rather than buying or selling goods would be of paramount importance.

## News Releases

A news release is far more complicated than a letter in that it might well be used by all three news media. However, these releases can be very effective for reaching a large audience. Remember, the audience is as varied as the total listening, viewing, and reaching audience of the area covered.

## Telephone Calls

With the exception of face-to-face meetings with park visitors, managers will probably have more personal contact with citizens by telephone than by any other single method. Here are some time-tested suggestions for using the telephone to improve public relations:

- Answer the telephone as quickly as possible and explain any wait or holding.
- Greet the caller pleasantly.
- Identify yourself.
- Find out and state whether or not the person being asked for is in or out before you ask who is calling.
- For callbacks, be sure to get the telephone number and the name correctly; if possible, record the subject matter.
- Be attentive.
- Use the citizen's name.
- Try to end the phone call on a pleasant note. Be brief. You are busy and should assume that the caller is also.

## The Employee

By far, the most important person in all public relations is the employee. All of the news releases, all of the emails and letters, and all of those excellent telephone conversations will not have one fraction the impact the agency employee will have, on or off the job. Employees are also members of the community, and as such they are ambassadors to that community. Therefore, the agency should inform its employees on policy matters and of the agency position on current debates in addition to insisting on neat appearance and politeness on the job. Employees should be periodically reminded of how important they are to the creation of a favorable image for the agency, both on and off the job.

## CONCLUSION

There is no replacement for the goodwill of the community, and the interaction with volunteers and groups, if properly handled, will help supply understanding and support for agency objectives. Volunteers have proven themselves very helpful in the past. During times of stringent budgeting, they are invaluable. Creative thinking involving both citizen and agency personnel on the subject of volunteer assistance is now more important than ever.

Park agencies and park managers must also be responsive to public opinion from beyond the volunteer ranks, and they should be legitimately active in forming that opinion. Involving citizens is the best way of both serving and pleasing them. Involving citizens also is a principle of sustainable park management. The richer the citizen involvement is for park management, the more likelihood that plans are responsive to needs and address diverse viewpoints and problem-solving strategies.

## REFERENCES

### References Cited

Bend Metro Park and Recreation District, Citizen Involvement, http://www.bendparksandrec.org/ Planning__Development/

California State Parks. (2003). Volunteer in Parks Program Guidelines, http://www.parks.ca.gov/ pages/735/files/vipp%20guidelines%202003.pdf

Department of Environment and Conservation has published an extensive Parks and Recreation Citizen Board Training Manual. See http://www.state.tn.us/environment/recreation/pdf/ cbtmanual.pdf

Friends of Hanauma Bay, http://www.friendsofhanaumabay.org/

Groves, Earl T. (1978). From a speech presented to National Recreation and Park Association. Asheville, NC.

Hartzog, George B., Jr. (1988). *Battling for the national parks.* Mount Kisco, NY: Moyer Bell Limited.

Minneapolis Parks and Recreation Public Meeting Procedures, http://minneapolisparks.org/default. asp?PageID=163

National Recreation and Park Association (2002). Independent Citizen Board Member Resource Guide. http://www.nrpa.org/uploadedFiles/Connect_and_Share/The_NRPA_ Network_%28Socnet_Function%29/Independent%20Citizen%20Board%20Member%20 Resource%20Guide.pdf

Oregon's Citizen Involvement Advisory Committee. (2008). Putting the People In Planning: A Primer on Public Participation in Planning. http://www.oregon.gov/LCD/docs/publications/ putting_the_people_in_planning.pdf

Stone Mountain Memorial Association, http://www.stonemountainpark.org/

U.S. National Park Service, http://www.parks.ca.gov/pages/735/files/vipp%20guidelines%20 2003.pdf

*Chapter Nine*

# Planning, Acquisition, and Development of Parks

Park managers have to deal with the consequences of planning in general and in more specific ways. This brief overview of planning, acquisition, and development, and the implementation process involved, will introduce the student or manager to an important phase of park agency operations. Insight into the responsibilities and difficulties may illuminate some park management problems.

Planning is a widely used process that cannot be defined narrowly. Planning not only plays into land acquisition and classification, but it is also inherent in areas covered in this book such as facilities, policy, fiscal management, personnel management, and citizen involvement. As a framework for addressing problems, planning is a major factor in maintenance and safety, environmental concerns, opportunities for vandalism, and visitor conflicts.

## PLANNING

There are many definitions of planning. It has been defined as "an activity concerned with the systematic collection, analysis, organization, and processing of technical information to facilitate decision making. Planning is the process of preparing in advance and in a systematic fashion, recommendations for policies and courses of action to achieve accepted objectives. It is important to note that the process of planning helps solve park and recreation problems, not the plan itself. The process allows stakeholders to discuss issues and come to some sense of agreement or understanding. The plan itself is a static document; the process is dynamic.

In order to save critical park open-space systems, it is imperative that park officials embark on a well-structured and process-oriented park planning effort to serve the needs of future generations. The U.S. National Park Service notes that NPS managers constantly make difficult decisions concerning:

- ways to preserve significant natural and cultural resources for public enjoyment,
- competing demands for limited resources,
- priorities for using available funds and staff, and
- differing local and nationwide interests and views of what is most important.

The NPS notes that planning provides methods and tools for resolving these issues in ways that minimize conflicts and promote mutually beneficial solutions that articulate how public enjoyment of the parks can be part of a strategy for ensuring that resources are protected unimpaired for future generations (http://planning.nps.gov/GMPSourcebook/WhyNPS.htm).

In this section, planning will touch on the process of determination of the need, the involvement of the manager, and the steps leading up to a plan document and site procedures. Development will encompass budget preparation, staffing, the review and approval process, and construction. A later chapter will deal with construction in more detail and will also address master planning.

In discussing planning and development, especially from the manager's viewpoint, all park areas could be said to fall into one of the following three categories:

1.  The park is well established. It is able to properly handle its visitor load, change activities, and use patterns with minimum stress on the resource and with only minor difficulties for the users and park staff.
2.  The park is well established but needs modification. Perhaps its facilities need updating (including changes to meet energy conservation, sanitation, or accessibility requirements), or perhaps it is a question of limiting the danger to the users or resources. Time and changing patterns eventually put most parks into this category.
3.  The area is a new one, still in the planning stage, with site design plans yet to be drawn up and approved.

In the last two situations, the contributions of a manager who is dealing with, or has at some time dealt with, a similar situation or site could be most useful. In agencies that have effective checks and balances and that follow proper procedures, a manager or another representative from the field staff is required to sign off on site plans at a certain point.

The National Park Service (http://planning.nps.gov/GMPSourcebook/WhyNPS.htm) provides a glimpse into the issues being faced by managers.

### Planning — Deciding about Tradeoffs, Priorities, Solutions

Are there parts of the battlefield at Gettysburg where rehabilitation would be preferable to preservation? To what extent should the natural values of the landscape be enhanced? What are the highest priority actions for restoring natural ecosystem functioning in Everglades National Park? How can traffic congestion be reduced at Zion National Park? Should visitors be encouraged or required to use a public transportation system? How can transportation alternatives enhance visitor experience opportunities? What role should the National Park Service play in partnership with the local community to preserve and interpret the history of New Bedford Whaling? What are the desired resource conditions and associated opportunities for visitor experiences at Saguaro National Park, where a 50% increase in use over the past 10 years is causing resource damage and significant conflicts among visitors seeking different types of experiences?

The questions are complex and not easily answered. It should be obvious that these issues can only be best answered through an informed and systematic planning process.

## PLANNERS

Due to the complexity of park and recreation planning and the several skills necessary to comprehend the planning of land use, planners come from many disciplines. They could be landscape architects, civil engineers, urban planners, geographers, or graduates of one of several planning programs now offered in Canada and the United States that address park management. Some planning tasks are handled by planners who are staff employees, while others are consultants. However, the best plans are produced with a team approach. Here the planner has access to expertise from foresters, soil specialists, historians, geographers, and archaeologists, i.e., persons from disciplines pertinent to the site in question, including the park manager and maintenance personnel.

Planners are not decision makers; the agency director, park board, or park commission has that responsibility. However, in their deliberations, these decision makers must rely on the planners' presentation of the situation, on those alternatives the planners have chosen to prepare, and on the planners' expertise. It is imperative, therefore, that planners provide data that is accurate and fairly analyzed. It is also imperative that these data were developed from extensive and exhaustive citizen participation.

## Planners Determination of Need

There are different levels within land-use planning, and these are primarily identified by the area addressed (e.g., nationwide, regional, state, provincial, agency, or area). Also, development or site-design planning should be considered on a separate level.

Planners at these various levels must anticipate the needs of the public from a process that engages the public, determine potentially suitable areas and their optimum capacities, and plan park facilities and services to meet public needs. They frequently must estimate costs for development and operations. This must be a continuing function that considers the total recreation requirements of their level of planning responsibility.

Information on inventory, classification, and use limits for current and projected parks must be gathered. Objectives are set in light of this information, and a program must be outlined for systematic accomplishment of the objectives. Attendance statistics and use data must be studied, keeping in mind that statistics are molded by the facilities available. The varying tastes of users for convenience, primitive situations, or some intermediate state of comfort must be assessed and taken into account. Different experiences are provided by various public land-managing agencies and by the recreational facilities offered by the public sector, and all these opportunities must be factored into determination of need.

Planners do have established mechanisms to help in determining need. In the United States, each state must have on file a Statewide Comprehensive Outdoor Recreation and Open Space Plan (SCORP), which provides the basic data for recreational acquisition and development by state and local agencies. The section of this chapter entitled "Land Acquisition" deals with the various methods by which an agency can acquire such lands.

Canada also has collected appropriate data for broadly based recreational planning, which began with the Canadian Outdoor Recreation Demand Study. Provinces have conducted similar studies and have produced provincial models of the Canada Land Inventory. Data from these studies helped establish system processes that continue to identify and provide a diversity of recreation experiences for Canadian citizens.

In addition to national plans, agencies may have their own outdoor recreation plans. Most parks have a master plan giving long-range direction for all facets of that park's development and management.

## Planning Concerns of the Manager

The following headings represent useful methods of sorting out the various ways planning affects managers. Perhaps these categories will also offer new insight into the planning process at the individual park level.

**Location.** The park manager shares with the planner a concern for the overall layout of the park. This includes an interest in circulation patterns, modes of transportation, and density levels of development. The planner, in consultation with the public, needs to locate facilities so the park staff can observe camping sites, picnic areas, and other high-use areas. The same attention needs to be given to visitor safety. Typical planning concerns here might be over the best locations for the water source, sanitary facilities, garbage-collection points that avoid attracting animals into sleeping areas, lighting fixtures where needed for safety as well as for surveillance to deter vandalism, and emergency exits from structures as well as from forested areas.

**Preservation.** Most managers express a sincere interest in the preservation of the resources of their areas, and they can speak with authority about the need to employ protective strategies in planning. For example, exposed tree roots, eroding hillsides, chewed-up shrubs, muddy pathways, and other signs of human and vehicular impact are typical management problems. These might be prevented or lessened by planning techniques based on a thorough knowledge of soil and vegetation types and the observation of visitor-use patterns. Planners' judgments and public comment about park location and correct layout of facilities are critical considerations in the matter of preservation.

**Operations.** The manager is responsible for the staffing of the park and its budget requirements. Therefore, this person will be very interested in personnel and operational costs of the facilities and use areas being designed by the planners. The distinction between development funds, needed on a one-time basis, and operation funds, needed annually, is important. After the planners and citizens have finished with plans, the manager must be able to supervise the results. Thus, the operating costs and staffing must be reasonable.

**Maintenance.** Considerations that suggest the need for manager-planner dialogue in operational matters hold equally true for maintenance. What is built must be maintained, and maintenance requires personnel and money. Careful consideration must be given to this consequence in the planning process so that maintenance costs will be kept within acceptable limits. Managers asked to review site design plans must seek advice from maintenance personnel if they themselves are not familiar with materials. Then managers must design possibilities that would be appropriate and economical at the sites in question.

## Production of General Plans

The standard planning phases are described here. These are by no means the only processes available to the planner and manager, but these steps do address key aspects of planning.

**Identifying goals and objectives.** As guides to specific action, goals state a desired end. Objectives must state an overall purpose, consider the implications of action to achieve that purpose, and identify a specific target and course of action to reach that target. These objectives should be measurable.

**Data collection.** This step is a complex set of requirements in terms of user data, surveys, observations, public input, analysis of needs, constraints, and opportunities. Pertinent data must be compiled on use and users, present and potential, and on the characteristics of the resource base.

**Analysis of data.** Examination of all data and their prospective interrelationships occur during this phase. This should be a consultative process with experts in such disciplines as ecology, economics, soils, transportation planning, and forestry, to name only a few. In addition, the analysis of data should include citizen interpretation of the findings. Planners compile data, and then work with citizens and special interest groups to interpret the findings. A reasonable understanding of the resource, the user, and the possible management strategies and patterns can be gained from these data for the development of the management plan.

**Alternatives and planning choices.** Several different courses of action, any of which will fulfill the stated objectives, should be delineated in the planning document. The planner's creativity, specialized knowledge, and citizen perspectives should find expression here, always guided by the objectives and channeled by economic restraints.

The different possibilities must be sufficiently developed in this synthesis so the decision makers can determine the advantages and disadvantages of each course of action and judge how well each might fulfill the objectives. Their choice of a plan, of a modification of a plan, or of a combination of plans is the final step in the synthesis phase.

**Adoption of a plan.** The selected plan must be elaborated upon. This includes the environmental impact statement and sometimes a social impact statement required by the jurisdiction in which the proposed park will lie. On occasion, a cost-benefit analysis will accompany the plan. The plan document should provide an accurate base map indicating existing conditions on the land as well as all proposed changes. These include boundaries, access and other roads, utilities, previous use, existing and proposed developments, vegetative cover, open space, unusual features, and soil types.

Facilities should be located precisely enough so that no substantial facility relocations should be necessary for the preparation of the more detailed site plans. There should be a written narrative report explaining what is in the plan and the justification for these elements. At certain stages of the procedure, there must be an opportunity for both public and agency feedback.

**Implementation.** Consideration of developmental phases, to include acquisition, capital investment projects, and environmental impacts are central to this task.

**Evaluation and revision.** This process should be operating during all phases of planning, but must be formally instituted at this point. Do the plan's results meet the stated objectives? Periodic review of monitoring results and attention to feedback from independent sources should enable evaluation and guide revision. Unfortunately, this step is rarely completed due to a lack of legal mandates, budget, or staffing issues.

More detailed site plans necessary to generate the development process are also required. Site planning, dealing with land not previously developed for recreation purposes, relies on the area or general development plan as the source of specifications for the plans. In some instances, of course, the park already exists and will be adding a new facility or having an existing facility modified, so this situation is then the genesis of the site plan.

Site planning locates structures and activities on the ground. Integration of the proposed facility into the web of environmental relationships requires sensitivity. This in turn demands the expenditure of time by several disciplines gathered into a team headed by the planner, usually and landscape architect in this case. The first result of their observations and decisions will be site plans, whether for a building or for another facility. Decision makers calling for agency or public review of the proposals and specifications, will eventually adopt and fund the development.

Table 9.1 presents a table of contents for a park and open-space system. As one can see, there are elements of the plan that address need, historical use and future trends and issues, as well as capital improvements.

## Land Acquisition

In order for people to participate in outdoor recreation, land and water areas must be set aside for this purpose. Parks agencies are racing to acquire enough lands and contiguous parcels for greenways due to development pressures. The factor of time cannot be ignored here. In areas near large population centers, other uses may well preempt recreational use if a well-planned program of acquisition is not employed to secure suitable land.

There are four important factors adding to the recreational space problem:

1. More and more international visitors are using park lands.
2. Our own citizens are using these same park lands more and more frequently.
3. There is far less open space owned by private citizens or companies available for our citizens and foreign visitors to use. This results in greater use of public parks and recreation areas.
4. Technology (web-based information) has made access to these lands easier and has vastly increased the demand for special areas to handle particular needs.

Despite strong statements from national leaders citing the need for more recreational areas, acquiring needed parklands has become increasingly difficult, particularly in urban areas where needs are greater, but where conflicting demands are formidable due to development pressures.

There are some positive aspects to the land-acquisition situation, however. Land is often zoned for recreation because experience has proven this to be the best use. For example, flood plains are an example of areas where other uses are not practical because of periodic flooding. Recreational uses on such lands can adjust to the inconvenience without danger to human life or serious economic loss.

Another bonus has resulted from the general decline in railroading, resulting in the disuse and abandonment of tracks in the United States. Citizens have recognized the recreation potential in this unexpected resource and have worked to acquire abandoned railroad rights-of-way. These long, narrow, often scenic strips of land have proven to be excellent sites for public hiking, cross-country skiing, and biking trails.

In terms of railroad rights-of-way, the Rails-to-Trails Conservancy has lead the way in the United States. Headquartered in Washington, D.C., with regional offices in California, Ohio, and Pennsylvania, and a state office in Florida, Rails-to-Trails Conservancy connects, builds, protects and promotes rail-trails and their far-reaching benefits.

- We advocate and influence policy at the national and state levels, making trail building possible.
- We provide information, technical assistance and training for local trail builders. We are the leader in protecting and increasing the federal Transportation Enhancements program—the largest source of funding nationally for trail development.

## Table 9.1. City of Bellevue Parks and Open Space System Plan 2003

**Table of Contents**

- We steadfastly defend the federal railbanking statute in the U. S. Congress and the courts as an essential tool to preserve unused rail corridors.
- We encourage trail use and development by providing trail access, information, maps and resources free to the public through our online trail-finder, www.TrailLink.com. (http://www.railstotrails.org/ourWork/index.html)

Another influential non-profit association, American Trails, has also advocated for trails and greenways. Their mission states "*American Trails is pursuing a national infrastructure of trails and greenways that serve a full range of activities. Through education, partnerships, and timely information resources, we promote the creation, conservation, and broad enjoyment of quality trails and greenways that offer places of solace, health, fitness, recreation and transportation for all Americans.*"

**American Trails envisions:**

- **Trails and greenways that are a part of everyday life**—a quality system accessible to all people including a broad range of abilities, economic, and cultural backgrounds within 15 minutes of every American home or workplace.
- **A diverse trail and greenway system**—serving urban areas as well as wild and rural landscapes.
- An Interconnected National System of Trails and Greenways—used regularly by Americans and foreign visitors.
- **Myriad trails and greenways uses**—with a full range of activities both nonmotorized and motorized.
- **Quality trail and greenway experiences**—that enable the appreciation of natural beauty, cultural and historic connections, and bring people back in touch with special places in the outdoors.
- **Trails and greenways that promote the conservation of resources**—with a system that optimizes wildlife preservation and land and water stewardship.
- **Trails and greenways that promote economic development**—enhancing property values, business opportunities, tourism and marketability of communities.
- **A trail and greenway system that is durable**—affordable to maintain with a sustainable commitment of resources. (http://www.americantrails.org/about.html)

## Methods of Gaining Ownership—Example Processes

There are several ways recreation or park agencies can acquire land. These include purchase, donation, stipulated deed, condemnation, easements, dedications, and transfer. There are also means of securing the use of an area without purchase. An agency must be willing to negotiate with the landowner. At the same time, the rules governing the availability of funds also govern the flexibility an agency has in such negotiations in terms of appraisals, relocation costs, use privileges, and time sequences. The following describes some typical federal and city processes for acquiring park lands.

**Identification processes for land protection by federal land management agency.** Federal guidance and agency-specific guidance mandate a process for identity of specific lands for protection in slightly different ways; however, the basic concept is similar. Common denominators to agency processes include: 1) identification of lands for protection based on detailed information from a variety of sources, 2) launching of processes at the local level, and 3) significant public participation and input. The Department of Interior-United States Department of Agriculture (2005) provided in a report to congress the following processes that each agency follows for land acquisition (DOI-USDA, 2005).

***Bureau of Land Management.*** The BLM identifies lands for acquisition or other forms of protection through collaborative land use planning processes. These collaborative planning efforts include Resource Management Land Use Plans or Special Area Management Activity Plans. The BLM land use plans generally identify acquisition needs by establishing criteria to use in evaluating land acquisition opportunities. These criteria are developed through public input as part of the planning process and supplement criteria that may be used by the BLM for ranking LWCF project priorities. The criteria encompass opportunities that may arise from land exchange, purchase, or donation proposals. Land use plans may also establish criteria for the acquisition of interests in land, such as acquiring access easements and water rights needed for implementing the plan's objectives and decisions.

*Fish and Wildlife Service.* Habitat and population objectives for threatened and endangered species, migratory birds, and a variety of other legislated trust responsibilities determine the footprint of a National Wildlife Refuge when it is developed. Lands identified for protection are a compilation of "layers" of habitat and population goals that were identified in specific legislation, national partnership plans, comprehensive conservation plans, and habitat management plans. A Refuge should be considered a project that contains a natural system providing nationally significant fish and wildlife habitat for plants and animals, invertebrates and vertebrates. Each of these systems or projects included in a Land Protection Plan contributes toward numerous habitat and population goals and objectives for a project on the same land base.

*National Park Service.* Congress directs the NPS to prepare a suitability and feasibility study for the inclusion of lands in the National Park System, which can be followed by a Congressional decision. Or in some cases, units can be established by presidential proclamation. After Congress has authorized a park, the NPS may prepare a Land Protection Plan concurrently with the General Management Plan to determine the degree of protection for the land located inside the Congressionally drawn boundary. When a land protection plan is prepared as a separate document, it becomes an action element of the general management plan when approved.

*United States Forest Service.* The primary driver for identifying which private lands need protection is the Landownership Adjustment Strategy (LAS) plan, developed in association with each National Forest or Grassland's Land Management Plan. The LAS plan provides the framework for assessing and prioritizing realty opportunities. Most LAS plans acknowledge that land purchases will be made only with willing sellers, therefore there will always be an expectation that accomplishment is often limited by opportunity. This does not assume that the FS is not proactive in seeking desired land acquisitions either through land purchase or land exchange. The FS is moving towards State-wide and regional versions of the LAS plans in the future that incorporate the key goals and objectives by State. These State-wide goals and objectives will then be blended into the individual LAS plans.

**State of Florida Acquisition Process.** Once it has been determined that the State of Florida will be able to work with a landowner toward acquiring a parcel, DEP's Division of State Lands' Bureau of Land Acquisition becomes involved. The Bureau of Land Acquisition is divided into two sections: 1) Negotiation Section; and 2) Closing Section. In the Negotiation Section, land acquisition agents negotiate full fee acquisitions, conservation easements, and other less-than-fee transactions. This section also assists with the acquisition of projects for DEP's Office of Coastal and Aquatic Managed Areas, Division of Recreation and Parks and Office of Greenways & Trails, as well as the Florida Fish and Wildlife Conservation Commission, Florida Division of Forestry and other non-conservation entities such as state universities and the Florida Department of Corrections. Basically, the land acquisition process consists of

- **Due diligence:** Through the use of private contractors, title work, an environmental site assessment and a survey are obtained to aid in the identification of any issues which may impact the title, boundary, value, manageability and long-term ownership of the property.
- **Issue resolution:** Staff reviews the due diligence products to identify and evaluate any issues. The seller must resolve those issues prior to closing. Staff may assist in the resolution of issues.
- **Closing:** This phase of the closing process consists of execution of all legal documents between the parties and the delivery of monies necessary to complete the transaction on the terms and conditions of the contract. Title is transferred to the Board of Trustees of the Internal Improvement Trust Fund of the State of Florida (Governor and Cabinet). (Source: Florida Department of Environmental Protection, http://www.dep.state.fl.us/lands/acqprocess.htm)

***A city example of gaining ownership.*** The City of Seattle has developed the following acquisition strategies for parklands. Notice the emphasis on form, design, greenways, and in-fill strategies.

1. The spirit and guiding principles of the original 1903 Olmsted Plan will be expanded through open space acquisitions, park development, and creation of new or improved boulevards and trails to serve as park connectors.

2. Acquisition and voluntary preservation of real property to expand Seattle's inventory of open spaces and parklands will be actively pursued.

3. With the diminishing availability of natural open space, urban property will be reclaimed and converted to park purposes for small neighborhood parks and major regional parks.

4. Private properties within greenspaces (greenbelts and natural areas) and other primarily natural areas such as stream corridors, and wetlands will be acquired to preserve such areas.

5. Preservation and acquisition of other open space will be planned on a geographic basis. The quantity of open space will be based upon the following considerations:
   (a) Distribution guidelines presented later in this document.
   (b) Two categories of open space, one for breathing room and one for neighborhood park (usable) space are to be considered. For breathing room space, total dedicated open space acreage on a citywide basis regardless of use, topography or access restrictions, but not including tideland or shoreland (submerged) park acreage shall be considered, as well as availability of public open space owned by others. For neighborhood park (usable) space, separate guidelines for primarily single-family areas and for higher density urban village areas shall be considered.
   (c) The open space functions of boulevard trails and green streets in meeting open space needs shall be recognized.
   (d) Unique characteristics of properties, user patterns (local, citywide and regional) and densities in the analysis of open space needs shall be considered.
   (e) Available opportunities, long-term budget impacts, and priorities as established in the city's comprehensive plan shall be considered in each potential acquisition.

6. In general, priority for the expansion of the open space network shall be given to areas of the city subject to population growth, including urban villages targeted for the largest share of residential growth and those areas not adequately served at present according to the population-based goals for open space.

7. The Urban Wildlife Habitat Plan shall be maintained and updated on a regular cycle. Grant monies shall be sought to realize important wildlife habitat acquisition and enhancement projects.

8. Public shoreline access will be regarded with the same degree of importance as open space and will be planned to ensure a reasonable amount of public access along each shoreline. A distribution guideline is presented later in this document.

9. The following methods may be used to preserve open space:
   (a) acquisition for park purposes through public funds and grants, donations, and community self-help;
   (b) acquisition of life estates, where appropriate, to protect current owners;
   (c) acquisition of voluntary conservation easements or similar mechanisms for preserving the open space qualities;
   (d) dedication or leasing from other public agencies, including the Seattle School District; and
   (e) If no other options are available, condemnation or removal of existing development will be pursued to preserve or re-create open space in highly developed areas lacking open space, although elimination of existing housing stock is generally to be avoided.

10. No-cost or low-cost methods to protect open space shall be pursued to preserve critical publicly owned open space that is not owned by the Department, recognizing the requirements of Washington state law in the acquisition of surplus utility property.

11. Work with the Department of Planning and Development (DPD) to ensure that land use code requirements are adequate to meet needs for on-site open space, provision of open space linkages, and protection of parklands and water features.

12. Encourage the private sector to join in providing adequate open space for residential developments and public open space for commercial developments. (http://www.seattle.gov/parks/Publications/Development/Plan2006.pdf)

## Outright Purchase of Land

Areas are acquired in fee title when all rights in the area are obtained. If the area is purchased in less than fee title, this implies some restrictions on rights. Frequently, for example, mineral rights are at issue. Bonds are one of the means by which park agencies can acquire land. Consider the East Bay Regional Park District's newest measure, Measure WW.

Of the $500 million raised by Measure WW, $375 million (75%) will fund regional park acquisitions and capital projects, with $26.2 million (7%) held in reserve for unanticipated future needs and opportunities.

In addition, $125 million (25%) of proceeds will go to cities, special park and recreation districts, and county service areas for their park and recreation services. Livermore voters are not part of this extension tax as Murray Township was not within the East Bay Regional Park District's jurisdiction in the initial bond measure. The Park District continues to serve this community through new acquisitions of parklands. (http://www.ebparks.org/planning)

## Federal Funding Sources for Purchase of Lands

The Final Department of Interior-USDA Land Acquisition Plan - 2005 (DOI-USDA, 2005). presents a variety of authorities and funding sources available to support the land acquisition goals and objectives of the U.S. Federal agencies. The following list of funding sources provides an introduction to each source, and briefly describes how priorities are set and decisions are made.

*The Land and Water Conservation Fund (LWCF, P.L. 88-578).* This fund was established for acquisition of lands or for other uses (determined by Congress) to ensure public access to outdoor recreational resources and to provide protection of critical resources. The NPS, FWS, FS, and BLM all utilize LWCF to support their agency goals and Departmental objectives. Each agency has created its own ranking system based on its mission to determine which projects should receive the highest priority for acquisition. These ranking systems are the primary tools by which agencies establish their annual land acquisition budget request.

*The Southern Nevada Public Land Management Act (SNPLMA) of 1998 (P.L. 105-263) and the Federal Land Transaction Facilitation Act (FLTFA) of 2000 (P.L. 106-248).* With the planning and enactment of these laws, the BLM has new authorities to generate funds from public land sales that may benefit land acquisitions by the BLM, FWS, NPS, and the FS. The revenues from public land sales in the Las Vegas area, under SNPLMA, are made available for land acquisitions, and for other local recreation and conservation benefits, to the agencies in Nevada without the need for separate appropriations from Congress. Between November, 1999 (first sale), and June, 2004 (most recent sale), 8,142 acres were sold, for a total of $1,383,744,611. FLTFA provides authority to the BLM to generate funds from public land sales that would be available for land acquisitions by the agencies without the need for further appropriations from Congress.

*The Migratory Bird Conservation Fund (MBCF).* This is another major funding source available to the FWS and is funded principally by the sale of "Duck Stamps" and import duties on arms and ammunition. Funds available from the Migratory Bird Conservation Fund for acquisition within existing refuge boundaries are generally in the range of $40 million to $50 million per year, and the goals and objectives for the land acquisition effort are driven by the wetlands and migratory bird habitat needs of the units in the National Wildlife Refuge System.

*The North American Wetland Conservation Act (NAWCA) of 1989 (P.L. 101-233).* NAWCA also provides some funding to the FWS for land acquisitions within approved boundaries to support the protection of wetlands habitat. This major source of federal funding is to encourage partnership efforts to protect, enhance, restore, and manage wetlands and other habitats for migratory birds and other fish and wildlife to carry out the objectives of the North American Waterfowl Management Plan. Funds available from NAWCA usually range between $40 million to $50 million per year; however, very few of these funds are used for refuge land acquisition, as most of the funding is allocated to partners in Canada, the United States, and Mexico.

## Other Common Tools for Land Acquisition—Fee and Less Than Fee Examples

**Condemnation.** The bad word! No one likes to wear the black hat and, like the villain closing in, foreclose or condemn. However, sometimes an agency must institute condemnation proceedings. Assuming for the moment that the agency head has such authority, he or she should use condemnation only when necessary. Some reasons why an agency might need the land for the public good and thus decide to institute such proceedings.

*Identified resources.* The first reason for condemnation is based on the agency's state or provincial plan, as discussed earlier in this chapter. An identified resource refers to land that has already been selected as suitable and necessary to the agency plan.

*Inholdings.* For various reasons, an agency may find itself with a private parcel inside the boundaries of one of its holdings. The owner might choose to develop a facility not in keeping with the park atmosphere or might prevent the park agency from accomplishing a logical development. To eliminate such problems, attempts to acquire the in holding should be made, and condemnation might be necessary.

*Natural boundaries.* Rivers, mountains, or lakes form natural boundaries for many land areas. Unfortunately, all too frequently an existing park's boundaries are artificially set; that is, they do not follow the natural boundaries. For instance, they may stop 30 feet (9 meters) from a wide river. Such intervening parcels of land cause many administrative problems, and agencies will sometimes condemn them to acquire them.

*Threats of incompatible use.* There will be a time when the possibility or actuality of incompatible use dictates acquisition, such as the threat of a motorcar raceway next to a natural area.

The actual condemnation process involves one or both of two actions. The first is establishing the right of eminent domain, which means, in essence, seeking a court ruling that states that the government entity needs the area for the welfare of the public. Need, as seen by the agency, has just been discussed under the types of condemnation. However, this does not mean that the court will see the situation in the same light. The agency will have to convince the court of this need. Should the court not rule in favor of the agency, the right of eminent domain has been established. The next phase is that of establishing the price.

Sometimes the landowner wants to sell the property but for considerably more money than the agency believes the parcel is worth. When such is the case, the condemner waives the right of forcing the government entity to prove eminent domain and enters into what is commonly called friendly condemnation. Condemnation is not desirable. It costs the agency time and money, and it sometimes causes resentment in a community. It frequently places hardships on those whose property is being condemned. For these and other reasons, it is highly desirable to identify the nature of the problem and attempt to resolve it in other ways.

Managers can perform a particularly useful service here in recognizing those areas that would affect the park if incompatible uses were established. They should strive to keep informed on projected sales or land use changes in the area, and should alert supervisors about them.

**Conservation bank.** A conservation bank is used to protect privately or publicly owned lands that contain endangered, threatened, or at-risk species. With a conservation bank, credits are established for the specific habitat or species that occurs on a site. In exchange for permanently protecting the banked lands, the bank sells habitat credits to developers and others who need to compensate for the environmental impacts of a project. The bank uses the funds to protect the environmental resources it holds. Conservation banks are typically used when it makes more sense for a developer to purchase conservation credits than to protect part of the area being developed (for example, when on-site conservation would result in small, isolated sites). A conservation bank, must be approved by a state or federal wildlife agency (such as the U.S. Fish and Wildlife Service). Not all states endorse conservation banks. A conservation bank is funded through an endowment created by participating landowners who deposit funds to maintain and manage the protected lands, which generates interest for management of the conservation bank. The U.S. Fish and Wildlife Service [www.fws.gov/endangered/landowner] is the primary source of information about conservation banks.

**Cooperative agreements.** Legal instruments defining administrative arrangements between two or more parties (usually federal agencies). They can result in the exchange of services or benefits such as access to managing natural or cultural resources, sharing responsibility for maintenance of structures and facilities, providing public access, management of wildlife or other resources, and providing law enforcement.

**Donations.** The giving of land, interest in land, or money for the purchase of land to the federal government by a state, individual, corporation, trust, or foundation.

**Easement acquisitions (interests in land).** Acquisition of a right or privilege to use the land of another for a specific purpose or the acquisition of an owners' right to use certain aspects of his/her property.

*Access easements.* Also called rights-of-way; this is the right a person or persons has/have to travel over a designated portion of another person's land.

*Conservation easements.* Acquired for conservation purposes and used to protect resource values on non-federal lands by restricting the type and amount of development or activities on land that is subject to the easement. Public access and use is seldom provided by the acquisition of a conservation easement. The term "conservation easement" is often used generically to describe a scenic easement, open space easement, historic preservation easement, agricultural preservation easement, etc. Restrictions on non-federal lands usually specify the activities in which the owner may not engage, such as felling trees, building structures, subdividing, excavating or draining the property.

*Prescriptive easements.* These are gained when an agency claims and is awarded the use of a parcel of land on the basis of a number of years of similar use by the public. For example, walking rights over a beach or across open space might be secured by such an easement.

*Scenic easements.* These are similar to development rights, but they differ in that the owner is paid the amount necessary to preclude any changes that would detract from the scenic aspect. Such an easement might involve a setback on a bluff overlooking a whitewater river, private land adjacent to a park, or an inholding next to a roadway. An examination of the U.S. Forest Service National Scenic Byways would be an example of these easements at the larger scale. There are many local and state examples as well. The National Scenic Byways Program is a voluntary, community-based program administered through the Federal Highway Administration (FHWA) to recognize, protect, and promote America's most outstanding roads. Through their state departments of transportation, communities can apply for designation as a State or National Scenic Byway for funding from the FHWA. In 1991, Congress established the program under the Intermodal Surface Transportation Efficiency Act (ISTEA) and strengthened it further with the passage of the Transportation Equity Act for the 21st Century (TEA-21) in 1998 and subsequently with the recent passage of the Safe, Accountable, Flexible, and Efficient Transportation Equity Act - A Legacy for Users (SAFETEA-LU), in 2005. (Scenic America, 2010, http://www.scenic.org/byways). One may visit the National Scenic Byways Program (http://www.byways.org/) to view the 125 designated scenic byways. The National Park Service St. Croix National Scenic Riverway is another example (http://www.nps.gov/sacn/parkmgmt/loader.cfm?csModule=security/getfile&pageid=81875

**Dedication.** Many states have laws or dedication ordinances allowing a local or county agency to require land for parks based on a formula of number of bedrooms in the housing development. Illinois and California have led the way with this acquisition method.

**Development rights**. This method assures the continuation of present use and does not involve purchase of the land. For instance, an agency might purchase development right from the owners of a golf course. That use, golf, and no other, would then prevail on that land. This is commonly done on farm lands to ensure the continuation of agricultural use.

**Donation.** Agencies often make known their need for recreation lands through public speaking engagements, interviews, and various media contacts in order to attract donations. Furthermore, agency personnel should attempt to alert attorneys and clergy to their needs, as these persons are frequently contacted by people interested in making donations of land. To be prepared for these opportunities, all agencies should have a list of needs with a wide range of probable costs.

Some provinces and states have established park foundations to seek and receive donations. These foundations can be of great assistance to an agency, as they help people realize the rewards associated with this sort of generosity. It is suggested that all land-managing agencies become well acquainted with the programs and personnel of natural land, non-profit land conservation organizations such as The Trust for Public Lands and The Nature Conservancy (see below).

**Exchanges.** An exchange of land or interests in land is a "trade" of real property between the government and an owner of non-government land. Usually the properties must be equal in value, approximately equal in value, or can be equalized with cash payments. Land exchanges are included in this list because they are the tool often used by both the BLM and the FS to acquire lands for resource benefits as well as to improve land ownership configuration for management efficiencies. These are authorized under the Federal Land Policy and Management Act of 1976 (P.L. 94-579) (coupled with the Weeks Act (P.L. 61-435) or the General Exchange Act (P.L. 67-173) for the FS) and are funded within existing agency appropriations. Land exchanges can also be used by the NPS and the FWS to acquire lands and may provide some opportunities to offset the need for LWCF appropriations from Congress for other agency land acquisition needs.

**Fee title.** Fee title purchases result in the deed to the subject being vested in the United States. In almost all instances these transactions involve the transfer of essentially all the interests in the property into the Federal estate. Often there are outstanding road and utility easements and, on occasion, other easements that do not preclude accomplishment of agency goals and objectives. An annual payment-in-lieu-of-taxes or federal revenue sharing payment (in the case of FWS) is made to counties for fee title land held by the United States.

**Grants.** The federal government provides financial assistance to states, local governments, or non-profit organizations for land acquisition, planning, development of outdoor recreation facilities, and/or for acquisition and protection of natural or cultural resources.

**Land trusts.** A land trust is a nonprofit organization that, as all or part of its mission, actively works to conserve land by undertaking or assisting in land or conservation easement acquisition or by its stewardship of such land or easements. Land trusts have been around for most of the last century. The trusts have proven to be very effective tools in conserving land. The trusts help interested landowners find ways to protect their land in the face of ever-growing development pressure. A land trust can be used to protect land that a community values; and the land can be farmland or scenic, recreational, or environmentally significant areas. See the example of TPL below.

**Leasing.** A contract by which one party conveys land (or other property) for a term of years (or life) for a specific amount of rent or compensation. Fee title is retained by the leasor. This arrangement is usually for a set period of time and for a specific purpose. The rental fee is commonly based on the value of the property and paid on an annual basis. An example would be the county leasing land from the state government for recreational use. Another example is the utilization of land belonging to the U.S. Bureau of Land Management or U.S. Forest Service for ski areas.

**Partnerships.** Relationships between two or more governmental or non-governmental parties involving the sharing of common interests, goals, expectations and philosophical beliefs. See the example below describing the role of the Trust for Public Land.

**Stipulated deed.** This is the method commonly used to give land to an agency when there are conditions as to what may or may not be done with the land. An example would be the donation of a parcel of land that must be used for recreation or it would revert to the owner. This would preclude using this parcel for sale or trade in order to consolidate holdings or lessen management problems.

**Transfer.** Transfer of jurisdiction between agencies and among local, county, state, provincial, and federal governments is a process frequently used in order to follow legislative mandates or to adequately represent all types of areas in systems planning. Hundreds of parks exist today as a result of the transfer process. As one can see in Figure 9.1, ownership of parks is dispersed across agencies. The planning, acquisition, and management of each level of park is different with varying legal mandates. In addition, a combination of some of the methods described in this section.

**Use permits.** These are issued usually at little or no fee for an indefinite period of time, but with a provision for revocation. Typical situations would be use of the space under electrical transmission lines for a trail of right-of-way or use of a bridge or pier for fishing.

**Zoning.** Zoning is based on the power of state and local governments to protect public, health, safety, and welfare by regulating the use of land. Local zoning can be used to limit the density, type, location, and character of private development. A type of zoning is the overlay zone can be used to protect particular natural, cultural, or built features in a community that are under pressure from development. Such zones can be used to carry out a variety of community objectives: to protect the character of a neighborhood, downtown, waterfront, or road corridor; to protect a scenic view, an aquifer recharge area, natural slopes, wetlands, and watersheds. (DOI-USDA, 2005. Final Department of Interior-USDA Land Acquisition Plan. http://www.fs.fed.us/land/staff/LWCF/ Final%20DOI-USDA%20Land%20Acquisition%20Report%20to%20Congress.pdf)

## An Example of Donation, Cooperative Agreements, and Partnerships

The Trust of Public Land (TPL) is a unique resource for land management agencies. The Trust for Public Land's Federal Affairs Department provides the following ways for threatened lands to be purchased and then transferred to government ownership:

- It builds bridges with important conservation partners, both private and public, to help create solutions for land conservation.
- It is the primary link between TPL, the U.S. Congress, federal administration officials, and national policy organizations.
- It provides information and guidance about federal policy and funding resources to a wide range of interested parties, including Congressional, administration, and agency staff, local and state land trust activists and government officials, and other national conservation groups.
- It works with Congress and the administration to secure funding and authorizations related to land conservation.
- It maintains partnerships with Congress, administration officials, and federal agency staffs.
- It provides guidance and assistance to TPL regional offices, as well as other local land trusts, community groups, and government offices, regarding federal funding and policy initiatives.

Trust for Public Lands also provides the following conservation services to aid park acquisition efforts. The Trust for Public Land conserves land for human enjoyment and wellbeing, from inner city to wilderness. Our five initiatives are listed below.

- **Parks for People.** TPL works in cities and suburbs across America to ensure that everyone—in particular, every child—enjoys close-to-home access to a park, playground, or natural area.
- **Working Lands.** TPL protects farms, ranches, and forests that support land-based livelihoods and rural ways of life.
- **Natural Lands.** TPL conserves places of natural beauty that preserve wilderness for our children's children to explore and that support other species with whom we share the planet.
- **Heritage Lands.** TPL protects places of historic and cultural importance that keep us in touch with the past and who we are as a people.
- **Land and Water.** TPL preserves lands that protect clean water and the natural beauty of our coasts and waterways. (http://www.tpl.org/tier2_kad.cfm?folder_id=3149)

Another excellent example is the New Jersey Department of Environmental Protection (DEP) Green Acres Program. This program also partners with the TPL. Like many other states, it provides the following example of combining scenic easements, zoning, and regulatory measures to protect park and open space, as noted on the following page.

The goal of protecting the scenic quality of Route 57 can be accomplished in a number of ways. Local master planning and conservation zoning may be used to steer future growth away from sensitive viewsheds. Design guidelines, such as those provided in this Toolkit, may be used to encourage compact community forms and attractive building types that harmonize with the surrounding landscape. Scenic overlay zoning may also help municipalities limit visual disturbances, by regulating such elements as building heights, parking, and commercial signs.

In some cases, certain views may be so highly valued by community residents that consideration can also be given to the outright acquisition of land for preservation purposes. Alternatively, landowners may be willing to grant scenic easements that protect views while allowing current activities to continue on a parcel. Public sector programs that may assist with the acquisition of specific parcels of land along Route 57 include NJDEP's Green Acres Program and Warren County's Department of Land Preservation. Private land trusts are another resource. Resources for acquiring preservation easements include the State Agriculture Development Committee's "Planning Incentive Grants" (PIGs), which target active farmland. Some of these programs require that the land in question be part of a municipal open space or farmland preservation plan. (New Jersey Department of Environmental Protection, Land Acquisitions and Easements: Route 57 Corridor Plan, http://www.state.nj.us/transportation/works/studies/rt57/pdf/LandAcquisitionandScenicEasements..pdf)

**Figure 9.1. Graph of Total Number of Wisconsin Parks by Land Ownership**

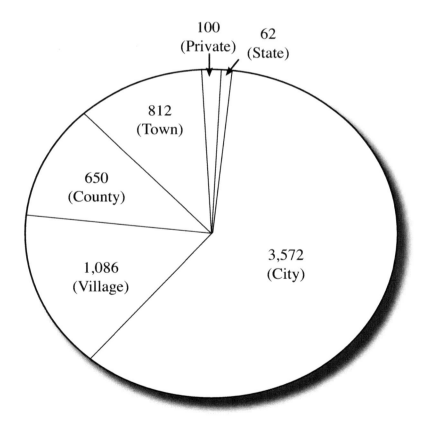

# DEVELOPMENT

Once the land envisioned in the area plan has been acquired and the planners have provided a plan document, a tangible structure or some other modification of the area will become a reality. Sometimes these areas have little or no development, based on the resources and needs. For example, linear greenways serving as wildlife corridors and floodplain management might only have trails.

Financing the costs of construction is a very important phase of development. Here final project features are illustrated and estimated construction costs are projected. At this point, too, the agency starts perfecting its capital budget for legislative review.

## The Capital Budget

Earlier information in chapters on fiscal management and on budget preparation is applicable here. More specifically, however, the capital budget must be considered at this time.

The capital budget request deals with monies for acquisition and development of new areas and facilities as well as major renovations and repairs to extend the life of existing facilities. (This is in contrast to the operational budget, which is the day-to-day money used to run the agency.) The development part of the capital budget is usually set forth in a long-range capital needs program of six to 10 years; the specific capital budget request that spans one or two years. The specific request requires much more specificity and should prove the need along with details on the proposed design.

## The Process of Development

**Staffing.** Though the exact number will vary with the size and scope of the capital development program, many people with professional and technical training will need to collaborate on budget preparation. These people must gather appropriate data to develop all documents necessary to implement the program. The personnel that typically stay on the project staff include planners, engineers, environmentalists, and at least one representative, perhaps a manager, from the field staff. The maintenance department should also be represented at some point.

**Environmental review.** Preliminary environmental project review must be undertaken. The environmental impact statement (EIS) consists of estimating the effect of the proposed construction on the site. This information is deduced from environmental data, such as studies of flora and fauna.

**Permits.** The agency will also review pertinent regulatory documents and move to obtain the required permits. In both planning and development, there are many situations that require permits before work can proceed. These fall under federal, provincial, state, and local agency rules and reflect the areas of concern for each level's responsibilities.

**Operations review.** Design features must now be reviewed by the field staff to identify estimations for start-up and annual operating costs. These cost figures are then to be placed with and become a part of the budget documents. They are to be added to the operating side of the appropriations if the capital request is funded.

Public input. There will be public input from many sources at different times during the planning process. Some will be provided during the "determination of need," and even more will be supplied during the "environmental review." Depending on the scope of the project, there will be a need for public meetings, comments, and hearings.

**Agency approval.** When these internal reviews are completed, this budget document takes it place with other agency budget documents and is assigned some point of priority within the agency budget request. Then, all agency budget requests are considered—compared—and submitted by "the authority" in his or her annual request to the legislative body. The "authority" will be the governor if the budget is from a state agency. In the case of a park district, that person would be the park director.

**Legislative approval.** Neither the legislative body, nor the board, manager, or other approving authority will consider a request for construction funds (capital budget) unless a plan has been adopted by ordinance or other legislative means. They will also demand a high probability of completion in a timely fashion if the funds are to be forthcoming.

## The Actual Construction

Considerable time elapses between the preparation of the budget request and its final legislative approval. Furthermore, even more time passes before the project can assume its place on the agency agenda. During this lag time, various events can occur that drastically change the scope of the job or even cause its cancellation. Therefore, the agency now needs to have a project review before construction begins.

**Project review.** The planner initiates this review, considers needed changes, summarizes the recommendations, and coordinates the review by other staff persons to promote their approval of the changes in the project. Unresolved differences of opinion over changes in the project are sent to higher level government, as necessary, for a final decision. These persons will likely be the same ones who originally approved the project. Following this review, there should be no further changes to the project without the approval of the chief of engineering and the legislative body.

**Construction schedule.** In order to ensure that all projects are started and completed within the appropriation period, a project implementation schedule designating specific time periods for each project phase (field data, permits, design, and construction) should be in place. The effective project schedule will have taken into consideration such items as weather, potential interference with public use, permit requirements (for instance, no work to be done in the streambed during spawning season), and any other requirements affecting the construction program.

**Permits.** It is now time to prepare the final environmental documentation and secure any permits not previously obtained. Sometimes minor revisions in project scope or design will be necessary to comply with permit requirements.

**Decision to proceed.** The final decision to proceed or not to proceed with project implementation is made after review of the final project design permits and environmental documentation. The agency budget and finance office needs to be contacted to verify that the funds for the project have been set up.

**Production of plans and advertising.** The engineering division is responsible for the production of plans and specifications. These documents must be sent to all who have indicated an interest. They must also be advertised for bids in the appropriate journals, in most places titled by the town or city name, such as the *Honolulu Advertiser.* This solicitation must be handled according to the public bidding procedures applicable to the particular province or state. Bid openings should be brief and conducted in a professional manner with all participants well oriented in standard bid-opening procedures.

The plans have been approved, the appropriations made, the bids let, and the contracts awarded. The contract documents must now be prepared. These documents include the contract, the performance bond, the bid proposal sheet, and a complete set of specifications. It is now time to start construction in accordance with the agency construction schedule.

**Inspection.** There are two stages of inspections during construction. That which is done during construction is known as "on-site," while inspections completed prior to the agency accepting the project is known as "final."

*On-site inspection.* The more major or complex the project, the greater the need to have an on-site agency inspector present during all construction hours. Regrettably, this is often impossible. Frequently, incorrect quantities or products of inferior quality are used. The on-site inspector should keep records of quantities and other items pertinent to payment. The inspector keeps a construction diary and lists any changes in the on-site construction due to unforeseen problems will need to be written up officially as a change order. This process is expensive and time consuming.

*Final inspection.* The final inspection is actually in two phases. A "punch list" is submitted by the agency inspector. This shows the contractor what the agency believes needs to be done before the project is accepted and the controls are paid. (There are different versions of the derivation of this construction jargon. One version is that a whole was punched beside each item on the list as it was completed.) Taking care of these requests constitutes the second phase. After the inspector believes the project is properly completed, the agency "signs off" as having accepted the project.

**Guarantees and payments.** Project failures that are a result of poor work, substandard materials, or faulty equipment (generally within one year of the project acceptance) are replaced at the contractor's or supplier's expense. The agency usually protects itself by requiring the contractor to accept a one-year performance bond. This type of bond, paid for by the contractor, is a financial assurance that the work will be done as specified, both as to quantity and quality. Each public works contract is backed up by 100-percent performance bond and liability insurance. In addition, the contract should specify a certain number of days for completion of the work.

In spite of all good intentions by contractors and agency inspectors, there will, in all probability, be something wrong with most new facilities. It would be optimistic to expect all projects to be built right the first time. The chances are the park manager will need to do a little rearranging or "fixing" even at new facilities, be they campgrounds or visitor centers.

## CONCLUSION

Few decisions made in park systems are more long lasting or obvious than those made in planning, acquisition, or development. It should be clear that many planning and acquisitions systems are in place to develop parks for use by the public. If mistakes are made, they seldom go away or lend themselves to easy solutions. All three of these phases require masterful orchestration of many processes. These processes are vulnerable to change and political exigencies. The appearance of a park complete with facilities ready to serve the public represents the culmination of a long and complex process.

## REFERENCES

American Trails, http://www.americantrails.org/mission.html

Colorado State Parks, Staunton Park Flow Chart, http://www.stauntonpark.com/documents/FinalOpenHouse/FlowChartIV10-16-09.pdf

DOI-USDA (2005). Final Department of Interior-USDA Land Acquisition Plan. http://www.fs.fed.us/land/staff/LWCF/Final%20DOI-USDA%20Land%20Acquisition%20Report%20to%20Congress.pdf

East Bay Regional Park District, Acquisition, http://www.ebparks.org/planning.

Florida Department of Environmental Protection, (2010) http://www.dep.state.fl.us/lands/acqprocess.htm

Gallatin National Forest, Project Flow Chart, http://www.maximtechnologies.com/newworld/flowchart.htm

Job Hazard Analysis: Identifying Risks Sooner Rather than Later, http://www.nps.gov/.../jha_pguide_010605.pdf, retrieved June 5, 2010.

McDonough, William, & Braungart, Michael. (2002). *Cradle to cradle: Remaking the way we make things.* New York: North Point Press.

National Park Service. (2006). St. Croix National Scenic Riverway Plan. Retrieved January 13, 2011 from http://www.nps.gov/sacn/parkmgmt/loader.cfm?csModule=security/getfile&pageid=81875

National Park Service (March 2008). General Management Plan Dynamic Document, http://planning.nps.gov/GMPSourcebook/WhyNPS.htm

New Jersey Department of Environmental Protection, Land Acquisitions and Easements: Route 57 Corridor Plan, (2010). http://www.state.nj.us/transportation/works/studies/rt57/pdf/LandAcquisitionandScenicEasements..pdf

Rails to Trails, http://www.railstotrails.org/ourWork/index.html

Scenic America. (2010). Scenic Byways. Retrieved from http://www.scenic.org/byways.

Seattle's Park and Recreation 2006 Development Plan, http://www.seattle.gov/parks/Publications/Development/Plan2006.pdf

U.S. Fish and Wildlife Service, (2010). www.fws.gov/endangered/landowner.

Xanterra, http://www.xanterra.com

# Chapter Ten

# Park Facilities

*"Recreational development is a job not of building
roads into the lovely country, but of building
receptivity into the still unlovely human mind."*

—Aldo Leopold
*A Sand County Almanac,* 1949

Park facilities include any modification of the landscape intended to facilitate access, use, and understanding of the park. All structures, roads, trails, signs, utilities, and parking lots, among other "improvements" are considered facilities. The location and design of facilities can help to interpret park resources; however, facility location and design can also contribute to the degradation of the resource. Facility location and design is one of the most important management techniques for the manager to guide the interface between visitors and the park. Careful consideration must be given to the location of every facility within a park to maximize use and control for user behaviors.

An understanding of facilities, their relationships, and their use is important to the design of new facilities or the remodel of existing facilities. In some instances, park managers inherit facilities that promote use that is detrimental to park resources. These may need to be relocated or removed. The process used for facility design is critical to creating a visitor experience that complements park resources.

## THE PLANNING PROCESS

A multidisciplinary team to collaborate on site and facility design options typically is needed to address multiple concerns for successful park operations. Management and maintenance staff will be responsible for the operation and maintenance of facilities and should be a part of the design team. Landscape architects, architects, and ecologists familiar with particular ecosystems and their functioning are also often needed on the design team. The perspectives needed on the design team depend on the nature of the site.

The planning and design process should include meaningful participation by the public. People who visit the same park year after year may do so because they like the park "just the way it is." They may feel possessive about a certain part of the park, even seeking out the same experience each year. A loyal clientele might suddenly become antagonistic if drastic changes are made. For example, visitors might come to a park because it offers good fishing on a lake where access to the water is by small car-top boats or canoes. The planner or manager might believe a further service could be provided if a boat launching ramp were installed to benefit all boaters, including those pulling water skiers. An astute manager would carefully determine the need for such a facility and would invite discussion on the change with present park clientele through workshops and public hearings before making such an "improvement."

Actively organizing public participation offers alternative avenues to creatively address management concerns. This expands the capacity of the managing agency and draws on community. resources Careful consideration must be invested in a public participation process that uses multiple techniques at multiple venues, and at a variety of times. Investment in an inclusive and responsive public participation process has multiple benefits and can expand ongoing volunteer assistance in park operations and a public more aware of ecosystem functioning and resource management issues.

## Site Design Considerations

Understanding the ecosystems functioning within the park and the interrelationships between systems is essential prior to locating and developing any improvements within the park. The manager must also have an understanding of the park within its regional context. The National Park Service identified six site design principles fundamental to sustainable site design within the context of the park setting (*Guiding Principles of Sustainable Design*, U.S. Department of the Interior, 1993):

- recognition of context,
- treatment of landscapes as interdependent and interconnected,
- integration of the native landscape with development,
- promotion of biodiversity,
- reuse of already disturbed areas, and
- making a habit of restoration.

Conservation agencies must look beyond political boundaries in site planning and design. Figure 10.1 displays the mapping of ecological assets that cross state boundaries. A sustainable approach to park management requires an ongoing curiosity with assessment, monitoring, and reevaluation. It is a cyclical process that informs future development and management strategies. An ability to assess projected inputs and waste outputs of a proposed facility should be determined prior to development. Inputs include energy, material, labor, and products that are necessary to support a development option. Outputs are solid waste, sewage effluent, and exhaust emissions that are a result of the development.

The Seattle Parks developed a sustainable approach to development by integrating design approaches, construction methods, project characteristics, technologies, and materials that concurrently promote environmental quality, enhance social benefit, and reduce the cost of ownership. The intent of the effort is to:

- reduce operational and maintenance costs
- reduce initial and ongoing adverse impacts to the environment
- increase the ecological function of landscape and natural areas
- increase the comfort, health and safety of parks visitors and building occupants
  (See http://www.seattle.gov/Parks/sustainable/default.htm for more detailed information)

General site design considerations can be applied to the initial steps of assessing the appropriate location of facilities in any area. Table 10.1 compares traditional vs. sustainable approaches to development (U.S. Department of the Interior, *Guiding Principles of Sustainable Design*,1993):

## Table 10.1. Comparison of Traditional and Sustainable Developments

|  | **Traditional Development** | **Sustainable Development** |
|---|---|---|
| **Activity Objectives** | Traditional development consists of identifying target customers and assessing their desires, and then trying to make visitors comfortable in familiar surroundings and in heavily manipulated environments. Typically much of the site is totally reconfigured with pools patios terraces, and vegetative compositions. The experience is very controlled and reflects the view that earth's resources are for human use. | Sustainable development for tourism focuses on the preservation and interpretation of indigenous natural and cultural resources rather than creating a contrived or artificial environment. The development accentuates the indigenous natural and cultural assets while respecting resource constraints.<br><br>The basic programmatic objective of sustainable development is to help visitors appreciate the natural and cultural uniqueness of a site by bringing them physically closer to it. To achieve this the development must be human-scaled and intimate so that sensory features of the native landscape such as sights, smells and sounds are appreciated and preserved.<br><br>The basic environmental objective is to achieve these experiences within acceptable limits of change. If these objectives cannot be achieved on the same site, the development cannot be justified. |
| **Site Planning and Design** | The traditional approach to site planning and design begins with collecting and mapping data pertinent to site development. A good geographic information system. (GIS) is a practical method for collecting data on biological (vegetation, wildlife) physical (topography, soils, climate) and cultural (ownership, legal, historical) factors. Analysis for preliminary design then combines and compares these data to determine the best areas for development and the areas in which development would be very difficult, costly, or environmentally unsound. | The sustainable approach to site planning and design goes beyond combining and comparing site inventories. A sustainable process attempts to determine the relationships between site factors and how those factors will adapt to change. Understanding these relationships also clarifies how development impacts from one area of the site will affect other areas. An evaluation of potential development impacts requires that a predevelopment baseline or environmental model be produced. This model will describe the essential functions and interrelationships of the individual site factors and will establish acceptable limits of change during and after construction. Selected environmental monitoring and testing will be done during construction. The entire build-out of the development will be phased to allow time between construction projects to monitor environmental impacts and adjust the baseline model. |
|  | The major steps in a traditional approach to site planning and design are as follows:<br><br>• Inventory site factors<br>• Analyze opportunities and constraints<br>• Design according to site suitabilities | The major steps in a sustainable approach to site planning and design are as follows:<br><br>• Model the ecosystem to establish an environmental understanding<br>• Ass social-economical context<br>• Establish acceptable limits of change<br>• Design facility within social and environmental thresholds<br>• Monitor site factors throughout construction<br>• reevaluate design solutions between development phases |

## Figure 10.1. Ecological Assets Map

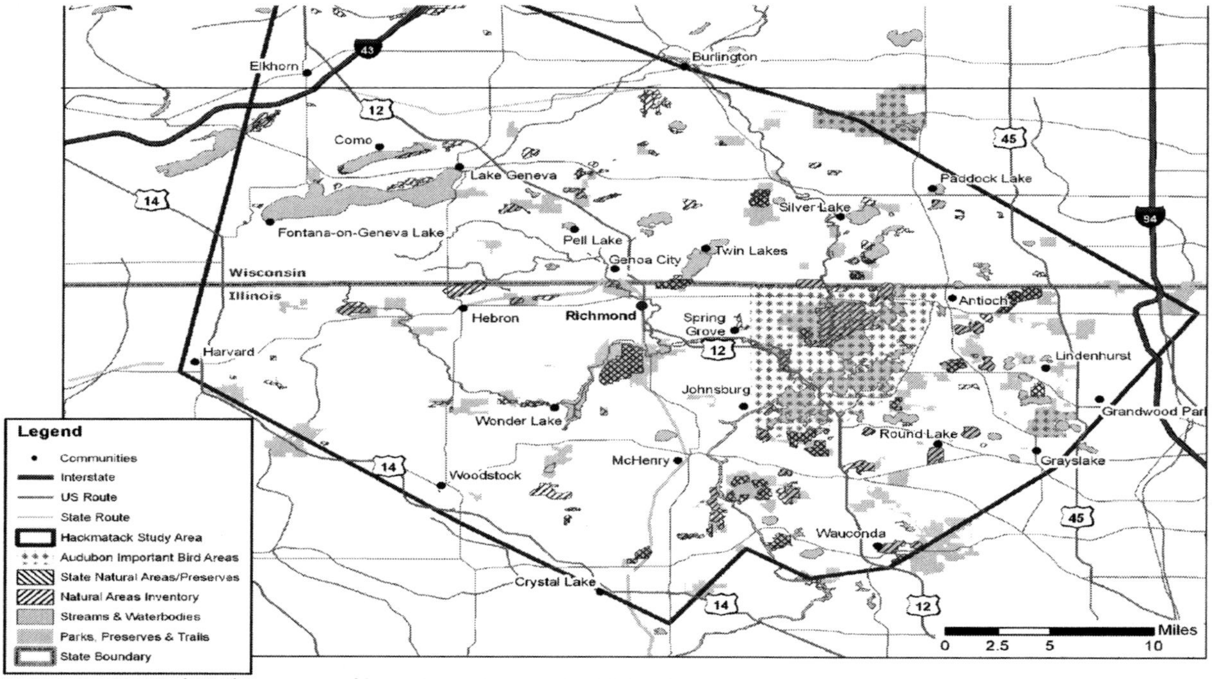

Note: Ecological Assets Map of the Hackmatack National Wildlife Refuge Visibility Study includes many communities in the states of Wisconsin and Illinois. The study area spans several jurisdictional boundaries. From Hackmatack National Wildlife Refuge Viability Study, 2010, Retrieved November 2010. Brenda Adams-Weyant, Fermata Inc. Reprinted with permission.

Site design for facilities is like putting together a three-dimensional puzzle where all surfaces must match. This puzzle includes natural, cultural, social, and operational characteristics. Site-specific characteristics will influence the location of facilities. Programmatically, the manager must have a sense of the demand for specific types of facilities. This information will assist in aligning use with the carrying capacity of the site, which in turn influences the density or extent of facilities developed. Natural characteristics such as climate, slopes, and vegetation will also influence the location and scale of facility development. Facility location becomes a question of access and whether access should or should not be provided and to whom. Access to natural attractions can become natural hazards. Access to natural and cultural features can initiate the degradation of these features. Careful consideration should be given to park access and the level of access provided. Facility development guides access.

### Universal Design and Barrier-Free Facilities

Outdoor recreation activities are appealing to a range of people with varying abilities. All areas in parks, forests, and reserves cannot be available to all visitors, but older facilities that are being refurbished and all new facilities being considered can eliminate most structural barriers by using universal design principles.

Universal design, also know as inclusive design, design-for-all, or human-centered design, provides a framework for designing places or products without special or separate accommodations. The universal design framework pushes park planning and design beyond minimum accessibility guidelines. The National Center on Accessibility (www.ncaonline.org) has developed a one-hour e-course as an introduction to the principles of Universal Design for park and recreation practitioners. The free course is offered through the Eppley Institute for Parks and Public Lands online learning site: www.parktraining.org.

In the United States, the Architectural Barriers Act of 1968 notes, "Any building or facility, constructed in whole or part by federal funds must be made accessible to and usable by the physically handicapped." This Act was followed by Section 504 of the Rehabilitation Act of 1973 and the Americans with Disabilities Act (ADA) of 1990.

The ADA addresses access to the workplace (title I), State and local government services (title II), and places of public accommodation and commercial facilities (title III). It also requires phone companies to provide telecommunications relay services for people who have hearing or speech impairments (title IV) and miscellaneous instructions to Federal agencies that enforce the law (title V).

To assist park managers to comply with ADA laws, the Access Board was established. The Access Board is an independent federal agency that was instituted to assist in the promotion of accessibility of parks. Meeting throughout the 1990s, the Access Board established 11 guidelines for developing accessible park systems:

1. Protect resource and environment
2. Preserve experience
3. Provide for equality of opportunity
4. Maximize accessibility
5. Be reasonable
6. Address safety
7. Be clear, simple, and understandable
8. Provide guidance
9. Be enforceable and measurable
10. Be consistent with Americans with Disabilities Act Accessibility Guidelines
11. Be based on independent use by persons with disabilities

In March 2010, the U.S. Department of Justice issued the 2010 ADA Standards for Accessible Design, Title II and Title III.

The Americans with Disabilities Act (ADA) requires the Department of Justice (the Department) to publish ADA design standards that are consistent with the guidelines published by the U.S. Architectural and Transportation Barriers Compliance Board (Access Board). The Department has adopted revised ADA design standards that include the relevant chapters of the Access Board's 2004 ADA/ABA Accessibility Guidelines as modified by specific provisions of the Department's revised rules implementing title II and title III of the ADA. To minimize compliance burdens on entities subject to more than one legal standard, these design standards have been harmonized with the Federal standards implementing the Architectural Barriers Act and with the private sector model codes that are adopted by most States. The changes to the design guidelines were adopted by the Access Board as a series of separate rules that were combined in the 2004 ADA/ABA guidelines. These rules addressed recreation facilities, play areas, state and local government facilities (detention facilities and courthouses), and, finally, the revision of the Access Board's 1991 guidelines. These changes have been adopted, with some modifications, as the 2010 Standards for Accessible Design. (U.S. Department of Justice. Retrieved from: http://www.ada.gov/regs2010/factsheets/2010_Standards_factsheet.html)

The 2010 Standards set minimum requirements—both scoping and technical—for newly designed and constructed or altered State and local government facilities, public accommodations, and commercial facilities to be readily accessible to and usable by individuals with disabilities. These ADA standards establish a revised reference point for Title II entities that choose to make structural changes to existing facilities to meet their program accessibility requirements; and it establishes a similar reference for Title III entities undertaking readily achievable barrier removal.

**Application of 2010 ADA Standards as Set Forth by the U.S. Department of Justice**

| *Compliance Date for New Construction or Alterations* | *Applicable Standards* |
|---|---|
| Before September 15, 2010 | 1991 Standards or UFAS |
| On or after September 15, 2010, and before March 15, 2012 | 1991 Standards, UFAS, or 2010 Standards |
| On or after March 15, 2012 | 2010 Standards |

From www.ada.gov/regs2010/2010ADAStandards/2010ADAstandards.htm#c10

Accessible facilities should display variation in design to accommodate a range of users. The National Center on Accessibility compares an example of "accessible design" and "universal design" of a camp site. An accessible design requires clear floor space which is firm and stable allowing an individual to move around a campsite and pitch a tent. A tent platform with a ramp increases accessibility. A tent pad that raises the ground level 17 -19 inches to pitch a tent increases use or accommodates a range of users. Examples of a range of universally designed facilities can be viewed at Indiana University's National Center on Accessibility at http:wwwncaonline.org.

## The Park Master Plan

The culmination of a thorough planning process for facility development is reflected in the park master plan. Some master plans present park objectives in the broadest terms, serving only as guides to the development of more detailed plans, including facility location. Other master plans, for small parks, may be so specific that they spell out in detail the location and type of roads, trails, utilities, buildings, and other facilities. Often park agencies combine these two types of plans and have specific plans for facility design and development within the general master plan. There must be consistency between the master plan and site-specific plans. The master plan guides site-specific plans; however, the development of site-specific plans can require a shift in the master plan. Appendix B t the end of this chapter shows an example of a master plan process.

The manager uses the master plan to:

- assure coordination between the park and its neighbors,
- establish land-use priorities,
- guide the designer in the preparation of detailed plans for each facility,
- show relationships between various park facilities,
- provide a basis for determining cost estimates,
- give agency administrators reference for preparing construction priorities, and
- provide the maintenance staff with a reference guide to all park facilities.

## FUNCTIONS OF FACILITIES

It is difficult to imagine the average park area without facilities. Facilities do the following:

- They serve the need of park visitors.
- They protect the park from visitor impact.
- They are necessary to the management and maintenance of the park.
- They create the park image, either favorable or unfavorable.

Although facilities may add to the appearance of a park, they also intrude on park resources. Facilities cost money to build, are expensive to maintain, and can be a focus for vandalism. Vandalism must be addressed by giving special consideration to the design, placement, and material make-up of facilities (see chapter 13). Where possible, facilities should be constructed of materials indigenous to, as well as in harmony with, the natural environment.

Facilities must not infringe on unique areas or be placed where there is unusual or endangered flora or fauna. In the past, too many parks were unduly manicured or overdeveloped simply because the park "looked better that way." Today, some park agencies make it a policy to have up to 80 percent of the park acreage in a natural condition, benefiting both wildlife and the people who wish to see wildlife.

## PLANNING FOR PARK FACILITIES

When determining the kind and extent of facilities, the planner must consider the following factors:

- How is the site to be used?
- What is the amount and kind of land and water available?
- Will the land support the expected visitor load and activities without excessive deterioration?
- Can the proposed facilities be maintained with a modest increase in the personnel and materials budget, or will substantial increases in one or both be needed?

### Facility Costs

The cost of a facility has many variables, including labor costs, distance from suppliers, availability of materials, weather factors, site conditions, required standards, and initial planning costs, which might include delays for public hearings and time spent on the filing and acceptance of environmental-impact statements. Most managers will have to depend on the agency headquarters to determine the cost of new and rehabilitated facilities through bidding and other contract procedures. The relationship of these costs to the available monies will determine the quality of the facility, its size, and many other factors, including whether or not it will be built at all.

Not all types of facilities are capital construction projects. Some, such as signs, picnic tables, fireplaces, or components for footbridges are made in prison industries, centralized agency workshops, or in the parks themselves, frequently during the off season.

### Facility Design

The four facility functions listed earlier illustrate that facilities provide user satisfaction and serve as management tools. Using these as criteria, the planner might look at proposed facilities under the following headings.

**Suitability to site.** Is there harmony between the proposed facility and the natural landscape? Is there harmony among the various facilities? How much of the natural setting will have to be altered to construct the facility?

**Adaptability.** Can the proposed facility be expanded to meet new demands at reasonable cost?

**Suitability for maintenance.** Will this design raise or lower maintenance costs? Has this design proven elsewhere to be relatively low in maintenance costs?

**Safety.** Do design and materials provide maximum safety for both visitors and staff?

**Vandalism potential.** Will the design leave the facility vulnerable to vandalism, or will it discourage vandalism? Will broken or defaced facilities be easily restored?

**Access.** Is the facility readily accessible to all visitors including persons with disabilities? Is traffic flow and directions obvious for both foot and vehicle traffic? Is night lighting adequate?

**Energy efficiency.** Is the facility designed for minimizing heat loss in cooler months? Does it make provision for cooling in the warm season? Are the energy requirements reasonable? Is lighting achieved with minimum wattage?

**Cost effectiveness.** Is the design actually the least expensive, or would spending more on the construction be offset by reduced maintenance and vandalism costs as well as increased life of the facility?

**Construction costs.** Does the design entail unnecessary or expensive constructions costs, such as earth removal and grading? Are the materials difficult to secure?

**Architectural character.** Do the facilities and structures help interpret the nature of the site and the cultural heritage of the area? Is the design compatible with existing facilities?

## EXPERIENCE WITH PARK FACILITIES

Does the fact that facilities are new guarantee trouble-free management? Assume that the planner has done his or her homework well. The planner has considered the climatic and topographic factors, the water availability, and the desirable and undesirable features of the site. After asking specialized user groups for comments on the facility design, a good plan with several options for the decision makers has been put together. The "best" design is picked, contracts are let for construction, and within a year or so, the new park with its shiny new facilities is dedicated with the local politicians in evidence, and the shake-down period begins.

The park, as it turns out, is far from complete. Construction scars need to be effaced and screenings must be planted. The visitors arrive and go into places the manager does not want them just yet. The sign system leaves something to be desired. What was designed for low density appears to be receiving high-density use. Some trails will need paving. Picnic table pads might be necessary. No emergency or overflow camping area was provided, but everything is already full. A vault toilet placed in a wet area is slowly surfacing. Some trees blow down during a windstorm. Initials are appearing in the smooth-barked trees in the campground. Children have to be rescued from nearby cliffs. The chlorinator in the water supply system breaks down. A tree catches fire because of fireplace location. A camper wedges his huge recreation vehicle between two trees, damaging everything involved. Someone has broken into the coin box in the shower house. A camper complains about the noise coming from the adjacent group camp and threatens to punch someone in the nose.

Fortunately, things ease up after a while. Not all of these hypothetical problems are a result of faulty design; some might be the result of faulty construction, some are policy related, others are due to inexperience or bad luck, and still others are caused by those few visitors who really do not care. A good facility design and location, however, can lessen or avoid at least some of these problems.

Facilities vary greatly from park to park. Areas near large population centers with high visitation differ greatly in their facility needs than parks located a considerable distance from major population centers. When the park was established also influences the types of facilities that have been developed. Space does not permit detailed information on the design of specific facilities. Our treatment here will stress manager-related concerns regarding buildings, day-use areas, overnight areas, and support facilities (needed in both day and overnight areas). However, there is no prescription for the types of facilities each park should develop and maintain. Facility location and design is dependent on the interface between the place, its natural and cultural resources, and the people who come to experience the place.

## BUILDINGS

These are difficult to classify, as they can be found in any of the categories that follow, but they do form a special unit of park facilities. Some buildings serve the public, but most are for park employees, serving park management and maintenance needs. These include administrative buildings, utility buildings, shop structures, employee residences and dormitories, entrance stations, and perhaps a historic building or two. Buildings intended for park visitor use include bathhouses, restrooms, visitor centers, and picnic shelters. Some parks have concession buildings for food service, lodging, or rentals of various kinds.

Since buildings stand out prominently, it is particularly important that design and construction materials should be selected for appearance, durability, and ease of maintenance. Building location should provide easy access yet be in harmony with the natural aspects of the area. Earlier in this chapter, it was suggested that facilities in general be constructed of material indigenous to the area and in accordance with the environment. This is particularly true for park buildings.

## DAY-USE AREAS

These offer facilities for picnicking, swimming, boating, trailheads and trails, impromptu games, interpretive areas, and winter sports areas. Day-use areas should be designed to be readily accessible, aesthetically pleasing, and functional. These areas should also require minimal maintenance. Facilities for each of the above uses will be considered separately.

### Picnic Sites

Picnicking, which basically involves eating outdoors, often with family or friends, is one of the most popular daytime recreation activities in North America. Some people prefer to picnic in isolation with their family, while others do not object to and may even enjoy large groups. Picnicking can take place anywhere, but it is enhanced if there is some shade, reasonably level ground, and an attractive view. At least some sites and the paths leading to them should be firm and level, equipped with totally accessible and usable facilities, and identified with the International Symbol of Access (see Figure 10.2).

### Figure 10.2. The International Symbol of Access

If the picnic area is near water, the sites should be set back, unless the sites are on rock, to prevent shoreline impact. Facilities include tables and fireplaces or charcoal grills at each site and a nearby trash receptacle, water supply, toilet, and central parking. These facilities keep people concentrated in areas designed for this use, consolidating the problems of cleanup and maintenance and confining soil compaction.

The fireplace or charcoal grill should be set away from trees and permanently anchored. The trash container should be obvious to the visitor and accessible to maintenance crews, but it should blend into the surroundings. The water supply and toilets are usually centrally located. Attempting to provide shade at each table is unwise, because picnic use puts too much compaction on the feeder roots of trees and eventually kills them.

Large group picnic areas should be separated from the family picnic area. In group areas, the tables are closer together and more formally arranged, and fireplaces or grills are not needed with each table. A picnic shelter containing stoves, water, and tables and providing overhead protection from sun or rain may be found in either group or family picnic areas.

The number of persons to be accommodated per acre in picnic areas is generally fixed by agency policy and is based on the park's proximity to population centers and the number that can be accommodated without deterioration of the site. The limitation to the number of people is referred to as carrying capacity or use limits, an approach used by many agencies to determine levels of use. This concept is discussed in greater detail in chapter 12.

Barrier devices or curbing will be necessary to confine vehicles to parking areas, for everyone wishes to drive right up to the tables, and will if not deterred. Signs will be needed for management purposes.

**Figure 10.3. This picnic facility allows users to view the surrounding areas while enjoying a shaded, level area to relax and eat.**

Photo courtesy of Hannah Lang.

## Swimming Areas

Swimming takes place in pools, ponds, lakes, reservoirs, streams, rivers, and oceans and is a major day-use activity. Freedom from pollution and hazards is essential. Beaches should not be developed where there are strong currents, steep drop offs, or other conditions that create a safety problem for swimmers.

Facilities might include a sandy or pebbled beach, a grassy area upslope from the beach, toilets, a change house or dressing room for each sex, a central parking area, trash receptacles, drinking fountains or hand pumps, an anchored float, and a roped-off area or buoy markers designating the outer boundaries of the swimming area. Approximately 75 percent of the swimming area should be in depths of five feet (1.5 meters) or less. Various signs will also be needed.

A small play area for impromptu games, such as frisbee tossing or touch football, contributes to the enjoyment of the area. A fast-food concession stand near the beach is a convenience some park visitors really enjoy, but it adds to the litter problem. Accessibility for persons with disabilities consists of a firm pathway or boardwalk built from the parking lot to the water's edge, with a rubber mat laid directly on the sand. Handrails give such swimmers an added assurance of safety. The clear tread width of a beach access route must be 36 inches (91.5 mm) at a minimum. The only exception to not developing an accessible beach route is when another beach access route exists within a half mile and under the management of the same authority.

## Boating Areas

Most park managers will be concerned mainly with boats that can be transported either by car-top or on trailers. The major facilities involved are launching ramps, docks, fuel facilities, parking for cars and trailers, adequate turn areas, and toilet and garbage facilities. Launching, boating, and fishing regulations must be posted. In some areas, fish cleaning facilities might be necessary. Facilities that accommodate trailers require a fairly large parking area. Trailer parking can be off-set from shoreline to reduce shoreline impact. Hardened parking areas near the shoreline should be graded to direct water away from surface water.

## Trailheads

The trailhead is a point where users transfer from road vehicles to trails or vice versa. Users could be hikers, walkers, horse or bike riders, or, in winter, snowmobilers, cross-country skiers, or snowshoers. From the facility standpoint, these areas are relatively uncomplicated. The trailhead consists of a central parking area convenient to the trail. Facilities may include toilets, drinking, water, garbage cans, an information bulletin panel, and trail-use signs. If horses are used on the trail, a hitch rack is usually necessary. A load/unloading ramp may be needed if commercial packers use the trailhead.

Care must be taken not to overdevelop a trailhead. The size of the parking area should be closely related to the designed use or optimum capacity of the trail system (see chapter 12, Environmental Impact). Also, the facilities here must be carefully considered in order to avoid unrelated use. If, for example, tables and fireplaces are provided at the trailhead, it is difficult to prevent the site from becoming a campground for other park visitors who do not intend to use the trail.

## Trails

Trails are linear corridors, usually well defined, generally leading the user away from and back to "civilization." The purpose is to permit visitor access to the resource with a minimum of impact. Walking trails are short and provide access to nearby points of interest for the casual hiker or stroller. A popular walking trail is the self-guided interpretive or nature trail. The walking trail should take full advantage of a variety of views, vegetation types, and other points of interest. Walking trail standards include such requirements as numerous bends in the trail, easy grades, benches, handrails near potential hazards, and footbridges or boardwalks over wet areas and sensitive sites. The tread should be treated with some surfacing material, such as wood chips, bark, or soil cement. Paving may be required in certain areas of heavy use.

Hiking trails, on the other hand, are designed for the more experienced and rugged hikers and encompass long distances and rougher terrain. Grades may be up to 12 percent or more. Reaching scenic vistas is an important consideration in hiking trail location. Since hiking trails run across hillsides to gain elevation, switchbacks as well as cuts and fills are usually necessary. Soil erosion must be held to a minimum by use of drainage techniques, such as culvers and water bars.

As a park manager, it is also imperative to develop trail systems that are accessible to all patrons. There are specific guidelines for trail planners to follow in order to comply with the ADA laws. It is important as a manager to use specific signs to clarify which trails are accessible. "Accessible trails" include those newly constructed and altered trails that meet all of the provisions. The table in Appendix A to this chapter lists the ADA guidelines for trails.

Other types of trails include equestrian, bicycle, snowmobile, and cross-country ski trails. Each type has standards of design, and the trail planner must understand these differences of construction, location, and vertical and horizontal clearing needs. As we will see elsewhere, keeping these users apart by time, season, or physical separation is frequently necessary. There are also likely to be problems with a trail leaving or entering a park. When crossing the border to or from another ownership, the user may encounter a different set of rules governing such actions as handling, pets, carrying guns, setting campfires, using motorized vehicles, and smoking while traveling.

Trails have become increasingly popular for exercise, wildlife viewing, and economic development. Trails linking destinations is becoming more common. Figure 10.4 demonstrates the level of funding support for Colorado State Parks. This trend is mirrored across the nation. Figure 10.5 represents the use levels of trails by activity in Colorado State Parks. Walking, hiking, and biking are the predominate activities, followed closely by snow-based activities, fishing and hunting, and backpacking.

## Playground Facilities

Not all agencies feel it necessary or appropriate to provide play apparatus. Most playgrounds are found in the activity-oriented structured recreation parks, but occasionally such facilities

## Figure 10.4.
## Level of Funding Increase in Colorado For Trails

| Fiscal Year | State Parks Lottery | GOCO* (State Parks share) | GOCO (Local govts.) |
|---|---|---|---|
| 99-00 | 100,000 | 500,000 | 500,000 |
| 98-99 | 100,000 | 468,000 | 513,400 |
| 97-98 | 100,000 | 355,000 | 402,100 |
| 96-97 | 100,000 | 360,000 | 400,000 |
| 95-96 | 100,000 | 350,000 | 750,000 |
| 94-95 | 150,000 | | 1,000,000 |
| 93-94 | 175,000 | | |
| 92-93 | 100,000 | | |
| 91-92 | 100,000 | | |
| 90-91 | 100,000 | *Great Outdoors Colorado* | |

From http://parks.state.co.us/NR/rdonlyres/4BF640F8-1780-46FE-B81B-3D835F8A8DA9/0/Trailsprogramstrategicplan.pdf.
Reprinted with permission.

## Figure 10.5. Distribution of Trail Use in Colorado State Parks

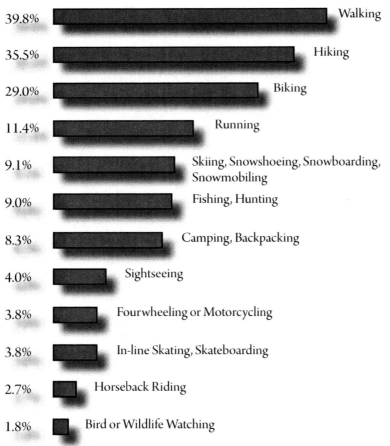

39.8%  Walking
35.5%  Hiking
29.0%  Biking
11.4%  Running
9.1%  Skiing, Snowshoeing, Snowboarding, Snowmobiling
9.0%  Fishing, Hunting
8.3%  Camping, Backpacking
4.0%  Sightseeing
3.8%  Fourwheeling or Motorcycling
3.8%  In-line Skating, Skateboarding
2.7%  Horseback Riding
1.8%  Bird or Wildlife Watching

From http://parks.state.co.us/NR/rdonlyres/4BF640F8-1780-46FE-B81B-3D835F8A8DA9/0/Trailsprogramstrategicplan.pdf).
Reprinted with permission.

are found in state and provincial parks. Some are even found in national recreation areas. The management purpose of these facilities is two-fold: to provide children with an opportunity to use large muscles and "let off steam" and to concentrate their activities in a small area, usually in or near a campground, picnic area, or wading water. Equipment includes simple culvert crawl through and hideaways, swings, sandboxes, whirls, climbing bars, overhead ladders, and slides.

## Impromptu Game Areas

Resource-oriented parks do not usually provide facilities for organized sports or athletic events. If they are provided, the standards are usually less than league requirements. The policy on providing sports facilities varies greatly even within agencies, however.

Once a pattern of use is established, it might be difficult to stop. For example, local pressure to provide space for a soccer field, complete with goal posts and white lines, could lead to tournament play and the need to provide more fields. A policy on such use is clearly needed.

Level, open space is usually sufficient invitation for visitors to start an impromptu game of softball, soccer, football, or to throw frisbees or discs, sail kites, or fly model airplanes. Such space should be separated from picnic areas and campgrounds if possible. Some parks provide backstops or goalposts, shuffle-board courts, and horseshoe pits. Visitors often bring their own equipment for badminton or volleyball. Sandy beaches and other small areas, including septic tank drain fields, are ideal for many of these uses.

## Interpretive Areas

Basic facilities for interpretive areas include simple bulletin boards or exhibit shelters and interpretive signs. Exhibit shelters may be located at trailheads, en route between parking areas and the attraction, and at the attraction itself. Interpretive trails, utilizing either signs in place or numbered posts keyed to leaflets, provide access with a minimum of disturbance to natural or cultural areas. These trails, designed for intensive use, require constant maintenance; for this reason they should be less than one mile (1.6 kilometers) long. Wildlife observation blinds and platforms provide access to native wildlife species for close study and photography. Some parks offer the convenience of a visitor center that contains restrooms, offices, an information desk, exhibit rooms, and an auditorium. The visitor center serves as the focus for park information. Here visitors can discover something about the cultural and natural history of the area in addition to learning what to see and do while in the park.

Most interpretive facilities are intended for day use. An exception is the amphitheater, designed for evening presentations on the natural and cultural history of the area. Seats, a projection booth, a screen, an amplification system with speakers, a fire circle, and a short access trail are usually components of such a facility. Newer units have a rear-screen projection system that eliminates the projection booth at the rear of the audience. Most amphitheaters are located in or near campgrounds and are reached by walking. Some may have a central parking lot for patrons coming from other areas.

## Winter Sport Areas

The criteria used to determine whether a site is suitable for winter sports activities include snow texture and depth, slope steepness, wind, temperature, avalanche potential, slope clearing costs, protection from erosion, electricity availability, and accessibility. Winter sports include such activities as downhill skiing, cross-country skiing, snowshoeing, ice skating, snowmobiling, and snow play. The area often requires warming facilities, a food and hot drinks concession, restrooms, equipment rental, a first-aid station, and lockers. These comforts and conveniences will require housing in a ski shelter, hut, or lodge.

Downhill skiing requires a lift device, and the types vary greatly from simple tow ropes to elaborate chair lifts, or cars (called gondolas or trams) suspended on wires. Cross-country skiing requires a safe system of relatively level trails that are separate from snowmobile trails. Both types of skiing will probably require plowed parking at the trailhead. Sliding areas for snow play must also be separated from other winter sports, and this activity must be confined to treeless slopes in order to avoid accidents.

## OVERNIGHT AREAS

Overnight areas include campgrounds, group camps, and lodging areas. Each should be designed to provide a pleasant experience for visitors and should be separated from day-use areas in order to avoid conflict between user groups.

### Campgrounds

The campground is perhaps the prime example of a park facility serving as a management tool. It limits visitor impact to a specific area, thus reducing damage to the overall recreation complex. It allows concentration of services, maximum surveillance and safety measures, and social interaction among users. From its beginning, the campground has been designed to accommodate automobiles, the channel most North Americans have used to reach these sites. The family car gave people the mobility to participate in the camping experience.

Even though extensively and carefully planned, the area supporting the campground will undergo considerable modification over time. Vegetation, soil, and wildlife population are all altered through initial construction and continued visitor use, as noted in chapters 11 and 12. Such deterioration is one of the costs of providing overnight accommodations for people in the natural environment. When a park is small and the campground is comparatively large, modification will be more apparent than in a park where the campground covers only a fraction of the total park acreage. If they bear in mind that the objective is to protect the rest of the park while confining the impact, managers can be more tolerant of visitor-imposed damage. Trees singed by campfires, shrubbery cut to make wiener sticks, roots exposed, land eroded from shortcutting, and land altered for enlargement of campsites to accommodate specific visitor needs are impacts that must be kept to minimum by wise and vigilant management, but they can never be stopped. These problems come with the convenience and control that campgrounds also provide. When one considers the alternative to the developed campground, such as extensive litter and sanitation problems, campfires out of control, intrusion of tents and vehicles everywhere, the campground, with all its problems, seems preferable in most situations.

Camping is an essential ingredient of outdoor recreation. Staying in a campground is the recreation experience for many patrons—the campfire, the cooking, the renewed contact with the elements, the change of pace, and the removal of some of the comforts and conveniences of home are all factors that contribute to the camping experience. On the other hand, campgrounds are regarded by some visitors as primarily inexpensive, convenient, and relatively safe stopovers in route to other places. For yet others, campgrounds are a base of operations, a place to stay while exploring, fishing, or hiking.

All this leads one to believe there should be a wide spectrum of campground designs to meet the needs of the camping public. Often diversity has been considered in the planning process. Park information should be detailed according to the types of services offered. Some developments, such as traveler's camps, have 15 sites per acre with campsites side by side. No attempt is made to screen out distractions or preserve the natural values of the area. Forest camps usually have 100-150 feet (30-50 meters) between individual sites, and the natural values are left reasonably intact.

Campground sizes vary greatly, as does the array of facilities offered. The purpose of the campground, the amount and kind of suitable land available, construction costs, demand forecasts, proximity to travel routes, and agency policy all dictate the general design of the campground. Design should allow for the closure of some units for vegetative rehabilitation as well as for convenience of fee collection and trash pickup during the off season.

The developed campground size ranges from a small area with three or four sites and a simple pit toilet to those with an elaborate road and sign network, several hundred units, flush toilets, showers, and an amphitheater. These large campgrounds require a sophisticated sanitation system. Local sanitation laws often dictate the type of sanitation facilities used in campgrounds.

A typical campsite or unit should consist of a parking spur and an adjacent use area containing a table, fireplace or grill, and tent space. Barriers may be used to confine the car to its parking space and protect the table from damage. More elaborate sites come with complete sewer, water, and electrical hookups for recreation vehicles. Areas with more than 24 camp units should have a holding-tank dump station. All these components will be considered under Support Facilities later in this chapter.

Campers seek different experiences from their camping. Some want the sociability and security of having other people nearby. Some bring with them most of the conveniences of home, including radios, ipods, and television. Others want isolation or at least peace and quiet. Purists bring with them only the essentials for sleeping and eating. It's all called "camping," and this variety of styles again shows the need for a diversity of offerings in order to satisfy the needs of the camping public.

The campground often becomes the park manager's main problem, because it is where people, many of them strangers, concentrate for overnight or longer. It's the city transplanted to the woods. Some problems are related to the design of the facility, and some are not. Aside from the social problems of noise, pets, and other annoyances, below are some common campground problems related to design.

- Confusing entrance and road layout
- Campsites and parking spurs not level
- Group camp too close to family campsites
- Materials chosen with no concern for ease of maintenance or protection from vandalism
- Campsites too close together
- Campground too close to a major hazard
- Campground size inadequate to meet demand
- Campground too close to day-use facilities
- High incidence of theft due to nearby road
- Shortcuts taken in design and construction materials in order to economize
- Water or sanitation facilities inconveniently located for many sites
- Campsites not diverse enough to accommodate a wide range of recreational vehicles
- All sites designed for single vehicles only
- No screening vegetation between campsites
- Insufficient parking for guests or visitors
- Inadequate campsite barriers
- Trail system poorly signed

Other problems, arising from policy decisions rather than the design of facilities, include those resulting from a differential fee system, an inadequate reservation system, and insufficient staffing and materials to properly maintain the campgrounds.

A simple welcoming sign stating that "This is your campground" may remind visitors of the reason the campground is there. This will encourage campers to assume some responsibility for its care and upkeep.

## Group Camps

Group camps, also known as organizational camps, environmental learning centers, and other similar names, are often found on public recreational lands. They are used for educational and social purposes by school, scouting, church, and other groups that have a common interest requiring members to live together for a few days. Demand for such areas is usually heavy, and reservations must often be made a year in advance.

Basic facilities include a road and trail system, parking lots, a sign system, a headquarters building for staff offices, kitchen facilities, a dining hall, a first aid room, cabins or bunkhouses for staff and campers, shower and toilet structures, a water supply for both domestic use and fire control, classrooms, a clubhouse, and other indoor recreational space. A swimming area is highly desirable as is outdoor space for organized sports, challenge courses, and nature activities. Miscellaneous facilities include shelters, fire circles, and perhaps a caretaker's residence.

Group camps should be isolated from all other park facilities to lessen distractions and assure privacy and safety for group campers. This also protects other park users from the noise associated with group camps.

Standards and safety practices for group camp facilities, particularly the water supply, sewage treatment, and living quarters, might be dictated by local health agencies. Information on standards and accreditation requirements for health and safety practices may be obtained from the American Camp Association (ACA) (2010).

## Lodging Areas

Such facilities range from simple housekeeping tent units to housekeeping cabins to elegant lodge facilities complete with opportunities for dining. The policy on guest cabins and lodges varies with agencies: some provide and maintain them, others build and then lease them to a concessionaire, others are concessionaire built and maintained and still other agencies leave the matter up to the private sector outside the park boundary. Some park agencies have found the operation of lodging to be a profitable business. These kinds of facilities increase the opportunity for a larger segment of the population to enjoy the park or recreation area. Not everyone cares to camp, and lodging areas provide an alternative.

## SUPPORT FACILITIES

Support facilities are those structures and amenities that provide water, sanitation, parking, safety, convenience, and access. These support facilities or utilities are needed in both day use and overnight areas as well as in the area housing park personnel.

Service facilities, shops, offices, and employee residences should be located away from recreational use areas and, where possible, confined to locations that do not have resource values attractive to the public. Electricity and telephone services will be required; lines should be placed underground.

## The Water Supply

Providing a continuous safe, clean water supply for the park and its visitors is a major task for park managers. The needs of visitors include drinking, cooking, washing, and sanitation. The park needs to include additional water for residences, fire protection, and irrigation.

Past inadequacies and present high standards cause public health agencies to speak a great deal about the park water supply, including its source, method of transport, storage, method of purification, and final dispersal to visitors. Water may be cold, taste good, and look clean, but these attributes are no guarantee that it is potable (safe to drink). Any water source can be contaminated, and all water must be tested frequently. Water taken from a lake, reservoir, or spring requires chlorination.

Early in the planning of a park, the average daily water needs as well as the peak demands must be estimated. Then it is necessary to determine whether this amount of water is available from either a groundwater or surface source. Groundwater is frequently more readily available and less costly to develop for use than is surface water. Whatever source is to be tapped into, a permit process may be required.

Water demand varies with the kind of facilities that are in place. A park with pit toilets has one level of demand, a park with flush toilets another. Add to this a shower house, laundry house, rental cabins, and a group camp, and the demand increases dramatically. For example, in a campground with pit toilets, the average daily requirement per person is about 5.5 gallons (21 liters). In a campground with showers and flush toilets, the daily requirement of water per person could be as much as 27 gallons (100 liters). Some writers estimate a much higher use.

In a given park, the water supply may come from several sources. In most instances, the preferred source is a drilled well with water pumped to various outlets. This requires electricity, of course. Sources other than groundwater are streams, springs, lakes, and reservoirs, this water reaching the area of use by gravity in most instances. Springs must be fenced, boxed, and covered with a lid. Hand pumps must be boxed to prevent contamination. Maintenance includes annual cleaning to remove sand, silt, algae, and salamanders. Often a collecting or storage tank is needed to provide a reserve supply for peak demand. In colder climates, provision must be made for weatherproofing or draining all pumps, pipes, and storage tanks to prevent freezing.

Where a water supply is utilized away from developed areas, such as along a trail, the visitor should be encouraged to boil or chemically treat any water obtained for drinking or cooking.

## Toilets and Sewage

Toilet facilities, ranging from modern flush toilets to primitive pits, are necessary for any recreation development. Toilet buildings should be well lighted, ventilated, and painted. The fixtures should be securely anchored to the floor or walls, and all pipes should be hidden from view in order to reduce vandalism. Skylights permit natural light to enter. In some regions, solar collector panels can be used to heat and cool the building or run fans.

**Dry toilets.** Dry toilets as their name suggests, do not use water. There are several types of dry toilets available.

***Composting toilets.*** A composting toilet has a large tank below the toilet room. Wastes enter the tank directly and decompose in an oxygen-rich environment. No water is used for the toilet, but a bulking agent (such as wood shavings) is added to improve liquid drainage and aeration, and to provide fuel. A small fan draws air through the tank and up the vent pipe to ensure adequate oxygen for decomposition and odorless operation. Internal components (such as ducts, baffles, and rotating tines) enhance the composting process. The finished compost can be removed from the lower end of the tank about once each year. It can be used as a fertilizer for soil.

**Pit or box toilets.** A pit toilet is a hole in the ground with a wooden structure over it. When the hole fills, the toilet is moved and the site is covered with soil. These structures have not disappeared from the park scene. They are used in such areas as small and remote campgrounds, picnic areas, trailheads, small swimming areas, and winter-use areas where freezing weather forces the closure of flush toilets. They are also used where soil percolation is poor and where water is unavailable.

**Vault toilets.** Similar to the pit toilet, the vault toilet is more costly to build, it must be pumped out periodically, and the pumping is a continuous cost. Also, it must be accessible to pump-out trucks that transfer the waste to sewage treatment plants. The main advantage is no need for relocation and more sanitation than a pit toilet. This type of toilet is particularly useful in areas with a high water table.

One of the major problems with vault toilets is improper use. As mentioned above, the vaults require pumping out. Beverage cans, plastic, rocks, sticks, rolls of toilet paper, and other debris that visitors throw into the toilet damage the pumping mechanism. This creates a serious management problem, because contracting firms will not pump at any price if their equipment is going to be damaged. The park manager must somehow convince visitors to use these facilities for the purpose intended and not as garbage cans. Here is an opportunity to use interpretation as a management tool; perhaps a sign could be devised that would persuade visitors to look after this facility for their own sakes.

Portable fiberglass box and hold tank toilets that sit on top of the ground are available commercially and might be necessary in very wet areas, at special events, or where permanent facilities have broken down. In some parks, a supply of these is kept on hand, and as the need arises, they are shifted around. This rotation might also include summer- and winter-use areas. These new toilets are miniature treatment plants, some injecting air into the holding tank to induce bacterial destruction of waste while others use recirculation of odorless oil to carry waste products through a settling tank. In the latter model, the waste sinks and the oil is filtered and used over again.

**Flush toilets.** These are costly to build, have a high water-use rate, and require a reliable water supply. Water is used as a carrier of the waste through pipes to a sewage treatment sytem. Waste can be treated anaerobically or aerobically.

***Anaerobic treatment.*** This type of treatment is handled through a septic tank and drain field. To accommodate a septic tank-drain field system, the soil must "perc," that is be suitable to filter and remove nutrients as the effluent makes its way to the groundwater or other bodies of water. To determine the suitability of the soil, a percolation test is performed.

The advantages for this type of system are easy installation, operation, and maintenance. However, septic systems are not suitable for treating high volumes of sewage over long periods of time. Septic tank solids must be pumped on a regular basis and transported to a sewage treatment system.

***Aerobic treatment.*** This type of treatment forces air through the waste to promote aerobic breakdown of nutrients. Aerobic treatment does not normally produce offensive odors, so the system can be located close to occupied areas. Aeorbic treatment is relatively rapid, requiring less holding time and subsequently less holding space. High-quality effluent can be produced for irrigation and recycled toilet flushing water.

There are several manufacturers of small aerobic treatment plants that are suited for harsh environments and isolated areas. These systems are quick to install, simple to operate and maintain, designed to use the fewest movoing parts, and consistent in effluent quality.

Research is continuing in the disposal of waste, particularly in backcountry areas, where high use in combination with thin soils creates serious problems.

## Dump Stations

Most recreational vehicles today are self-contained, which means they possess toilet holding tanks. To prevent people from emptying these tanks along lonely country roads, provisions must be made for convenient dumping stations. A few gasoline stations offer customers the service of draining their holding tanks. However, to be more effective, the service must be available where the toilet is being used, in the park itself. Dump stations are usually placed somewhat inconspicuously on a pull-through just inside the park on the exit side of the road system. The station itself is quite simple. It consists of a concrete pad over which the recreational vehicle is driven. The pad contains a drain hole leading to a huge holding tank. There is also a hose and water supply used for washing down any spills and for replenishing the vehicle's holding tank.

## Trash Receptacles

The all-important garbage can, litter barrel, or trash receptacle is usually made of metal or plastic. Those made of metal might be steel oil drums with one end removed, aluminum cans, or wire baskets designed to hold trash. Some parks have a take-it-home policy and do not provide such receptacles. Most park managers find it impossible to get along without them.

These cans must be readily available to visitors and maintenance people alike. Most are painted green and have the litter logo on the outside. To prevent loss, they must be chained in place. Even if not anchored with a lock, having a special mounting or base suggests to park visitors that cans should not be moved closer to their site or taken home with them. A supportive base also prevents animals from tipping cans over, a major irritation to employees who have to clean up the mess. This speaks well for having tight-fitting lids in order to keep rodents, flies, and birds from entering the container. The relatively inexpensive, but durable 55-gallon drum has the disadvantage of being heavy when empty; it becomes a backbreaker when full.

Heavy-duty plastic liners make pickup and disposal of garbage a more efficient and less unpleasant task and keep the cans cleaner. Trucks are available today that make loading easy. Some parks now use large containers and self-loading compaction trucks, particularly where visitor use is heavy and great amounts of garbage are generated daily. Private contracting of refuse pickup should be considered where practical. This frees employees for other duties and relieves the park from having to dispose of mountains of garbage. Park managers should keep abreast of up-to-date solid waste disposal concerns and, where possible, to initiate some degree of recycling in their parks.

Raccoons, porcupines, rodents, and even domestic dogs can become a nuisance if waste is not handled properly. Extreme care must be exercised in placement of cans or dumpsters if the area is a bear habitat. Deaths and injuries can result from attracting bears to camping areas.

## The Road System

Roads provide access and introduce human use to remote areas. Even the construction of the road can introduce undesirable plant species to the park. The National Park Service for Hawaii Volcanoes National Park prescribed construction protocol for road contractors to minimize the introduction of exotic species. Road location must be carefully considered to avoid affecting sensitive areas.

The park road system includes entrance roads, public access roads, service roads, and through roads. As these roads provide the main circulation and access to park features, their location must be carefully considered to avoid affecting sensitive areas.

Roads should be located to take best advantage of the topography and scenery with a minimum of disturbance to park features. Designers try to keep cut-and-fill slopes to an absolute minimum in order to reduce road scarring. Where the scenery is favorable and the topography permits, parking is provided to enable visitors, particular the driver, an opportunity to view the scene in a more relaxed manner. These overlooks may include drinking water, toilets, interpretive signs, picnic tables, and a trailhead for a short walking trail.

Park roads are built to different standards than major highways and are not designed for high speeds or exceptionally heavy vehicles. They may have sharper curves, steeper grades, and narrower widths because they are intended for restful, leisurely driving. These standards also make park road construction less expensive than highway construction.

**Entrance roads.** Unfortunately, some drivers do not realize that road standards are different within the park, and therefore they do not adjust their speed. On the road leading into the park, appropriate signage should emphasize the fact that the visitor is entering a territory requiring different driving behavior. A sign merely posting the park speed limit does not tell the driver why he or she should go slower, and results can include frequent confrontations with park rangers, or worse yet, frequent accidents. Interpretive skills will be required to communicate this message. Entrance roads should be few in number to limit administrative problems.

**Access roads.** Access roads provide visitors admittance to campgrounds, picnic areas, food sites, lodging sites, and other developed recreation opportunities. Here again, speeds are much reduced for safety reasons. The use of speed bumps might be appropriate.

**Service roads**. Use of service roads is usually limited to park employees for maintenance, fire control, or other emergency access. These roads are posted as service roads and often have physical barriers at their entrances to keep visitors out.

**Through roads.** Roads that provide transportation to both sides of a park by going through the park rather than around it are difficult to deal with. The degree of difficulty increases if the maintenance of such roads is paid for by another entity. This is especially true if this responsibility is located in a higher level of government, such as state over county, or federal over state.

**Maintenance.** From a maintenance standpoint, the road system requires considerable attention. For every unit of road, there is double the roadside to maintain. Vegetation keeps invading the roadside, loose soil fills the drainage ditches, catch basins and culverts fill with blocking debris, trees fall across the road, and visitors keep tossing out garbage that we politely call litter. The signs need replacing, the grass and weeds must be mowed, the road surface must be patched, and the center stripe must be repainted. Gravel roads need to be bladed to control drainage, remove loose material, fill ruts, and level washboard. Dust might have to be controlled in heavy-use areas. The road system requires constant attention from the park staff.

## Parking Areas

Parking lots are intended to provide temporary storage for visitors' cars in an area where the planner and, presumably, the manager want them. They are also an excellent management tool for regulating numbers of people, distributing them evenly over the park, and protecting the rest of the park from damage.

Parking lots are a major component in the design of any park layout. The size and shape vary because of basic requirements. Most are for grouped day-use activities, such as picnicking and swimming, and often one lot can be designed to serve several activities. On the other hand, some lots serve a specific activity, such as boat launching. In the case of overnight camping, a private parking slot comes in the form of a spur or pull-through. Most park visitors, particularly those staying overnight wish to be close to the vehicle that brought them to the park, both for convenience and for security reasons. Parking lots are also found at trailheads and specific points of interest, such as overlooks.

In locating a parking lot, the planner must consider several factors: the traffic problem it will create or solve, the proximity of the lot to the activity it serves, the extent of intrusion on the activity, the intrusion on the natural landscape, the size, the potential for expansion should it be needed, and the impact on the site.

The construction and use of a parking lot impacts any site, but it may bring other problems as well. A classic example is seen in Arizona's Petrified Forest National Park. If people can park near the fossilized wood, it disappears. If people have to walk any distance from the petrified wood to their car, the wood remains undisturbed. A site known as Crystal Forest illustrates this point. The park roadway bisects this area. One side of the roadway has a parking lot, and the other does not. The side adjacent to the parking lot is nearly bare of small pieces of petrified wood; the side without the parking lot area appears in sharp contrast.

Large lots may be necessary where heavy use demands the accommodation. Where possible, the planner tries to break up solid parking areas with a median strip between the parking lanes and to blend the development into the natural surroundings. Tree plantings provide shade, manage run-off, and soften the harshness of paving and rows of cars, providing a suitable transition to the more natural area beyond. To prevent problems, such as cars slipping their brakes, all parking areas should be level.

Special care should be taken in the design and construction of parking areas for amphitheaters to ensure that vehicle lights will not interfere with the presentation on the screen.

The parking facility cannot be designed to accommodate peak holiday use. Even on ordinary weekends, the lot may fill and people will have to be turned away. On such days, traffic will become congested at park entrances and people will park along the shoulders of the approach roads, thus causing problems in another jurisdiction. Parking must be limited to the designed capacity of the parking lot; limitations were imposed to operate in just such situations to protect the resource from overuse.

## Traffic Control and Parking Barriers

These are intended to keep cars where the planner and the manager want them, on the roads, parking lots, and parking spurs. Individual barrier devices made of a variety of materials include native rock boulders, precast concrete posts, wood posts, logs, concrete curbing, or wood curbing. Guardrails made of steel or wood are another type of barrier. These are mounted on concrete or masonry posts. The purpose of the traffic control device, as the name implies, is to protect the visitor from dangerous places, and to protect park resources from visitors. Rows of trees and shrubs serve as living barriers along roadways, but are not too effective in campgrounds, where continuous abuse form autos eventually kills barrier vegetation. The simplest yet most effective barrier is street curbing. Urban dwellers understand its purpose. In contrast to this, the large log or boulder presents a challenge. Visitors seem to want to move such barriers out of the way as though they were there by chance and simply represent an inconvenience. Barriers should be esthetically pleasing, or at least not offensive, while meeting safety and administrative requirements.

## Signs

Visitors depend on signs for guidance, information, and safety. Managers use signs to inform visitors of hazards, to denote regulations, and to control traffic. Where recreational uses might overlap, signs are necessary to assist in the avoidance of conflict. Signs should intrude as little as possible on a site yet be conspicuous where needed. The size of the sign and letter size varies with use and agency policy. A person on foot reading a sign has a different need than someone traveling in a car. Wording should be brief and positive, and the text should be in lowercase letters. Some parks maintain an electronic file of sign messages. The scripts are easily retrievable and do not need to be rewritten should the sign be stolen or damaged and need replacement. A note of caution: The wording on a sign might be grounds for a lawsuit in case of an accident. It is essential that the agency legal staff review the proposed wording on any signs used so as to avoid lawsuits.

Sign materials are usually wood or metal or a combination of the two. Posts are made of concrete, metal, or durable or preservative-treated wood. The choice of materials is often ruled by problems of weathering, vandalism, maintenance, and replacement costs. Park or agency policy also may be decisive; for example, some agencies require all sign panels be made of metal. In others, particularly the older parks, the signs are all made from wood. The lettering is sometimes routed directly on the wood, or it might be painted or silkscreened on the wood or metal.

Carefully maintained signs foster an attitude of respect for the park and its facilities. Directional signs leading to the park are most often the responsibility of another agency, usually the Highway Department or Department of Transportation. Where possible, a sign manual covering agency policy on specifications, construction methods, maintenance, and ordering procedures should be used. If none exists, one should be written following examples already established by some agencies.

## The Community Kitchen or Picnic Shelter

Used by small to large groups in inclement weather or hot sun, this concrete-floored structure is usually roofed with open sides. It commonly contains large, wood-burning stoves or metered gas or electric stoves, sinks equipped with running water, serving counters, and picnic tables. This facility is usually located near the group picnic areas. If constructed of wood, it must be made of pressure-treated timbers to extend its life and reduce maintenance costs.

The design should fit the landscape. Some modern shelters are constructed of precast concrete frames and laminated wood beams and can accommodate anywhere from one to more than 50 picnic tables.

## Picnic Tables

The picnic table is the basic facility in picnic areas and campgrounds. The style and condition of the tables are major factors in the appearance of the site. They must be sturdy to withstand concentrated abuse and exposure to the weather.

Picnic tables are commonly made of pressure-treated wood, precast concrete, masonry, fiberglass, metal (usually galvanized iron pipe or aluminum tubing), or a combination of these materials. The hardware should be rust resistant. On those parts of the table and bench where bare skin or food comes in contact with wood, toxic preservatives, such as pentachlorophenol should not be used. A high-quality wooden table is usually finished with exterior varnish, plastic, or other synthetic finish.

The choice of table design is governed by suitability and availability of materials, custom, cost, and the type of park and landscape. For example, massive rustic tables usually blend with the scenic qualities and withstand the demands of a national park or forest, whereas a light wooden and metal table may better fit a neighborhood park.

A standardized design within a park or park system is advantageous because it allows for interchangeable parts, ease of transportation and storage, and most important of all, mass production in construction. Some park agencies construct their own tables during the slack season, others depend on institutional labor, and still others purchase their tables from commercial suppliers.

The popular wooden table of a few years back utilizing round, peeled logs for the under parts and machined wood for the seats and tops, is giving way to the all-machined wooden table or to one with pipe legs simply because the latter models lend themselves better to mass production methods and generally cost less to maintain.

Maintenance is important in determining the life of a table. The tables and benches should be constructed so planks can be removed every few years for refinishing. A smooth surface is more attractive, easier to wipe clean, and less likely to snag clothing. Also, a defaced or weathered surface may invite more carving or other abuse. Broken and unsafe parts, loose hardware, and unsightly surfaces should be promptly repaired.

Lighter tables are more convenient for park personnel, but also make it possible for visitors to move the tables. Generally the policy is to anchor tables in place to prevent theft and the tendency for ever-expanding site deterioration. In heavily used areas, the table site should be hardened with a concrete pad, gravel, or wood chips.

It is also important that managers are aware of requirement to include accessible tables for patrons who may have disabilities. If one fixed table is provided, it is necessary to supply a table for accessibility reasons. Park managers must disperse these tables among a variety of areas and not seclude them to a particular setting. The choices for seating areas should be similar to those of the able-bodied visitors. An average accessible table has the dimensions of ten feet long by two and a half feet wide. Each seating space will provide knee space of at least 30 inches wide, 19 inches deep, and 27 inches from ground to the bottom of the table top. As for clearance, it is required that there is a 36-inch minimum clear space surrounding the usable sections of the table. Park managers must become knowledgeable and aware of the requirements necessary for all visitors to equally participate in outdoor recreation.

## Outdoor Stoves and Grills

The dream unit that could be used for an evening campfire, be converted to a waist-level cooking stove, and be theft proof, indestructible, and easily fabricated in the park shop is not yet on the market. Some designers have come close, but in the meantime, compromise is still necessary.

Probably no park facility has undergone a more complete transition than the park stove or fireplace. It has gone from a simple ring of rocks to an elaborate fireplace with firebox, grill, and chimney to the all-metal, waist-level, pipe-supported grill that can be swiveled to face the wind. Several ground-level stoves have been built that permit easy cleaning, swivel to face the wind, have adequate flat surface to hold several pans and do not disintegrate when cold water is thrown on hot parts, but they are still backbreakers when used for cooking.

The waist-level charcoal grill is convenient for cooking but is not practical for the evening campfire. Perhaps it's asking too much of a facility to serve both cooking and campfire purposes. Therefore, perhaps one should place the high grill in day-use areas and the ground stove in overnight sites. The design is a matter of meeting local needs. The manager can expect complaints from both kinds of users.

## Fireplaces or Stoves

These are found in the community kitchen or picnic shelter. The design includes a chimney for smoke draft, a metal or brick firebox, a steel grill, and brick or native stove masonry on the outside. Perhaps there will be a built-in fuel bin. Such a facility is expensive to build and subject to damage from freezing and thawing in cold climates. Once common outside, they are gradually being replaced with cheaper ground-level stoves. Their use in picnic shelters is probably not as great as it once was, because there are now many convenient ways of cooking and transporting hot food. It is no longer necessary to fire up the big stove and cook on site.

## Fire Ring

The fire ring is used largely at night for "recreational fires" for social gatherings, wiener or marshmallow roasts, or warming. It is constructed of plate, metal, or corrugated culvert set in the ground. The ring size varies depending on use from two feet (0.6 meters) for family groups to six feet (two meters) for small campfire programs or skating pond warming fires. The fire ring is usually circled with benches or logs.

## Trail Bridges

Trail bridges must serve hikers, bicyclists, horseback riders, and maintenance vehicles. In some instances, one bridge must do all of these, and in other places, it may be designed to support foot traffic only. Materials for trail bridges include concrete or wood supports, wood stringers, and wood decking. Laminated arch beams are also used. All wood must be seasoned and treated with preservatives. Most footbridges over shallow stream crossings need not have handrails; however, a footbridge over three feet (one meter) high should have at least one handrail. Rustic-style footbridges are suitable in a forest setting and are often photographed as backgrounds for family pictures.

**Figure 10.6. This bridge was designed to support a variety of recreation activities, such walking, biking, and blading, and it provides access for maintenance.**

Photo courtesy of Hannah Lang.

## Docks

These are needed to provide access to water for swimming, fishing, or boat mooring. One dock should not be expected to serve all three purposes because of the conflict between uses and the specific design needs. Use should be limited to that for which it was designed; for example, swimming should be prohibited from fishing and boat docks.

Bottom and water conditions vary greatly. Some bottoms are soft and will accept driven piles; others, because they are rocky, will not. The water surface may fluctuate greatly between summer and winter or even daily in tidal areas. In some areas, there will be thick ice that can rip a dock apart.

Some docks must be designed to float in order to fluctuate with the water level. Flotation is provided by large steel drums, Styrofoam, or logs. Other docks, of a cantilever design, are built out over the water and can be raised above the ice level in winter. Some use permanent rock cribs as foundations; here the decking is removed before the lake freezes over. In others, everything is portable and must be removed before the winter freeze. Where winters are mild and the lake level remains relatively constant, docks can be built in a more permanent manner.

## Boat Ramps

The ramp, usually constructed of reinforced concrete slabs, should be at least 10 to 15 feet (three to 4.5 meters) wide and be long enough to be usable at any water level. On some reservoirs, this can be a considerable distance during the drawdown. The preferred grade is between 8 and 15 percent. The water beyond the ramp should be free of hidden obstacles. A trailer parking area is necessary; boaters will appreciate one designed with drive-through stalls.

Separating the ramp from the swimming area will reduce conflicts and minimize swimmer contact with propellers or pollution from oil spills.

## Lifeguard Towers

These structures are used by lifeguards while on duty at swimming beaches. They should be high enough to provide an unobstructed view of the entire swimming area because the lifeguard is in charge of all beach and water activities.

A sign should state that these towers are intended exclusively for the use of lifeguards. No one else should be on them, whether or not the guard is on duty. A sign should also inform the public of the hours during which lifeguard protection is available.

A roof or umbrella should be available to shade the person on duty. Other equipment needed by the lifeguard includes a megaphone, a first-aid kit, blankets, a stretcher, a surfboard or torpedo buoy with rope, and a lifeboat with oars. A two-way radio is advantageous if the park uses such a system.

## The Bathhouse

The bathhouse is a changing facility for swimmers and may include lockers, a hose or shower, toilets, and separate dressing rooms for men and women. When a food concession is part of the bathhouse operation, the concessionaire usually is responsible for this facility. The one exception would be the first-aid room, which is usually the lifeguard's responsibility.

In parks where the visitor load is relatively small, a simple changing shelter may be all that is necessary. The structure is often roofless so that it can be dried by sunlight. Care must be exercised that nearby trees or cliffs do not provide "viewpoints."

## Bulletin Boards

These are located at roadside pull offs, overlooks, trailheads, trail sides, historical structures, or other points of concentration in parks where essential information or interpretive messages are provided for visitors.

A wide overhanging roof provides protection from rain and helps reduce glare. The plate glass covering, which protects the materials, should slope outward at the top to further reduce glare and annoying reflections. This sloping surface also reduces the amount of bird droppings that accumulate on the glass.

Materials used vary greatly. Some consist of outdoor plywood and metal posts, while others use sturdy timbers and a roof of shakes or shingles. Massive structures of timber and stonemasonry are found in areas of heavy snowpack.Useful bulletin board materials include maps and a list of park services and regulations. Information on what to see and do and where to purchase camp items should also be posted, and there should be space for visitors to leave each other messages (see chapter 17). Interpretation, if offered, should be concerned with features in the immediate area.

**Vegetation**

Plants are facilities also, in the broad sense, as many shrubs and small trees are brought in and planted. Plantings beautify an area, break up monotonous developments, provide shade, and control traffic and erosion. Vegetation between campsites provides privacy and screening, and in other areas it can hide landfills or maintenance buildings and equipment.

Plants are also a focus for problems. Theft and damage are ever-present possibilities. In parking lots, trees shed their leaves, break up pavement with their roots, or drop their limbs. Trees will eventually fall and are thus a liability, as discussed in chapter 4, Recreation Laws and Liabilities.

## ENERGY AND FACILITIES

Certain park facilities require energy in the form of fuel or electricity for heat or light. The cost of energy will in all probability continue to increase, so energy-saving devices should be considered in the design of all new park buildings. This would include the use of insulation, weather-stripping, and building materials that resist heat transfer. It is also possible to use solar panels in the roofs of park buildings; the water supply for restrooms, shower facilities, and pools can be heated in this way. Park managers along coastal areas, mountains, prairies, or other windy areas should consider the use of windmills to generate electricity. Park agencies should assume a leadership role in utilizing solar heating and wind systems. Park facilities often have the required acreage to support the installation of thermal heating systems. Thermal heating reduces consumption requirements and in turn, operational costs.

How can the park manager contribute to energy conservation? Stopping waste is one way. Other methods include having employees walk or ride bicycles when possible rather than driving, turning off lights when not needed, turning down building thermostats, checking insulation in all appropriate areas, reducing water consumption to save both water and electricity for pumping and heating, and promptly repairing dripping faucets. Recycling aluminum cans, glass, paper, and other materials should be considered a requirement except in unusual circumstances. Solid waste management is covered in the next chapter.

Energy conservation will require cooperation from both employees and park visitors. Imaginative interpretation could assist in making energy conservation goals important to both groups. Managers must have a firm commitment and be willing to inconvenience themselves in order to set a good example.

## CONCLUSION

Park facilities may be built to prevent visitor impact, channel visitor use, provide convenience to visitors, prevent theft or vandalism, fulfill safety requirements, enhance the quality of the park experience, provide utilities, assist in management operations, or comply with the law. Maintaining these facilities and seeing that they are not misused is an essential part of the manager's job.

Managers come and managers go, but the facilities stay, aging and enduring. Eventually they will wear out or perhaps lose popularity, and other facilities of one kind or another will replace them. In both planning and replacement, informed choices are necessary in order to avoid basic problems.

## REFERENCES

**References Cited**

Allwood, J., & Taylor, R. (1980). "Signs of the Times," *Parks Magazine, 5*(1):20-21.

American Association of State Highway and Transportation Officials. (1999). *Guideline for the Development of Bicycle Facilities* (3rd ed.).    https://bookstore.transportation.org/item_details. aspx?ID=104

American Camp Association. (2010). Accreditation and Standards. http://www.acacamps.org/accreditation

Douglass, R. W. (1982). *Forest recreation* (3rd ed.). Elmsford, NY: Pergamon Press, Inc.

Federal Register 26CFR Part 1195. (2007). Architectural Barriers Act (ABA) Accessibility Guidelines for Outdoor Recreation Developed Areas. http://www.access-board.gov/outdoor/preamble.htm.

Hill, D. E. (1966). *Percolation testing for septic tank drainage.* Bulletin No. 678. New Haven: Connecticut Agricultural Stn.

Landsberg, H. H. (1964). *Natural resources for U.S. growth.* Baltimore, MD: Johns-Hopkins.

National Park Service. (2010). Accessible to Everyone. http://www.nps.gov/pub_aff/access/index.htm

National Trails Training Partnership. (2010). Accessible Trails. http://www.americantrails.org/resources/accessible/ADAcoloDec.html

Patterson, J. C., & Rodgers, C. (1979). "Static Pile composting–A Waste Treatment Alternative," Grist. *Park Practice Program, 23*(3):17,23-24.

U.S. Access Board. (2010). ADA Standards. http://www.access-board.gov/ada/index.htm

U.S.Access Board. (2010). Outdoor Developed Areas. http://www.access-board.gov/outdoor/index.htm

U.S. Department of Justice. (2010). 2010 ADA Standards for Accessible Design. http://www.ada.gov/regs2010/2010ADAStandards/2010ADAstandards.htm

U.S. Department of the Interior. (1980). *A guide to designing accessible outdoor recreation facilities.* Ann Arbor, MI: Heritage Conservation and Recreation Service.

U.S. Department of the Interior. (1993). Guiding Principles of Sustainable Design, www.andropogon.com/www.accessiblenaturetravel.com

**General References**

American Camping Association. (1980). *Camp standards with interpretations for the accreditation of organized camps.* Martinsville, IN: ACA.

Fight, R. D. (1980). *Planners guide for estimating cost per user-day of proposed recreational facilities.* General Technical Report PNW-110. Portland, OR: USDA Pacific Northwest Forest and Range Experiment Station.

Goldthorp, A. (1980). "Access Requirements for Disabled in National Parks," *Parks Magazine, 4*(4):13-15.

Good, A. H. (1990). *Directory of technical assistance materials for trails, development and assistance.* Washington, D.C.: American Hiking Society.

Jubenville, A., Twight, B. W., & Becker, R. H. (1987). *Outdoor recreation management: Theory and application.* State College, PA: Venture.

Little, C. E. (1990). *Greenway for America.* Baltimore, MD: Johns Hopkins.

Morton, W. B., & Hume, G. L. (1979). *Standards for historic preservation projects.* Washington, D.C.: Department of the Interior.

National Park Service. (1990). *Keepers of the treasures.* A report on Tribal Preservation Funding Needs. Washington, D.C.: NPS.

Olson, D. (1981). "Energy Saving in Ohio State Parks," *Trends Park Practice Program, 18*(2):12-17.

"Trends in Energy Management." (1982). A complete issue of Trends consisting of 16 articles devoted to energy and park management. *Park Practice Program 18*(2).

Wagar, J. A. (1963). *Campgrounds for many tastes.* Ogden, UT: USD Intermt. Forest and Range Exp. Stn.

# Appendix A

## Comparison of American Association of State Highway and Transportation Officials (AASHTO) Guidelines for Bicycle Facilities and the Proposed Guidelines for Trails

| Outdoor Developed Areas Accessibility Guidelines | AASHTO Guide for the Development of Bicycle Facilities |
|---|---|
| T303.3 Surface: Firm and stable | Bicycles need the same firmness and stability as wheel chairs; skaters usually require a smooth, paved surface. Most shared use paths are paved, although crushed aggregate surfaces are used on some paths. |
| T303.4 Clear Tread Width: 36 inches (3 feet; 915 mm); exception for 32 inches (815 mm) | Shared use paths usually require a minimum 3 meter (10 foot) width, plus a 0.6 meter (2 foot) safety buffer on both sides. A 2.4 m (8 foot) width may be allowed in low use facilities. Posts or bollards installed to restrict motor vehicle traffic should be spaced 1.5 m (5 feet) apart. Posts or bollards should be brightly painted and reflectorized for visibility. When more than one post is used, use an odd number, with one on the centerline to help direct opposing traffic. |
| T303.5 Openings (Gaps): To prevent wheelchair wheels and cane tips from being caught in surface openings or gaps, openings in trail surfaces shall be of a size which does not permit passage of a ½ inch (13 mm) diameter sphere; elongated openings must be perpendicular or diagonal to the direction of travel; exception to permit parallel direction elongated openings if openings do not permit passage of a ¼ inch (6 mm) sphere; second exception to permit openings which do not permit passage of a ¾ inch (19 mm) sphere. | The AASHTO Guide does not specify a maximum for a surface opening, but openings should be minimized. Openings should not permit a bicycle wheel to enter. Grates should be flush with the surface, and elongated openings should be perpendicular to the direction of travel (diagonal openings are more difficult for bicyclists to negotiate). Where openings are unavoidable, they should be clearly marked. |
| T322.1 Protruding Objects: T405 provide a warning if vertical clearance is less than 80 inches (2030 mm) | Protruding objects should not exist within the clear tread width of a shared use path. Vertical clearance on shared use paths should be a minimum of 3 m (10 feet) or the full clear width including safety buffers. Where vertical barriers and obstructions, such as abutments, piers, and other features are unavoidable, they should be clearly marked. |
| T303.6 Tread Obstacles (Changes in level, roots, rocks, ruts): Up to 2 inches (50 mm); exception up to 3 inches (75 mm) | Tread obstacles are hazardous to bicyclists and skaters. The surface of a shared use path should be smooth and should not have tread obstacles. |
| T303.7 Passing Space: At least 60 inches (1525 mm) width within 1,000 foot (300 m) intervals. Advisory recommends more frequent intervals for some trail segments | Shared use paths should have a minimum clear width of 3 m (10 feet); exception for 2.4 m (8 feet). |

## Appendix A (cont.)

### Comparison of American Association of State Highway and Transportation Officials (AASHTO) Guidelines for Bicycle Facilities and the Proposed Guidelines for Trails

| Outdoor Developed Areas Accessibility Guidelines | AASHTO Guide for the Development of Bicycle Facilities |
|---|---|
| T303.3 Surface: Firm and stable | Bicycles need the same firmness and stability as wheel chairs; skaters usually require a smooth, paved surface. Most shared use paths are paved, although crushed aggregate surfaces are used on some paths. |
| T303.4 Clear Tread Width: 36 inches (3 feet; 915 mm); exception for 32 inches (815 mm) | Shared use paths usually require a minimum 3 meter (10 foot) width, plus a 0.6 meter (2 foot) safety buffer on both sides. A 2.4 m (8 foot) width may be allowed in low use facilities. Posts or bollards installed to restrict motor vehicle traffic should be spaced 1.5 m (5 feet) apart. Posts or bollards should be brightly painted and reflectorized for visibility. When more than one post is used, use an odd number, with one on the centerline to help direct opposing traffic. |
| T303.5 Openings (Gaps): To prevent wheelchair wheels and cane tips from being caught in surface openings or gaps, openings in trail surfaces shall be of a size which does not permit passage of a ½ inch (13 mm) diameter sphere; elongated openings must be perpendicular or diagonal to the direction of travel; exception to permit parallel direction elongated openings if openings do not permit passage of a ¼ inch (6 mm) sphere; second exception to permit openings which do not permit passage of a ¾ inch (19 mm) sphere. | The AASHTO Guide does not specify a maximum for a surface opening, but openings should be minimized. Openings should not permit a bicycle wheel to enter. Grates should be flush with the surface, and elongated openings should be perpendicular to the direction of travel (diagonal openings are more difficult for bicyclists to negotiate). Where openings are unavoidable, they should be clearly marked. |
| T322.1 Protruding Objects: T405 provide a warning if vertical clearance is less than 80 inches (2030 mm) | Protruding objects should not exist within the clear tread width of a shared use path. Vertical clearance on shared use paths should be a minimum of 3 m (10 feet) or the full clear width including safety buffers. Where vertical barriers and obstructions, such as abutments, piers, and other features are unavoidable, they should be clearly marked. |
| T303.6 Tread Obstacles (Changes in level, roots, rocks, ruts): Up to 2 inches (50 mm); exception up to 3 inches (75 mm) | Tread obstacles are hazardous to bicyclists and skaters. The surface of a shared use path should be smooth and should not have tread obstacles. |
| T303.7 Passing Space: At least 60 inches (1525 mm) width within 1,000 foot (300 m) intervals. Advisory recommends more frequent intervals for some trail segments | Shared use paths should have a minimum clear width of 3 m (10 feet); exception for 2.4 m (8 feet). |

# Appendix A (cont.)

T303.8.1 Cross Slope:
1:20 (5%) maximum; exceptions for open drains up to 1:10 (10%)

For drainage, shared use paths should have a minimum 2 percent (1:50) cross slope on a paved surface. On unpaved shared use paths, particular attention should be paid to drainage to avoid erosion. Curves on shared use paths may require super elevation beyond 2% (1:50) for safety reasons. The Guide suggests limited cross slope for accessibility reasons.

T303.8.2 Running Slope:
1:20 (5%) any length
1:12 (8.33%) for up to 200 feet
1:10 (10%) for up to 30 feet
1:8 (12.5%) for up to 10 feet
No more than 30% of the total trail length shall exceed 1:12

Running slopes on shared use paths should be kept to a minimum; grades greater than 5 percent are undesirable. Grades steeper than 3 percent may not be practical for shared use paths with crushed stone or other unpaved surfaces. Where terrain dictates, grade lengths are recommended as follows:
< 5% (< 1:20) any length
5-6% (1:20-16.7) for up to 240 m (800 feet)
7% (1:14.3) for up to 120 m (400 feet)
8% (1:12.5) for up to 90 m (300 feet)
9% (1:11.1) for up to 60 m (200 feet)
10% (1:10) for up to 30 m (100 feet)
11+% (1:9.1) for up to 15 m (50 feet)

T303.9 Resting Intervals:
Size: 60 inch (1525 mm) length, at least as wide as the widest trail segment adjacent to the rest area. Less than 1:20 (5%) slope in all directions. Resting areas are required where trail running slopes exceed 1:20 (5%), at intervals no greater than the lengths permitted under running slope (see T302.6.2 above).

The Guide does not address resting intervals.

T303.10 Edge Protection:
Where provided, 3 inch (75 mm) minimum height. Handrails are not required.

The Guide does not address edge protection. Some kinds of edge protection may be hazardous to bicyclists and skaters. The Guide has minimum railing height recommendations when needed for safety reasons.

T222 Trail Signs:
Accessible trails require designation with a symbol of accessibility, and information on total length of the accessible segment. No traffic control sign information.

Guidance on signing and marking is provided in the Manual on Uniform Traffic Control Devices (MUTCD), incorporated by reference as a Federal regulation (23 CFR 655.601). A proposed amendment for Part 9 (Traffic Controls for Bicycle Facilities) was published in the Federal Register on June 24, 1999 (64 FR 33802).

The "Guide for the Development of Bicycle Facilities" is available through the American Association of State Highway and Transportation Officials (AASHTO), 444 North Capitol Street, NW, Suite 249, Washington, DC 20001, (202) 624-5800, fax (202) 624-5806, https://bookstore.transportation.org/ Reprinted with permission)

# Appendix B

## Critical Path for Developing the Park and Recreation Master Plan
### Waterloo, Iowa

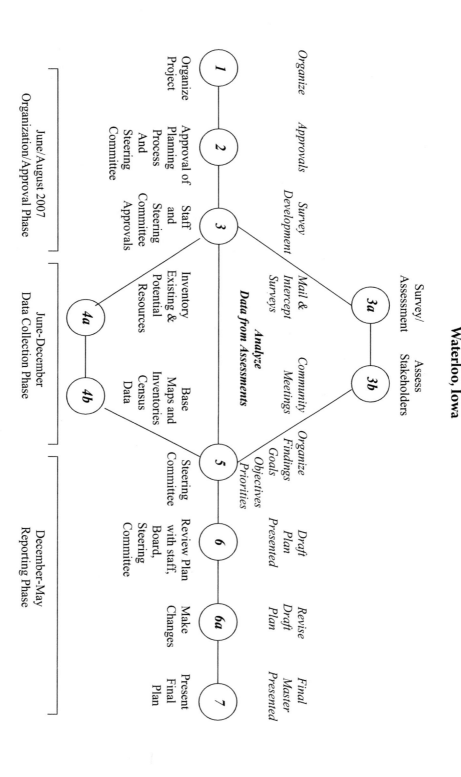

*Chapter Eleven*

# Environmental Management Issues

## THE PARK ECOSYSTEM AND NATURAL SYSTEM

Park managers and the public need to be aware of the environmental issues that pertain to the land and water areas in which they visit and work. Importantly, there needs to be an understanding of the notions of conservation, ecosystems, and the natural environment, as well as some of the management strategies.

The natural environment encompasses all living and non-living things occurring naturally within a region. There are two general components, the ecological units (vegetation, wildlife, soils, geologic structures etc.) and natural resources such as air, water, climate, etc. This can be contrasted with the built environment that humans influenced.

Ecosystem refers to the combined physical and biological components of an environment. Typically, it is an area within the natural environment in which physical (abiotic) factors such as rocks and soil, function together along with interdependent (biotic) organisms, such as plants and animals, within the same habitat. Some parks have specific ecosystems that are not found in other places on the planet, creating the need for aggressive park-management strategies.

Conservation is concerned with resource use, allocation, and protection. This is a primary function of park management. Generally speaking, conservationists attempt to monitor and maintain the health of the fisheries, habitats, and biological diversity. Conservationists are also concerned with energy and materials use. Park managers may be referred to as conservationists. It is important to note that conservation implies use of the resource.

A nature reserve (natural reserve, nature preserve, natural preserve) is a protected area of importance for wildlife, flora, fauna, or features of geological or other special interest, which is reserved and managed for conservation and to provide special opportunities for study or research. Nature reserves may be designated by government institutions in some countries, or by private landowners, such as charities and research institutions, regardless of nationality.

The Wilderness Act states: "A wilderness, in contrast with those areas where man and his own works dominate the landscape, is hereby recognized as an area where the earth and its community of life are untrammeled by man, where man himself is a visitor who does not remain (http://wilderness.nps.gov/factsnew.cfm, 2010). Wilderness has two dimensions that create the need for specific park-management strategies: (1) A place that is mostly biologically intact, and (2) A place that is legally protected so that it remains wild and free of industrial infrastructure, and open to traditional indigenous use, or low-impact recreation (http://www.wild.org/main/about/what-is-a-wilderness-area/). It should be noted that a wilderness may not be pristine, as humans have impacted nearly every place on the planet. Yet, the preservation of areas that have had minor impact may qualify a large tract of land to be within a wilderness preserve. Wilderness areas are protected for a broad range of biological, social, economic, spiritual, and recreational benefits.

### Environmental Management Issues

As attendance at park areas increases, greater pressure is put on fragile park ecosystems. What limitations should the manager impose on the number of visitors in order to reduce this pressure? What level of damage is tolerable? How does the manager judge the point at which crowding or trampling is destroying the very park resources the visitors came to enjoy? Is this concern with limiting use the province of the park manager? There are no clear-cut answers to these questions. Agencies vary in their ability to react to problems of this kind. However, park managers must address these issues. These issues concern not only land-based parks, but marine life parks and aquatic areas as well.

All natural resources are subject to human manipulation, overuse, or inappropriate use. Unfortunately, past environmental alterations have sometimes been characterized by opportunism and inadequate planning. The consequences of this in regard to soil, water, vegetation, marine and aquatic life, and wildlife have frequently been disruptive of natural processes. Dumping of raw industrial and municipal waste into streams and lakes, destruction of soil through poor agricultural practices, eradication of cover, and intensive unregulated hunting are examples of negative manipulation. A recent assessment of the natural resources of the national park system documented six common issues of concern (National Park Service, 2006).

1.  Exotic, feral, and pest animals and plants are changing park ecosystems.
2.  Park ecosystems still show effects from historic, disruptive activities and need rehabilitation.
3.  Recreational visitors are affecting park ecosystems.
4.  Consumptive uses within parks are affecting park ecosystems.
5.  Watershed development, air shed development, and other activities outside parks are affecting park water and air resources.
6.  Urban development along park boundaries is affecting park ecosystems and interrupting larger ecosystems on which parks depend.

These issues are not unique to national parks, but apply to most parks and protected areas at all levels of public or private management. In 2009, the National Park Service Director, Jonathan Jarvis, described climate change to Todd Wilkinson of *The Christian Science Monitor* as "the greatest challenge ever to face national parks."

Jarvis hopes boosting the agency's $2.5 billion budget will help fund scientific research and education efforts about global warming, Wilkinson reports. Jarvis, the first park service director to be trained as a biologist, says the parks could sequester carbon, serve as sanctuaries for species facing extinction, and bring to public attention the ways global warming is transforming the environment. His first goal, Wilkinson writes, is "to ensure that peer-reviewed science plays a foundational role in management decisions, especially in confronting climate change" (http://irjci. blogspot.com/2009/10/new-park-service-director-global.html).

The following broad and *general issues of ecosystem management* have become primary concerns for park management.

*   **Ecosystems**—biodiversity, coral bleaching (harvesting corals for profit and for fishing by using bleach),  wildlife habitat destruction that also results in forms of fragmenting large habitat areas, and the larger issue of global warming
*   **Fishing**—Blast fishing, gill netting, illegal and unregulated fishing, overfishing, and marine pollution
*   **Forests**—clear cutting, deforestation, and illegal cutting of trees
*   **Resources**—general depletion of natural resources and exploitation for profit from the resources, such as development of open space, logging, mineral extraction, and collecting items (rocks, gems, shells, corals) for sale to tourists
*   **Species**—habitat destruction from development, roads, trails and facilities, introduction of Invasive species and the lack of ability to control these species, poaching,  species extinction, delisting of animals such as wolves and grizzly bears for hunting, and wildlife trade

Some broad environmental issues due to human activities are impacting the natural environments of parks and preserves are also becoming prominent concerns for management.

- **Anoxic waters**—from chemicals and lack of replenishment leading to hypoxia, (ocean and lake de-oxygenation) and the resulting in dead zones
- **Climate change**—resulting in warming of arctic areas, severe weather patterns, flooding, drought, rising sea levels, ocean and lake acidification, and disruption of marine and mammal migrations
- **Conservation**—concerns for species extinction, coral reefs and marine life, water practices and mitigation measure, and endangered wildlife
- **Dams**—environmental impacts of dams
- **Energy**—energy conservation, renewable energy, efficiency, extraction and generation of energy
- **Environmental degradation**—eutrophication, habitat destruction, and invasive species
- **Environmental health**—air quality (indoor and outdoor) resulting in lung diseases and increases in asthma, electromagnetic fields, and radiation
- **Genetic engineering**—genetic pollution, genetically modified food controversies
- **Intensive farming and illegal growing of marijuana**—overgrazing, irrigation, monoculture, pesticide drift, diversion of water and use of chemicals for growing marijuana
- **Land degradation**—general land pollution and litter, desertification
- **Soil**—soil conservation, erosion, contamination, and salination
- **Land use**—urban sprawl, gateway development near parks, habitat fragmentation, and destruction
- **Overpopulation**—causing increased burial sites, water crises, tragedy of the commons
- **Pollution**—light, visual, noise pollution, nonpoint and point source pollution
- **Water pollution**—Acid rain, eutrophication, marine pollution and debris, ocean dumping and plastics, oil spills, urban runoff and storm water management, oil spills, urban water runoff, water crisis, ship and boat pollution and wastewater, fish kills and algae blooms
- **Air pollution**—smog and ozone depletion, indoor air quality, particulate matter
- **Resource depletion**—exploitation of natural resources
- **Consumerism**—consumer capitalism, and over-consumption
- **Fishing**—blast and cyanide fishing, bottom trawling, ghost nets, illegal, unreported, and unregulated fishing, overfishing, shark finning, whaling
- **Logging**—clearcutting, deforestation, and illegal logging
- **Mining**—acid mine drainage, mountaintop removal mining, slurry impoundments
- **Toxins**—chlorofluorocarbons, DDT, endocrine disruptors, Dioxin, toxic heavy metals, herbicides, pesticides, toxic waste, PCB, bioaccumulation, biomagnification
- **Waste**—e-waste, litter, waste disposal incidents, marine debris, medical waste, landfill, leachate, recycling, incineration, Great Pacific Garbage Patch

From a marine park perspective, Guam has recognized the impacts of recreational use on their coral reef system, which has in turn caused depletion of the diversity of fish in the area in Table 11.1.

**Table 11.1. Examples of Recreational and Commercial Impacts
on Coral Reef Systems in Guam**

| Activity | Actual and/or Potential Impacts |
|---|---|
| Snorkeling | Kicking up sediment, which increases turbidity and reduces light levels; Physical damage (breakage, lesions) due to:<br>• Touching or accidentally finning<br>• Poorly selected points of entry<br>• Standing or resting on corals |
| SCUBA diving | Physical damage (breakage, lesions) due to:<br>• Poor buoyancy control<br>• Wearing of excessive weight<br>• Touching or accidentally finning<br>• Poorly selected points of entry<br>• Standing or resting on corals<br>• Chasing or harassing marine life |
| Fish feeding | Alters wildlife behavior and increases Dependency |
| Boating | Physical damage from anchoring and grounding |
| Kayaking/Canoeing | Physical damage due to paddle strikes and accidental grounding |
| Paddle-boating | Physical damage from accidental grounding |
| Collecting (shells,corals, etc.) | Threatening survival of rare species and contributing to over-exploitation |

From Department of Agriculture, Guam http://www.marinepreserves.com/. Reprinted with permission.

As one can comprehend from the above information, park management also has become more involved in the broad field of environmental management. Randolf (2004) notes that environmental management is the means of controlling or guiding human-environment interactions to protect and enhance human health and welfare and environmental quality. These interactions can affect human welfare and the environment in the following ways (Randolf, 2004):

- The environment poses certain natural hazards to human society. Examples include range and forest fires, floods, and landslides due to developments in located in flood plains and high fire areas.
- Society generated pollution impacts human health through the environment. Examples include contaminated drinking water, swimming areas with high e-coli counts caused by inadequate sanitation.
- Society exploits economically important natural resources at unsustainable rates. Examples include energy and mineral extraction, logging, grazing, groundwater recharge, and fisheries. Sustainable management is called for to enable these "working landscapes" to be more sustainable. For example flood control and wetlands management and vegetation restoration.
- Pollution and overuse undermine productive natural systems and ecosystems. These include hard to define and measure noneconomic natural resources such as species habitat and biodiversity.

Some states such as Colorado have scoped the issues of environmental change and have assessed the impacts on recreation in their parks. This work is examining the larger context of global environmental issues and how the impacts might negatively impact individual recreation experiences in the parks. Figure 11.1 provides an example of these challenges.

---

## Figure 11.1. Colorado Parks System and Environmental Change

### Issue # 1: Effects of Environmental Change on Recreation and Tourism

*Goal 1: Address and/or minimize the potential negative effects of environmental change on recreation and tourism.*

**Objectives and Supporting Actions**

**Objective 1.1 Develop a better understanding of how climate change may impact recreation and tourism in Colorado.**

- Secure necessary funding and partners to conduct new research or compile existing information to more clearly identify potential effects of climate change on recreation and tourism. Reports should include specific indicators, mitigation strategies, alternatives for existing recreation activities that will be heavily impacted, and surveys of visitor perceptions about climate change and related impacts to their experience.

**Objective 1.2 Lessen the impact of future climate change on Colorado's recreation and tourism economy, while dealing with some of the impacts that are likely to occur.**

- Request that the Western Climate Change Initiative include an outdoor recreation component in their planning process.
- Incorporate mitigation of and adaption to climate change into agency strategic and operational planning processes. Agencies should lead by example, reducing their own carbon emissions, modifying recreational facility design and engineering standards (e.g., trails, structures, roads, water and power infrastructure), and using low-emission vehicles. Design standards should also anticipate expected future conditions, such as more heat, more severe weather, periodic flooding, and drought.
- Engage the ski industry (and other winter sports stakeholders and outfitters) to collaboratively plan for an initial increase in visitation (due to eventual lack of snow in European countries) and an eventual decrease in winter skiers and visitors. (The effort should also include expanding summer-based recreation, such as mountain biking and hiking).
- Encourage employees' professional development to learn how to better communicate and educate others about their impacts of future climate change on Colorado's recreation areas. Seek additional resources for outdoor recreation organizations to effectively teach about the complicated topic of climate change and make it relevant to youth and adult community program participants throughout Colorado.
- Protect and restore critical fish and wildlife habitat that provides important refuge, breeding grounds, and migration corridors.
- Work with the Governor's Energy Office to fund alternative modes of transportation projects as a means of offsetting carbon production.
- Incorporate green building standards into grant applications for COCO and Colorado State Trails Program, with respect to trails, recreation facilities, or infrastructure.
- Create eco-tourism or green-minded vacation packages for visitors. (This could be modeled after Volunteers for Outdoor Colorado (VOC) stewardship adventures. Could also be focused on offsetting the impacts of vacations by offering carbon offsets to tourists at the airport, car rental counters, ski resorts, Colorado Welcome Centers, etc.).

**Objective 1.3 Support efforts to mitigate and manage wildfire and infestations (e.g., bark beetle and non-native invasive species) that will impact the overall quality of Colorado's recreation opportunities.**

- Work with potential funding sources (federal agency appropriations, OEDIT, DNR, etc.), to expedite removal of dead-standing trees in burned and bark beetle infestation areas (particularly in campgrounds, picnic areas, parking lots, and along popular trails). Secure funding and plan for active forest management and fish/wildlife/vegetation habitat management and adaptation strategies.
- Support efforts to prevent the spread of invasive plant species (e.g., tamarisk) and plant/tree pathogens. Implement early detection and rapid response mechanisms.
- Educate stakeholder groups about how to contain the spread of invasive species and prevent potential infestations by sharing the impacts of zebra mussel infestations; help them identify mussels and sanitize their boats.
- Support educational outreach efforts to school-aged children, Colorado residents, and tourists to inform them of the realities of bark beetles and related potential wildfire—focusing on a positive message about healthy forests and the need for active management, including prescribed burning and thinning.

From Colorado State Parks. Reprinted with permission????

## Soils and the Park

Why should soils be a concern of the park manager? Park lands are not commonly managed for agricultural crops, forest products, meat, or other consumptive purposes. Therefore, managers might not expect park lands to deteriorate in any way while under their care. Unfortunately, park lands also suffer from overuse. The park manager must be able to recognize and try to control overuse, as management implies stewardship of all resources.

Often lands not available for anything else are made available for outdoor recreation. Millions of acres of forest and grass-covered lands in North America have been found to be substandard for agricultural purposes; these are lands that never should have been plowed. Most have reverted to grasslands for grazing, to timber-producing lands, and to a lesser extent, to park lands, with some being used for intensive outdoor recreation. Failure as crop land or timber land probably means the fertility was low, or the growing season was too short. The suitability of such lands for recreation may be questionable, but often they are only lands available for that purpose. This is one reason managers have difficulty retaining covering vegetation.

Most park managers take charge of areas that have been long established, so these managers were not there when campgrounds, picnic sites, park trails, waste management systems, or other facilities were first located. Possibly topography, slope, drainage, and other factors were considered at that time, but mistakes may have been made. Unforeseen circumstances may now frustrate the original plans. This is particularly true of those circumstances related to visitor impact, such as soil compaction and erosion. Managers, then, often inherit some tenacious problems.

The National Park Service has extensive involvement in soil management systems to deter erosion and minimize flooding. The NPS Soil Resource Management Objectives follow from the overall resource management objectives in NPS Management Policies (http://www.nature.nps.gov/geology/soils/index.cfm):

1. Preserve intact, functioning, natural systems by preserving native soils and the processes of soil genesis in a condition undisturbed by humans to the extent possible.
2. Maintain significant cultural objects and scenes by conserving soils consistent with maintenance of the associated historic practices, and by minimizing soil erosion to the extent possible.
3. Protect property and provide safety by working to ensure that developments and their management take into account soil limitations, behavior, and hazards.
4. Minimize soil loss and disturbance caused by special use activities and ensure that soils retain their productivity and potential for reclamation.

Soils are a basic resource of natural systems, and variations in soil conditions usually are evidenced in related parts of the system. A change in soil type, for example, may be associated with changes in vegetation, water quality, or erosion potential.

For these reasons, soils play an important role in recreation planning. Some knowledge of their properties is useful to the manager. Soil texture or particle size distribution is an important property that affects soil management. Below are categories of the various soil particle sizes and their engineering capabilities.

1. Gravel is coarse, with particles over two millimeters in diameter. It is well-drained, stable material that will support heavy loads.
2. Sand is 0.05 to 2 millimeters in diameter and is gritty to the touch. It also drains well and holds up under heavy loads. When dry, sand lacks cohesion and must be confined. Fine sand is less stable when saturated and tends to flow if not confined.
3. Silt is 0.002 to 0.05 millimeters in diameter, is barely visible, and feels smooth to the touch. When dry, it lacks cohesion, remaining stable but compressing under loads. When wet it becomes very unstable, and it heaves when frozen. In a disturbed state, it is subject to wind erosion.
4. Clay is under 0.002 millimeters in diameter, and individual grains are invisible to the naked eye. When dry, it is cohesive and supports heavy loads. When wet, clay becomes plastic, slippery,

and impervious. Porous soils lying over clay are subject to slippage on slopes greater than 10 percent. Clay is also subject to wind erosion if powdered, such as on trails or roads.

5. Peat soils are of origins, fibrous to the touch, dark in color, and they lack cohesion. They are unstable and will not normally support development. They are usually associated with high water tables, either at present, or at some time in the past.

There is a direct correlation between the type of soil and the feasibility of such recreation developments as roads, trails, building foundations, or sewage drainfields. Yet we must look beyond particle size and engineering properties and consider other aspects of soils as they affect management practices. These aspects include erosion, compaction that induces flooding from runoff, and cracking of surfaces and structures.

Park managers need not feel uncomfortable about lack of soil knowledge. Soil scientists with government agencies are available to assist in classifying, mapping, and describing soils so that they may be used to their best purpose. In soil survey work, the soil scientist walks around the area, stopping frequently to dig into the soil and study its properties. The field work is supported by laboratory testing of soil samples collected in the field. Soil maps are made with accompanying descriptions. These show the planner and manager the location and extent of different soils. From this, decisions can be made on safe uses of the soil or adjustments and corrections of present use. Soil maps are especially informative to the manager wishing to expand facilities in the park. Soil surveys show soil wetness, overflow hazards, depth to bedrock, hardpans, tight layers, erodibility, clay layers that crack when dry and swell when wet, and hazard of slippage on slopes. Surveys show the location and extent of different soils and provide information about their properties to a depth of about six feet. Soil maps are available for most of the United States and the populated regions of Canada.

Table 11.2 demonstrates the map symbol, soil component and name, and the types of soils in Black Hawk County, Iowa, for suitable use in urban and recreation conditions. As one can see, there are indications of soil types and if they are appropriate for camp areas, paths and trails, etc. These conditions can be mapped by the service. The Cooperative Soil Survey (http://www.soilsurvey. org/survey/selectstate.asp) has online the soil conditions for all states and counties and even cities within the United States. This service is provided by the U.S. Department of Agriculture, Natural Resource Conservation Service (http://websoilsurvey.nrcs.usda.gov/app/).

Most countries have some type of soil survey. For example, Agriculture and Agri-Food Canada has a similar service at (http://sis.agr.gc.ca/cansis/nsdb/detailed/intro.html), European Commission Land Management and Natural Hazards at (http://eusoils.jrc.ec.europa.eu/data.html), and Australia Department of the Environment, Water, Heritage and the Arts at (http://www.anra.gov.au/topics/ soils/asris/). The Queensland Government (http://www.derm.qld.gov.au/land/management/erosion/index.html) has posted on the web guidelines for mitigating soil erosion from runoff and how to determine runoff rates, and design areas and facilities to minimize runoff to avoid erosion.

The U.S. Department of Transportation, Federal Highway Administration also has useful soil suitability information for trail development.Table 11.3 provides information on the soil components (factors) and their general capability for trails (http://www.fhwa.dot.gov/environment/fspubs/02232821/page02.htm).

## Table 11.2. 2007 Soil Survey of Black Hawk County, Iowa
### Urban and Recreation Interpretations Thundersheet

| Select all/none Map Symbl / Component Name Select all/none | Off-Road Motorcycle Trails | Camp Areas | Picnic Areas | Paths and Trails | Playgrounds |
|---|---|---|---|---|---|
| Marshan (75%) 1152 | Very limited | Very limited | Very limited | Very limited | Very limited |
| Selmass (5%) 1152 | Very limited | Very limited | Very limited | Very limited | Very limited |
| Shandep (5%) 1152 | Very limited | Very limited | Very limited | Very limited | Very limited |
| Lawler (70%) 1226 | Very limited | Very limited | Very limited | Very limited | Very limited |
| Marshan (10%) 1226 | Very limited | Very limited | Very limited | Very limited | Very limited |
| Burkhardt (40%) 1285G | Somewhat limited | Very limited | Very limited | Very limited | Very limited |
| Bassett (34%) 1285G | Somewhat limited | Very limited | Very limited | Very limited | Very limited |
| Chelsea (20%) 1285G | Somewhat limited | Very limited | Very limited | Very limited | Very limited |
| Colo (100%) 133 | Very limited | Very limited | Very limited | Very limited | Very limited |
| Coland (100%) 1585 | Very limited | Very limited | Very limited | Very limited | Very limited |
| Aquolls (15%) 1585 | not rated | not rated | not rated | not rated | not rated |
| Marshan (10%) 1585 | Very limited | Very limited | Very limited | Very limited | Very limited |
| Sigglekov (55%) 1586 | Very limited | Very limited | Very limited | Very limited | Very limited |
| Fluvaquents (30%) 1586 | Not rated | Not rated | Not rated | Not rated | Not rated |
| Aquents (15%) 1586 | not rated | not rated | not rated | not rated | not rated |
| Finchford (90%) 159 | Somewhat limited | Somewhat limited | Somewhat limited | Somewhat limited | Somewhat limited |

From U.S. government report from the Soil Conservation Service.

## Table 11.3. General Guidelines on Trail Site Suitability and Sensitivity to Impact

| Soil factor | Poorly suited (highly sensitive) | Limited suitability (moderately sensitive) | Generally suitable (slightly sensitive) |
|---|---|---|---|
| Soil texture | All organic soils; soils with an organic surface layer thicker than four inches. | Silt greater than 70 percent or clay greater than 40 percent in the soil surface layer; sand component is greater than 80 percent in the surface layer. | Soils with a high percentage of gravel or rock in the surface layer. |
| Soil temperature | Ice-rich permafrost is within 40 inches of the surface; soils at or near freezing. | Low ice permafrost within 40 inches of the surface. | Deeply frozen soils (winter activities) |
| Soil moisture | Poorly or very poorly drained soils; the water table is 12 inches of the surface; water is ponded at the surface; soils are at or near saturation. | Somewhat poorly drained soils; the water table is between 12 and 24 inches of the surface. | Well- and moderately well-drained soils; the water table is deeper than 24 inches below the surface. |
| Type of surface cover | All wetland vegetation communities; permafrost-influenced vegetation communities; alpine tundra communities | | |
| Root mass | Fine, thin, poorly developed root mass. | Root mass that is two to six inches thick, primarily fine roots. | Root mass is more than six inches thick with a high percentage of woody roots. |
| Soil depth | -- | Less than two feet to bedrock. | More than two feet to bedrock. |
| Slope | Slopes steeper than 40 percent if the slope length is longer than 50 feet; slopes 20 to 40 percent | Slopes between six and 20 percent (with appropriate water control). | Slopes less than six percent (with appropriate water control). |
| Landscape position | North-facing aspects in some climatic conditions. | Ridgelines (if shallow soils); foot and toe slopes (if wet or there are seep zones); floodplains (seasonal flooding); slopes (depending on percent of slope, see above). | South-facing aspects; gravel bars, terraces, and alluvial benches; outwash plains; alluvial fans (depending on slope) |

From U.S. government report from the Soil Conservation Service.

## Soil Erosion

One of the park manager's biggest environmental problems may be soil erosion. Because it takes anywhere from 50 to 100 years to build one inch (2.5 centimeters) of soil, this vital resource must not be wasted. All soils erode, but some do so more quickly than others. The rate of erosion is dependent on several factors: vegetation, soil characteristics, precipitation, topography (soil slope), wind, animal impact, and visitor impact.

The influence of soil characteristics on erosion is difficult to determine in that soil factors are difficult to isolate in the presence of vegetative factors. The dynamics of soils themselves are not completely understood.

Wind erosion is most common in arid and semiarid regions, but also occurs in humid areas, particularly during dry weather periods. Wet soils are not susceptible to wind erosion. When the moisture content of soils is lowered by hot, dry, winds, wind erosion may take place. Vegetative cover is the best way to alleviate wind erosion in park areas. In dry regions, windbreaks of trees and shrubs and picket fences are useful in reducing wind velocities and trapping drifting soil.

Water is the chief cause of erosion; over a period of centuries, water action can level mountain ranges. Running water is the major contributor to erosion; however, raindrop splash serves to detach soil and, under conditions, to transport it. Vegetative cover is a major deterrent to raindrop impact and erosion. On bare soils, raindrop splash provides the detaching force that begins erosion. Level soils or soils at a low angle are subject to soil splash but actual soil transport is minimal even when rainfall intensity is high. Downhill transport increases with slope angle and reaches its maximum where slope steepness and rainfall intensity are the greatest. Sand-size material is especially susceptible to splash erosion.

## Recreation Impact on Soils

Recreation development is often the cause of soil erosion through topographic modification as well as the clearing of vegetation. Heavy equipment used in construction alters soil porosity, which affects the infiltration rate. Site wear indicators are bare soil, soil compaction, loss of ground vegetation, dead trees, wind throw, trees with exposed roots, and an increase in site size. Physical changes are not easily noticed unless there is some form of environmental monitoring such as photographs of the same site taken every few years. Manning indicates the detrimental effects of trampling may be described in a seven-step soil impact cycle.

In the Quetico-Superior canoe country of Minnesota and Ontario, studies showed the A horizon of campsites was reduced in thickness an average of 65 percent below that of adjacent unused control areas. This loss of litter and humus was attributed to loss of ground vegetation, mechanical reduction resulting from trampling, surface runoff that increased with soil compaction, and the practice of raking litter to improve the appearance of the campsite and reduce fire hazards.

Recreation area soils must support heavy traffic by people, vehicles, and sometimes, horses. Helgath, in her study of trail deterioration in the Selway-Bitterroot Wilderness in Idaho and Montana, noted trail location to be more important than the level of visitor use in causing deterioration in trails. A trail system with the same amount of use throughout showed variable amounts of deterioration depending on a variety of site factors. She noted some trail grades of 15 percent eroded more easily than steep 30-percent grades, the variable being the soil type through which the trail ran. One stretch of trail had only a five-percent grade, but because it was located on a fine-textured soil, it suffered very serious erosion. Rerouting the trail around the vulnerable soil type of installing planking across it would correct this.

Intensive recreation use does affect underlying soils, but there is some difference of opinion regarding the nature and extent of this influence. The primary change seems to be through the physical compaction of soils from either pedestrian or vehicular traffic. Such compaction causes changes in bulk density, soil moisture, and infiltration rates. Ketchledge and Leonard also point out that hiking boots with cleated rather than smooth soles cut and roughen the soil surface. The soil loosened by these boots is easily eroded by runoff water. Many park managers are encouraging park visitors, as well as their employees, to switch from heavy lug-sole boots to lighter boots with flat soles or even running shoes. The use of light shoes results in less damage to trail treads and actually requires less energy for hiking.

According to Lull (1959), the amount of compaction depends on five major factors: weight of the compacting agent, previous use, soil type, amount of organic matter, and moisture content. Moisture content is mentioned as most important because resistance to compaction decreases as moisture content increases. The moisture acts as a lubricant, weakening adhesion between particles.

Once land is stripped of vegetation, most soils have little resistance to erosive forces. Rainstorms of high intensity can be expected to generate tremendous quantities of sediment. Dirt roads and trails both deteriorate from rain splash erosion when there is not protective tree canopy overhead to absorb rain energy. Vegetation, then, is an important deterrent to soil erosion through its interception of raindrop impact and through its root system, holding soil in place. Unfortunately, vegetation is often difficult to maintain in recreation areas where human use is heavy.

Given the information that recreation use changes certain soil characteristics, what are the implications for managers of recreation areas? Probably the most important is that soil information must be utilized in the process of planning any new recreational developments, and when considering changes in existing areas. In locating trails for hiking or other uses, care should be taken to avoid unstable or highly erodible soils. This should lessen the impact of trails and make them less costly and easier to maintain. The Queensland Government (http://www.derm.qld.gov.au/land/management/erosion/index.html) has posted on the web guidelines for mitigating soil erosion from runoff and how to determine runoff rates and design areas and facilities to minimize runoff to avoid erosion. The National Park Service has produced a soil resource management document that addresses planning and facility design and siting based on soil capability.

## Water and Outdoor Recreation

Most recreation activities are directly dependent on water; it is difficult to imagine an outdoor recreation area without it. Water is important for many reasons, the most basic being for drinking. Water is essential in most kinds of recreation area sanitation systems. It is also the limiting factor in whether an area can support swimming, boating, sport fishing, waterfowl hunting, and such winter sports as skating, skiing, tobogganing, and snowmobiling on ice or snow. Water has great attractive powers, whether it is at rest as a pond, lake, or reservoir, or in motion as a flowing creek, a river, pounding ocean surf, a geyser, or a waterfall. Hearing the sound of water is also part of the recreation experience. Water, for many of the uses just cited, will need to meet certain federal, state/provincial, and local standards for quality, often stated in biological, physical, or chemical terms. The quality of water available as a recreation base might be lowered both by natural processes and human influence. Visitors to the park may contribute to water pollution. An oil or gas spill caused by careless use of an outboard engine causes pollution. Soil erosion also contributes to the deterioration of water quality.

Industrial, agricultural, or urban pollutants often enter a river upstream from a recreation area and render the water useless for all purposes except enhancement of the view. Even this esthetic value may be impaired if it is known that the water is polluted.

Sediments carried into lakes affect plant life in two ways: by obscuring sunlight and thus interfering with photosynthesis, and by burying plants. Silt pollution also smothers fish eggs and may seriously affect aquatic insects that serve as fish food. Chemical wastes kill plant and animal life, often many kilometers from the source. Thermal pollution, the release of hot or cold waters into lakes or streams, affect the fish population. Diseased animals are also sources of waterborne diseases that cause intestinal disorder in humans. A fecal parasite, *Giardia lamblia*, is known to exist in wildlife throughout North America, particularly in the Cascade and Rocky Mountain regions, and it can be transmitted to humans through water. It causes *giardiasis*, perhaps better known as beaver fever or backpacker's disease.

Evidence of pollution includes water discoloration, floating materials, oil slicks, and objectionable odors. Sometimes the water looks and tastes all right, but diarrhea or abdominal pain in users signal contamination. Pollution should also be suspected if there is a change in aquatic life, especially in plant species and population. When pollution is found within the park, the manager must ensure that adequate warning is given to park visitors in order to protect visitor health.

Parks on large lakes may be exposed to pollution, particularly if the lake is used for industrial purposes, if it is ringed by agricultural lands, or if it is used for transportation. Though park managers must rely on local, state, provincial, or federal environmental legislation to eventually alleviate such problems, they should be aware of existing regulations and be able to discuss any infraction of them when called on to do so. At the same time, managers must do all in their power to prevent or terminate part-related pollution and must notify the authorities if a problem arises.

The manager should not confuse lake eutrophication with pollution. Eutrophication is the natural aging process of lakes that takes place independent of human activity. In this process, a lake traps nutrients draining in from the surface of the surrounding basin and from groundwater inflow. According to Greeson (1969):

> Enrichment and sedimentation are the principal contributors to the aging process. The shore vegetation and higher aquatic plants utilize part of the inflowing nutrients, grow nutrients, grow abundantly, and, in turn, trap the sediments. The lake gradually fills in, becoming shallower by the accumulation of plants and sediments on the bottom and smaller by the invasion of shore vegetation and eventually becomes dry land. The extinction of a lake is, therefore, a result of enrichment, productivity, decay, and sedimentation. Regardless, human activity can increase the eutrophication process and is referred to as cultural or artificial eutrophication.

The park manager can extend the life expectancy of a lake by controlling those factors that speed up eutrophication. For example, the excessive fertilization of park lands with nitrogen and phosphorus contributes to algae growth. Keeping roads and trails away from a lake shore and using other erosion control methods will help reduce sediments. Keeping a tree cover around the shoreline keeps water temperature down. Dredging is a direct means of reversing the eutrophic process.

## VEGETATION

Native vegetation is considered a valuable resource for any park. Its presence at park entrances, along roads, around buildings, and generally throughout the park is often perceived as that factor that makes the area "park like." It usually stimulates appreciation for the park environment, particularly when the area outside the park has been noticeable modified. Unfortunately, some parks are devoid of much of their original vegetation. Many areas have previously been used for farming, timber production grazing, military purposes, or industrial production. "Such uses have often drastically modified the area. On the other hand, some parks are established where vegetation has been relatively unmodified by human activity.

**Vegetation and visitor interest.** Visitors to parks are often more than casually interested in the vegetation found in park environments, particularly the varied tree, shrub, and wildflower species. Some parks have unusual or rare plants, large trees, or vegetation having cultural significance. The park manager can enhance visitor enjoyment by interpreting the vegetation through the various media cited in chapter 17.

**Plants and energy.** In the presence of sunlight, the leaves of plants take in carbon dioxide from the air and water from the soil. Through a chemical reaction called photosynthesis, plants produce a carbohydrate that is sent to all parts of the plant less than a year old. This new growth contains stored energy that is used by other living things. Oxygen, a by-product, is released into the atmosphere, where it becomes available to all forms of plant and animal life for respiration.

**Plants and wildlife.** In addition to providing food and oxygen for wildlife, vegetation serves another important function. It provides wildlife habitat. As land outside parks becomes increasingly modified by urban sprawl and through farm and forestry practices, certain wildlife species become even more dependent on park land for suitable cover and nesting sites. Vegetation usually provides this needed habitat.

**Vegetation and soil.** Plants eventually die and decay, their remains becoming available to other plants. When decomposed, vegetation increases the water-holding capacity of the soil. Plants also facilitate soil aeration through root decay. Some plants add nitrogen to the soil through nitrogen-fixing bacteria that fasten on the root nodules of the leguminous plants as well as on the root structure of some trees.

**Vegetation as a site indicator.** Certain species of trees, shrubs, and other plants grow in poorly drained soils. Others are found only in dry sites. Still others are found in open sunlight, while some tolerate total or partial shade. Lists here would be pointless, because the species combination varies widely throughout North America. A local list of vegetative site indicators should be obtained and studied by the manager.

**Vegetation and microclimate**. Plants serve as indicators of microclimate. The species that occur, their growth rate, and their health are all indices of subtle climatic changes. Plants differ according to the direction the slope faces, and they also indicate frost pockets and windy sites by composition and condition. Taller vegetation also modifies the microclimate, as one readily notices when moving from direct sunlight into the shade of the forest canopy.

**Vegetation as a screen.** Plants can effectively cover unsightly areas or special park operations such as dumps, maintenance sheds, or service areas. They can serve as screens along park boundaries and provide privacy around employee residential areas. Thorny species are also used to channel visitor movement.

**Vegetation as a sound barrier.** The ability of vegetation to impede sound transmission is not great, so it should not be relied upon for sound reduction where the sound source is close by. To be most effective, special planting must be made (i.e., shrubs in the foreground, trees in the background) to complement a specially constructed, centered landform of sufficient height to screen the sound source. Where distances are great [1,000 feet (300 meters) or more], trees may be only slightly better for absorbing sound than the same distance left in open space. The effectiveness of the trees to absorb sound varies with their size, density, type, and position relative to the sound source.

**Vegetation and wind velocity.** Trees dissipate the force of wind by acting as vertical barriers in its path. The best examples of this are the windbreaks or shelterbelts of the great plains, where the winds are affected on the leeward side for a horizontal distance of over 40 times the height of the trees. Soil evaporation is reduced, transpiration from vegetation is diminished, drifting snow is checked, and the movement of soil is lessened. Picnic sites or campgrounds in windy areas might benefit from such plantings.

**Miscellaneous contributions.** Though not as important in parks as in areas under cultivation, vegetation's greatest contribution to human is in providing foods (fruits and vegetables), fuel, plant pigments (dyes), shelter (forest products), fibers, clothing, spices, beverage plants, decorations, latex, chemical derivatives, containers, furniture, wood novelties, tobacco, and drugs. Only in unusual circumstances are any of these projects of significance in park areas, although some outdoor recreation opportunities might be available in certain commercial forests and farms, and berry picking and mushroom collecting are allowed in most recreation areas.

## Vegetation, Recreation Impacts and Management Options

Some plants are classified as weeds, perhaps because no one has found a use for them. Often it is because they are not indigenous, and having no natural controls, they crowd out native species or harm our well-being, our livelihood, or our recreational activities. Currently, exotic water plants that choke lakes and waterways and bring boating and swimming to a halt in certain areas. Water intakes are clogged, fishing is made difficult or even dangerous, and ecological relationships are seriously disturbed.

Visitors coming in with boats and trailers must be persuaded to examine their equipment for any plant fragments of any kind before putting their equipment into the water. Interpretive assistance should be sought in order to design the most effective signs possible, and other media should also be considered to help alert the public to the problem and elicit cooperation. Although the spread of these weeds seems inevitable, attempts can be made to slow their spread until more effective controls can be developed.

When considering impact on vegetation, a distinction should be made between the overstory (trees) and the understory (ground cover). The latter contains the reproduction of tree species, as well as woody shrubs and herbaceous vegetation. Certain activities impact one layer but not the other; the degree of impact differs, and certain impacts can be injurious to one but beneficial to the other layer.

Some of the impact of recreational use on vegetation is apparent. Consider trees that have been scarred by initials or branches broken off of trees and shrubs for firewood. Axe blazes and other wounds serve as entry points for disease and insect infestation.  A study of the Quetico-Superior canoe country of Minnesota and Ontario found that many pine saplings had been cut for tent poles by canoeists, only to be  burned for a campfire by a following party not needing the poles. More saplings were cut by later parties, and this essentially reduced the number of pines in the younger age classes (LePage, 1967).  It was interesting to note in the same study that campers preferred sites with pine cover; however, that cover type will eventually disappear if this depreciative use continues.

The recreation impact on vegetation is primarily caused by trampling. The above study found that 80 percent of the ground cover was lost with only light use. Both cover abundance and the number of plant species present were reduced. In a study in a new campground in northwestern Pennsylvania, LaPage found that the original ground cover, not able to withstand continued pressures from trampling, was replaced by more resistant species. Grasses have a greater tolerance to trampling than do dicotyledonous herbs.

Even light use eventually results in loss of ground vegetation at campsites. Observers of a new area can expect to find a reduction in the abundance of cover within a year or two, as well as a reduction in the number of plant species present. In his Pennsylvania study, LePage found campsites that had received 150 camper days of use throughout the first summer averaged less than 10 percent loss in the vegetative cover; however, loss of vegetation increased to 60 percent for 300 camper days of use. It was thought that restricting the average amount of use to 200 campers or less per season might minimize loss of cover. However, such restrictions may not be feasible in view of continuing demands for recreation space.

When managing areas for recreation, consideration must be given to the ability of native and suitably introduced species to withstand recreational use and abuse. Studies by LePage (1967) show that such plants as blue grass (Poa), path rush (Juncus), and clover (Trifolium) demonstrate tolerance to trampling.  Rehabilitation methods include delaying the opening of sites early in the spring when the ground is damp and easily compacted and the spreading of thin layers of straw on bare sports at the close of the season to trap windblown seed and hold it in place until spring. Consider loosening and aerating the soil, bringing in new topsoil, or adding mulch. Re-vegetate bare areas with species resistant to drought and trampling. It may be necessary to close damaged sites for a year or two in order to effect rehabilitation.

It would be advisable to look for resistant characteristics in indigenous species. Woody shrubs may be more desirable than herbaceous ground cover due to their greater durability. Species with thorns or dense branching serve well to define site boundaries. Jute matting is useful in site rehabilitation as it helps hold soil in place and gives new plants a chance to get started beneath a protective covering.

The recreation manager must carefully consider and evaluate the nature and degree of visitor use and abuse as well as the impact of planned management actions. As suggested earlier, much of the attraction of a recreation area is of an esthetic nature, and thus the vegetative character can have an influence on the level of user satisfaction derived from the area. Silvicultural treatments are used on commercial stands to produce timber; it might be possible to adapt these treatments to produce healthy vegetation that enhances the quality of recreation.

Although each visitor contributes to the deterioration of a recreation site, there is no general awareness of this unless, of course, the damage is deliberate. Any management attempt to restore damaged sites or to extend their period of usefulness must be accompanied by an interpretive visitor-education program. Visitors should be made fully aware of the problem through park interpretive programs and informed of how they can assist in slowing the deterioration. Vegetation itself can be used as a management tool. It can be used for fencing, screening, controlling users, attracting wildlife, stabilizing soil, and modifying microclimate.

**Air**

As with other management issues, interpretation has an important role here. Interpretation can both enhance discussion of the effects of pollution within the park or recreation area and educate the public about ways to help guard this invaluable resource. Local monitoring and research methods are also subjects of high interest. Small parks may not have interpretative staff, but all personnel can be made aware of current issues and the park's place in the larger scene.

## WILDLIFE

Wildlife forms the basis of certain types of recreation and can be a complement to still other recreation activities. The recreational enjoyment of wildlife can be separated into non-consumptive uses (wildlife photography, bird watching, and other generalized or specialized wildlife observation) or consumptive uses (fishing, hunting, and trapping). Both types of uses may fall within the spectrum of activities that a given area offers to recreationists, especially if they occur at different seasons.

At present, the per-capita hunting population is on the decline in the United States. At the same time, the proportion of people interested in watching wildlife without killing it is on the increase. Traditionally, financial support for wildlife has come from license fees paid by fishermen and hunters and the federal taxes on guns, ammunition, and fishing tackle. Because of the increase in numbers, this wildlife is also seen and enjoyed by the non-hunting public. Competition between the consumptive and non-consumptive user of wildlife will no doubt increase in the years ahead, and more confrontations between the two groups can be expected. A case in point is the bison and wolf populations in the Yellowstone ecosystem, which are hunted by way of federal laws. In Alberta, Canada, there are proposals to allow hunting of the grizzly bear. Here is where recreation area managers could use interpretation as an effective tool to reduce the number of such confrontations. Through interpretation, the non-consumptive users can learn the values of hunting and other wildlife management techniques.

**Problems With Wildlife**

Wildlife provides pleasure for park visitors but also creates problems for them as well as for park managers. Animals may leave the park and feed in nearby orchards or on field crops, or a park may become overpopulated with a species that causes damage to park vegetation. Beaver and muskrat build dams and may back water into adjacent landowners' property as well as into park lands. Beaver have been known to leave the park area and cut down trees on nearby residential lands. Beaver and muskrat also transmit a disease commonly known as "beaver fever," *Giardia lamblia*, through contaminated water. Lyme disease and Rocky Mountain Spotted Fever are transmitted by ticks which infest various animals. Park wildlife might transmit disease to livestock on adjoining lands. Certain mammals such as skunks, foxes, and bats might endanger the lives of park visitors because these animals are subject to rabies. Rattlesnakes, copperheads, and other poisonous snakes create problems in campgrounds and along trails. Bears are a serious problem in many larger parks, as are moose, elk, and deer in the rutting season. Deer are frequently killed in collisions with vehicles, and serious injuries often result to the drivers, passengers, and cars. Wildlife might be harassed, chased away, or killed by visitor-owned domestic pets. Many problems with varying degrees of hazard have been mentioned. Park managers must acquaint themselves with problems whose occurrence is significant or even possible in their area, and see that a policy for dealing with these is effective and consistently carried out.

In order to maintain ideal wildlife populations in a park, the manager will have to maintain a suitable habitat, which includes food, water, nesting and escape cover, and bedding, roosting, and feeding areas. One of the greatest threats to wildlife everywhere is the disappearance of such habitats. Wildlife dependent on a particular habitat will usually perish if that habitat is altered or eliminated.

Some larger parks provide considerable habitat, particularly those with areas of minimal development or access. Birds such as woodpeckers depend on old-growth trees provide cavity-nesting areas. Many of the land-use practices available to farmers, ranchers, and foresters are available to the park manager. These would include food production, water development, and cover and wetland improvement.

Food production is the practice of planting tree and shrub species that produce fruit and browse (the leaves, twigs, and shoots of trees and representative shrubs) beneficial to wildlife. Oak, hickory, beech, gum, cherry, mountain ash, dogwood, wild plum, crab apple, persimmon, and service berry all produce wildlife food, called mast. Providing browse is another means of assuring food for wildlife. The wildlife department in your area can recommend suitable species for browse planting.

Water developments are projects designed to supply water for the purpose of improving wildlife habitat. Such devices include reservoirs, small ponds, and water catchments. Professional assistance is advised for such projects.

Cover improvement includes providing both protective cover and nesting cover. Protective cover offers hiding places from severe weather and safety from predators. Hedgerows, brushpiles, and plantings for roosting are part of protective cover planning. Nesting cover includes providing ground cover, den and nesting trees, and, where indicated, artificial nest structures. Diversity of habitat is the key consideration.

Wetland improvement provides wetland for waterfowl and fur-bearing mammals by means of developing marsh interspersed with open water areas. Controlling water levels through ditching and dredging and the use of such structures as dikes and spillways is also part of wetland improvement.

## Water and Animals

**Fur mammals.** Aquatic fur-bearing animals, such as otter, mink, muskrat, and beaver usually elicit great visitor interest. Laws vary as to whether or not these mammals are protected in parks. Where possible, the habitat of these interesting aquatic creatures should be managed in a manner that contributes to their survival, while making them available to visitor observation. This may be effected through the park interpretive program.

**Aquatic birds.** Marsh or aquatic birds also have great appeal for visitors, and their habitats should be maintained through the usual conservation practices of controlling soil erosion and pollution, as well as the provision of adequate pond development and nesting opportunities. Park managers should consider means to protect such birds as geese, ducks, swans, coots, rails, and other shorebirds. Examples of protection include provision for vegetative cover, domestic animal control, and isolation from visitors.

**Fish.** Some park areas provide for visitor viewing of fish populations in small ponds or through windows on stream profile chambers. Most park areas with fish populations permit fish harvesting, with the take usually being regulated by fixed seasons and catch limits. Because of the popularity of recreational fishing in park areas, visitor impact on the resource is usually heavy, and fish management measures are often necessary.

The environmental needs of fish include cover for protection from their enemies, adequate space, suitable spawning sites, favorable water temperatures, and a year-round food supply. Possible stream-management techniques are the regulation of water flow, temperature, and water fertility; the control of competitor fish; watershed protection to prevent siltation and reduce high-water damage; and pollution abatement. Pools can be built of logs or boulders; these can provide hiding and resting places in streams. The stocking of game fish is necessary in lakes and streams where waters are deficient in either food or suitable habitat, and sport fishing is an established usage. Advice from fish specialists is advisable before considering stream channel manipulation or other fish improvement projects.

## MANAGER RESPONSE TO ENVIRONMENTAL IMPACT

Visitor impact is largely from visitors doing exactly what they want to do, although poor park design can contribute to impact. With a continued increase in use on the same land base, and without skillful management, it can be assumed people will eventually trample, pollute, de-vegetate, and disturb the wildlife throughout the park systems. The need for more intensive management becomes apparent. The park manager may employ direct control measures, indirect control measures, or a combination of the two. These techniques are described in the chapter on conflict and capacity. However, there are a number of organizations working with parks and park managers. One in particular, the International Union for Conservation of Nature (IUCN), is conserving biodiversity by addressing three categories: species and their sub-populations, genetic diversity, and ecosystems. Hundreds of projects are underway around the world aimed at saving species and ecosystems and providing the knowledge needed for successful conservation action. IUCN's biodiversity conservation work is carried out by its various programs including Water, Forests, Marine, Species, Ecosystem Management and Protected Areas (http://www.iucn.org/what/tpas/biodiversity/solutions/).

## CONCLUSION

Without some milepost or benchmark, deterioration and its rate are difficult to determine. Studies and photographic records should be made of an area when it is new to determine what is there and in what quantity and condition. The environmental impact of visitors must be measured over time; it cannot be a single-point determination. Several years of observation are usually needed before an assessment can be made regarding the resistance of the site and the severity of the impact. Historical photos can help, as well as writings and personal accounts, but unless studies of some sort have been made, impacts must be measured with the park's present condition as the criterion.

Ecological transects and plots, photographs, and elaborate lists of plants and animals and their abundance and sociability are needed to determine present levels. It becomes the responsibility of the park agency to determine the seriousness of the environmental impact by seeking advice from specialists who can offer management suggestions and to make management decisions based on science, observation, and common sense. Law enforcement and interpretation are other tools available to the manager to help protect park landscapes from excessive deterioration. Park design and the proper number and location of facilities are also factors the manager should be able to count on to help stave off unacceptable levels of damage.

## REFERENCES

**References Cited**

Agriculture and Agri-Food Canada, 2010, Soil Information Survey, (http://sis.agr.gc.ca/cansis/nsdb/detailed/intro.html)

Colorado Parks, 2010, Issue and resolution for environmental impacts of Colorado State Parks. http://parks.state.co.us/NR/rdonlyres/07BCFAC1-269B-42CC-BDDF-7B1EA3FA556D/0/Section7SCORPStrategicPlanandConclusion.pdf)

European Commission Land Management and Natural Hazards, European Soils, (http://eusoils.jrc.ec.europa.eu/data.html)

Greeson, P. E. (1969). "Lake Eutrophication: A Natural Process," *Water Resources Bulletin*, American Water Resources Association, 5(4):16-30.

Guam Marine Preserves, 2010, Limits of Acceptable Change http://www.marinepreserves.com/

International Union for Conservation of Nature, http://www.iucn.org/what/tpas/biodiversity/solutions/

Na Ala Hele, 2001, Soil Erosion on Trail to Manoa Falls, Honolulu, HI, Hawaii Trail Analysis, http://www.state.hi.us/dlnr/dofaw/pubs/TrailAnalysis/NAH_study.pdf

National Park Service, 2006, Natural Resource Year in Review. http://www.nature.nps.gov/yearin-review/yir2006/01_b.html.

National Park Service, 2010, Gateway to the National Park Service Wilderness, http://wilderness.nps.gov/factsnew.cfm

National Park Service, 2010, Soil Resource Management Objectives,    http://www.nature.nps.gov/geology/soils/index.cfm

The Queensland Government, 2010, Soils and Land Management, http://www.derm.qld.gov.au/land/management/erosion/index.html

Randolf, J. (2004). Environmental land use planning and management, Washington, D.D.: Island Press.

The Wild Foundation, 2010, Wilderness, http://www.wild.org/main/about/what-is-a-wilderness-area/

U.S. Fish and Wildlife, Coastal Program, U.S. Fish and Wildlife Program Soil Stabilization Project, http://www.fws.gov/coastal/

U.S. Department of Transportation, Federal Highway Administration, Managing Degraded Off-Highway Vehicle Trails in Wet, Unstable, and Sensitive Environments Soil--The Stuff Under Foot, Hoof, and Wheel, http://www.fhwa.dot.gov/environment/fspubs/02232821/page02.htm

## General References

Agee, James K., & Johnson, Darryll R. (Eds.). (1988). Ecosystems management for parks and wilderness. Seattle: University of Washington Press.

Alldredge, Rendel B. (1973). "Capacity Theory for Parks and Recreation Areas," *Trends Park Practice Program, 104*(4):20-30.

Atchkinson, Stewart W. (1977). Some Effects of a Campground on Breeding Birds in Arizona. *USDA Forest Service General Technical Report RM-43*:175-182.

Armson, K. A. (1977). *Forest soils: Properties and processes*. Toronto: University of Toronto Press.

Australia Department of the Environment, Water, Heritage and the Arts, 2010, Soils, (http://www.anra.gov.au/topics/soils/asris/)

Bucknam, Harry O., & Brady, Nyle C. (1974). *The nature and properties of Soil* (8th ed.). New York: Macmillan.

Bury, Richard L. (1976). "Recreation Carrying Capacity – Hypothesis or Reality?" *Parks and Recreation, 11*(1):22-25, 56-58.

Barton, Michael A. (1969). "Water Pollution in Remote Recreational Areas," *Journal of Soil and Water Conservation, 24*(4):132-134.

Beardsley, Wendell G., & Herrington, Roscoe B. (1971). Economics and Management Implications of Campground Irrigation – A Case Study. *USDA Forest Res. Note INT-129*. Ogden, UT: Intermt. Forest Range Exp. Stn.

Bogucki, Donald J., Malanchuk, John L., & Schenck, Theron E. (1975). "Impact on Short-term Camping on Ground-level Vegetation," *Journal of Soil and Water Conservation, 30*(5):231-232.

Bradley, Jim. (1979). "A Human Approach to Reducing Wildland Impacts," in  Ruth Ittner (Ed.), *Recreational Impact on Wildlands Conference Proceedings*. Seattle, WA: Forest Service UADA, National Park Service USDI.

Chubb, Michael, & Ashton, Peter. (1969). Park and Recreation Standards Research. *Technical Reports No. 5 Dept. of Park and Recreation Resources*. East Lansing: Michigan State University.

Clark, Roger N., &  Stankey, George H. (1979). "Determining the Acceptability of Recreational Impacts: An Application of the Outdoor Recreation Opportunity Spectrum," in Ruth Ittner (Ed.), *Recreational Impact on Wildlands Conference Proceedings*. Seattle, WA: Forest Service USDA, National Park Service USDI.

Cohen, Robert. (Ed.). (1985). *An environment agenda for the future*. Washington, D.C.:Agenda Press.

Cole, David N. (1978). "Estimating the Susceptibility of Wildland Vegetation to Trailside Alteragtion," *Journal of Applied Ecology, 15*(1):281-286.

Cole, David N. (1981). "Managing Ecological Impacts at Wilderness Campsites: An Evaluation of Techniques," *Journal of Forestry, 79*(2):86-89.

Cole, David N. (1982). Wilderness "Campsite Impacts: Effect of Amount of Use. *USDA Forest Service Research Paper INT-284.* Ogden, UT: Intermt. Forest and Range Exp. Stn.

Cook, David I., & Van Haverbeke, David F. (1972). "Trees Shrubs, and Landforms for Noise Control," *Journal of Soil and Water Conservation, 27*:259-261.

Cowgill, Peter. (1971). "Too Many People on the Colorado River," *National Parks and Conservation Magazine, 45*(11):10-14.

Davis, Gary E. (1990). "Monitoring Natural Resources," *Trends Park Practice Program. 27*(4):32-37.

Davis, Gary E. (1990). "Monitoring Natural Resources." *Trends Park Practice Program. 27*(4):32-37.

Dawson, J. O., Countryman, D. W., & Fittin, R. R. (1978). "Soil and Vegetation Patterns in Northeastern Iowa Campgrounds," *Journal of Soil and Water Conservation, 33*(1):39-41.

Dotzenko, A. D. (1967). "Effects of Recreation Use on Soil and Moisture Conditions in Rocky Mountain National Park," *Journal of Soil and Water Conservation, 22*(5):196-197.

Elder, Hayes. (1971). *Way.* Brussels, Belgium: Forum-Environment.

FitzPatrick, E. A. (1980). *Soils: Their formation, classification and distribution.* New York: Longman, Inc.

Frissell, Sidney S., Jr., & Duncan, Donald P. (1965). "Campsite Preference and Deterioration in the Quetico-Superior Canoe Country," *Journal of Forestry, 63*(4):256-260.

Farmer, Eugene E., & Van Haveren, Bruce P. (1971). *Soil Erosion by Overland Flow and Raindrop Splash on Three Mountain Soils*, USDA Forest Service Research Paper INI-100. Ogden, UT: USDA Intermt. Forest Range Exp. Stn.

Garrahan, Kenneth A. (1989). "Fight the Bite: Ticks and Lyme Disease." *Proceedings,* 1989, St. Paul, MN: National Interpreters Workshop.

Geockermann, K. (1972). *"Physical Change on Newly Established Wilderness Campsites,"* unpublished master's thesis, University of Minnesota, MN: College of Forestry.

Helgath, Sheila. (1975). Trail Deterioration in the Selway-Bitterroot Wilderness, *USDA Forest Service Research Note INI-193.* Ogden, UT: Intermt. Forest Range Exp. Stn.

Herraman, Raymond, & Craig, Turi. (1986). *Proceedings: Conference on Science in the National Parks.* Washington, D.C.:George Wright Society.

Herrington, Roscoe B., & Beardsley, Wendell G. (1970). Improvement and Maintenance of Campground Vegetation in Central Idaho. *USDA Forest Service Paper INT-87.* Ogden, UT: Intermt. Forest and Range Stn.

Hester, Eugene F. (1990). "Preserving Natural Resources: Introduction," *Trends Park Practice Program. 27*(4):31.

Holmes, Daniel O. (1979). "Experiments on the Effects of Human Urine and Trampling on Subalpine Plants," in Ruth Ittner (Ed.), *Recreational Impact on Wildlands Conference Proceedings*, Seattle, WA: Forest Service USDA, National Park Service USDI.

Jackson, Bill, Kimball, Dan, West, Barbara, Williams, Owen, & Ponce, Stan. (1990). "Managing Water Resources," *Trends Park Practice Program. 27*(4):26-31.

Joseph, David. (1990). "Air . . . A Natural Resource." *Trends Park Practice Program. 27*(4):22-25.

Ketchledge, E. H., & Leonard, R.E. (1970). "The Impact of Man on the Adirondack High Country," The Conservationist, *Soil Science Society American Journal, 25*(2):14-18.

King, J. G., & Mace Jr., A. C. (1974). "Effects of Recreation on Water Quality," J. Water Poll. *Cont. Federation, 46*(11):2453-2459.

Larsen, James A. (1980). *The Boreal Ecosystem.* New York: Academic Press.

Leet, Don L., & Judson, S. (1971). *Physical Geology* (4th ed.). Englewood Cliffs, NJ:Prentice-Hall.

Legg, Michael H., & Sneider, G. (1977). "Soil Deterioration on Campsites: Northern Forest Types," The Conservationist, *Soil Science Society American Journal, 41*(1):437-441.

Leonard, Raymond E., & Parr, Sally B. (1970). "Trees as a Sound Barrier," *Journal of Forestry, 68*(5):282-283.

Leonard, Raymond, & Plumley, H. J. (1979). "The Use of Soils Information for Dispersed Recreation Planning," in Ruth Ittner (Ed.), *Recreation Impact onWildlands Conference Proceedings,* Seattle, WA: Forest Service USDA, National Park Service USDI.

LePage, Wilbur F. (1967). Some Observations on Campground Trampling and Ground Cover Response. *USDA Forest Service Research Paper NE-68.* Upper Darby, PA:Northwest For. Exp. Stn.

Lime, David W., & Stankey, George H. (1971). "Carrying Capacity: Maintaining Outdoor Recreation Quality," Proceedings, Forest Recreation Symposium, Syracuse, NY. Upper Darby, PA: LUSDA Forest Service Northeastern Forest Exp. Stn.

Lull, Howard W. (1959). Soil Compaction on Forest and Range Lands. *USDA Forest Service Misc Paper 768.* Upper Darby, PA: Northeastern Forest Exp. Stn.

Mann, Donald L., & Dull, Ken. (1979). "Six Years of Site Restoration at Lyman Lake," in Ruth Ittner (Ed.), *Recreational Impact on Wildlands Conference Proceedings*, Seattle, WA:Forest Service USDA, National Park Service USDI.

Manning, Robert E. (1979). "Impacts of Recreation on Riparian Soils and Vegetation," American Water Resources Association, *Water Resource Bulletin, 15*(1):30-41.

Matheny, Sandy J. (1979). "A Successful Campaign to Reduce Trail Switchback Shortcutting," in Ruth Ittner (Ed.), *Recreational Impact on Wildlands Conference Proceedings,* Seattle, WA: Forest Service USDSA, National Park Service USDI.

Merriam, L. C., Jr., C. K. Smith, D. E. Miller, et al. (1973). Newly Developed Campsites in the Boundary Waters Canoe Area: A Study of Five Years' Use. *University of Minnesota Agriculture Experimental Station Bulletin 411*, U.S. Forest Service.

Pfister, Robert E., & Frenkel, Robert E. (1975). *The concept of carrying capacity: Its application for management of Oregon's scenic waterway system.* Salem, OR:Oregon State Marine Board.

Ream, Catherine H. (1980). Impact of Backcountry Recreationists on Wildlife: An Annotated Bibliography, *USDA Forest Service General Technical Report INT-84*, Ogden, UT:USDA Intermt. Forest and Range Exp. Stn.

Reynolds, George. (1987). *Promise or a threat? A study of greater Yellowstone management.* Riverston, WY:We Care.

Ripley, Thomas H. (1962). Tree and Shrub Response to Recreation Use. *USDA Forest Service Research Note No, 171.* Asheville, NC: Southeastern Forest Exp. Stn.

Schultz, Richard D., & Bailey, James A. (1978). "Responses of National Park Elk to Human Activity," *Journal of Wildlife Management, 42*(1):91-99.

Settergren, C. C., & Cole, D. M. (1970). "Recreation effects on soils and vegetation in the Missouri Ozarks," *Journal of Forestry, 68*(4):231-233.

Settergren, Carl D. (1977). "Impacts of River Recreation Use on Streamband Soils and Vegetation – State-of-the-Knowledge," Proceedings: River Recreation Management and Research Symposium. *USDA Forest Service General Technical Report NC-28.* January 24-27, 1977.

Sharpe, Grant W., Hendee, Clare W., & Sharpe, Wenonah F. (1984). *Introduction to forestry* (5th ed.). New York: McGraw-Hill.

Shields, James T., & Swanson, Gustav A. (1971). "Places to Fish and Hunt – The Problem of Access," in Richard D. Teague (Ed.), *.A manual of wildlife conservation.* Washington D.C.:The Wildlife Society.

Stankey, Geroge H., & Lime, David W. (1973). Recreation Carrying Capacity: An Annotated Bibliography. *USDA Forest Service General Technical Report INT-3.* Ogden, UT: Intermt. Forest and Range Exp. Stn.

Sudia, Theodore W., & Simpson, James M. (1973). "Recreational Carrying Capacity of the National Parks," Guideline. *Park Practice Program. 3*(3):25-34.

Taylor, Robert E. (1990). *Ahead of the curve.* New York: Environmental Defense Fund.

Teschner, D. P., DeWitt, G. M., & Lindsay, J. J. (1979). "Hiking Impact on Boreal Forest Vegetation and Soils in Vermont's Northern Green Mountains." *Research Note SNR-RM 6.* Burlington, VT: University of Vermont.

Tracy, D. M. (1977). *"Reaction of Wildlife to Human Activity Along the Mount McKinley National Park Road,"* unpublished master's thesis, Fairbanks, AK: University of Alaska.

Wagar, J. Alan. (1974). "Recreational Carrying Capacity of Wildlands for Recreation," *Forest Science Monograph 7.*

Wagar, J. Alan. (1974). "Recreational Carrying Capacity Reconsidered," *Journal of Forestry, 72*(5):274-278.

Waggenet, R. J., & Lawrence, C. H. (1974). "Recreational Effects on Bacteriological Quality of an Impounded Water Supply," *Journal of Environmental Health, 3*(1):16-20.

White, Ray J. (1971). "Stream Improvement," in Richard D. Teague (Ed.), *A manual of wildlife conservation*, Washington, D.C.:The Wildlife Society.

Wilkins, Bruce T. (1971). "Non-harvest Aspects of Wildlife Management," in Richard D. Teague (Ed.), *.A manual of wildlife conservation*, Washington, D.C.:The Wildlife Society.

Wondra, Phil. (1990). "Using Geographic: Information Systems to Manage Natural Resources," *Trends Park Practice Program.*

Wright, Gerald. (1990). "Managing Wildlife in National Parks," *Trends Park Practice Program. 27*(4):17-21.

Yoakum, James D. (1971). "Habitat Improvement," in Richard D. Teague (Ed.), *A manual of wildlife conservation*, Washington, D.C.:The Wildlife Society.

Young, Robert A. (1978). "Camping Intensity Effects on Vegetative Ground Cover in Illinois Campgrounds," *Journal of Soil and Water Conservation,33*(1):36-39.

Zaslowsky, Dyan. (1981). "Looking Into Soles and Other Weighty Matters," *Audubon, 83*(2):60-63.

*Chapter Twelve*

# User Conflict Management

The recreation area manager will be primarily concerned with three different scenarios, each with some variation depending upon the park being managed: the conflicts between recreational and non-recreational users of the land, the conflicts among recreation users themselves, and the conflicts between park managers and other entities. A number of reasons exist as to why these conflicts happen, such as grazing and extraction activities, crowding, expectations of users among other things. For example, in Table 12.1, the Wisconsin State Parks has identified the following conflicts within their park system in rank order in its State Comprehensive Outdoor Recreation Plan (SCORP). As one can see, there are issues both within and among users, agency and administrative issues, and park manager issues.

---

### Table 12.1. Ranked Recreation Conflicts in Wisconsin

| | |
|---|---|
| Environmental damage | Wildlife |
| Trails | Ordinance |
| Landowners | Access |
| Activity ban | Viewscapes |
| Management actions | Bills (legislative) |
| Local parks | Budget/fees |
| Safety | Water levels |
| Noise | |

---

In any case, the important issue is how conflict is managed will determine its toxicity; thus, the conflict-management process is of imminent importance (Dustin & Schneider, 1998). An example of placing managers in a position of conflict resolution is oftentimes the result of multiple overlapping and conflicting organizational goals. For example, Cole (1989) examined the rafting business on the Colorado River within the Grand Canyon. He noted that the management objectives for the River in the Grand Canyon focused on providing quality experiences, solitude, and natural quiet. A seemingly conflicting objective was to provide users of all ages, abilities, and conditions opportunities to float the river. What is the manager to do? Limit use so some receive the expected benefits of solitude and natural quiet, or serve the masses? The picture below presents a number of questions to be answered. Did these boaters realize the extent to which this beach is used? Is this beach at capacity, and are there conflicts with other boaters, fisherman, homeowners along the shoreline, and other types of water users (jet skis, speed boats, kayaks)? How is this use level in compliance with management objectives for the area?

To get a sense of perspective, an understanding of the historical context will assist in seeing current conflicts calmly as part of an ongoing adjustment in land use and user values and attitudes.

## A BRIEF HISTORY OF LAND-USE ATTITUDES

The following quote from Ernie Swift (1958) in the National Wildlife Federation's book, *The Glory Trail*, outlines the early conflicts. "Land was given to the states, to the veterans of successive wars. . . . The creation of the Forest Service did not end the fight, but it marked the high tide of exploitation and the meager beginnings of resource management and some restraints."

Public and political interest were stimulated during the 1860s and 1870s as a result of two trips west. In 1859, Horace Greeley not only went west but also publicized his trip to Yosemite. The portentous exploration of Yellowstone country by the Washburne-Langford-Doane expedition took place in 1870. Citizen interest in the West increased. Political pressure to arrest exploitation grew mainly through the efforts of conservationists and publishers. One manifestation of this interest and pressure was the effort to establish national reserve lands.

In 1864, administration of the Yosemite Grant was transferred to California in order to better protect it. It became a national park in 1906. Yellowstone was set aside in 1972 but without any funds to operate it. In 1891, the forest reserves, later called national forests, were established. The Antiquities Act of 1906 gave the executive branch a method of protecting choice lands until such time as Congress might be persuaded to mandate protection.

Free access or free use of forest resources was taken as a right by industrial, agricultural, and individual interests throughout the West during the nineteenth century. Each time regulations and restrictions were proposed or enacted, conflicts were generated. Timber, mining, grazing, and railroad fortunes were involved, huge payrolls were affected, homesteaders were shut out, taxpayers were concerned with new demands on the budget, and the esthetic conservationists began to organize.

In the early twentieth century, recreation on public lands was typified by automobile and tent campers as well as by hunters, fishermen, and hikers. However, it was limited by the Great Depression in the 1930s. At the same time, the federal government assisted outdoor recreation through the work for the Civilian Conservation Corps and Works Progress Administration.

In the aftermath of World War II, the stimulated economy brought a higher standard of living and a wider range of travel. Increased mobility within our society as well as economic and social trends helped to create a desire for outdoor recreational opportunities. Leisure ceased to be defined in negatives, and vacations became mandatory. The idea of "getting away from it all" somehow became entangled with the admonition "Be prepared!", and recreational vehicles were hatched. These were soon followed by off-road vehicles (ORVs), trail bikes, and snowmobiles, and later by hang gliders and jet skis.

During the 1960s, there was a sharp increase in the recreational use of public lands. This increased use was not always taken into account in federal or state agency budgeting or by management and other personnel, who were often slow to adjust attitudes and methods in order to cope with the influx. The Outdoor Recreation Resources Review Commission (ORRRC) outlined what resources were available and how people would want to use them. From this, and from a growing body of research, an understanding of the North American situation has finally emerged. Subsequent commissions, such as Americans Outdoors, have strengthened that understanding. Land and water must be managed to protect the resource, park visitors must be educated and regulated to provide for their understanding and safety, and the ensuing conflicts must be researched and met in a manner reasonable acceptable to all.

In many ways, the development of land-use attitudes in Canada paralleled those of the United States. Historians of the conservation movement have observed two streams of thought in the early days of the park movement in both the United States and Canada. One group argued for a "usefulness" type of conservation—the "rational" use of natural resources. The second group called for strict control of natural resource exploitation and the preservation of unique environments. In the United States, the national parks adhered more closely to the preservation theme, whereas the national parks of Canada followed the usefulness stream of conservationist thought, at least in the early years. The first national park in Canada was established at Banff Springs in 1885, just 13 years after the establishment of Yellowstone National Park in the United States (Nicol, 1968). The creation of Algonquin Provincial Park in Ontario, which occurred in 1893, stressed the desirability of "government regulated logging, wildlife protection, and the potential for hotel- and cottage-style vacationing (Morrison, 1979)."

Camping out and all its related activities (hiking, skiing, swimming, boating, running, biking, and even the use of recreational vehicles in park settings) are now perceived as necessities by millions of North Americans as well as visitors from other continents who come here to partake of these outdoor amenities. Some enthusiasts want space, quiet, solitude, pure air, and trails through vast tracts unmarred by human endeavor; others expect well-groomed interlocking trail systems leading off from conveniently located facilities with hot water and electrical outlets. These groups will be in conflict with one another at times. Motorized groups bother hikers and equestrians, and, on occasion, even each other. It seems that one person's recreation may be another person's annoyance.

The struggle over recreational lands is not limited to user groups but affects administration, too. New agencies dealing with these lands have been created. Established agencies have awakened to the extent of their involvement. An excerpt from *Reality and the Middle Ground*, regarding conflict follows:

> Conflicts also develop between various entities of government and between existing resource uses contesting for the available capital. Higher levels of government are frequently able to establish higher priorities and exercise authorities over lesser levels of government. Such priorities and authorities have on more than one occasion been exercised to the detriment of recreation. Additionally, the resource allocations are nearly always made in favor of the use for which identifiable and quantifiable benefits can be calculated. Here again, recreation is virtually assured of being relegated to a secondary role. (Ramsey & Schnell, 1970).

The above paragraph was written in 1948, but the problem of intergovernmental wrangling is still with us. Even though there is now more land set aside and, relatively speaking, more money available for recreation, the skirmishing continues between agencies and user groups and among the agencies themselves, with constantly shifting alliances. In all probability, these conflicts will continue. However, their intensity and scope will no doubt vary with changing economic, social and political conditions.

## An Understanding of Conflicts in Recreation from the Social Sciences

There have been many advances in examining user conflicts in outdoor settings and understanding the ways in which park managers can address the conflicts. Some reasons include the lack of public land for recreation, restricted access, growing populations, and trends in recreational pursuits. Marcouiller, Scott, and Prey (2005) noted that there are two perspectives in which managers must be aware of and able to address. First, there is the issue of alternative and competing recreation uses within a confined land base, as noted by Carothers et al. (2001) and Manning and Valliere, (2001). This is in part driven by new technology and motorized vehicles according to Roe and Benson, (2001), and Wang and Dawson, (2005). The second arena of conflict noted arises between outdoor recreation and other forms of land use (Clawson 1974; Marcouiller 2000). This inter-use conflict impacts how open space develops, and the competing economic land based interests such as residential, commercial, industrial, agriculture, and forestry.

Conflict has been traditionally viewed as a result of goal interference among users (Jacob & Schreyer 1980; Ivy et al. 1992; Ruddell & Gramann 1994; Gibbons & Ruddell 1995; Vaske et al. 2000; Vaske et al. 2004; Wang & Dawson 2005). Jacob and Schreyer's (1980) goal interference model identifies four major factors that contribute to recreation conflict: (a) the meaning individuals attach to the activity, (b) the significance of the resource to the individual, (c) the extent to which the individual is focused on the environment or activity, and (d) the users' acceptance of different lifestyles. Differences in social values (Adelman et al. 1982; Saremba & Gill 1991; Watson et al.

1994; Vaske et al. 1995; Carothers et al. 2001; Whittaker et al. 2001), emotional state of the user (Lee and Shafer 2002; Vitterso et al. 2004; Lee et al. 2005) or sense of place (Stokowski 2002), also explain variation in conflicts among users. Finally, Vaske et.al. (2000) noted that another concept besides goal interference is also useful in some situations. For example, when multiple groups share the same physical space, safety concerns may influence conflict (Blahna, Smith, & Anderson, 1995), especially for high-speed activities that attract large numbers of participants in relatively confined areas such as ski resorts (Finley, 1990; Hughes, 1988).

In a conceptualization of conflicts among users, Marcouiller, Scott, and Prey (2005) noted that interactions among users fall into four basic categories along a spectrum that include (a) complementary, (b) supplementary, (c) competitive, and (d) antagonistic (van Kooten 1993). In light of the above frameworks, Vaske et al. (2000) developed the model in Figure 12.1 and empirically tested the model with alpine skiing and snowboarders. The model was confirmed in their research. Basically, the activity style of the user, the resource base, lifestyle tolerance of participants, safety and mode of experience lead to two types of conflicts, out-of-group and in-group conflicts. In-group conflicts could be surfers vying for the best wave surf. Out-of-group conflicts would include surfers, body surfers, sailboards, and bodyboarders competing for waves at the same break (Lankford, Hetzler, & Lankford, 1995).

## Figure 12.1. Social Carrying Capacity Model

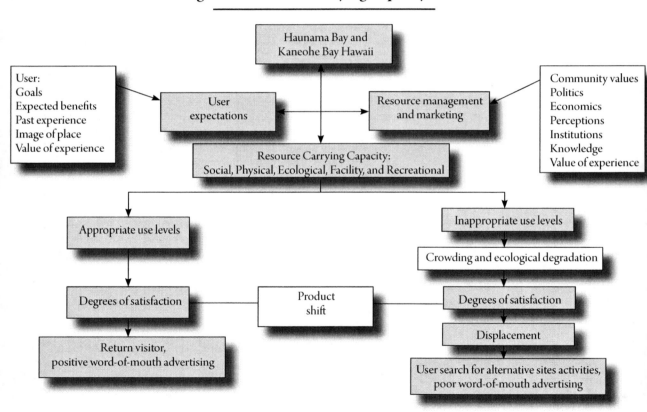

From Lankford, S., Inui, Y., Whittle, A., Luna, R., Tyrone, D. (2005). *Sustainability of Coastal/Marine Recreation: Modeling Social Carrying Capacity for Hanauma Bay, Hawaii.* Paper funded by a grant/cooperative agreement from the National Oceanic and Atmospheric Administration, Project # R/FM-8, which is sponsored by the University of Hawaii Sea Grant College Program, SOEST, under Institutional Grant No. NA86RG0041 and NA16RG2254 from NOAA Office of Sea Grant, Department of Commerce. The views expressed herein are those of the author(s) and do not necessarily reflect the views of NOAA or any of its subagencies. UNIHI-SEAGRANT-OP-02-001. Retrieved from http://www.uni.edu/step/reports/hb_seagrant_final.pdf.

In response to conflicts and capacity issues, the United States Department of Agriculture Forest Service has led the way in research on the social and behavioral issues within conflict management in natural resource areas. Their long-term research will focus on four categories: changing recreation patterns; values, attitudes, behaviors, and conflict related to natural resources; communication related to recreation and natural resource use; and social and recreation aspects of fire; and fire management. The Research and Development–Social Science Research Unit (http://www.fs.fed.us/research/social_science_research.shtml) has developed the following structure to research and inform managers on the best means of managing conflicts.

A. **Community research** is conducted by social scientists with specialties in rural and urban sociology, environmental and social psychology, human geography, and political science. This research provides knowledge about human relationships, demographic changes, and social forces and institutions that influence natural resource protection and management. Community research may be conducted at the local community scale, or at larger "community-of-interest" regional and national scales. Topics of research include:

1. Community well-being: contribution of forest-based industries to community well-being; impacts of social and land use change associated with the urbanization of rural areas; understanding community resiliency
2. Social networks: characteristics of collaborative stewardship and implications for forest management; development of effective public participation processes; local institutional capacities related to natural resource management
3. Social trends: systems for monitoring the social environment; implications of changing demographics for forest management
4. Values and perceptions: conflicting values and perceptions related to forests and forest management; sense of place; social and political models of resource valuation

B. **Cultural heritage research,** which relies primarily on the sciences of anthropology, cultural geography, and archaeology, to provide knowledge about the characteristics of sustainable societies, the cultural dimensions of ecosystem management, and the management and enhancement of heritage resources. The major topics of research include:

1. Traditional local cultures: role of traditional practices in maintaining cultural identity and economic health, use of traditional ecological knowledge
2. Human populations and environmental change: sustaining communities and management institutions in the face of conflict, climate change, and resource change; historic human influences on landscape development

C. **Economics research** provides information for evaluating the consequences of resource management policies and decisions. A wide range of topics are being studied, including the following:

1. Economic impacts of forest management: role of wood products, non-timber products, and recreation and tourism in local and regional economies
2. Fire economics: fire budgeting and program analysis, large fire costs, fuels management, public preferences and perceptions of fire management, economic impacts of wildland fire on local communities
3. Forest policy: sustainable forest management, international trade and environmental policies; effects of taxes, laws, and regulations on forest management
4. Forest product markets: supply of and demand for forest products; effects of technology change, economic feasibility of processes and products; U.S. competitiveness
5. Forest values: monetary and non-monetary valuation of market and non-market goods and services

6.  Nonindustrial private forest management: effects of natural resource policies on landowner behavior; economic efficiency of alternative management strategies

D.  **Outdoor recreation research** provides information about recreation use of forests, supply and demand of recreation opportunities, and impacts of resource management activities and landscape change on recreation activities. A broad range of topics are studied including:

1.  Relationship between ecological conditions and recreation activities: impacts of fire on recreation activities
2.  Cultural differences in outdoor recreation use: minority participation in outdoor recreation; access to leisure and urban open space opportunities
3.  Psychological and social dimensions of the recreation experience: human values and perceptions associated with recreation activities; sense of place and recreation management; experiential aspects of wilderness; impacts of criminal activity in forests on recreation; use of recreation fees; recreation visitor conflicts
4.  Recreation assessment and trends: visitor service quality assessment; national recreation assessment and trend analysis (NSRE); national visitor use monitoring (NVUM); scenic quality assessment

E.  **Resources Planning Act (RPA) Assessment.** The Forest Service has the responsibility to prepare the Forest and Rangeland Renewable Resources Planning Act of 1974 (RPA) Assessment. This periodic report examines status and trends for natural resources and their management on all forest and rangelands in the United States. The Assessment is used to track trends in the extent and condition of resources, and the supply of and demand for renewable natural resources. Supporting documents provide detailed information on specific resource areas or topics, such as recreation, water, wildlife, fisheries, range forage, timber, minerals, urban forests, climate change, and forest resource statistics. Assessment documents are available on the RPA website in pdf format (http://svinet2.fs.fed.us/pl/rpa/).

F.  **Wildland Recreation and Urban Cultures Research Unit** examines recreation activities, management decision making, and evaluates management strategies, especially at the wildland/urban interface with a focus on: changing recreation use patterns, including those derived from ethnicity and technological changes; values, attitudes and behaviors, as well as barriers or conflict, related to natural resources; communication related to recreation and natural resource use; and the social and recreational aspects of fire and fire management. Created in 1987, the unit has a primary focus on non-traditional recreation activities, non-traditional visitors, and heavily used wildland areas.

## EXAMPLES OF CONFLICTS BETWEEN RECREATION USERS AND NONRECREATION USERS

An area that is ripe for conflict is one that must be shared by those seeking enjoyment and those earning a living. Several entities are affected by this type of controversy.

### Timber Management

Some hikers, backpackers, and other recreationists are disturbed by timber harvesting and silvicultural methods that severely alter the ground cover. Many fishermen are irritated by the effects of logging practices and road construction on the fish habitat. Swimmers complain about manufacturing wastes that adversely affect the appearance and quality of the beach as well as the water. The concern for air quality and fuel conservation has brought about increased criticism of slash burning, while debate continues about the practice of clear cutting.

**Possible controversy.** As with all conflicts, there is another side to the story. Many forest fires are started by thoughtless campers or sparks from ORVs. Snowmobiles damage the terminal buds of snow-buried evergreens, causing tree regeneration problems similar to those caused by deer or elk. Vandalism continues to plague landowners; broken gates and locks, stolen or damaged logging equipment, and damaged signs are common problems. And if clear cutting bothers the environmentalists, tree theft angers timber growers.

Logging has been practiced in several Canadian parks and is very controversial. In the past, timber harvesting has taken place in Strathcona Provincial Park (B.C.) and in Quetico Provincial Park (Ontario), but current management policies have eliminated logging activities. Logging is still practiced in Algonquin Provincial Park (Ontario), and some adverse impacts have been recorded (Hegens, 1980). Selective cutting of hardwoods has resulted in very poor browse for large ungulates, such as the deer. Because tourists come to Algonquin Park expressly to view deer, it is apparent that logging practices, although perhaps well intended, have been counterproductive to recreation objectives.

This issue of forest fire management is contentious, at least in the Ontario Park System. While many people realize that timber-management practices such as controlled burns approximate natural processes, these have not been used by the Ontario Park System; instead, natural fires are suppressed. Fire suppression in the past has led to stagnant forests in which natural forest fire hazards are severe. To allow natural forest fires to run their course would be catastrophic.

**Ways to minimize conflicts.** Certainly it is true that wood and paper users—and this includes all of us—have to recognize that the accustomed comforts of civilization require raw materials and that a clear-cut hillside has a very direct connection with our comfortable, even luxurious, North American standard of living. Also, certain recreational activities are in part dependent upon clear cuts or are facilitated by logging roads. Fortunately, there are the following ways to minimize the undesirable effects, both real and perceived, of timber harvesting.

1. Interpretation of timber practices to provide an understanding of management methods and goals. These groups most concerned about timber management should be approached with carefully chosen methods. A slick color film is not going to convince knowledgeable backpackers. They need show-me trips, short slide presentations by on-the-spot personnel, and a chance to pose hard questions and get honest answers.
2. Provision of buffer zones to screen the more unsightly stages of timber regeneration especially from major highways and, where possible, from trails.
3. Use of irregularly shaped cutting units that more nearly conform to natural clearings.
4. Use of greater care in transport of logs and disposal of debris near fish-breeding waters.
5. More imaginative efforts to make use of logging slash. No matter how convincing the economic argument, burning huge amounts of air-polluting fuel simply to get rid of it cannot be unquestioningly accepted in today's fuel-conscious and environmentally aware society.

## Watershed Management

As with timber management, there are also conflicts among people of sincere convictions over watershed management. Watersheds include the original smaller streams of rainwater or melted snow that feed into larger bodies of water, such as rivers and lakes. Watersheds vary greatly in size and shape.

**Possible controversy.** Watershed management programs usually benefit the whole of society in one way or another. Yet the very magnitude of watersheds causes most people to identify benefits and drawbacks from the same project. For example, dams provide irrigation and power, control floods, and create a reservoir for water-based recreational activities. These same dams also destroy steam fishing, some forms of hunting, and the beauty of the free-flowing rivers, although they replace the latter with their own forms of beauty.

Watersheds for municipal drinking water are sometimes placed off limits to recreation users, and this often causes confusion, because in some areas, where tertiary treatment of water is undertaken, watersheds are open to recreation. Conflict not only exists between the watershed managers and the potential users, but also involves medical people and other public health specialists who are concerned with overuse, contamination, and litter.

The development for the James Bay Power Project in northern Quebec altered several major river systems and their environments. Although not designated as a wilderness area or park, this type of ecosystem is currently underrepresented in the Parks Canada system's planning strategy, and so there is controversy over its development.

In Ontario, the Madawoska, Spanish, and Missinaibi are outstanding recreational rivers, but their future is constantly debated in terms of their potential to supply hydroelectric power. In British Columbia, the Stikine River faces similar pressure. Also in British Columbia, the Campbell River on Vancouver Island was damned in the past to provide hydroelectricity for the island. When this damn was constructed, the watershed was logged according to specifications of the time. The reservoir, known as Buttle Lake, is a significant feature of Strathcoma Provincial Park. Unfortunately, when water levels are low, the stumps of this logged-off watershed are visible and detract from the spectacular landscape.

This same problem exists in many reservoirs in the United States. At the time of logging, specifications for stump height were not as stringent as they are now. The issue of relicensing looms large as many licenses issued during a time of relatively uninhibited resources use now expire. Washington State alone contained three instances. In Olympic National Park, a proposal to restore the Elwah River drainage ecosystem was receiving high-level support. At Lake Cushman bordering Olympic National Park, a power company was preparing to trade land to the Park Service to eliminate an impoundment trespass. In North Cascades National Park, yet another major power company agreed to pay for environmental mitigation in its effort to relicense two existing dams.

**Ways to minimize conflicts.** Some of the conflicts over dams of various kinds can be minimized by stressing the contributions of the project to the residents of the area through interpretation. This should be on site for visitors to the project, off site through slide programs made available to clubs and other group, and by means of publications and articles in newspapers.

Various remedies for specific problems related to dams and reservoirs are available, such as trapping and trucking anadromous fish around dams and creating shallow impoundments in reservoirs to provide natural plant feed for birds.

In case of watersheds containing municipal water reservoirs, limiting the type of recreation equipment and the type and amount of use allowed as well as providing suitable sanitation facilities should be considered. Managers of recreation areas involving dams and reservoirs should not be insensitive to the controversial nature of these projects even though the necessity of the project might seem undeniable. Present-day visitors may be sophisticated consumers, but they are frequently disinterested in, if not downright hostile to, such mechanics of civilization as irrigation or power generation. Managers must seek to identify the nature of conflicts and misunderstandings with an eye to alleviating them, and should try to interest the public in the way such utilities function.

## Highways and Roads

Environmental problems and inflationary pressures have brought new superhighway building to a virtual halt. Some highways and access roads are still being constructed, however, and repair and rebuilding continues, in parks and other recreation areas.

**Possible controversy.** The majority of U.S. and Canadian citizens are wedded to their cars but are becoming hesitant about disrupting wildlife habitat or destroying wetlands for construction. Further extension of logging or fire access roads is also a troublesome issue; one that generates lively debate.

**Ways to minimize conflicts.** Certainly park managers need to be alert to point out the potential impact of any new roads or highways on their areas and be ready to try to mitigate harmful effects if construction of these is unavoidable.

Ways are being found to convey visitors about the parks by jitney buses and aerial trams. Federal funds have been provided for highway beautification and abutting bicycle routes. Scenic and recreational highway systems are being created in some jurisdictions. Roadside rests in some areas are places of beauty and enjoyment with interpretive and directional materials available.

The situation calls for intelligent long-range policy decisions, as indeed, do all of the conflicts dealt with in this chapter. A political climate that fosters professional expertise and allows for wide public input will serve the resource and the recreationist best in the long run.

## Mining

Mining and recreation activities conflict in several ways, although usually not as dramatically as in previously mentioned conflicts.

Today, we find many abandoned mines and accompanying mine shafts in wilderness areas. It must first be noted that mining is a congressionally approved activity within most wilderness areas under the Wilderness Act, and it is also allowed in certain classes of Canadian national parks. Where mines are still active, they bring criticism for pollution and visual disruption, but such mines must operate under certain restrictions, and a climate of mutual tolerance should be fostered.

**Possible controversy.** Abandoned shafts create serious safety hazards to hikers and ORV users and many constitute "attractive nuisances" to explorers. To some, old mining machinery is an eyesore, while to others it is a reminder of a moment in history. The results of strip mining continue to offend the travelling public, not to mention the local environmentalists.

Another conflict is caused by water passing through shaft mines and running over and out of open-pit mines. Depending on the type of mine, adjacent streams may be found to have quantities of metals lethal to waterfowl.

**Ways to minimize conflicts**. There are very few if any practical ways to minimize the adverse effects of mine-caused water pollution except to post the area. However, there are ways of alleviating the safety and esthetic problems of mines. Boarding up mine shafts will usually be short-lived in effectiveness as enterprising explorers will soon open the most entrance-proof of barriers. High barbed fencing is one of the best deterrents, especially when accompanied by explanatory signing.

Historical interpretation gives recreationists a better understanding of the importance of mining today, as well as in the past. Proper screening of open-pit mines and strip-mined areas, along with planned landscaping, can mitigate the visual impact.

## Livestock

Cattle grazing is occurring with greater frequency on recreation lands. Areas having profuse growth of grasses are vulnerable to range fires in the dry season, and grazing can reduce the accumulation of fuel. Having become accustomed to the cowboy mythology, we may take cattle grazing on the open range for granted, but there are those who believe that grazing causes undesirable changes and perhaps unacceptable damages to the range ecosystem. Certainly it subjects the range plants to the selective pressure of cattle grazing in addition to that already exerted by native species such as deer, antelope, and elk.

**Possible controversy.** The desire of sheep ranchers to exterminate predators (especially coyotes) has resulted in confrontations with environmentalists, nature enthusiasts, and recreationists. Exploding "coyote getters" are dangerous to hikers, campers, and anyone else using public lands. Poisoned carcasses create esthetic as well as contamination problems, especially near fishing streams popular with campers. Poisons kill nontarget species of birds and mammals. Predator control programs upset recreationists who consider their outdoor experiences enhanced by the presence of any and all wildlife. Recreationists and conservationists anger sheep ranchers who consider their livelihood threatened by these species and by what they consider to be the environmentalists' selfish and ill-informed meddling.

Competition for food between livestock and big-game animals results in conflicts between hunters and ranchers. Species such as deer, elk, and bighorn sheep sometimes compete for the same foods as domestic sheep and cattle.

**Ways to minimize conflicts.** The resource manager will have little influence on the management of livestock that is grazed on private lands. Those resource managers who manage open or range lands will be exposed to the difficulties, but will also have some channels for minimizing conflicts, including (a) being certain that all such lands have established animal month units (AMU), which estimate the number of animals that can graze in a given period of time without damage to the vegetation, (b) careful posting of these lands so the general public will be aware of the presence of livestock, and (c) interpretive programming aimed at targeted conservationist and rancher organizations and presented at their meetings. This task must be handled by open-minded, well-informed personnel who can stand firm amidst the crossfire of outraged animal lovers and furious ranchers.

## Wildlife

Prohibition of hunting does not necessarily mean wildlife populations are undisturbed. In even the most natural settings conflicts emerge, and some situations can be dangerous to humans.

**Possible controversy.** Where park rules preclude hunting or allowing natural fires to burn, changes have taken place in the faunal composition that negate the policy of leaving the area unchanged. Large populations of elk have created overgrazing problems, for example, in Yellowstone National Park and the Canadian Rocky Mountain parks. Exotic animals, such as the burros in the Grand Canyon and the mountain goats in Olympic National Park, have caused problems for visitors, as well as for native fauna and flora. In early 1900, the USNPS finished an extensive study of goat impact, and, as a result, set out to rid the park of the goats. Two years of successful live capture and transplant had to be stopped because of the danger to personnel as well as the goats. The Park Service has held public meetings and assembled a team of experts to help decide how to resolve this issue. The same is true for the reintroduction of the wolves in the Yellowstone ecosystem. The controversy between park users, local ranchers, and communities is an extremely debated issue and has drawn international attention to the perceived issues of wildlife in and around population centers.

**Ways to minimize conflicts.** Park managers need to be abreast of agency policy as well as public sentiment on these matters, and must act with discretion. Where the large herbivores and carnivores move beyond park boundaries, it may be necessary to establish buffer zones to prevent conflicts with adjacent ranchers. In some instances, it may be necessary to fence certain areas. In addition, resource managers should (a) listen to and converse with people on both sides of these issues, (b) seek and study the technical advice of scientists, (c) consult with other groups who are involved in the same situation, and (d) develop carefully worked-out policies and seek to make them intelligible to the communications media and to the general public. It is of greatest importance that visitors to parks with dangerous species be adequately forewarned and instructed in safety procedures.

## Native Rights

In Canada, many provincial and national parks have been established in areas where native groups live or continue to hold some form of tenure or land-use privileges. In these parks, and also in the new national parks and monuments in Alaska, native people retain the right to hunt, fish, or trap for subsistence foods or materials. Their subsistence activities for the most part have not jeopardized wildlife or natural features, and so it can be argued that the continued subsistence activities of native people is a part of this natural environment. Conflicts, of course, are bound to occur from time to time between park managers, hunters, and native groups over resource extraction within parks.

## Nonconforming Uses

All of the foregoing topics involve conflicts between recreational and nonrecreational use of the land. There is another type of conflict brought about when the resource agency receives a request for a nonconforming use, often to erect a structure that is not related to recreational pursuits. Such structures might well include television or radio station antennae, civil defense buildings, or housing for personnel not employed by the park agency.

To handle such problems, most agencies adopt policies that assert that the agency is firmly opposed to the placement of any facilities that will adversely affect public recreation or despoil the natural environment. While such policies declare that public recreational needs and park values are paramount to any other use, they usually contain some statement that might allow exceptions. For instance, it might state that conflicting uses shall be considered only when no feasible alternative exists and public welfare, safety, or the integrity of park lands should be defensible.

## Conflicts Among Recreation Users

Even though there are and always will be conflicts between recreational users and nonrecreational users of the lands under management, by far the greatest clash of personalities and the most vigorous forwarding of mutually exclusive objectives occurs among the users themselves. There is even conflict among devotees of the same sport, as levels of expertise and degrees of specialization exist within all activities. These problems can only increase, because in the future there will be less and less land on which to recreate and, presumably, there will be more people desiring to do so. Further complications will arise from the fact that people will probably have even more time and more money to spend in recreational pursuits. Less gasoline at higher prices will also increase the intensity of the conflict by narrowing the choice of area available for recreation.

The following examples of conflicts among user groups relate to specific uses, types of development, and areas. The list is not meant to be inclusive, but rather to provide examples of a variety of conflicts.

### Trails and Hikers

There is a recognition that there are some differences in multiuse trail management due to location, various environmental factors, types of usage, and urban and rural influences, among other factors. At study by Gambill (n.d.) for the American Trails found many similarities among agencies surveyed with respect to both problems and solutions in user-group cooperation and resource management.

**Possible controversy.** Managing conflict among trail user-groups, and controlling the impacts of overuse associated with crowding or misuse of the trail system. Tour guides in Hawaii market trails to tourists, yet the fragile soil structure erodes when too many hikers use an area in conjunction with the heavy rainfall. The study by Gambill (n.d.) cited user-group conflicts occurring in all geographic areas of the country represented by the survey. Survey data on 28 multiuse trails in northeastern Illinois and on 43 trails in other states was analyzed. Through the use of a different questionnaire, input was solicited from trail user, trail advocacy, and conservation organizations on their policies concerning multiuse trail issues. Overall, the most prevalent user-group conflicts were perceived to be: (a) pedestrian/bicyclist (both tour and mountain bike); (b) equestrian/mountain bicyclist; and (c) cross-country skier/snowmobiler.

Respondents in the trail impact study also evaluated overall environmental impacts to the trail path and adjacent lands due to trail use activities in a similar fashion. The majority of all respondents assessed some minor problems due to trail-use activity on their sites. Forty percent of the respondents evaluated overall impacts as causing moderate or major problems, such as soil erosion, soil compaction, vegetation damage, off-trail abuse, and impacts from activity on wet trails.

The three most important social/behavioral causes of user-group conflict were perceived to be: (a) "reckless or unsafe behavior"; (b) "incompatibility of user-group values (e.g. attitudes toward nature, appropriateness of trail use activities)"; and (c) "user-group causing environmental impacts" and/or "user-group going off-trail." Other respondents noted: "reckless or unsafe behavior" was rated as the most important cause; for Illinois respondents, "user-group causing environmental impacts" and "user-group going off-trail" were rated equally as being the most important cause of conflict. "Crowding" was rated by the majority of all respondents as the most important trail-related cause of conflict. In general, social/behavioral factors were rated as being more important causes of conflict than were trail-related factors.

**Ways to minimize conflicts.** Respondents from all states surveyed assessed the following as the most important measures to reduce conflict:

1. "More education of user groups by user-group organizations and media on proper trail use and trail etiquette" was rated as the most important by the majority of all respondents
2. "More education to be provided by trail-managing agencies"
3. "More brochures, maps, and other trail-related information for dissemination to trail users"
4. "More communication between trail-managing agencies and user-groups." Respondents rated "more patrolling or monitoring" as among the next most important measures needed to reduce conflict on their multiuse trails. In general, light-handed measures, (i.e., education, communication, etc.), were rated as the most important ways to reduce conflicts among trail user-groups.

Approximately 50 percent of all respondents indicated that their agencies now provide some type of formal trail user education; however, most of this appeared to be in the form of brochures and signage. Twenty-eight percent of respondents advised that they provide other types of education including presentations by park rangers, barricade programs, bicycle rodeos, group meetings with agency staff, forums, nature or awareness programs, and public relation campaigns.

Additional recommendations made for management of user-group conflict included:

1. involve user groups in the decision-making process,
2. use volunteer patrols, and
3. involve user groups in trail maintenance.

Recommendations for controlling adverse impacts of trail use included:

1. appropriate trail design and maintenance,
2. seasonal closures and closures during wet conditions, and
3. education of the trail user.

## Hunting

There are basic conflicts between those who hunt and those who don't hunt as well as conflicts among the hunters themselves. Some nonhunters are not necessarily against hunting, but do view hunting as a single-use activity and are critical of the large amount of land it requires.

**Possible controversy.**  There are other nonhunters who object to hunting itself. These people generally lodge their complaints in one of the following three sweeping indictments:

1. The animals need to be saved from hunters. The balance of nature will keep the population in check without interference from the hunters.
2. Hunters lose their sense of judgment when pursuing wildlife and endanger other land users, as well as themselves.
3. Hunters trespass, vandalize signs and buildings, strew litter, start uncontrolled fires, harm livestock, and illegally cut trees for firewood, camp furniture, and tent poles.

On one hand, hunters feel strongly about their rights, and point out the following:

1. They pay their own way by purchase of expensive licenses.
2. They also help pay the way of nonconsumptive users such as birders, photographers, and backpackers.
3. They provide food for their families through their own efforts.
4. They help control excess numbers of animals.

The hunters themselves have conflicts concerning such items as length of the hunting season, the best methods of conservation, and how to instill outdoor manners in those careless hunters who give the rest a bad name.

**Ways to minimize conflicts.** Hunters, nonhunters, and resource management personnel must continue to strive to reduce these conflicts. Possibilities include: (a) increased enforcement to protect private property from trespass and vandalism, (b) separate seasons or zones for various types of hunters, (c) hunter information, training and safety programs, and (d) more widespread information for the general public on the place of hunting in wildlife management.

## Off-road Vehicles

Off-road vehicles include dune buggies, motorcycles, and snowmobiles, and any other motorized land vehicle capable of travel in areas without roads. Nearly all of the conflict related to ORVs is between those who ride them and those who don't. There is very little disharmony among the ORV users themselves, except perhaps between the two wheelers and four wheelers.

**Possible controversy.** As previously noted in this chapter, ORV users are accused of many illegal and irresponsible acts. Complaints against these riders include frightening wildlife, stampeding cattle, making too much noise, creating hazardous situations for horseback riders, destroying vegetation, damaging roads, dropping litter, and invading the privacy of hikers, campers, canoeists, cross-country skiers, and snowshoers. Although some of the accusations made against them are not substantiated, there can be little doubt that they cause serious management problems and that most other recreationists have a difficult time accepting ORVs as a harmonious part of the backwoods scene.

**Ways to minimize conflicts.** ORVs are often used in areas not designed to accommodate them. Manager often lack sufficient enforcement authority, funds, and personnel to cope with the problems presented. As far back as 1976, Bury, Wending and McCool suggested, ORV policy should be directed by management objectives that will determine the amount of ecological change that can be tolerated and the types of outdoor experiences to be provided.

Ideally, ORV areas and trails should be located and designed in a way that minimizes disturbance to the natural environment, to other recreationists, and to local residents. The location, size, and design of such areas should be planned in close cooperation with various ORV user groups, foot and horseback trail users, environmental experts, and affected public and private landowners. A park manager opening a section of an existing park to ORVs should carefully study all of the potential ramifications of such use.

ORV users should be reached by off-season interpretive programs tailored for their group. Acquainting ORV users with agency problems, stressing the need for self-regulation and informing them on subjects of interest will often result in excellent cooperation. The ORV organizations emphasize within their membership ways to promote a positive image through responsible use.

## Horseback Recreation

In metropolitan and suburban areas, horses need exercise and so do their riders. However, space is often limited for one horse and rider, much less several. In other areas, the use may be backcountry trips of one or more weeks' duration, with a large group of horses and riders.

**Possible controversy.** Parks and recreation areas close to cities are experiencing problems of overuse. As areas urbanize, there usually is an increase in riders with a corresponding decrease in available land. ORVs conflict with horseback recreation through the creation of noise, which can spook horses. Backpackers who carry sleeping bags high on their packs and mask the human silhouette, and those wearing raingear over their packs and themselves also scare horses. Mountain bikes, which move fast and silently, can suddenly come upon a horseback rider, scaring both the horse and the rider. On the other hand, few hikers who have traveled a trail also used by horses have not complained about mud, manure, and the startling effect of a horse and rider suddenly looming up as one rounds a turn.

Overgrazing of meadows, damage to tree roots and trunks where horses have been tied, and damage to wet trails early in the season are chronic problems for managers. Rider groups complain of inexperienced park personnel and improperly planned facilities.

**Ways to minimize conflicts.** In some areas, it may be necessary to prohibit early-season use of trails until they dry out. Careful construction of horse trails may help reduce this sort of erosion also.

These conflicts, like so many others, can be minimized by better education of the user groups themselves to the problems or the resource needs of other users. Most organizations have newsletters, and these can be an effective means of communication for the resource managers involved. The horse group can improve its image by practicing minimum impact, offering help with backcountry projects, and appealing to the trail-ride leaders to police their own groups when traveling in the backcountry.

The manager can, in consultation with the horse groups, provide properly constructed trailer turnarounds, campgrounds, trails, and hitching racks; limit their group size; and perhaps require that feed be carried for all stock. When possible, off-season use should also be encouraged. Other users of these areas must learn tolerance and realize that horseback groups have a right to use public lands as indeed do motorized groups.

## Primitive Versus Developed Recreation

Conflicts between primitive and developed recreation exist in issues of land allocation and in the management of areas already set aside for nature preservation or dispersed recreation. These conflicts are evidenced both in philosophy and in actual practice, and they manifest themselves when new areas are under consideration and when any changes are proposed in the development of, use of, or access to existing areas.

**Possible controversy.** Often the struggle centers around whether to improve public access to an area or leave it undeveloped for those willing and able to travel by primitive means. Easy access means loss of solitude and contact with primitive natural conditions. Dispersed recreation advocates want to exclude mass recreation.

**Ways to minimize conflicts.** One obvious method is to locate the developed campgrounds on forest or park fringes and the primitive recreation sites in the interior, providing a range of opportunities for campers. These areas would be in addition to designated wilderness areas, which should try to preserve natural conditions by avoiding any development. Separation of the two sorts of uses should help reduce conflicts in management philosophies and reduce recreation pressures on designated wilderness areas. Some of these more remote areas should contain no facilities, some should contain trail systems with shelters, and others should have trail systems with hostels. Access should be provided also to important scenic areas and natural attractions through controlled public transportation, such as aerial trams, cog railways, and buses. These would provide a window on primitive areas without impacting them, and allow the general public some sense of participation in, and enjoyment of, these reserves.

The same solutions must be tried here as in other conflict situations: good communication with user groups, perhaps even asking them for input on problem solving. Skillful use of volunteers might help provide control of some situations. Observation of other areas with similar problems often generates fresh thinking and might lead to some regional solutions. Professional workshops on these conflicts are also helpful.

## Water-based Recreation

Problems here consist primarily of wind surfers, surfers (in the case of ocean recreation), operators of personal watercraft, water skiers, and other motorboat operators disturbing activities such as canoeing, river floating, fishing, or swimming.

**Possible controversy.** Adverse effects of motorboats, with or without water skiers, include noise, wave action that erodes banks, oil film left on the water, disturbance to fishing, and safety hazards to other boaters as well as to swimmers.

Swimmers, including snorkelers and scuba divers, need a safe environment and do not want to be threatened by fishing boats, ski boats, or other motor boat use. They are vulnerable to injury from propellers of motor boats as well as from the gas and oil film resulting from operation of these boats.

Many problems associated with water skiing are simply those of motorboats. These problems are magnified due to the larger motor size needed to pull a skier, the surface area requirements of water skiing, and the problems of driving the boat with sufficient caution when concentrating on the skier's needs.

Another source of conflict in water-based recreation is river traffic, including hand-propelled crafts, jet boats with short-run sightseers, kayakers, and river floaters on rubber rafts. The people in hand-propelled crafts may well resent the noise and numbers of users associated with rafts and motorboats of all types, while bank and boat fishermen may be disturbed by any intrusion into their fishing areas. On the Island Kauai, Hawaii, tours by kayakers have created an uproar with the communities along the rivers due to privacy, noise and partying.

**Ways to minimize conflicts.** The interface between land and water naturally attracts large numbers of users, so this area must be zoned where several uses coincide. Zoning can be by size of boat, horsepower or space, time, and a combination using shoreline geographic locations. Fishing and water skiing could be allowed in the same waters by alternating days of use, or by time zoning, which permits different activities at different times of the day. Water skiing and boats with large motors could be kept off small lakes and ponds by limiting the allowable speed or simply by excluding ramp facilities. On small ponds, prohibiting use of all but electric motors would eliminate the problems of noise, excessive speeds, and fuel pollution. The use of booms, buoys, signing, and educational approaches also help to alleviate problems, particularly those of safety.

The sanitation problems associated with river floating can be overcome by portable toilet devices. Zoning on rivers can assist the different user groups in finding space to enjoy their particular form of boating with minimal distraction. Interpretation aimed at making peace among the users and protecting the resource has proven to be helpful in some areas.

### Bicyclists, Roller Skates, Skateboarders, Joggers, and Pedestrians

People in these five categories, plus automobile drivers, all travel at different speeds. When they use the same route there is bound to be conflict.

**Possible controversy.** In the city, neighborhood streets and sidewalks were designed to separate pedestrians and vehicular traffic for safety reasons. Joggers or runners frequently must make do with streets or sidewalks even though these hard surfaces are not desirable and here they must compete with established uses. Some use school or gymnasium tracks, but park settings with soft running surfaces and more pleasing surroundings are preferred.

Bicyclists and skateboarders also frequently have to use streets and sidewalks not designed to accommodate them. Special bicycling, jogging, and walking paths are being constructed in many areas. Unfortunately, removing the car from the scene does not solve all the problems, for these uses are sometimes in conflict with each other.

**Ways to minimize conflicts.** Green Lake Park in Seattle, Washington, contains a paved, circular path that accommodates pedestrians, joggers, skaters (roller, blade, and board), and cyclists. This path is a heavily used facility, three miles (5 km) long and approximately 10 feet (3 m) wide, circling Green Lake. The asphalt path has a white striped lane down the middle and stenciled signs designating the inside lane for foot traffic and the outside lane for nonmotorized cycle or skating use. Cycle and skater use is restricted to counterclockwise, one-way traffic with a speed limit of 10 mph (16 kilometers per hour). Joggers and walkers are restricted to clockwise and may use the surface path or the jogger-beaten strip adjacent to the paved surface.

Even with this separation of users, conflicts persist, including: (a) bicyclists, pedestrians, and joggers riding, walking, and running in the wrong lanes; (b) bicyclists riding in the wrong direction; (c) bicyclists exceeding the speed limit; (d) groups of users occupying the entire width of the path and blocking movement by others; (e) dogs, on or off leashes, running back and forth across the path without warning; (f) park users, especially small children, stepping into or across the path without looking first; (g) inexperienced bicycle riders weaving and making abrupt stops; and (h) bicyclists and joggers weaving in and out around slower traffic.

Originally the path around the lake was used by strollers, and they objected when bicyclists invaded their quiet paths. These users adjusted, only to be complicated by joggers. More recently, roller skaters, roller bladers, skateboarders, and joggers pushing baby strollers, caused a new flurry of accidents and complaints, and people, including the park department superintendent, were being attacked with fists (Koch, 1979).

Several on-site inspections in 1991 revealed that conflicts were increasing; apparently 40 percent of the walking users will not go in the designated direction. As a result, in 1993, the park department and city council held a series of public meetings that led to more positive signing and the addition of lanes with dividers.

To assure proper use and control of a 10-mile-long bike path on the island of Longboat Key in Florida, the town commissioners adopted the following set of rules.

- Bikers should exercise caution, courtesy, and common sense.
- The path may be used only by cyclists, pedestrians, joggers, and baby carriages.
- Motorcycles, mopeds, golf carts, and any other type of motorized vehicles are prohibited from the bike path.
- Cyclists should observe a 15-mph speed limit.
- Bicyclists must have a horn or bell and a rearview mirror.
- At night, bicycles are required to have a front light and rear reflectors.
- Bicycles shall not tow other vehicles on the path.
- Pedestrians should use caution when crossing the path.
- Users of the path should slow down at intersections.
- Bicycles should be walked across the business parking lots.
- No part of any vehicle may be parked on the path.
- No more than one person may be carried on a bike unless it is equipped properly for an extra rider.

## CONFLICTS BETWEEN PARK MANAGERS AND OTHER ENTITIES

Certainly the foremost use of recreation lands is to provide a place for people to have a good time. The means of having fun varies greatly with the user, and the use ranges from passive to active forms of recreation. Troubles arise when a person's recreation is in conflict with the managers need to make the area available to all users and to protect it from undue impact.

If park managers see their job primarily as protecting the resource from the visitor, the impact will appear even greater. Managers must realize nearly all park visitors have a degree of impact, some more than others. Consider trail users for a moment. Equestrians' heavy mounts create impact with their metal horse shoes; off road bikers, with or without motors, can cause rutting and erosion with their soil-gripping knobby tires. Even hikers with their lugged soles can cause erosion in soft soil. In wet areas with poor drainage, the damage in considerable. All visitors have the potential to contribute to the litter problem, cause vandalism, or place excessive demands on the manager's patience. From the visitors' standpoint, this is what parks are for, a place to have fun doing their own special brand of recreation. In their minds, the manager may simply be the custodian who gets paid to clean up. Broader understanding is needed by both sides. Managers have to expect a certain amount of wear and tear. Visitors need to be induced to behave in a way that helps their recreation resource withstand repeated assaults.

Although there are a great many recreational activities available, all forms cannot be pursued within a single park. Some areas lend themselves nicely to certain types of recreation, and others do not. Some parks were established specifically to accommodate certain kinds of recreation, while other areas were discovered by user groups, who then established their own use patterns. Park visitors, influenced by advertising, continue to bring new kinds of recreation equipment or modifications of traditional forms. Some of these innovations may be compatible with existing activities; some may be in direct conflict. Organized and vocal user groups exert political pressure on park managers and their agencies through comments, letters, and public hearings. Lobbyists insist that their group's type of recreation be well provided for. For the park manager, the recreation activities scene is one of constant change and challenge.

Throughout this book, we have seen how conflict is resolved, or at least reduced, through politics, policy, planning, design, interpretation, law enforcement, and training of personnel. However, visitors may not be totally happy with the compromises, and the manager soon hears about it, either directly or through channels.

Local problems involving other jurisdictions may cause difficulties for park managers. Officials of another agency sometimes end up at cross purposes with park managers over personality conflicts or the refusal of nearby residents to follow park regulations.

The picture is frequently more complex than complaints over local problems. Often hard but necessary decisions on park policy are made at the higher levels of authority. These may well contravene the wishes of some local park users. For example, a decision to exclude snowmobiles from park roads or trails satisfies cross-country skiers, but antagonizes the local snowmobilers who have been using the area for years. Though the conflict in this instance is between user groups, it's the manager who must attempt to carry out directives.

## VISITOR USE—THE CASE OF ROCKY MOUNTAIN NATIONAL PARK

The following section presents various excerpts from the Rocky Mountain National Park Final Masterplan (http://www.nps.gov/romo/parkmgmt/upload/final_master_plan.pdf, 2010). This section illustrates the complexity of issues and the management response to those conflicts. One can see many of the issues described previously in this chapter being recognized as conflicts and challenges to managing the park and visitors.

Trends on a park-wide scale are amplified by the steadily increasing numbers of people: 1,774,000 visitors in 1962, rising to 2,520,000 in 1972. It now exhibits the greatest increases in the spring and fall along with the usual summer vacation peak period. There is an increasing impact on the environment as measured by the effects on vegetation and wildlife. And there is a growing impact on the experience, as demonstrated by crowding and conflicts in lifestyle.

Both the land resource and man's experience are endangered, and a way must be found to perpetuate the resource base, while enriching the park experience. The solution should be generated from the patterns of use that have developed around different parts of the park, ranging from drive-through viewing from the Trail Ridge Road, to the adjacent day-use areas, and into the less accessible backcountry.

Here, two basic premises must be stated. One is that all visitors do not want the same park experience. The other is that all use zones are interrelated, For example, many people will be satisfied with looking at distant peaks from their automobile, while others want nothing less than climbing those peaks in an area devoid of manmade facilities. Yet, both activities are based on the same resource, and differ primarily in the means used to satisfy the end. Thus, each area within the park, by virtue of its ease of access or its existing facilities, falls into a definable pattern of use. And each use zone can be designed to provide the man/land experience for which it is most suited. Where conflicts occur, either from excessive stress on the physical environment, or through high human density, management priorities must defer to the basic character of a given zone. With different priorities established for each zone, high-density use can be accommodated where necessary, and the maintenance of natural conditions can be given preference in the more primitive portions.

Three broad zones can be identified in the park: the scenic viewing or drive-through zone, the day-use zone, and the primitive or backcountry zone.

The scenic viewing or drive-through zone is experienced by most visitors. Because the park is easily accessible by two major east-west interstate highways (70-80) with minor north-south connectors from the developing front-range cities, it provides the opportunity for a scenic drive or loop for both cross-country travelers and regional residents. Cross-country travelers, especially those going west, find a scenic drive through the mountains a welcome change from the long drive across the nearly flat plains states. They normally enter at one side of the park and exit at the other. Regional residents, however, usually enter and exit from the east side. Because Trail Ridge Road is one of the few roads crossing the Rockies over a ridge, rather than through a valley, it offers a spectacular scenic drive. This is a unique experience and is a valuable interpretive opportunity in itself. Trail Ridge Road will thus be retained. However, alternatives to private automobile use on the park road network, especially during the "summer vacation" peak period, must be considered. A Fall River Road/Trail Ridge Road loop by means of public transport should also be considered as an alternative. The private automobile should be eliminated from the dead-ending Bear Lake Road during peak use periods. Access, then, to this heavily used area should be by public transport. Transportation studies are required to determine the location of the necessary staging areas— probably outside the park boundaries—their relationships,scheduling, and related interpretive opportunities.

The day-use zone is the area normally used in association with existing roads. Day-use activities such as picnicking, day-long walks, short walks, horseback riding, cross-country skiing, wildlife observation, and interpretive activities enrich a short visit and will be encouraged. The demand for such activities is accelerating dramatically and needed land is at a premium. Overnight vehicle camping competes for the same type of land, requires more extensive support facilities and can be accommodated outside of the park. Hence, overnight vehicle camping should not be expanded and should even be reduced in those areas where it competes directly with the need for day-use activities. A greater portion of tent-camping facilities should be provided in existing campgrounds. This will diversify the overnight experience. The primitive-use or backcountry zone offers a range of experiences, from total isolation in a trailess area to a short walk-in experience. Activities include short- and long-distance hiking, backpacking, cross-country skiing, horseback riding, and overnight tent camping. This use often involves an extended visit accompanied by the desire for a "wilderness experience." Increasing numbers of people are using this zone. Already it has become necessary to issue backcountry permits for designated campsites in order to limit and control the impact of use. There is a continuing need for education in backcountry use for neophytes whose lives have been primarily urban-oriented, This education/information should be made available in the day-use zone of the park and in surrounding urban areas.

### Resource Management
Rocky Mountain National Park will be administered and managed under the policies, rules, and regulations for a natural area. In the past, its resource management has been guided along a path similar to that of many other large western parks. As in most areas, the National Park Service did not acquire a complete ecological entity, free from manmade factors originating outside the park lands. The activities of the early residents of the front-range eliminated the gray wolf, Colorado grizzly, and bison. Ranching, resort developments, summer homes, gold and silver mining, lumbering, water diversion, and man-caused fires all altered the landscape prior to the park's establishment."

## CONCLUSION

Many conflicts may be minimized if park users can be educated or made to recognize the needs to nonrecreational users as well as those of other recreationists. However, not all standards and methods apply in all situations, and some users may be more than careless in their actions and use of parks. For example, Knotek, Watson, and Christensen (n.d.) reported evidence of social and behavioral experiences of users and how that type of information is important and necessary for establishing management direction, setting standards and implementing relevant monitoring for such diverse recreation experiences in one unique place. They noted for instance, "Limits of Acceptable Change social indicators in the Bob Marshall Wilderness and their standards apply equally for horseback riders and hikers (USFS, 1987), and in the Frank Church-River of No Return Wilderness they apply to both rafters and kayakers along the primary rivers and streams (USFS, 2003). In Denali, however, the two main user groups in the study area have very different recreation experiences, making selection of common indicators more complex. It actually raises the question of whether a strategy for establishing common indicators is even possible."

Separation by time or space and regulation through limiting access and facilities often help resolve conflicting uses. Education through interpretation should also be provided by signs and brochures and by off-season, off-site presentations and special on-site programs designed to befriend and educate user groups. This is particularly important because recreationists are likely to ignore even the most imaginatively designed solutions if they don't understand their purposes.

Careful records of complaints and accidents should be kept so that patterns of use and conflict can be delineated. These should prove useful for researchers as well as managers, and researchers may be able to suggest new ways to circumvent conflicts. To keep informed of new developments, managers should attend workshops and read professional publications. They could also try to come up with some ingenious ideas of their own to help abate these conflicts.

In analyzing the park conflict situation, the following questions may assist the manager (adapted from Marcouiller, Scott & Prey, 2005):

1. In general, how do the primary outdoor recreation activities interact with one another (to include geographic scale, asymmetry, and thresholds)?
2. How effective have current tools been in minimizing competitive and antagonistic interactions? What new tools could be crafted to alleviate conflict?
3. How effective are current policies to enhance the amount of complementary and supplementary in the recreation options present in the park system? What new tools could be crafted to maximize the beneficial types of interaction?
4. What key issues exist between recreation and alternative land uses such as residential development, forestry, and agriculture?

## REFERENCES

**References Cited**

Blahna, D. J., Smith, K. S., & Anderson, J. A. (1995). Backcountry llama packing: Visitor perceptions of acceptability and conflict. *Leisure Sciences, 17*, 185–204.

Bury, R. L., Wendling, R. C. & McCool, Stephen F. (1976). *Off-road Recreational Vehicles: A Research Summary, 1969-1975.* College Station, TX: Texas Agric. Exp. Stn. Texas A & M University.

Cordell, K. H., & Tarrant, M. A. Forest-Based Outdoor Recreation Southern Research Station, USDA Forest Service, http://www.srs.fs.usda.gov/sustain/draft/socio6/socio6.htm, retrieved June 6, 2010.

Everhart, W. C. (1972). *The National Park Service.* New York: Praeger.

Hegens, L. E. (1979-1980). From a series of articles in *Park News.* Toronto: National and Provincial Park Association of Canada.

Hope, J. (1972). "The Invasion of the Awful ORVs," *Audubon* (Jan.):37-43.

Gambill, P. (n.d.). Multi-Use Trail Management Policy: User-Group Conflict and Resource Impact Issues. http://www.americantrails.org/resources/ManageMaintain/ActionArticGambill.html, retrieved June 6, 2010.

Hughes, K. (1988, March 22). Surfboarding shifts to the ski slopes, and cultures clash. *Wall Street Journal,* p. l.

Jacob, G. R., & Schreyer, R. (1980). Conflict in outdoor recreation: A theoretical perspective. *Journal of Leisure Research, 12*, 368–380.

Knotek, K., Watson, A., & Christensen, N. Diverse Recreation Experiences at Denali National Park and Preserve, NPS, Science for Management, retrieved from http://www.nps.gov/.../knotek.pdf, June 6, 2010.

Koch, M. (1979). Personal Communication. Senior Supervisor, Seattle, WA: Green Lake Community Center.

Lloyd, R. D., & Fischer, V. L. (1972). Dispersed Versus Concentrated Recreation as a Forest Policy. Presented at the Seventh World Forestry Congress, Buenos Aires, Argentina, Oct. 4-18.

Marcouiller, D., Scott, I., & Prey, J. (2005) *Addressing Recreation Conflict: Providing a Conceptual Basis for Management, Working Paper 05-2.* Madison: University of Wisconsin Department of Urban and Regional Planning, 2005.

Miller, K. (1961). *Our native land.* New York: Education Department, National Association of Manufacturers.

Morrison, Ken. (1979). "The Evolution of the Ontario Provincial Park System," *Park News.* Toronto: National and Provincial Park Association of Canada.

Nicol, Jack I. (1968). "The National Parks Movement in Canada," in J. G. Nelson (Ed.), the *Canadian National Parks: Today and Tomorrow.* Calgary: University of Calgary.

Ramsey, M. D., & K. P. Schnell (Ed.). (1970). *Reality and the Middle Ground.* A Report on Outlook 70-Knoxville Institute of Agriculture, The University of Tennessee and Tennessee Valley Authority.

Ryan, M. (1992). "The Historic Canyon Creek Charcoal Kilns." From The Origins of the National Forests: A Centennial Symposium. Harold K. Steen (Ed.). Durham, NC: Forest History Society.

Rocky Mountain National Park Final Masterplan, http://www.nps.gov/romo/parkmgmt/upload/final_master_plan.pdf, retrieved June 6, 2010.

Schneider, I. E. (2000). Revisiting and revising recreation conflict research. *Journal of Leisure Research, 32*, 129–132.

Stokowski, P. (2002). Languages of place and discourses of power: Constructing new senses of place. *Journal of Leisure Research 34*, 4: 368-382.

Swift, E. (1958). *The Glory Trail.* Washington, D.C.: The National Wildlife Federation.

U.S. Department of Agriculture, Forest Service. (USFS). (1987). *The Bob Marshall, Great Bear and Scapegoat Wildernesses Recreation Management Direction.* USDA Forest Service, Flathead, Lolo, Helena, and Lewis and Clark National Forests.

U.S. Department of Agriculture, Forest Service. (USFS). (2003). *The Frank Church—River of No Return Wilderness Management Plan.* USDA Forest Service, Intermountain Region.

van Kooten, G. C. (1993). *Land resource economics and sustainable development: Economic policies and the common good.* Vancouver: UBC Press.

Vaske, J. J., Carothers, P., Donnelly, M. P., & Baird, B. (2000). Recreation Conflict among Skiers and Snowboarders, 22, *Leisure Sciences*, 297-313.

Watson, A. E. (2001). "Goal interference and social value differences: understanding wilderness conflicts and implications for managing social density." *USDA Forest Service Proceedings RMRS-P* 20: 62-67.

Watson, A. E. (1995). An analysis of recent progress in recreation conflict research and perceptions of future challenges and opportunities. *Leisure Sciences, 17*, 235–238.

Watson, A. E., Niccolucci, M. J., & Williams, D. R. (1994). The nature of conflict between hikers and recreational stock users in the John Muir Wilderness. *Journal of Leisure Research, 26*, 372–385.

Watson, A. E., Williams, D. R., & Daigle, J. J. (1991). Sources of conflict between hikers and mountain bike riders in the Rattlesnake NRA. Journal of Park and Recreation Administration, 9, 59–71.

Watson, A., Zaglauer, H., & Stewart, S. (1996). Activity orientation as a discriminant variable in recreation conflict research. In Proceedings of the 1995 Northeastern Recreation Research Symposium (Gen. Tech. Rep. NE-218). Saratoga Springs, NY: U. S. Department of Agriculture Forest Service, Northeastern Forest Experiment Station.

Wisconsin Department of Natural Resources. (2005). SCORP, http://www.dnr.state.wi.us/planning/scorp/plan/WIS_2005-, retrieved Jun 6, 2010.

## GENERAL REFERENCES

Adelman, B. J. E., Heberlein, T. A., & Bonnicksen, T. M. (1982). Social psychological explanations for the persistence of a conflict between paddling canoeists and motorcraft users in the Boundary Waters Canoe Area. *Leisure Sciences 5*, 1: 45-61.

Anderson, D. H., & Brown, P. J. (1984). The displacement process in recreation. *Journal of Leisure Research 16*, 1: 61-73.

Baldwin, M. F., & Stoddard, Jr., D. H. (1973). *The off-road vehicle and environmental quality* (2nd ed.). Washington, D.C.: The Conservation Foundation.

Brewer, J. E., & Fulton, D. L. (1974). *A Review of Recreation Land Allocation on the Mark Twain National Forest.* Outdoor Recreational Research: Applying the Results. USDA Forest Service General Technical Report NC-9.

Bryan, H. (1979). *Conflict in the Great Outdoors. Sociological Studies No. 4.* Bureau of Public Administration. University, AL: The University of Alabama.

Butler, R. W. (1974). "How to Control 1,000,000 Snowmobiles," *Canadian Geogr. Journal, 88*(3):4-13.

Carothers, P., Vaske, J., & M. Donnelly. 2001. Social values versus interpersonal conflict among hikers and mountain bikers. *Leisure Sciences 23*, 1: 47-61.

Chambers, T. W. M., & Price, C. (1986). Recreational congestion: some hypotheses tested in the forest of Dean. *Rural Studies 2*, 1: 41-52.

Chubb, M. (Ed.). (1971). *Proceedings of the 1971 Snowmobile and Off-road Vehicle Research Symposium.* Technical Report No. 8. East Lansing, MI: Michigan State University.

Clawson, M. (1974). Conflict, strategies, and possibilities for consensus in forest land use and management. In M. Clawson, (Ed.), *Forest policy for the future: Conflict, compromise, consensus.* Washington: Resources for the Future.

Cole, D. N. (1989). The Grand Canyon of the Colorado: a challenge to float, a challenge to manage. *Western Wildlands 15*(3): 2-7.

Dailey, T., & Dave R. (1975). *Guidelines for Roadless Area Campsite Spacing to Minimize the Impact of Human-related Noises.* USDA General Technical Report PNW-35. Portland, OR.

Ditton, R. B., & Goodale, T. (1973). "Water Quality Perception and the Recreational Uses of Green Bay, Lake Michigan," *Water Resources, 9*(3):569-579.

Dustin, D. L., & Schneider, I. E. (1998). The widening circle: The role of democratic deliberation in outdoor recreation conflict management. *Trends, 35*(2), 27-30.

Donnelly, M., J. Vaske, Whittaker,D., Shelby, B. (2000). Toward an understanding of norm prevalence: A comparative analysis of 20 years of research. *Environmental Management 25*, 4: 403-414.

Gibbons, D. R., & Salo. E. O. (1973). *An Annotated Bibliography of the Effects of Logging on Fish of the Western United States and Canada.* USDA Forest Service General Technical Report NW-10.

Gibbons, S., & Ruddell, E. (1995). The effect of goal orientation and place dependence on select goal interferences among winter backcountry users. *Leisure Sciences 17,* 3: 171-183.

Hall, T., & Shelby, B. (2000). Temporal and spatial displacement: Evidence from a high-use reservoir and alternate sites. *Journal of Leisure Research 32*, 4: 435-456.

Hammitt, W. E., McDonald, C. D., & Noe, F. P. (1984). Use level and encounters: Important variables of perceived crowding among nonspecialized recreationists. *Journal of Leisure Research 16*, 1: 1-8.

Hendee, J. C. (1972). "Management of Wildlife for Human Benefit," Western Proceedings, 52nd Annual Conference, Western Association State Game and Fish Commission, Portland, OR, pp. 175-181. Reproduced by USDA Forest Service.

Ivy, M. I., Stewart, W. P., & Lue, C. C. (1992). Exploring the Role of Tolerance in Recreational Conflict. *Journal of Leisure Research 24*, 4: 348-360.

Jacob, G. R., & Schreyer, R. (1980). Conflict in outdoor recreation: A theoretical perspective. *Journal of Leisure Research 12*: 368-380.

Johnson, A., & Dawson, C. (2004). An exploratory study of the complexities of coping behavior in adirondack wilderness. *Leisure Sciences 26*, 3: 281-293.

Kuentzel, W. F., & Heberlein, T. A. (1992). Cognitive and Behavioral Adaptations to Perceived Crowding: A Panel Study of Coping and Displacement. *Journal of Leisure Research 24*, 4: 377-393.

Lee, B., Shafer, C., & Kang, I. (2005). Examining relationships among perceptions of self, episode-specific evaluations, and overall satisfaction with a leisure activity. *Leisure Sciences 27*, 2: 93-109.

Lee, B., & Shafer, C. S. (2002). The dynamic nature of leisure experience: An application of Affect Control Theory. *Journal of Leisure Research 34*, 3: 290-310.

Lime, D. W., & Stankey, G. H. (1971). "Carrying Capacity: Maintaining Outdoor Recreation Quality," Recreation Symposium Proceedings, Warren T. Doolittle (Ed.). Upper Darby, PA: USDA Forest Service Northeast Forest Exp. Stn.

Lindsay, J. J. (1974). *Outdoor Recreation Conflict in Vermont, 1973*. Research Report SNR-RM2. Burlington, VT: School of Natural Resources, University of Vermont.

Manning, R., & Valliere, W. (2001). Coping in outdoor recreation: Causes and consequences of crowding and conflict among community residents. *Journal of Leisure Research 33*, 4: 410-426.

Manning, R., Walliere, W. V., & Wang, B. (1999). Crowding norms: Alternative measurement approaches. *Leisure Sciences 21*, 2: 97-115.

Manning, R. E., & Ciali, C. P. (1980). Recreation Density and User Satisfaction: A Further Explanation of the Satisfaction Model. *Journal of Leisure Research*: 329-345.

Marcouiller, D. W. (2000). The compatibility of timber production with forest-based recreation: Developing a basis for evaluating user conflicts. Working paper 00-01, Department of Urban and Regional Planning, University of Wisconsin–Madison. http://urpl.wisc.edu/people/marcouiller/projects/clearinghouse/Applied%20Research%20Clearinghouse.html#clearinghouse

Owens, P. L. (1985). Conflict as a Social Interaction Process in Environment and Behaviour Research: The Example of Leisure and Recreational Research. *Journal of Environmental Psychology 5*: 243-259.

Rasor, Robert. (1977). *Five state approaches to trailbike recreation facilities and their management*. Westerville, OH: American Motorcyclist Association.

Robertson, R. A., & Regula, J. A. (1994). Recreational displacement and overall satisfaction: A study of central Iowa licensed boaters. *Journal of Leisure Research 26*, 2: 174-181.

Roe, M., & Benson, J. (2001). Planning for conflict resolution: Jet-ski use on the Northumberland coast. *Coastal Management 29*, 1: 19-39.

Ruddell, E. J., & Gramann, J. H. (1994). Goal orientation, norms, and noise-induced conflict among recreation areas users. *Leisure Sciences 16*, 2: 93-104.

Saremba, J., & Gill, A. (1991). Value conflicts in mountain park settings. *Annals of Tourism Research 18*: 455-472.

Shelby, B., Bregenzer, N. S., & Johnson, R. (1988). Displacement and product shift: Empirical evidence from Oregon rivers. *Journal of Leisure Research 20*, 4: 274-288.

Shelby, B., Vaske, J., & Donnelly, M. (1996). Norms, standards, and natural resources. *Leisure Sciences 18*, 2: 103-123.

Shelby, B., Vaske, J. J., & Heberlein, T. A. (1989). Comparative analysis of crowding in multiple locations: results from fifteen years of research. *Leisure Sciences 11*: 269-291.

Shindler, B., & Shelby, B. (1995). Product shift in recreation settings–findings and implications from panel research. *Leisure Sciences 17*, 2: 91-107.

Sincock, J. L., Smith, M. M., & Lynch, J. F. (1974). "Ducks in Dixie," in Joseph P. Lindusk (Ed.), *Waterfowl tomorrow*, USDI Bureau Sport Fisheries and Wildlife. Washington D.C.: U.S. Government Printing Office.

Stankey, G. H. (1973). *Visitor perception of wilderness recreation carrying capacity.* USDA Forest Service Research Paper INT-142.

Stankey, G. H., & McCool, S. F. (1984). Carrying capacity in recreational settings: Evolution, appraisal, and application. *Leisure Sciences 6*, 4: 453-473.

Vaske, J., M. Donnelly, K., & Laidlaw, S. (1995). Interpersonal versus social-values conflict. *Leisure Sciences 17*, 3: 205-222.

Vaske, J., Dyar, R., & Timmons, N. (2004). Skill level and recreation conflict among skiers and snowboarders. *Leisure Sciences 26,* 2: 215-225.

Vaske, J. J., Donnelly, M. P., & Heberlein, T. A. (1980). Perceptions of crowding and resource quality by early and more recent visitors. *Leisure Sciences 3*, 4: 367-381.

Vaske, J. J., Graefe, A. R., Shelby, B., & Heberlein, T. A. (1986). Backcountry encounter norms–theory, method and empirical evidence. *Journal of Leisure Research 18*, 3: 137-153.

Vitterso, J., Chipeniuk, R., Skar, M., & Vistad, O. (2004). Recreational conflict is affective: The case of cross-country skiers and snowmobiles. *Leisure Sciences 26*, 3: 227-243.

Wang, C., & Dawson, C. (2005). Recreation conflict along New York's Great Lakes coast. *Coastal Management 33*, 3: 297-314.

Watson, A. E., Niccolucci, M. J., & Williams, D. R. (1994). The nature of conflict between hikers and recreational stock users in the John Muir Wilderness. *Journal of Leisure Research 26*, 4: 372-385.

Westover, T. N., & Collins, J. R. J. (1987). Perceived crowding in recreation settings: an urban case study. *Leisure Sciences 9*: 87-99.

Whittaker, D., Manfredo, M., Fix, P., Sinnott, R., Miller, S., & Vaske, J. (2001). Understanding beliefs and attitudes about an urban wildlife hunt near Anchorage, Alaska. *Wildlife Society Bulletin 29*, 4: 1114-1124.

Whittaker, D., & Shelby, B. (1988). Types of norms for recreation Impacts: Extending the social norms concept. *Journal of Leisure Research 20*, 4: 261-273.

Wagar, J. A. (1974). "Recreational and Aesthetic Considerations," in *Environmental Effects of Forest Residues Management in the Pacific Northwest: A State-of-Knowledge Compendium,* Owen P. Gramar (Ed.). USDA Forest service General Technical Report PNW-24.

# Chapter Thirteen

# Vandalism

*"Vandalism" has been used as a label for a broad range of negative behavior, from accidental or trivial incidents to actual criminal activity.*

—**Monty Christiansen**

The cost of vandalism is rising for park and recreation agencies. Deterring and tracking the cost of vandalism is an additional expense agencies cover. The City of Boise spent $42,000 in FY2009 and projects the cost will rise to nearly $54,000 in FY 2010 (http://www.cityofboise.org/Departments/Parks/PDF/Caring/2009VandalismReport.pdf). The estimated cost of vandalism in county parks in Knox County, Tennessee, is approaching $100,000, and the county spends additional funds using video cameras to deter destruction of park property (http://www.knoxcounty.org/current09/parks_deter_vandalism.php).

King County Washington, not unlike many parks management organizations, is having its share of problems (King County Parks and Recreation, 2005).

It's the kind of scene that makes you shake your head. A public restroom in King County's Big Finn Hill Park smashed to pieces by vandals. Not far from the restroom, another dismal scene –a natural area damaged and scarred by mountain bike riders installing jumps. It's a sight that's becoming all too common. Every summer defaced property in our King County parks adds up to an ugly, expensive problem.

Last year, it cost county taxpayers more than $21,000 to clean up property damage left behind by vandals. A total of 36 different sites were hit. Damage ranged from defaced signs to completely destroyed facilities. It took county parks crews more 519 labor hours to repair the damage.

It adds up and it's discouraging because we work hard to keep our trails and parks attractive and safe," said Bobbi Wallace, Park Resource Section Manager. "They are supposed to be places where children and families can come and enjoy themselves. I can't imagine why anyone would want to destroy public property just for fun.

Another more recent issue is the closure of state parks and the resulting threat of vandalism. These closures are certainly adding a unique challenge to park managers and park boards. The *Arizona Daily Star* (2010) reported:

State parks officials are struggling to figure out how they're going to keep closed state parks free of vandals and looters. The first wave of closures forced by state budget cuts is set to begin this week, with the Homolovi Ruins near Winslow and Lyman Lake near St. Johns closing today.

Parks officials say they will post signs telling visitors about the closures, and a ranger is expected to be on hand to answer questions. But officials still don't know how to secure the park perimeters and protect their assets. The parks staff is particularly worried about Homolovi, which was a playground for looters and vandals before the parks system acquired it in 1986. Dirt roads from the Navajo Reservation and nearby ranches run through the 4,000-acre site, which contains the remains of four ancestral Hopi villages and a host of cultural treasures. Officials recall finding looters with backhoes digging up the earth in search of valuable clay pots. Parks officials must now decide how to block access points while keeping the site accessible to staff members and volunteers who will patrol it. Securing the 1,500-acre Lyman Lake site presents similar challenges, parks officials said. "No one's ever done this before," said Ellen Bilbrey, a parks spokeswoman. "They weren't designed to be closed."

Vandalism is a significant management issue with far-reaching impacts on community, aesthetics, staffing, security, and budgetary concerns. Youths on their way home after the taverns close don't decide to vandalize the street tree plantings, they just decide to have a little fun by clipping off the young trees with their car bumpers.

Teenagers out for a day at the state park want to leave a memento of their visit there and of their feelings for each other. They aren't vandalizing; they're just carving their names together on an aspen tree. Even the more violent acts of destruction, such as wrecking restrooms, are no doubt exciting games and challenges to those involved. Their older brothers did it, or the guys from another high school or town "wasted a rest stop on the interstate," so they, too, want to show their strength and daring.

The point here is that the term "vandalism" represents the view from the top. It is a term used by the establishment: owners, managers, taxpayers. It is not used by the perpetrators. Because of this one-sided view, and because the term generalizes and thus masks a complex of acts and motives, it is imprecise. Its imprecision tends to confuse the issue when one is searching for motives or means of abatement.

Users of the words "vandal" and "vandalism" should remember these are not accurate descriptions of a person or an act. It is no wonder that many writers spend a lot of time trying to define and categorize these terms. We will do this too, but let us remember to use these words advisedly and try to see beyond to the person, the setting, and the motive.

## WHO ARE THESE "VANDALS"?

There is, perhaps, no such thing as a "typical vandal." It nevertheless seems to be true that most persons apprehended in connection with vandalism are male, and many are in their teens. Petty's (1966) early study of vandalism in national parks and forests found that over half of all apprehended vandals lived within 35 miles of the vandalized site. Less than one-fourth lived between 35 miles and 100 miles, and the remainder lived over 100 miles away.

Research on vandalism generally pertains to vandalism in schools, churches, public transportation facilities, private automobiles, and homes, but it can be applied to vandalism in park environments as well. Vandalism generally requires no skill or body of knowledge as do more complicated crimes. Given access and the requisite physical strength, almost anyone is capable of vandalism, although at times great ingenuity is used to defeat protective measures.

### Vandalism Defined

Vandalism is defined here as any act that willfully defaces or destroys some part of an outdoor recreation area and results in increasing costs to the manager or lessening the appeal of the area to the visitor. More specifically, vandalism is the damage or defacement of facilities, such as buildings, picnic tables, benches, signs, and other interpretive devices, or of natural, cultural, or geological features.

In order to arrive at effective preventive techniques, it is important to consider the different types of motives that underlie vandalism. A comprehensive review of vandalism by Cohen (1973) delineated five motivational categories: acquisitive, tactical, vindictive, playful, and malicious. Madison (1970) suggested an additional category, which he calls erosive, making six in all. He sees the first three as having an objective; they are not mindless, wanton, or meaningless—as he feels is true of the last three—but are committed for personal gain, to attract publicity, for revenge, out of spite, or in protest. Although they were formulated on a more general basis, these categories are also directly applicable to outdoor recreation situations.

## Causes of Vandalism

There is a lot of folklore about vandals and vandalism. The typical vandal appears to be an elusive persona, ranging from the child of deprived economic and social conditions, to the bored and idle youth or adult. A report by Beaulieu (1981) suggests six larger causes of vandalism (unranked):

- Social decay
- Inadequate parenting
- Lenient courts
- Boredom
- Peer pressure
- Developmental factors

Because we can't readily control or alleviate these factors, let's look at the established categories of vandalism. One way to remember these six categories is through mnemonic device **All Parks Must Evaluate Vandalism Thoroughly**, in which the bold letters stand for the kinds of vandalism.

## Kinds of Vandalism

**Acquisitive vandalism.** Acquisitive vandalism consists of destroying property in the process of illegally obtaining money or other desired objects. Examples include looting jukebox coin boxes, metered gas stoves, soft drink and candy machines, fee-collection boxes, electricity meters, and telephone coin boxes. Also included are thefts of park equipment, such as park signs and nameplates (for souvenirs), valuable metals (such as brass, copper, aluminum, or lead, usually for resale), athletic equipment, swing seats, garbage cans, picnic tables, and vehicle parts and supplies, including gasoline, tires, batteries, and tools.

**Playful vandalism.** Playful vandalism is the outgrowth of a group play situation and accounts for a relatively large percentage of the vandalism found in parks. The destructive act is not planned, but grows out of "interstimulation," where one individual excites the others, who in turn further encourage the first person's excitement. Members of the group feel a sense of security in numbers and regard their vandalism as simply mischievous fun. Peer pressure causes many individuals to participate in acts of vandalism that they might not otherwise commit.

Playful vandalism may become a game of skill to see who can do the most damage, such as spray painting the windshield of a park vehicle, breaking windows in a park building, or breaking insulators on utility poles. Such competition leads to considerable damage, yet participants are often genuinely surprised to learn that their actions are considered serious destruction of property. In many instances, the actions are cumulative but not continuous; in other words, successive groups contribute to the destruction of facilities.

**Malicious vandalism.** The stereotype of a vandal is drawn from this category because it includes those who seen to derive enjoyment and satisfaction from plundering, ransacking, and annihilating. Malicious vandals appear to vandalize for the pure excitement of it; wanton destruction is the charge laid against them.

Examples of malicious damage to parks include smashing restroom facilities or office equipment, setting fire to maintenance equipment, running equipment over a cliff or into a lake, sabotaging construction equipment, blowing up pit toilets, plugging sinks and then tying water valves open to cause flooding, and pulling up shrubs around park buildings.

Cohen (1973) cited several of the feelings that might precede malicious vandalism: "boredom, despair, exasperation, resentment, failure, and frustration." The exasperation, resentment, and frustration would in this case be directed against life in general rather than against a particular agency or person. The violence seems almost cathartic in these cases; perhaps this is why some judges treat it lightly, as long as no individuals were hurt nor private property damaged. As suggested in the opening paragraph of this chapter, drinking often plays a part in this behavior.

**Erosive vandalism.** An individual act of erosive vandalism might not be damaging, but when repeated by large numbers of people, such acts can cause substantial damage. Erosive vandalism may be the result of ignorance, but it may also result from neglect or from disregard for the values of the park. The individuals probably do not regard their actions as harmful or may feel they are justified in breaking this rule. Examples of erosive vandalism including shortcutting trails, walking off paths through sensitive vegetation, collecting park objects for souvenirs, picking wild flowers, littering, writing on rocks or walls, carving names on wood surfaces and tree trunks, and similar acts of depreciative behavior.

**Vindictive vandalism.** Vindictive vandalism is motivated by a desire for revenge on an individual, an organization, or simply the "system." Here vandalism seems to be an outlet or release of emotions for someone smarting under actual or imagined unfair treatment. It may also represent a chance to settle a grudge without resorting to personal violence. Being fired from a job, being discriminated against in job selection, receiving a traffic ticket, or being expelled from the park are frequently cited reasons for vindictive vandalism. The person being victimized is usually an authority figure, such as the manager, a park ranger, or a youth leader, and the active aggression is against property belonging to that individual or to the agency he or she represents.

Vindictive vandalism includes such act as spilling paint over a privately owned automobile or placing bottles under the tires of park vehicles. Smashing park windows or destroying office equipment are other means of obtaining revenge. Sometimes parks are damaged even when they are not involved in the employee-employer situation. An employee dismissed from a sawmill later stole a log loading machine and used it to demolish an adjacent park's facilities.

**Tactical vandalism.** Tactical vandalism, like acquisitive vandalism, is premeditated but is not for the purpose of acquiring money or property. Nor is it an expression of anger; tactical vandalism serves rather as a means of attracting attention or gaining publicity for a special cause. Such attention-getting vandalism may stem from psychological problems, often manifested by excreting in sinks or on toilet floors or by setting incendiary fires. These must be distinguished from "spite" fires. Publicity-oriented vandalism, as contrasted with attention-getting vandalism, most often takes the form of names or slogans written on park buildings. Some authors feel this is a form of territoriality. Smashing windows in order to be arrested and thus obtain food and shelter is another example of tactical vandalism. In addition, employees might purposely jam or break a machine in order to obtain a rest period; this also falls into the category of tactical vandalism.

## How Vandalism Occurs

### Sequence of Acts in Group Behavior

Another way of examining vandalism is through the psychology of the group, since certain types of vandalistic acts are rarely solitary and seldom happen spontaneously. Wade suggests that there are five general steps in group acts of vandalism.

**Waiting for something to turn up.** This is the free, unsupervised time when the group is waiting for an action-provoking suggestion from one of its members.

**Removal of uncertainty: The exploratory gesture.** At this point a suggestion, either cautious or bold, stimulates action within the group. Boredom disappears as interest develops. Vandalism can be prevented if some group members are convincing enough in the advice to "let it alone" or are able to divert the attention to a less destructive form of activity at this stage.

**Mutual conversion.** This stage may be brief, assuming agreement is reached, or it may include the need for more persuasion. Here, resisting individuals are under pressure. Should they stay within the norms of society at large, or yield to the standards of this smaller group? Their courage and "manliness" are being tested by their peers; a dare is usually enough to convince them to go along with the crowd. Any resistance at all is often met with the taunt "chicken." Once the decision is made in favor of the peer group, the stage of mutual conversion is complete.

**Joint elaboration of the act.** Whether the vandalism will be simple or will develop into substantial destruction depends on how the group interacts. For example,  competition to see who can do the most damage, contributes to the magnitude of the act.  So, instead of breaking a single window, for example, the group breaks all the windows in the building. Once the vandalism begins, it is difficult for any member of the group to slow it down. Instead, vandalism gathers momentum until everything vulnerable is destroyed or until the group is apprehended or chased from the scene.

**Aftermath and retrospect.** The fact that nothing is stolen during most of these acts of vandalism reinforces the perpetrators' rationalizations that they are merely pranksters, not criminals. Even if they are apprehended, such persons are consoled by the knowledge that they have peer approval for their actions. Guilt is further lessened by thinking along the lines of "It's only park property," or "The crew wouldn't have anything to do if it weren't for us."

## Some Typical Acts of Vandalism

What sorts of acts cause problems for managers in North American parks? The following list is representative of the acts of vandalism that have taken place in recreation areas in recent years.

Bark stripped from live trees.
Boards of nature trail ripped up.
Boating safety signs shot up.
Bottles smashed in picnic shelter.
Bulletin board chopped with an axe.
Cars and engine of miniature train overturned.
Cars driven repeatedly over newly planted turf.
Cylinder locks jammed with wood splinters.
Doors on restroom ripped off.
Doors to pump house pried off with tire irons.
Drinking fountains plugged with sand.
Drinking fountains smashed with sledgehammer.
Electric lights shot out (outside lighting).
Electric meter glass cover broken.
Entrance gate rammed with truck.
Fire weather station shot up with rifle bullets.
Fires built in restrooms.
Fireworks shot off in outdoor exhibits, breaking plate glass.
Garbage cans and picnic tables thrown over cliff.
Garbage from cans strewn around park.
Group camp building burned to ground.
Initials carved in smooth-barked trees.
Interpretive exhibit shot up.
Landscape shrubbery uprooted and left to die.
Lifeguard tower destroyed.
Lipstick smeared on restroom wall.
Locks shot off gates.
Logs and rocks rolled down on park road.
Mirrors smashed in restroom.
Names and dates spray-painted on boulders, trees, and statues.
New tabletop carved with knife.
Paint smeared on walls of historic buildings.
Paper towels stuffed in flush toilets, resulting in flooding.
Park benches smashed.
Park interpretive signs damaged with chains.
Park trail directional signs stolen.
Petroglyphs defaced.
Picnic tables chopped for firewood.
Pit toilets blown up with dynamite.
Pit toilet burned to ground.

Pit toilet walls riddled with bullet holes.
Protective railing of bridge removed and thrown into river.
Road signs defaced.
Seats in outdoor amphitheater destroyed.
Shower fixtures pulled out of wall.
Spray paint used on park building walls.
Stalactites in cave smashed.
Sugar poured into gasoline tanks of park vehicles.
Toilet bowls and sinks smashed.
Toilets plugged with plastic bags containing pebbles.
Vegetation destroyed by vehicle leaving designated road.
Wildflowers picked.
Windows broken in comfort station.
Wood shingles ripped loose from shelter.
Wooden bumper rails smashed with automobile.
Wooden interpretive sign repeatedly smashed by cars.

DesJean and Wilson (n.d. retrieved June 5, 2010) cited vandalism reports ranging from a Natchez Trace ranger observing a SCUBA diver in the Tennessee River working on an area of a submerged Indian mound and village and later removing artifacts from the diver's boat, to another ranger at Stones River observing two individuals, one with a pick axe, the other with a metal detector who, upon being questioned, stated that they were not aware that they were on federal property and that they were in the field looking for golf balls. The individual with the metal detector added that he did not want to leave it behind in the car. Other reports deal with people on Cumberland Island digging in historic dumps for bottles; people sawing up wood from an exposed shipwreck on the beach at Cape Hatteras; and rangers pursuing two individuals at Cumberland Gap who dropped their backpacks which, besides clothing, contained notes about digging and Civil War artifacts.

Reading about the various acts of vandalism and remembering one's own youthful pranks might be enough to discourage anyone from wanting to work in parks. It may, on the other hand, be viewed as an opportunity to match wits with that section of the public commonly known as vandals, accepting the problems posed as a challenge. If the latter is the case, knowledge of psychology and sociology will help as will an understanding of parks and facilities design and an appreciation of the need for prompt maintenance. Personnel in heavily vandalized parks are often depressed about the situation and consider combating vandals as a hopeless task because more keep coming as others grow up.

**Where and When Vandalism Takes Place**

Vandalism can take place anywhere and at almost any time, but is most likely to occur at certain favorable times and places.

**Where these acts occur.** Public property is more likely to be vandalized than is private property because it is depersonalized and more readily abused by persons who rationalize that it "belongs to everyone," including them. Parks that are heavily vandalized are frequently secluded, dark, and covered with trees; vandalism, of course, is greatest in areas that are infrequently patrolled and hidden from public view. Areas with extensive facilities suffer more vandalism than do areas with few facilities. Flimsy facilities also encourage vandalism as do facilities inappropriately located. Placing a visitor information exhibit shelter in the middle of a space once used as an impromptu athletic field is asking for vandalism. Facilities in disrepair are often looked upon as far game. Vandalism is also frequent in buildings that are nearing completion, are closed, or are abandoned.

**When these acts occur.** Vandalism increases during the spring and summer. In early spring, near the end of the school year, high school and college groups often hold beer parties in parks, and damage often results. As weather grows warmer and park attendance rises, the incidence of vandalism rises, too. Vandalism is also to be expected on or before Halloween, because the tradition of disturbing both public and private property at that time persists. The park manager should be on the lookout at all times of the year for announcements of festivals, initiations, parties, and sporting events, the eve or aftermath of which may contain potential for vandalism. The superintendent of a Canadian city park in Halifax states that vandalism happens mostly late at night, after 2 or 3 a.m., and when school terms are starting or finishing.  Finally, facilities left unprotected overnight or longer (such as over weekends) are most susceptible to vandalism. Even in the daytime, little-used areas or facilities are in danger of being damaged when there is no one in the vicinity to discourage or report the behavior.

## THE PARK MANAGER'S OPTIONS

It is ultimately the responsibility of the park manager to prevent or reduce vandalism in parks. Yet what works in one situation may not in another, and reading the available literature on the subject will not necessarily provide a specific solution. In fact, popular articles on vandalism may give rise to false hopes of easy success, while after more extensive reading, the manager might be so confused as to not know what approach to take. Unfortunately, much of the writing on vandalism is based on wishful thinking rather than on facts.

The writers of design articles feel that better designed park facilities are the solution. Equally strong arguments are presented by the authors favoring maintenance, law enforcement, education, and other options. Clark (1971) urged caution in searching the literature for "an answer to vandalism," pointing out that there is no single solution to the problem. He suggests that the manager weigh each solution carefully in terms of the specific situation, identifying unsubstantiated claims and avoiding reliance on data that are the result of poorly conceived research.

Faced with these problems, what can managers do? Identifying the major causes and then creating opportunities to communicate with people who visit parks just to let off steam, have a little fun, or show off in front of their peers is a start. Learning to recognize the potential vandal without suspecting every park visitor is also important. These are public relations goals toward which conscientious park managers must strive.

A recent example of addressing vandalism includes the State of Montana Fish, Wildlife, and Parks being authorized to require convicted vandals to pay damages and to also revoke their hunting, fishing and trapping privileges. According to the *Helena Independent Record* (2010):

> The law went into effect one year ago in early April, just in time to apply to widespread vandalism at the Dailey Lake Fishing Access Site in the Paradise Valley. The vandalism included driving over 12 signs, the visitor kiosk, five windscreens surrounding the latrines, and several sections of jackleg fencing, as well as ramming the iron ranger fee-collection box, which was set in one cubic yard of concrete.

The perpetrator was caught and charged with felony criminal mischief for the vandalism. He was ordered to pay restitution of $7,330, and his hunting, fishing, and trapping privileges were revoked for a minimum of 24 months or until restitution is paid in full. However, it was reported that it took $10,000 to replace the signs, kiosk, fencing, and windscreens, and to reset the fee collection box.

"Unfortunately, these crimes are becoming more common and replacing or repairing damaged public property costs FWP, and therefore Montana sportsmen and women, tens of thousands of dollars each year," said Regional Warden Captain Sam Sheppard. "I hope this makes someone think twice about destroying public property and the consequences of losing hunting, fishing, and trapping privileges" (Helena Independent Record, 2010).

Vandalism in parks causes great financial loss. Some agencies report spending between 10 and 20 percent of their entire budget on vandalism repairs amounting to many millions of dollars annually. Vandalism, however, also affects the visitor's experience in several ways. Repair or replacement costs must often be met by funds that have been diverted from visitor services or from expansion of park facilities. For example, $25,000 expended for vandalism repairs would contribute substantially to a park's interpretive program. Vandalism also increases park employees' workloads, taking them away from other maintenance chores and thus lessening the beauty and appeal of the park. The visitor also suffers when irreplaceable objects or unusual resources are destroyed. Disfigurement and scarring of park features is irritating and unsightly, and obscenities scrawled on walls detract from the enjoyment of many families visiting a park. Finally, visitors lose when facilities that can contribute to the understanding and enjoyment of an area are not installed because of vulnerability to vandalism.

Understanding and friendship toward park visitors is always a wise policy. Christensen and Clark (1978) point out that managers' attitudes are often part of the problem. Developing a good relationship with the local schools is another long-range approach. Sponsoring special events such as photo contests, park cleanup days, improvement projects, environmental education opportunities, and other means of attracting youth into the local park for constructive activities can help reinforce a sense of ownership and propriety.

## Suggestions for Reducing Vandalism

Although attempts to reduce vandalism are difficult and discouraging, a passive approach is even less satisfactory. Successful long-range reduction of vandalism may be possible on further research into its causes; in the meantime, programs to encourage citizen responsibility both in children and adults should also help alleviate the problem. Some interesting possibilities now being considered include various curriculum changes in schools and well-thought-out television publicity campaigns. Another approach is live-in host caretakers. The fact that someone is nearby to hear and report damage immediately seems to have a deterrent effect. Yet, in remote areas hosts are sometimes intimidated and threatened by local vandals.

There is a strong possibility that we will always have to endure a certain level of vandalism, but perhaps it can be reduced. In the meantime, the following suggestions, both tested and untested, might have some bearing on the reader's situation. Further ideas on vandalism control are found in the references listed at the end of the chapter.

### Design of Facilities

An extreme solution would be to remove all facilities from park areas. However, because facilities are put in parks for the comfort and convenience of park visitors and for protection of the park environment, removing them would be a drastic solution. At any rate, this is not possible under most agency public service mandates.

Better-designed facilities are often proposed as a solution to damage caused by vandalism. Poorly designed facilities and soon becomes aware of their vulnerability to vandalism. When facilities are replaced, the strongest materials available should be used. Architects should consult with seasoned park managers about facilities and vandalism. Both the architect and the manager should also be aware of new materials that offer some degree of protection from vandalism assault.

**Buildings.** Buildings and their interiors are common objects of carelessness, depreciative behavior, or outright vandalistic attack. Making buildings visually pleasing, yet physically strong enough to withstand vandalism is difficult, and is probably not the manager's responsibility. Nevertheless, the manager must often approve design plans and should be acquainted with recent advances in vandalism prevention. For example, building design and location should make it impossible to gain access to the roof by climbing fences, walls, trees, or the outside of the building itself. This precludes footholds on outside walls and strong shrubs or trees near buildings.

Buildings themselves, particularly wooden pit toilets, are vulnerable. Where possible, these should be replaced with concrete block toilets; however, wooden pit toilets will probably remain part of the park scene in small campgrounds and as a winter toilet facility when flush systems must be closed because of freezing weather. Tipping over pit toilets is the classic act of vandalism, and park managers probably should resign themselves to it, possible classifying it as nostalgic vandalism.

Building walls are often defaced with graffiti applied with lipstick, felt markers pens, crayons, pencils, and pens. Preventive measures include using wall material with textured rather than smooth surfaces. Outside walls must be able to withstand weathering and yet be inexpensive to maintain.

Suggested outdoor materials include brick, concrete blocks, and rock. Inside, a smooth, nonporous material such as tile is preferred because it is easy to clean and requires no painting. Glazed brick with a smooth surface is difficult to write on and is also easy to wash.

Spray paint represents another problem. Special coatings protect against some sprays, as they will wipe clean. The use of commercial paint removers of the water-washable type is recommended. Frequently, a supply of the various types of solvents is needed to deal with different types of sprays. Regardless of the material, it is important that the graffiti be removed as soon as possible.

**Restrooms.** Restrooms are the favorite target of many vandals. Grosvenor (1976) gives an interesting history of the response of Forest Service architects to these assaults, emphasizing design and materials. Suggestions for safeguarding these facilities include hiding all sink drain pipes from view, removing glass mirrors and paper towel holders and using metal mirrors and electric dryers, and using push-button faucets, bathroom fixtures, and shower fixtures that protrude as little as possible. Glass windows should be covered with heavy wire (hardware cloth) screens or replaced by heavy plastic or thick glass brick windows. Windows with shutters or fiberglass skylights might also be used. Sinks and bowls made of reinforced thermo-setting polyester resins are comparable to steel in strength and weight. Stall doors have been removed in many toilet facilities, sacrificing privacy in order to reduce depreciative behavior.

**Tables and benches.** Wooden tables and benches are attractive, inexpensive, and comfortable to picnic or sit on, but are tempting to carve. Using wood planks for seats and tops in combination with precast concrete or pipe bases makes refinishing or replacement of parts easier and less expensive. New materials of plastics, which resist carving, may also be used for seats and tops.

**Drinking fountains**. Survival of the drinking fountain depends on both construction and location. There is probably no fountain that is completely vandal proof, as the vertical shape, the spout, and the necessity for a drain makes it particularly vulnerable. Masonry and rock structures have always been the most popular, but they are more expensive than the commercial porcelain type. All types present some people with irresistible challenges.

Location can deter vandalism to some extent. A fountain out in the open with paved paths is less subject to damage than is a secluded one near sand or rocks that can be used as ammunition to demolish it or to plug up its drain. Although not the most handsome model, a pipe attached to a wooden post is the least expensive water fixture to install or replace.

**Fireplaces and grills.** These are usually waist-level charcoal stoves mounted on a standpipe, or ground-level forms of various descriptions. The waist-level types need to be theft proof, since the stove could be used at home in the backyard. The ground-level fireplace must be of material that can withstand sudden heat changes such as dousing with cold water to put out the fire. A simple grate set in concrete works best. The British Columbia Provincial Parks Branch uses an elegantly simple concrete ring for its amphitheater fireplace to confine the fire and the toxic effect of the ashes.

**Signs.** Signs are necessary for welcoming visitors and informing them about park facilities and features. They point out hazards and scenic areas and carry regulations and interpretive messages. Signs are vital to park management; unfortunately, they are also easily vandalized. Signs with negative messages, such as "Don't walk on the grass," as opposed to "Please use the paved paths" are most frequently vandalized. Briefly explaining the reason for the regulation may lessen vandalism and obtain a greater degree of compliance. For example, "Please wash dishes at your camp. Washing dishes here eventually causes the gravel drain to plug with grease" is better than "No Dishwashing!" This strategy will probably do nothing to deter the malicious vandal, but should decrease the ignorance or resentment that results in depreciative behavior.

Construction material should be considered carefully. Hand-routed wooden signs are pleasingly rustic, but are expensive to replace. Wooden and metal signs can be mass produced at low cost using a silk-screening process. Metal signs are good if their surface is scratch resistant, but they make a satisfying noise when shot at and are therefore less desirable where hunting is permitted.

Sign location and the lighting of signs could reduce vandalism. They should be well anchored in concrete and protected from vehicles by barrier posts.

The Idaho Transportation Department has developed and tested some innovative approaches to roadside rest area signage and vandalism reduction. One test is having classical music piped in. Who could vandalize with Mozart present? Their signs are equally classic.

**Park lighting.** In cities, floodlights set atop tall poles provide security for public property. Lighting has also been found to be an effective deterrent to vandalism and theft in parks. High-intensity discharge lighting systems (HID) provide a source of light covering a very large area. The presence of such lights in a building compound helps protect the visitor as well as park property. Letting lights burn all night in restrooms also acts as a deterrent to vandalism. Of course, lights are a favorite of vandals. Bulbs can be protected by screens or high-impact plastic.

**Plantings.** Trees and shrubbery are often damaged by the "playful" vandal and are frequently stolen for use elsewhere or for resale. Where the planting of exotic species is not forbidden, thorny trees and shrubs such as thornapple, honeylocust, wild rose, bayberry, prickly as, cat briar, and pyrocanthus are discouraging to these vandalistic acts. Such plantings also eliminate what Knudson (1967) calls "involuntary vandalism: (i.e., erosive vandalism) by keeping people on trails as much as possible.

**Maintenance.** There is circumstantial evidence that good maintenance practices discourage vandalism. The manager certainly hears about it from park visitors when an area is not clean and well maintained, but whether good maintenance actually prevents vandalism is unknown because no controlled research has yet been conducted. It can't be denied that clean and recently installed facilities do get vandalized, but vandalism seems to be reduced by keeping an area clean and immediately repairing or replacing vandalized objects. It often happens that carvings in picnic tables or signs and writing on restroom walls inspire imitation. Once the first mark or remark is there, others follow in short order. While the influence of prompt maintenance on control of vandalism needs more study, it should certainly be practiced as a matter of policy, along with other preventative methods.

### Removal of Temptation

Managers should see to it that their employees do not tempt vandals and thieves by leaving doors unlocked, tools at job sites, or keys in vehicles or construction machinery. Vending machines with their tempting coin boxes should be placed in hallways or other areas open to public view so that visitor traffic, can help discourage theft. If theft from vending machines continues unabated, managers may have to remove them completely. Some success has been achieved by labeling vending machines with signs such as "This machine is emptied of all cash each evening," or "This machine equipped with a silent alarm."

Closing little-used areas as the season draws to an end is another way to remove temptation from some potential vandals, but on the other hand, users who find a favorite camping spot blocked off may vandalize gates and vegetation in their attempt to get to it. Valuable artifacts must not be placed where theft is possible. Replicas should be exhibited and should be so identified in order to discourage the would-be thief.

### User Fees

Some managers have reported less vandalism in areas where a user fee is imposed, but others believe that fees increase vandalism by making users feel they have the right to do as they wish. Fees are usually imposed on sites that are more developed (i.e., areas that have more facilities), such as traffic counters, fee-collection stations, traffic barriers, a water supply, and flush toilet buildings. In contrast, free areas may have only tables, pit toilets, and a water source.

There are no reliable data to support the opinion that fees reduce vandalism or that they increase it. It is difficult to attribute reductions in vandalism to the fee system alone. The fact that a fee is collected means that park personnel are present at least periodically, and their mere presence may act as a deterrent. On the other hand, some managers are convinced that even minimal user fees have a positive effect on the type of visitors an area receives. The collection of fees is usually a policy matter, differing with each agency. Rather than being conceived of primarily as a method of vandalism control, the imposition of a fee usually aims at several objectives, including the recovery of some operational costs.

## Surveillance

Surveillance is nothing more than keeping watch over facilities and people in parks, and is no doubt the greatest deterrent the park manager has against any form of vandalism. Specific areas must be visited frequently, with increased patrolling during known problem periods. However, a varied schedule and travel pattern and occasional use of unidentified vehicles is recommended to throw the potential vandal off guard. Special patrols with well-trained personnel are necessary in troublesome areas. Caretakers, night security guards, and citizen patrols are good supplements to the regular park staff in reducing vandalism. Park employees should have training in surveillance and should know how to recognize potential vandals or thieves.

Special equipment is sometimes useful in park areas where the incidence of vandalism is high. Radio contact between key employees and ranger patrol cars is helpful. Monitoring areas or buildings with closed-circuit TV is also useful. Larger parks or those near cities may have access to helicopter surveillance during critical periods.

The campground host program has had favorable results in several ways, according to reports. Apparently an increase in voluntary compliance with the campground fee system was noted, as was improved protection of the area.

## Law Enforcement

One key to reducing vandalism in its various forms is law enforcement. It is important that park employees know the laws pertaining to vandalism and that they operate within them. In order to be in any way effective as a deterrent to vandalism and other crimes in parks, law enforcement must end in punishment so that potential vandals know they will face punishment of caught.

The chances of capturing the culprits are enhanced if surveillance is strong, but unfortunately, capture does not always guarantee a conviction. In prosecuting a case of vandalism, two things must always be demonstrated: first, that the damaged property had a value, and second that the act was willfully committed with intent to harm or destroy. In minor acts of vandalism, the elements necessary for prosecution do not exist.

Many prosecutions and judges are unfamiliar with the extent of serious vandalism problems in parks. The prosecutor also has considerable discretion as to whether or not to prosecute. The park manager must have a working arrangement with local police in order for park employees, often not trained in police work, to know how to handle the apprehended individual suspected of a crime in the park. The park manager must understand that if he or she decides to drop charges on a person apprehended for vandalism, these former charges cannot be taken into consideration if the vandal is apprehended again. There is much to know about making an arrest, holding persons once they are arrested, making a search, collecting evidenced, and testifying in court. Where laws are enforced, presumably crime goes down. The cooperation of the news media is helpful.

## Education and Public Involvement

Education and public involvement are long-range methods that try to reach the public with messages that will presumably lessen vandalism. The intent is to instill a positive attitude toward parks and other public areas. Park environments have an advantage over other public areas in that they offer natural settings that can be appreciated in many different ways. Managers and interpretive staff can encourage positive attitudes toward park values, particularly natural and cultural history offerings, through a well-planned series of slide programs and show-me tours of the park. If signs are used, the wording should tell the visitor why he or she can't do something, rather than simply listing negative imperatives. The public, including potential vandals, can better appreciate parks and other natural areas if they are informed as to the correct attitude and behavior in these settings.

## Teenager Involvement

Youth programs aimed at park improvement are worthwhile and include, as mentioned above, park cleanup days and other improvement projects that develop a sense of pride and identification with the goals of the park. The likelihood of youngsters vandalizing something they have helped create seems quite remote. However, a manager who is unnecessarily hostile to teenagers can expect retaliation. As has already been noted, much vandalism is committed by males approximately 15 years old who live less than 30 miles from a park. The following suggestion has worked in some city parks, but may not be appropriate in more remote areas: managers have permitted certain walls in parks to be used for self-expressive and decorative graffiti; here teenagers can vote for their favorite musical group or express various shades of feelings for their peers and the world in general.

## Parent and Community Involvement

When parents ask what they can do, the manager can suggest that parents know where their children are during visits to the park. The manager should also put together a set of slides on vandalism in the park to inform the local community. Discussing records of annual repair costs and showing how they have prevented the park from constructing facilities or have forced early closure could also be effective. It is the people's park, so the manager should share the problems with them.

## Visitor Involvement

Researchers have found that recreational visitors prefer not to get involved in stopping vandalism or other acts of depreciative behavior they may witness. Indifference, fear of personal threat, and unfamiliarity with how to report an incident are among the reasons for this noninvolvement, and so is the attitude, "That's what rangers get paid for." Clark (1976) suggested people be shown how to handle the situation themselves and be encouraged to report suspicious activity to park rangers so the rangers can take action. This is done by telling the visitor in advance, "We have a problem with violations of park rules. If you see any violations, please report them to a ranger." A sign reading "Report Vandalism Here" would help. Some visitors will report observed violations when questioned about an incident. The use of cell phones has helped to report vandalism to park authorities. Offering a reward for information about vandals has also been suggested. In any case, the knowledge that their concern will be courteously heard and investigated might well encourage people to be more cooperative. Visitors should be encouraged to think of parks as well-ordered places of beauty and relaxation that should be defended against vandals. In situations involving erosive vandalism, pointing out the result of certain behaviors to other visitors and the value of setting a good example can be helpful.

The following example of visitor involvement is from the Minneapolis Department of Parks and Recreation of suggestions to the public to curb vandalism (http://www.minneapolisparks.org/default.asp?PageID=647).

The Minneapolis Park Police needs your help to prevent vandalism and apprehend individuals who vandalize our parks and recreational facilities.

**Why is important to stop vandalism?**
If you think vandalism isn't your problem, think again. Here are a few reasons why vandalism hurts everyone. Vandalism destroys what your tax dollars have created. Each year vandals destroy thousands of dollars' worth of park facilities and equipment funded by tax dollars. A few minutes of destructive "fun" can add up to huge losses for our City's parks.

**Vandalism takes dollars away from recreational programs and facilities**. It costs money to repair or replace whatever a vandal's actions have destroyed. For example, the cost of removing writing from a cement or brick wall can easily reach $1,000 for sandblasting costs. Replacing a destroyed bench involves high labor repair costs. Even damaged boulevard trees are costly to replace at a value at $1000 or more.

**Vandalism is not cool.** Damaging public property through vandalism is both cowardly and uncool. Individuals who tag or use spray paint for artistic expression on public property are breaking the law and are no "cooler" than the person who breaks a window or basketball hoop on purpose.

### Help Stop Vandalism

Here's what you can do to help prevent and address vandalism.

- Always call 9-1-1 to report any crime in progress, including vandalism.
- If you have information about a crime that has occurred in a park, but that does not require an immediate police response, please call 612-230-6550.
- To provide information about a crime that did not occur in a park, when an immediate police response is not needed, call the local precinct station.
- Finally, if you want to remain anonymous, you may want to call 45-C-R-I-M-E. You will not be asked your name and instead will be assigned a number that will make you eligible for a reward if an arrest occurs.

## CONCLUSION

Park environments lend themselves to certain types of behavior, some of which may lead to vandalism. Some damage to park property is unavoidable, often accidental, and must be regarded as part of the cost of running an outdoor recreation area. On the other hand, much depreciative behavior is preventable; even costly deliberate vandalism can sometimes be circumvented. Park managers need to exert their best efforts to curb this drain on their budgets and time. If a manager has success in dealing with a problem, he or she should let other managers know about it. Although solutions may not always be exportable, beleaguered managers need all the help they can get. There is research being done on these problems; managers would be well advised to seek out and read some of the many reports available, some of which are cited here in this chapter. Perhaps cooperating with researchers can provide some feeling of detachment and control in an otherwise frustrating situation.

## REFERENCES

**References Cited**

*Arizona Daily Star.* (2010). Vandalism, Looting a Worry as Parks Close. February, 22, 2010. Retrieved June 5, 2010, http://azstarnet.com/news/state-and-regional/article_8676c7f0-2961-5c6b-ba27-556094f5e999.html.

Alfano, Sam S., & Magill, Arthur W. (1976). "Recommendations," Vandalism and Outdoor Recreation: Symposium Proceedings. Berkeley, CA: *USDA Forest Service General Technical Report PSW-17*. Pacific Southwest Forest and Range Exp. Stn.

Alfano, Sam S., & Magill, Arthur W. (1976). Technical coordinators of Vandalism and Outdoor Recreation: Symposium Proceedings. Includes 24 papers giving an overview of vandalism in outdoor recreation areas. *USDA Forest Services General Technical Report PSW-17*. Berkeley, CA: Pacific Southwest Forest and Range Exp. Stn.

Beaulieu, L. (1981). "Task Force on Vandalism: Province of Ontario." *Vandalism in Calgary.* Vandalism Task Force, Calgary, Alberta: City of Calgary.

Butler, James R. (1980). The Role of Interpretation as a Motivating Agent Toward Park Resource Protection. Unpublished doctoral dissertation, Seattle, WA: College of Forest Resources, University of Washington.

Campbell, Frederick L., Hendee, John C., & Clark, Roger N. (1968). "Law and Order in Public Parks," *Parks and Recreation, 3*(12):28-31, 51-55.

Christensen, Harriet H., & Clark, Roger N. (1978). "Understanding and Controlling Vandalism and Other Rule Violations in Urban Recreation Areas." *Proceedings of the National Urban Forestry Conference*, Washington, D.C.

Christensen, Harriet H., Johnson, Darryll R., & Brookes, Martha H. (1992). Vandalism: Research, Prevention, and Social Policy. Includes 22 papers presented at the first International Symposium on Vandalism in North America, in Seattle, Washington. *USDA Forest Service General Technical Report PNW-GTR-293.* Portland, OR: Pacific Northwest Research Station.

Christensen, H. H., & Clark, R. N. (1983). "Increasing Public Involvement to Reduce Depreciative Behavior in Recreation Settings. *Leisure Sciences, 5*:359-379.

Christiansen, Monty L. (1983). *Vandalism control management for parks and recreation areas.* State College, PA: Venture.

City of Boise, Parks and Recreation Department. (2010). Vandalism in the Parks. Retreived December 14, 2010. http://www.cityofboise.org/Departments/Parks/CaringForParks/ ParkServices/page5968.aspx

Clark, Roger N., Hendee, John C., & Campbell, Frederick L. (1971). Depreciative Behavior in Forest Campgrounds: An Exploratory Study. *Bulletin PNW-161.* Portland, OR: USDA Forest Service, Pacific Northwest Forest and Range Exp. Stn.

Clark, Roger N., Hendee, John C., & Frederick Campbell. (1971). "Values, Behavior, and Conflict in Modern Camping Culture." *Journal of Leisure Research, 3*(3): 143-159.

Clark, Roger. (1976). "Control of Vandalism in Recreation Areas – Fact, Fiction, or Folklore?" in Vandalism and Outdoor Recreation: Symposium Proceedings. Berkeley, CA: *USDA Forest Service General Technical Report PSW-17.* Pacific Southwest Forest and Range Exp. Stn.

Clark, R. N., Hendee, J. C., & Campbell, F. L. (1971). "Values, Behavior and Conflict in Modern Camping Culture." *Journal of Leisure Research, 3*:143-159.

Clinard, Marshal B., & Quinney, Richard. (1973). *Criminal behavior systems: A typology* (rev. ed). New York: Holt, Rinehart and Winston, Inc.

Clinard, Marshal B. (1989). *The sociology of deviant behavior* (7th ed.). New York: Holt, Rinehart and Winston.

Cohen, Stanley. (1973). "Property Destruction: Motives and Meanings," in Ward, Colin (Ed.),*Vandalism.* New York: Van Nostrand Company.

Cordell, H. K., Hartman, L. A., Watson, A. E., Fritschen, J. D., Propst, B. & Siverts, E. L. (1987). *The Public Area Recreation Visitor Survey: A progress report* in Cordell, H. K., & McDonald, Barbara (Eds.), Proceedings, Southeastern Recreation Research Conference, Asheville, NC.

DesJean, T., & Wilson, R. (no date). Vandalism behavior in the Southeast National Parks: Diagnosis and Treatment. Retrieved June 5, 2010, http://www.nps.gov/seac/coping/2-des-wil.htm

Donahue, Ron. (1968). "How to Handle Vandalism," *Camping Magazine, 40* (May): 24-25.

Dopkeen, Johnathon C. (1978). *Managing vandalism.* Boston, MA: Parkman Center for Urban Affairs.

Eliot, Martha M. (1954). "What is Vandalism?," *Federal Probation, 18*(1):3-5.

Fridgen J. D. (1980). "Environmental-Behavior Research: Implications for the Study of Leisure and Recreation Behavior," in Iso-Ahola, S. E. (Ed.), *Social psychological perspectives on leisure and recreation.* Springfield, IL: Charles C. Thomas.

Furno, O. F., & Wallace, L. B. (1972). "Vandalism: Recovery and Prevention," *American School and University, 44*(11):19-20, 22.

Gaines, Dan M. (1972). "Lighting Up the Parks," *Parks and Recreation, 7*(5):34, 49-50.

Grosvenor, John. (1976). "Control of Vandalism—An Architectural Design Approach," Vandalism and Outdoor Recreation: Symposium Proceedings. Berkeley, CA: USDA Forest Service and Range Exp. Stn.

Harrison, Anne. (1982). "Problems: Vandalism and Depreciative Behavior," in Grant W. Sharpe (Ed.) *Interpreting the environment* (2nd ed.). New York: MacMillan.

Hartman, L. A., Freilich, H. R., & Cordell, H. K. (1989). "Trends and Current Status of Participation on Outdoor Recreation." In: *Proceedings, Benchmark 1988: An Outdoor Recreation and Wilderness Forum.* Tampa, FL.

*Helena Independent Record.* (2010). New Law Makes Vandals Pay. http://helenair.com/news/ article_3ed0079e-438b-11df-818b-001cc4c002e0.html, retrieved 5 June 2010.

King County Parks and Recreation. (2005). Park vandalism costs county taxpayers plenty: King County asks for public's help in curbing senseless crime. Retrieved December 14, 2010. http://www.kingcounty.gov/environment/dnrp/newsroom/newsreleases/2005/june/0613Parkvandalism.aspx

Knox County Parks and Recreation. (2009). Knox County Parks and Recreation Uses Technology to Deter Vandalism. Retrieved December 14, 2010. http://www.knoxcounty.org/current09/parks_deter_vandalism.php

Knudson, George J. (1967). *Techniques to reduce vandalism on nature trails.* Annual Workshop of the Association of Interpretive Naturalists, Oglebay Park, Wheeling WV.

Madison, Arnold. (1970). *Vandalism: The not-so-senseless crime.* New York: The Seabury Press.

Matthews, Robert P. (1970). "Theft and Vandalism in Western Washington Forest," *Journal of Forestry, 68*(7):415-516.

National Park Service. (1990). *Keeper of the treasures: Protecting historic properties and cultural tradition on Indian lands.* Washington, D.C.: N.P.S.

Petty, Paul (1966). "Vandalism in Natural Forests and Parks," unpublished master's thesis, Fort Collins, CO: Colorado State University.

Reeves, David E. (1972). "Protecting Against Fire and Vandalism," *American School and University, 44*(9):62-66.

Reitelman, Michael. (1979). Personal Communications with Jim Nickerson, Superintendent, Point Pleasant Park, Halifax, Nova Scotia.

Reynolds, Jesse A. (1967). "Public Disregard, Vandalism, Littering, Increase Workload," *Parks and Recreation, 2*(10):39, 40, 50.

Scott, Chester C. (1954). "Vandalism and Our Present-day Pattern of Living," *Federal Probation, 18*(1):10-11.

Sharpe, Grant W. (1988). "Reducing Vandalism Through Interpretation." *Proceedings.* 1988 NAI National Interpreters Workshop. San Diego, CA. Edited by Debra Erickson, NAI.

Sissons, Ron. (1976). "Can We Stop Vandalism in Our Parks?" *California Parks and Recreation, Feb./Ma., 32*(1)33-34.

*Chapter Fourteen*

# Law Enforcement

## UNDERSTANDING LAW ENFORCEMENT

One of the most challenging aspects of park management is insuring protection of visitors, resources, and facilities. Managers and staff face philosophical issues between the traditional view of resource preservation and study and the necessity of law enforcement. Enforcement of either park regulations or general statutory laws poses unique problems as urban crime such as cultivation of marijuana transferred to remote areas (http://www.npr.org/templates/story/story. php?storyId=103866520). Increasingly, job descriptions for park employees include police training (https://www.avuecentral.com), not only for the protection of resources and the public, but for the protection of park employees.

Public recreation areas have attracted large numbers of visitors on an increasing scale in the past several decades. Campgrounds and public facilities, particularly during heavy-use periods, resemble small communities and experience many of the same problems. Among these problems are actions of the few that depreciate the recreational experience and violate the rights of others.

Depreciative behavior is a serious problem and is one that is increasing in scope and cost annually. The term "depreciative behavior" may refer to a wide variety of activities ranging from simple nuisance acts like improper water disposal to serious legal violations, such as theft, drug use, drug sale, vandalism, and assault, which sometimes results in injury to officers and others (http://www.csmonitor.com/2005/0808/p03s01-ussc.html). There has been an increase in crime, particularly those related to the growing, manufacture, and dumping of drugs, and resultant threats to personnel and the environment (http://www.fs.fed.us/psw/publications/documents/psw_rp253/psw_rp253.pdf). National parks located near borders provide pathways for smuggling of drugs, arms, and people due to easy access and low law enforcement presence, as noted in many news stories.

While not every park experiences large amounts of crime, two nationwide surveys conducted by PRC/Public Management Services, Inc. (1974) for the U.S. Army Corps of Engineers and the American Parks and Recreation Society indicate several factors that may explain why certain areas experience more problems than others. The studies show that crimes are more likely to occur:

- In a developed area as opposed to an undeveloped area.
- Near an urban atmosphere or a simulated urban environment.
- At a well-attended facility.
- On weekends.
- Between the hours of 8 p.m. and midnight.
- During the summer months.

## LAW ENFORCEMENT: PAST AND PRESENT

Offenses against park and forest regulations and violations such as the illegal taking of wildlife are not new. Having employees working in an enforcement posture dates back to when the military was the custodian of parks such as Yellowstone and Yosemite. Park staff commissioned as peace officers is a more modern phenomenon.

General statutes that originally created many park systems and established agencies to manage those lands often used very broad language. General charges such as "protection of visitors and lands" were common, but charges specifically delegating police authority were rare. In some instances, all agency employees were charged with the duty of protecting park and forest facilities without any of these employees being specifically commissioned to exercise law enforcement powers. In some agencies, this general charge still holds true.

Historically, the National Park Service has enforced all laws applicable to the parks where they exercise exclusive (the only law enforcement responsibility) or concurrent (shared law enforcement responsibility) legislative jurisdiction. The more serious cases, however, have usually been turned over to the FBI after initial investigation because they are federal lands. In areas of proprietary (having control of the land) jurisdiction, law enforcement is restricted to the rules set forth in Title 36 of the Code of Federal Regulations. This requires law enforcement to be primarily the responsibility of local law officers unless the park ranger is deputized by the local sheriff. Partial, the fourth type of jurisdiction, occurs when specific state responsibilities are released to other agencies, such as county or municipal agencies.

The National Park Service acquired the legislative mandate to commission its rangers with full law enforcement authority (http://www.nps.gov/policy/dorders/dorder9.html). The enforcement capabilities and authority of many other federal agencies have historically been low key or nonexistent, with agencies relying almost exclusively on local assistance, though this is changing toward internal law enforcement and rescue personnel since many local agencies lack appropriate training and equipment suited to the unique needs of remote parks.

### Assistance from Other Agencies

Most park agencies rely heavily on assistance from outside law enforcement departments even when they have internal personnel. The services that the agency can provide vary a great deal depending on the jurisdiction. Familiarity with a particular recreation agency's practices, combined with an understanding of traditional law enforcement departments, is the key to proper coordination.

Local park managers must learn who has primary responsibility and the most adequate capabilities to deal with a particular problem. A wildlife protection officer would be called for an offense concerning wildlife, while state police or the county sheriff would be summoned for an act of theft or vandalism. Also, with the exception of a very few national parks, such as Yosemite, Yellowstone, and Glacier Park, most areas do not normally maintain detention facilities. Coordination must be made with other agencies for this type of assistance.

In cases involving exclusive federal jurisdiction, federal law enforcement units (i.e., the U.S. Marshal Service or the Federal Bureau of Investigation) must be called for assistance.

Park managers and their respective agencies have sometimes entered into more formal agreements. In 1971, congress passed the cooperative Law Enforcement Program Act (P.L. 92-82), which allowed the U.S. Forest Service to appropriate money for local sheriffs' departments to provide additional visitor protection services for forested lands. This type of agreement can be thought of as a contract with local law enforcement departments.

Crimes against persons and property are the concern of local and state law enforcement agencies, but park law enforcement also investigates and prosecutes crimes involving historical artifacts and defacement of primitive sites and other resources (http://www.fletc.gov/training/programs/). One such investigation in the Four Corners area of the western United States in 2009 resulted in 24 arrests of people suspected of trafficking in Indian artifacts (http://www.sltrib.com/news/ci_14947390).

An agency employee has two enforcement alternatives: reactive (negative) contacts or proactive (positive) contacts. Flickinger (1976) found that in Ohio State parks, the majority of contracts were reactive as opposed to proactive, and he found that sufficient emphasis on a preventive program for both serious crimes and park rule violations was lacking. He points out that law enforcement can and should be "a constructive means of education and protection and must not be equated with repression and vengeance." This obviously includes proactive and positive interactions from the staff to the visitor.

## Enforcement Psychology

Public relations are a very important factor in a successful program. Even park employees who have little or no enforcement duty are often in uniform, and they soon realize that the public regards them as persons of authority. An employee in uniform may be regarded as a positive or negative presence. In a study indicating that uniformed rangers are held in high public regard, Moeller, et al.(1974) interviewed 157 campers and 281 boaters at a national forest reservoir and found that 80 percent felt regular patrols by uniformed officers were desirable.

**Avoiding the "cop" image.** The park ranger is not in the park to reform the public. Every effort should be made to remain objective and impartial in dealing with park visitors. The ranger has several roles to play, with enforcement being only one. While an extremely visible law enforcement presence may better deter crime, other roles that the ranger must fill may be adversely affected.

**Federal law enforcement agencies.** The United States is one of the few countries that does not have a national police force. When Congress creates a law enforcement body, the legislation also establishes specific jurisdictions and authority. The Federal Bureau of Investigation, for example, deals with 180 specified crimes plus crimes on government reservations, and no others. Many of these agencies below are now supervised by the Department of Homeland Security in the wake of terrorist attacks on September 11, 2001:

- Federal Drug Enforcement Administration
- Federal Bureau of Investigation
- Border Patrol
- Secret Service
- U.S. Coast Guard
- U.S. Marshal
- U.S. Park Police
- Various units with Departments of Agriculture, Interior, Commerce, Labor, etc.

**State law enforcement agencies.** Unlike the federal government, states can maintain law enforcement agencies that have general police powers within the state. State police forces operate under various names, such as State Police, State Patrol, or Highway Patrol.

The state may also provide for various delegations of restricted law enforcement duties to a number of other departments. These law enforcement units may be utilized by the park manager in various situations, including the following:

- Fish and game protection
- Environmental protection
- Fire protection
- Drug enforcement

**Local law enforcement agencies.** Law enforcement at the local level consists of either county or municipal agencies. County law enforcement is usually by either a sheriff's department or a county police department. County police departments are usually based on a consolidation of a county sheriff's department and municipal police department in an urban area. The sheriff's position is enabled through the state constitution. Because the sheriff's position is an elected one, however, the quality of professional services can vary a great deal from department to department. Park managers should be aware of the capabilities of their local sheriff's department.

County police and municipal police may be considered almost synonymous. While municipal police departments make up 37,000 out of 40,000 nationwide law enforcement departments, their services are seldom available to park lands in rural areas. Although assistance from various agencies is available in theory, local law enforcement budgets and rural locations make prompt assistance difficult.

### Formal Training

Historically, the National Park Service has been the agency most extensively involved in formal law enforcement training. The 1980s saw significant increases by other federal land management agencies in their law enforcement training. Each agency now has specific law enforcement commissioning requirements for permanent and seasonal employees. Permanent employees having law enforcement responsibilities receive approximately ten weeks of formal training at the Federal Law Enforcement Training Center (FLETC) (Flet-see) at Brunswick, Georgia (www.fletc. gov). The course, entitled "Basic Law Enforcement of Land Management Agencies," is aimed at personnel whose duties are concentrated in non-urban areas and who are full-time federal employees of participation land management agencies. Since the founding of FLETC, law enforcement has improved considerably in each of the federal agencies involved.

## LAW ENFORCEMENT TOOLS

Tools to minimize violations of rules, regulations, and laws in parks are many and varied. The best are preventative and positive in nature and will mitigate most adverse effects on staff, visitors, and image of the park or agency responsible for the park.

### Preventive Measures

Eldefonso et al. (1968), in *Introduction to Law Enforcement*, point out three factors necessary for a violation or crime to occur:

* The desire to commit the act.
* The will to commit the act.
* The opportunity to commit the act.

Preventive measures in parks deal with eliminating one of these three factors. Education about the park, its historic or physical characteristics, its significance, and the reason it was created as a park all contribute to a sense of ownership on the part of the visitor. Physical design and proactive behavior on the part of the staff also contribute to reducing opportunity for crime. Examples of such measures are preventive ranger patrols, park access control, facilities design control, increased lighting, posting of regulations, immediate repairs to vandalized areas, alarms, installations of barriers, and visitor education. The McCalls (1977) point out preventive measures should be "low key, such as disseminating information about campground rules and regulations." They also indicate that campground regulations should be handled in positive fashion, not by listing negations.

An initial contact with a visitor can be very effective in stopping participation in a violation. Contact concerning nuisance behavior is most frequently an attempt to effect compliance through education. This may consist of verbal or written warnings, or may include a citation and notation of observed behavior, each level of official response an escalation in seriousness and consequences.

### Patrols

One of the important purposes of the patrol is the presence and visibility of the employee. Much does not happen because of the presence, even though it is a friendly and helpful presence.

Besides its deterrent function, patrol is the means by which availability is assured for education, detection of violations, and visitor assistance.

The patrol is carried out in many ways depending on the terrain to be covered, the focus of the patrol, and the agency's policy. Patrol may be on foot, by bicycle, on horseback, by canoe, or by motor vehicle. Motorized transportation may include pickups, sedans, four-wheel drives, power boats, ATVs, helicopters, or airplanes.

The utility of patrol operations has not gone unquestioned. Very little research exists comparing hours spent on patrol and types of patrol used with actual number of crimes.

## Crime Scene Protection

When a crime occurs, a park employee may often be the first official person to arrive at the scene. Although a specialist will be needed, the employee can make a significant contribution to the investigation by making note of who was present, what happened and when, where the incident took place, and how it took place.

Except where an injury has occurred and treatment is necessary, the actual scene of an incident must be preserved intact for the ultimate collection and examination of all evidence. Preserving the scene of an incident means keeping the site in the same physical condition as it was when left by the perpetrator. The official in charge must apply safeguards to bar all forms of disturbance until photographs, sketches, and the final collection of information are made. Unauthorized persons, even other park employees and officials, must be excluded. All articles that are, or may be, of value as evidence must be collected. Articles that need documentation or collection may include fingerprints, tool impressions, foot and tire marks, weapons, glass fragments, stains, and clothing.

The full range of legal procedures and police action is available to trained and commissioned park employees in the United States. The park manager is encouraged to develop good relations with all law enforcement entities within and without his or her agency to protect people and resources and meet operational goals.

## THE CANADIAN APPROACH

For the most part this chapter deals with law enforcement in the United States. The Canadian approach differs somewhat and is not uniform from province to province. Canadian parks may have fewer visitors overall, but they experience similar problems, particularly in Banff and Jasper National Parks. However, for the most part, park rangers and supervisors in Canada can concentrate on park management while keeping a relatively low profile on hard-core law enforcement. A professional police organization, the Royal Canadian Mounted Police (RCMP), is authorized to enforce all of that country's laws and serve as the provincial police force in many areas.

The RCMP is regarded as *ex officio* park staff and, as such, routinely patrols parks. The federal government charges the individual provinces for this police service through a fee structure based on a per-capita assessment, so there is no direct expense to the individual park. The RCMP serves both provincial and national parks.

To a greater or lesser extent, depending on the provincial situation, park rangers or wardens still have many of the same duties of their U.S. counterparts. These include enforcing checkout times, leash laws, letter laws, and traffic laws; evicting drunks and rowdies; seizing illegal firearms, drugs, and alcohol; and enforcing dozens of other regulations listed in their agencies' respective park acts. The park officer is also responsible for detaining violators, protecting evidence, and providing other assistance to the RCMP staff in addition to pinpointing troublesome times and places so that RCMP patrols can be increased when needed.

In some provincial park systems, there are park rangers who possess special constable appointments and who are authorized to enforce statutes beyond those cited in the local park act. In such instances, they take initial action on all unlawful acts committed in the parks, calling in members of the local RCMP detachment only when backup is needed.

## Parks Outside Canada and the United States

Law enforcement in parks outside the two countries examined here varies tremendously. National police forces in many countries take the lead in enforcing laws and regulations in the country and in parks. In Africa, a continent noted for unique resources, national police provide protection and sometimes even maintenance (http://www.african-parks.org/). Systems of justice in these counties may not have the same provisions as those in the United States. Tourists and visitors in many of these destinations have noted the presence of security personnel who are heavily armed for a variety of reasons. Each sovereign country determines the appropriate methods for enforcing laws in its own territories.

## Conclusion

Proper and adequate procedures in law enforcement depend on professional training, adequate supervision, and irreproachable employee conduct. Professional handling of operations, especially procedures involving law enforcement, is not only necessary for maintenance of good visitor-agency relations, it is also required by law. Agencies involved in law enforcement that provide less than adequate training and supervision of field employees leave themselves, their field employees, and the visiting public unnecessarily vulnerable.

Park rangers are diplomats and public relations officers in uniform. Even when they do not have a peace officer's commission, carry no weapons, and lack the power of arrest, they still have a challenging variety of tasks related to keeping the peace and assuring good order.

## References

**References Cited**

African Parks, 2010, http://www.african-parks.org/, Retrieved June 9, 2010

Christian Science Monitor, 2010, http://www.csmonitor.com/2005/0808/p03s01-ussc.html, Retrieved June 9, 2010

Eldefonso, Edward, Coffey, Alan, & Grace, Richard C. (1968). *Principles of law enforcement.* New York: Wiley.

Federal Law Enforcement Training Center. www.fletc.gov/training/programs/, Retrieved June 9, 2010

Flickinger, Theodore Blair. (1976). "Crime and Law Enforcement in Ohio's State Parks," Unpublished doctoral dissertation, Columbus, OH: Ohio State University.

McCall, Joseph R., & McCall. Virginia M. (1977). "Through Appreciation Protection," *Outdoor Recreation, Forest, Park and Wilderness*. Beverly Hills, CA: Benzinger, Bruce & Glencoe, Inc.

Moeller, George H., Larson, Rodney G., & Morrison, Douglas A. (1974). *Opinions of Campers and Boaters at the Allegheny Reservoir*, USDA Forest Service Research Paper NE-307. Upper Darby, PA: Northeast Forest Exp. Stn.

National Park Service. http://www.nps.gov/policy/dorders/dorder9.html, Retrieved June 9, 2010

National Public Radio. http://www.npr.org/templates/story/story.php?storyId=103866520, Retrieved June 9, 2010

PRC Public Management Services, Inc., U.S. Army Corps of Engineers. (1974). *A Study of Law Enforcement Needs and Means of Providing Visitor Protection at Corps of Engineers Lakes*. Washington, D.C.

Salt Lake City Tribune. http://www.sltrib.com/news/ci_14947390, Retrieved June 9, 2010

U.S. Forest Service. http://www.fs.fed.us/psw/publications/documents/psw_rp253/psw_rp253.pdf, Retrieved June 9, 2010

## General References

Department of the Treasury. (1991). *Basic law enforcement for land management agencies.* Syllabus. Glynco, GA: Federal Law Enforcement Training Center.

German, A. C., Day, Frank D., & Gallati, Robert R. (1966). *Introduction to law enforcement.* Springfield, IL: Charles C. Thomas

Gunderson, Dennis F. (1988). *Communication of law enforcement.* Lanham, MD: University Press of America.

Johnston, Les. (1991). *The rebirth of private policing.* New York: Routledge.

National Park Service. (1989). *Law enforcement policy and guidelines*, Section II, Chapter 3. Washington, D.C.

Riekes, Linda. (1992). *Understanding law enforcement.* (2nd ed.). St. Paul, MN: West Publishing.

Vetter, Harold J., & Simonsen, Clifford E. (1976). *Criminal justice in America: The system, the process, the people.* Philadelphia, PA: W. B. Saunders Co.

# Chapter Fifteen

# Fire Management

Prehistoric fires probably burned most of North America at one time or another. The primeval conifer forests that were found here, with their associated deciduous components, were largely fire-dependent ecosystems. Native Americans used fire extensively on an annual basis for large-scale land management. Fire served multiple purposes to improve a variety of food and fiber resources, maintain plant diversity and vitality, kill plant parasites, and improve habitat for large game, among other benefits. Fire has been used as a management tool throughout the world. Inhabitants of European descent used fire largely to clear land for agricultural purposes rather than to increase productivity of a native landscape. The experience of how to use fire as a management tool as well as the memory of the effect on the landscape faded, and a different perspective of fire evolved. Damage and loss by human-caused fires prompted the formation of strong fire-suppression organizations, and anti-fire campaigns were established by federal, state, and provincial governments. But fire exclusion produced an unnatural forest, at least in those areas of North America where fire was once a relatively frequent natural event. Whole ecosystems have evolved in response to the lack of fire.

Fire is now considered an effective management tool. Although effective, fire burning out of control (wildfire) can create hazardous conditions. Parks generally include large areas of mixed vegetation with a few buildings interspersed. Most of the vegetation, at least during some part of the year is flammable. Most park managers have some other organization, such as the state or provincial forestry agency, which serves as the park's first line of defense. However, should a wildfire occur, the protection of human lives, public property, and natural resources are still the responsibility of park managers, even though help may be on the way. Park management must plan for and be knowledgeable about the use of fire in managing park resources and understand the threat posed from surrounding lands.

Several terms are useful to understand the nature of fire management. A distinction must be made between "controlled burns" and "wildfires." Fire management includes fire prevention, fire suppression, and the use of fire for specified purposes, such as controlled burns or prescribed burning, wherein fire is used as a management tool. Land management plans must address vegetation management to minimize fuel accumulation. Wildfires are fires burning out of control. They are commonly called "forest fires" or, in areas devoid of trees, "brush or grass fires." Another term used is "wildland fires."

## Fire Management Plan

The term "fire management" implies that fires in the park can have positive and negative consequences. For example, the same fire can be good for some parts of an ecosystem but bad for the forest industry or the safety of the public. Fire management is designed to deal with such conflicts by recognizing that the factors of time, location, fuel flammability, ecology, and economics make fires in the park or wildland either tolerable or intolerable. Planning for the appropriate use and response to fire is conducted through the fire management plan (FMP). The FMP includes strategic and operational elements to respond to unplanned ignitions, hazardous fuels and vegetation management, burned area emergency stabilization and rehabilitation, prevention, community interaction and collaborative partnership roles and monitoring and evaluation programs. The National Wildfire Coordinating Group provides a FMP template that structures the organization of the plan and facilitates interagency coordination. The structure assists a variety of agencies to address fire management systematically. The plan structure includes:

1. Introduction
2. Policy, land management planning, and partnerships
3. Fire management unit characteristics
4. Wildland fire operation guidance
5. Monitoring and evaluation

The first section of the agency FMP must provide a general introduction to the planning area including land ownership, significant resources, mission, and management designation of area. The second section must address policy, land management planning, and partnership. This section links high level planning, legislation, and policies to action and ensures consistency and coordination. The third section of the FMP must break the area into fire management units (FMU) and describe characteristics of each unit. A FMU divides a complex landscape into small geographic areas based on physical, biological and social characteristics. Subsequent sections of the plan are developed for specific use by each agency. The detailed outline can be found at: http://www.nwcg.gov.

**Prescribed Fire**

The "prescribed fire" is a tool to achieve land management goals for an area. It is widely used today, not only in North America, but also on other continents. In Australia, large areas are burned annually by igniting from aircraft the accumulated biomass that fuels wildfires. In Kruger National Park in South Africa, areas up to 100 square miles (258 km) are burned at one time.

Land managers use fire to prepare a favorable site before planting tree seedlings, to provide more suitable habitat for wildlife, to control weeds, to eliminate disease and insects, and to remove logging slash. Fire is also used under controlled conditions to eliminate accumulations of forest fuels (dead and dying trees, dense undergrowth, and stands of smalls trees) before these assume hazardous proportions as flash fuels. Prescribed fires may also be called controlled burns or management fires.

The objectives of prescribed fire in land management generally are as follows:

* hazard reduction (presuppression),
* nutrient release,
* undesirable species control,
* cover type conversion,
* grazing improvement,
* planting site preparation,
* sanitation (eliminating diseased or insect-infested trees), and
* wildlife habitat improvement.

Each controlled burn requires a burn plan  based on characteristics of the fire management unit described in the fire management plan. Safety, cost, fuel type, weather conditions, available manpower, topography, and objectives of the burn are considered.

Park managers should research the historical use of the prescribed or controlled burn and determine whether this management practice might benefit the park landscape. Burning of undergrowth and dead trees under controlled conditions is preferable to an uncontrolled wildfire, and this limited slower burning gives wildlife a chance to escape the area. Controlled burning may also stimulate germination and growth of species favorable for wildlife.

The public may be unaware of the benefits associated with controlled burning. Typically, negative perceptions are attached to all fires. It is critical for managers to include fire as a management tool in their public education or interpretive programs. The historical use, techniques, and advantages of fire as a landscape management tool can be addressed. Park managers must also consider the smoke generated by controlled burns in education, reservation, and other informational materials. Smoke can limit visibility and have adverse health effects for some who suffer from respiratory problems. Potential users should be informed of controlled burn seasons scheduled in the park. The National Park Service keeps the public updated with a website posting information about fires located within all national parks. Information includes: cause of fire, location, acreage treated, resources committed, estimated completion date, park status and updates, overview, activity in last 24 hours, strategy, vegetation affected, air/smoke issues, benefits of the burn, values to be protected, partners involved, and contact information. More detailed information can be found at http://www.nps.gov/fire/public/pub_firenews.cfm.

The California state park system provides a good example of a fire management program through vegetation management. This system has over 200 park units in a great variety of vegetative types. Many of these have a high potential for destruction by wildfire because of the large accumulations of fuel. Because of the placement of campgrounds, picnic areas, residences, trails, roads, and other developments within areas of high fire potential, the state adopted a policy to:

- protect state park units and visitors from major wildfires sweeping in from outside,
- prevent damage from wildfires originating within park lands, and
- accomplish well-defined environmental management objectives involving vegetation, soils, wildlife, scenic, and esthetic considerations.

The fuels of certain parks are modified or broken into smaller manageable units by a system of narrow, 10-foot-wide (3 meters) firebreaks, or wider 100 to 300 foot (30-90 meter) shaded fuelbreaks. Fire management in California state parks is essentially a fuel management program.

Fire management also encompasses the concept of permitting some lightning-caused wildfires to burn without direct suppression. This "natural fire" policy has gained acceptance in the larger western national parks and forests as well as in national wildlife refuge wilderness areas. This idea is relatively new to land management agencies in the United States, but has been practiced in Canada for many years. As stated above, fire has always been an important element in maintaining natural ecosystems. In such areas as these, which are managed to maintain natural conditions, fires started by lightning may be allowed to burn as long as human life, public developments, or other agencies' lands are not being threatened. However, before the decision is made to control or not control a fire, the manager must be in a position to predict what will be the result of a given course of action.

Many large parks today possess fine stands of trees that no one would wish to see destroyed, but these trees are extremely vulnerable. Because of careful protection in the years since the parks were established, the understory fuel often has built up to the point where these stands would be destroyed should a major fire break out. As the vast 1988 fires in Yellowstone National Park proved, the decisions about when to fight wildfire and when to let it burn are difficult and contentious. In this fire, nearly 794,000 acres burned for several months.

## Wildfires

A wildfire is a freely burning conflagration. This sort of fire consumes millions of acres of forest annually in North America. Attempts are made to limit and extinguish most of these fires, especially those that are human caused and that are located in areas where damage to human life, property, and perhaps even recreational values exceed long-term ecological considerations.

**Causes of wildfires.** Because fires may start outside the park boundaries and spread into the park or vice versa, it is important for the park manager to have some knowledge of the causes of fires. Uncontrolled fires are quite a different matter from controlled burns, and they nearly always come at a time when any conflagration in the park would be dangerous. Although statistics specifically related to parks are not available, the causes of wildfires in the United States have been classified under nine headings. Lightning accounts for 10 percent, and the other 90 percent are caused by humans. Each cause is considered here.

*Lightning strikes.* Approximately 10 percent of all wildfires start from lightning. Most occur in the Rocky Mountain and Pacific Coast states. Unlike the fires mentioned in the eight following groups, these are not preventable.

*Incendiary fires.* This is the largest category of human-caused fires in the United States, and it accounts for approximately 28 percent of the wildfires. An incendiary fire is one set purposely on someone else's land without the owner's permission. The reasons for setting such fires include gaining employment as a firefighter, improving hunting conditions, killing insects or snakes, paying back a personal grudge against the landowner, diverting attention from other illicit activities, or committing an unprovoked act of vandalism.

*Debris burning.* This cause of wildfires is responsible for 22 percent of human-caused fires. This is a traditional and widespread land management practice that many landowners are loath to give up. No doubt their forbearers also burned dead leaves in the spring or dead grass in the fall. Unwillingness on the part of the burner to obtain the necessary labor force to contain debris fires or misjudgment as to weather and wind conditions when burning, results in the fire escaping to adjoining land. Sometimes this may be park land, and thus managers must be aware of adjoining owners' practices in this regard. Legislation regulating air pollution may reduce this percentage in the future.

*Smokers.* Fires of this origin average about 11 percent of each year's total. Smokers include park users, including hunters, fisherman, berry pickers, truck drivers, picnickers, and others who may be passing through the park.

*Children.* Accounting for about nine percent of the designated total are wildfires caused by children less than 12 years old. Playing with matches is still one of the major risks in children-caused fires.

*Railroads.* Railroad operations account for about six percent of all these wildfires. Sparks from overheated brake shoes, smokestacks, burning rights-of-way, and any other activity causing fires related to railroads are included in railroad fires. Where railroad tracks skirt the boundaries of a park area, the park manager must be aware of this potential hazard.

*Campers.* This category, responsible for about three percent of all human-caused wildfires, includes campfires for cooking, warmth, and light. Very few such fires, of course, start in developed campgrounds with standard fireplaces or stoves. Most camper fires are caused by hikers, hunters, fishermen, and other backcountry users.

*Equipment uses.* These wildfires, some four percent of the designated total, are caused by any mechanical equipment other than that used in railroad operations. Power saws, bulldozers, and other construction and logging equipment are included.

*Miscellaneous.* These wildfires, which account for about nine percent of the total of human-caused fires, cannot be classified under the other categories of wildfires. Cabin fires, autos leaving the highway and burning, sparks from a chimney—all these are grouped under miscellaneous causes.

There are regional variations in these totals. For example, incendiary fires account for 39 percent in the southeastern states and 10 percent in the Pacific states, but only two percent in the Rocky Mountain states. On the other hand, lightning fires account for 61 percent in the Rocky Mountain states, 31 percent in the Pacific states, and only two percent in the southern states.

## Wildfire Prevention

Land management, building management, community education, and fire danger warnings are all components of a comprehensive fire prevention program typically addressed through the fire management plan. Considering the fact that nearly nine out of 10 wildfires are caused by people, it is important to invest in a targeted prevention program through community education. The National Wildfire Coordination Group sponsored by the U.S. Department of Agriculture, U.S. Department of the Interior, and the National Association of State Foresters has developed prevention strategies based on the most common causes of fires. More information can be found at http://www.nwcg. gov/pms/docs/wfprevnttrat.pdf

**Prevention programs**. An effective fire prevention program must be multifaceted and address employees, adjoining landowners/managers, special interest groups, and the general public through a variety of strategies including education, engineering, enforcement, and administration. NWCG has several guides available online to assist in developing effective fire prevention programs. Guide topics include conducting school programs, event management, wildfire prevention marketing, wildfire prevention strategies, effective wildfire prevention patrol, exhibits and displays, and field trips and tours.

Most state and provincial forest land is under some type of organized fire protection. Thus, when a fire occurs and is detected, it is attacked by a fire control agency. In most areas, the state or provincial forestry agency is ultimately responsible for wildfire control unless the fire is on federal land. In either case, in the park areas, the initial attack may be the duty of the park staff.

Park employees are critical to an effective prevention program. As noted earlier, many fires are started by people camping or smoking in the backcountry. Park managers with trail systems, fishing streams, or boat-access forested sites should attempt to warn user groups before they leave the front country. Posting signs at trailheads reading "No Smoking While Traveling" and reminding users to "Drown Your Campfire" at backcountry sites must be counted as minimum endeavors. During the critical seasons, the park personnel at the entrance stations and information desks, as well as those conducting interpretive activities, should be stressing fire danger. Fire permits for backcountry users detailing fire regulations and emphasizing fire hazard conditions can be helpful. Signs displaying the fire danger, located along the road to or just inside park entrances, are another means of keeping the public informed at critical times. Off-site, off-season programs targeted to reach specific user groups are often effective in reducing backcountry fires in the subsequent season.

The park manager may have to curtail backcountry use during critical fire danger periods. Keeping hikers out of the woods during extremely severe fire conditions by posting the area closed due to extreme fire hazard not only reduces the fire risk but also protects the hikers themselves, who might be trapped should fire break out. On the other hand, backcountry users can be effective fire detection agents.

*Fire risk.* Wildfire prevention deals with the reduction of both fire risk and fire hazard. Fire risk is the means by which forest fuels catch fire. It refers to the causative agent, such as a lightning strike, a cigarette, a match, or an abandoned campfire. Although nothing can be done to control the lightning strike, there are ways to lessen other forms of risk, such as the area closure example above.

*Fire hazard.* Dead leaves along a trail, dry grass along a roadside, or snags and slash in a forest constitute fuel that can be easily ignited. This fuel and its condition with respect to ignition and flammability is called the fire hazard. Fire hazard reduction is a part of fire prevention, and it can be accomplished by removing fuels from areas exposed to high fire risk. The park manager can reduce the fire hazard by removing fuel from a plowed strip along the park boundary, especially where the boundary runs next to a road where smoker fires could start. This firebreak might also guard the park from adjacent farmland or urban land where debris burning is practiced. Some park managers remove light ground fuels through periodic prescribed burns. Fire hazard can be reduced by converting or changing the dominant vegetation type of an area, such as annuals to perennials or brush to grass. This may require approval from higher authorities, and it presupposes an informed visitor clientele. The land management plan or fire management plan may prescribe mechanical, chemical, or biological (i.e., livestock grazing) methods to reduce hazardous fuels.

The cost of hazard reduction is often high and should be considered carefully. When both risk and hazard are high, it follows that such an area should receive attention, whereas one of limited risk and hazard might be better placed at a lower priority (Sharpe, Hendee, & Sharpe, 1984).

**Fire Behavior.** Before discussing presuppression, suppression, and post fire activities, there should be some understanding of how a fire can be expected to behave once it is started. No two fires are alike, of course, but generally speaking, an experienced firefighter can predict what a fire will do.

Basically, fires tend to burn in the direction the wind is blowing and uphill. They move slowly in heavy fuels such as logs and large limbs, but they often burn more intensely here. Fires burn faster in light fuels, such as grass, leaves, and fine brush. In the absence of wind and on flat topography, a fire will spread out uniformly, assuming the fuels it encounters are similar.

A fire that burns slowly through the forest organic matter below the surface is termed a ground fire. A fire that consumes the loose debris and smaller vegetation on top of the ground is termed a surface fire. When a fire burns between the surface and crown, it is referred to as an understory fire. If the fire rises to the branches and foliage of the forest and moves forward through the treetops, it is called a crown fire.

Most wildfires start as surface or ground fires and may eventually become crown fires. Embers from the crown can fall to the forest floor and start new surface or ground fires. All three may occur at the same time. A fire whose heat is lifting and blowing embers ahead of itself, generating new, separate fires, is said to be developing spot fires.

When a fire is crowning and burning several hundred acres at once, it creates tremendous heat and often generates its own weather, including small tornadoes. In such a situation, the course of the fire becomes unpredictable, and the danger to firefighting personnel is great. This kind of fire is sometimes called a blowup. Fire behavior is affected by topography, temperature, relative humidity, wind speed, wind direction, fuels, and a host of other factors.

*Fuel and its effect on fire behavior.* Fuel includes all burnable material in the forest such as duff, roots, rotting wood, stumps, leaves, needles, bark, branches, and standing trunks. Included are also the many forms of grasses and other herbs, as well as shrubs and small trees. The rate of spread through fuels varies with such factors as moisture content; fuel quantity, size and arrangement; fuel continuity; pitch and resin content; season of the year; and whether the fuel is alive or dead. Therefore, a knowledge of fuels is important in predicting fire behavior. Even more to the point, fuels are one component of the fire triangle that can be manipulated. This can be done through the construction of firebreaks, by reducing fuel volume, or by converting vegetation from one type to another through prescribed burning.

*Wind and its effects on fire behavior.* Wind is also an important factor in fire behavior, for it supplies oxygen to the fire, dries out fuels, and increases the rate of speed exponentially proportionate to the wind speed. Fire-created whirlwinds lift burning embers aloft and then drop them, producing spot fires up to half a mile ahead of the fire.

Winds associated with frontal systems can quickly change the direction of a fire. With the passing of a cold front, the wind may become turbulent, changing its direction about 90° to the right. This can create havoc with established fire lines.

Local winds may determine fire direction and rate of spread. Local winds known as "mountain winds" tend to flow down slope at night after the sun goes down and upslope in the morning after the sun warms the valley. Additionally, winds blow off bodies of water as sea breezes toward land in daytime and toward the water from the land surfaces at night.

*Topography and its effect on fire behavior.* Topography affects fire behavior in several ways. Fire moves upslope in a manner similar to a fire moving before a strong wind. The steeper the slope, the closer the flames to the fuel. Preheating is accelerated and the fire spreads faster.

Slope affects fuels in another way also. Compass direction of slope, or aspect, can influence fuel moisture. North and northwest slopes tend to be more moist than the sun-facing south and southeast slopes. Thus, fuels on the southern exposures usually burn faster than those on wetter northern slopes.

Elevation, another aspect of topography, also influences fire. Most fuels at lower elevations dry out first and may be ready to burn, while those at higher elevations may still be covered with snow. Also, fuel quantity tends to be less at higher elevations. Topography may also influence wind patterns in that wind moves faster in valleys oriented parallel to the direction of the prevailing wind than it does in valleys that lie at right angles to it.

**Presuppression Activities**. *The organization and fire control protocol.* A park with a small staff often must rely on another agency to handle major fire control activities. A cooperative agreement should be established between the park and that agency. In most instances, however, park personnel are responsible for the initial attack on park fires and then must cooperate with the fire control forces of other agencies when they arrive.

The fire control protocol is part of the fire management plan and details operational information to respond to unplanned fires. The fire control protocol should state who is responsible for detection, when the fire lookout personnel are to be on duty, what the priorities are for crews in fire dispatch, and what mutual aid agreements exist with neighboring agencies. It should also include evacuation plans for residences, campgrounds, and backcountry. In addition, necessary training should be coordinated, who should get it and how much, and what qualifications are needed for various firefighting positions.

Personnel should be familiar with the characteristics of each fire management unit. Ideally this data has been gathered on park topography, vegetative cover types, risk and hazard, weather patterns, equipment and labor availability, transportation routes by road and trail, communication facilities, and visitor-use patterns. A history of past human-caused and lightning-caused wildfires, including their behavior, should be compiled for risk analysis and other purposes.

Fire control duties are not separate from other employee duties. They should be integrated into the organization plan so that not only the maintenance division but also the entire park staff can quickly assume a readiness or standby posture. When the alarm sounds, people with fire control assignments leave what they are doing and become the fire control force. Regularly scheduled fire drills should be a standard procedure in order to achieve and maintain efficiency.

*Fire training.* Seasonal help must be given preseason instructions on the safe handling of flammable liquids and fire tools and the proper use of pumper and hose equipment. Other fire school training should include map interpretation, compass reading, weather instruments usage, radio and telephone procedures, and general fire-control techniques. The training course should also include general familiarity with park features such as road and trail location, sources of water, topography of the park, location of fire tool caches, and areas of high risk and hazard.

Fire line duty is extremely demanding physically. A crew may be in the field long hours working as hard as they have ever worked in their lives. The physical fitness of members of the initial attack crew must be taken into consideration by the dispatcher.

It is vital that personnel be thoroughly checked out on the operation and maintenance of specialized equipment, such as hand pumpers, small engine pumps, hose connections, and pumper trucks. The very nature of fire presumes emergencies; therefore, training and practice sessions must be conducted by persons who can imbue the employees with that degree of interest and urgency required to facilitate learning. As with other safety practice sessions, boredom and a false sense of security must be overcome by skillful training techniques.

Permanent park personnel in any park with a fire threat should attend local or regional interagency fire-suppression training courses. These courses are available through both federal and state fire control agencies.

*Detection.* An efficient detection system is essential to fire control in order to respond while the fire is small. Small parks can and do depend on visitors as detectors, asking them to report the fire at ranger or warden stations or by telephone. Larger parks may have a fixed-point detection system —the lookout cabin or tower—where a fire watch is posted during critical fire periods. A mobile ground detector may also be used. This person patrols on foot, bicycle, motorcycle, or truck in areas of high risk and hazard.

Larger parks, or those in a cooperative pact with other landowners, may rely on aerial detection during periods of high fire danger. Smoke spotted from aircraft can be scouted at close range, and information on access to the fire, fuel types, natural barriers, and other data can be reported. In some areas a combination of ground and air detection is used.

*Communication.* Communication between the person who spots the fire and those concerned with suppressing the fire is a vital link. A fire spotter such as a fire lookout or airplane spotter, should have a two-way radio connection to park headquarters. Cell phones are also used, particularly when a park is dependent on visitors to report fires. It is important to know where there is no reception.

Information on where to report fires should be posted. Park personnel must be notified by the dispatcher; this too requires a communication network. Usually it is done by two-way radio and telephone.

*The dispatcher.* Someone in the park organization must serve as the fire dispatcher. It is this person who determines the location of the fire by plotting received information on park maps. The dispatcher also asks questions about the size of the fire, the fuel type it is in, the topography, the wind direction, the speed, the nearness of water, and anything else that will be useful in determining the size of the crew necessary to attack the fire.

*Transportation.* The getaway time is the time it takes for a crew to leave once it is notified of a fire by the dispatcher. The firefighting equipment must be ready and available so there is a minimum of delay. The time between leaving and arrival at the fire is called travel time. To minimize this, the dispatcher must have travel maps prepared. These maps show the road and trail system and cross-country routes necessary to reach the fire. Vehicles must be able to avoid unnecessary delay. For this reason, it should be standard practice to fill pumper trucks with water and to fill all gas tanks before trucks are parked for the night. By the same reasoning, personnel must make periodic radio contact with headquarters when working away from vehicles in more remote areas.

*Equipment.* Appropriate equipment, tools, and provisions must be available for fire control. Caches of tools should be located in strategic points around the park. Often these are sealed in red painted boxes. On days of high fire danger, certain equipment must be kept in readiness for immediate use in fire suppression. Reliable water supplies and access must be noted.

Small parks may need only a modest cache of hand tools and pump cans. A large park may require power saws, pumper trucks, and bulldozers to fight its building or forest fires, but it too must have caches of hand tools in certain areas. Frequent inspection is necessary to guarantee that the tools are instantly available. Tools set aside for fire suppression should not be used for any other purposes. They must be kept sharp and in good condition.

Fighting fire by hand is laborious, and crews prefer to have the bulldozer do their work for them. It can construct fire lines quickly, save property, and sometimes save human lives. In parks, however, compared with the more precise hand tools, a bulldozer is a blunt weapon; necessity, not convenience, should dictate its employment on the fire line. However, the wide path a bulldozer carves may result in serious soil slippage at a later date as well as leaving an unsightly scar for many seasons to come.

*Interpreting fire danger.* Another presuppression activity is the measurement of conditions that affect fire danger. A park manager wishing to keep track of fire danger must keep records of environmental factors such as temperature, relative humidity, wind direction and velocity, fuel moisture content, conditions of vegetation, sky condition (clear or overcast, number of days since the last precipitation, and amount of precipitation. These factors affect the ability of a fire to start, the rate of its spread and the difficulty of control. Even though there is a National Fire Danger Rating System available from the Forest Service, park managers must know how to gather and interpret data in order to apply this to their particular area.

**Suppression activities**. A wildfire has been detected and reported, and a crew has been dispatched to suppress it. On arrival at the scene, the fire boss or crew chief must asses the fire with respect to the character of the fuel, the slope, the wind direction and speed, the volume of heat, and anything else that characterizes this particular fire. Is it a ground fire, surface fire, or crown fire? Is it small enough for this crew to contain, or will additional help and equipment be needed? Are people or buildings in danger?

Methods of bringing wildfires under control are based on the theory that removing any one of the sides of the fire triangle—fuel, temperature, or oxygen—will cause the fire to go out. The fuel is removed by raking or digging a cleared line across the path of the fire, thus breaking the continuity of the fuel supply. The fire is also deprived of its fuel when this side of the triangle is made nonflammable by applying chemicals, water or dirt.

The attack on the fire is usually made frontally. If there is danger of the fire running or crowning, and thus endangering firefighters, it must be approached from the flanks. This strategy attempts to pinch off the fire at the head when it reaches a natural barrier or when the wind changes direction.

The crew must construct the fireline by clearing brush and grass down to mineral soil, thus forming a break wide enough to prevent the fire from reaching the other side. On fires that are advancing rapidly, the fireline must be constructed well in advance of the fire, and when possible, tied in with natural breaks such as ridges, streams, rockslides, or a roadway, if one exists. Trees along the fire side of the break must be felled if overhanging limbs could permit sparks to fly across the line. In some instances, the fuel inside the fire break is ignited or backfired to rob the advancing fire of its sustenance, thus removing a side of the fire triangle.

**Post suppression activities.** After the fire is contained, mitigation and restoration begin. A reduced crew must remain to patrol the lines in order to take care of any sparks that may jump the fire break. When the burned area has cooled sufficiently, the mop-up crew must reenter the site and make sure that all burning materials within the boundaries of the fire are extinguished. Snags must be felled, logs rolled over, partially burned wood chunks dispersed to safe sites, and all smoke smothered with dirt or water. Many fires have been contained only to break out again because of inadequate mop-up in conjunction with an unexpected wind. Undetected "hot spots" often become active during the hottest time of the day.

The National Park Service (NPS Director's Order #18 and Reference Manual #18) has prepared minimum impact suppression guidelines that should be reviewed for application in specific parks. An example of how a specific park has applied these guidelines can be found in the Rocky Mountain National Park Fire Management plan http://www.nps.gov/romo/parkmgmt/fire_mgmt_plan.htm.

Mitigation measures to reduce impacts on natural resources are easier to implement on controlled burns. Detailed training with regard to the fire management plan/fire control protocol would include covering these measures. A complete list of mitigation measures for the Rocky Mountain National Park can be found on the above website. Examples include:

- Park vehicles in specified areas and have crew walk to project sites
- Insure only portions of watershed are burned in any given year to reduce potential erosion and sediment delivery to streams
- Do not conduct activities in wetland areas
- Do not move slash for upland sites into a wetland

**Reports/evaluations**. Fire records must be carefully kept. As soon as a fire is suppressed, a report should be filled out. This contains a detailed record of the tools and equipment used and the number of members in the crew. It should also include such information as location, size of area burned, estimated damage, cost of suppression, probable cause of the fire, and any problems or weak spots noted in the execution of the fire control protocol.

An assessment of the burned area by appropriate technical specialists should be completed to initiate a program of rehabilitation and monitoring. Staff will need to comply with reporting requirments associated with the area.

## Structural Fires

The fighting of structural fires is very different from wildfire suppression. Structures may have flammable fuels stored inside, electrical circuits make fighting fire with water dangerous, falling beams and walls make entry dangerous, and the fuel itself presents special problems. The fabrics in furniture and carpets can create toxic smoke that is especially dangerous in confined spaces. There is the possibility of people being trapped inside. Firefighters trained in wildfires suppression will probably find their background inadequate for combating structural fires.

Periodic inspection is mandatory to check for weaknesses in the fire prevention system. Hazards such as stored volatile liquids, flammable materials close to stoves, gutters full of combustible debris, firewood stacked adjacent to structures, tree limbs near chimneys, and vegetation, especially highly flammable vegetation, adjacent to structures all contribute to the potential for fire and the unchecked spread of fire.

Structures in parks consist of employee housing, ranger stations, and other administrative offices, warehouses, storage sheds, visitor centers, and restrooms. Most are made of wood framing and wood siding, and they often have wood shake or wood shingle roofs. The buildings are often clustered, and forest cover, along with other vegetation, may be close by. Herein lies the firefighters' problem. Structural fires can spread from the buildings into the vegetation, or wildfires can work their way toward developed areas through the vegetation.

**Implementing a defensible space.** Defensible space is the space surrounding a structure that provides the firefighter adequate room to defend the structure from an advancing fire. It may also provide the opportunity to prevent a fire from spreading from the structures to the nearby forest. A distance of 30 to 40 feet on level ground, cleared of vegetation, should be adequate under normal conditions. Because fires burn uphill faster than on flat land, the structure on a slope needs more defensible space. Even with a substantial defensible space, a fire burning under extreme conditions of strong winds and hot dry weather can send burning embers onto roofs, under eaves, and into vent openings.

When a wildfire gets into a compound of buildings and buildings ignite either directly from fire or from radiant energy, there is much confusion. Residents are often taken by surprise, especially by the speed with which the fire spreads. Salvaging personal belongings causes delay in evacuation plans. Fire equipment may be committed elsewhere and timely help may not be forthcoming. Someone has to make the decisions about which buildings to sacrifice and which to wet down. Park managers would be well advised to address the potential of wildland fire entering the park building complex. Knowing it can happen, taking preventative steps, and having a fire protection plan worked out may avert a disaster.

**Implementing a fire protection plan for park structures.** Fires in park compounds start from the same sources as fires in urban residential areas: burning trash, smoking, children playing with fire, falling powerlines, improperly used gasoline equipment, defective electrical equipment, and even arsonists. Hot dry winds or a lack of spring rains can contribute to the fire hazard. Most rural parks depend on the state or provincial forestry agency for major fire control, but they must be prepared for initial attack and suppression implementation until help arrives.

**The fire control plan and safety checklist.** *Personnel.* Inform and train personnel regarding their duties in case of fire. No one—permanent, seasonal, concession, or voluntary—should be allowed to engage in fire suppression without adequate training. Send them to fire school. Evidence of qualification is possession of a Red Card. Here the bearer shows he or she is qualified as a wildland firefighter and has recently passed the required fitness test.

*Roads.* Roads should be wide enough to provide fire truck access and serve as a safe escape route. Check access and egress roads and remove hazard trees and snags that could block roads.

*Water.* Have water available in swimming pools, ponds, or storage tanks. Provide adequate access for a fire truck to reach the water.

*Wood storage.* Pile firewood a safe distance away from buildings, preferably uphill.

*Power lines.* Make sure trees are cleared from below power lines. Remove snags or danger trees from near power lines.

*The ring of safety.* Keep dried vegetation or flammable species away from structures. The fire break does not have to be bare ground but can include green lawn, ornamental shrubs, or individual trees whose limbs do not touch the ground.

One way to develop an effective protection plan is to enter into an agreement with other agencies, forming a cooperative organization to work together in prevention and suppression efforts. The U.S. Fire Administration has publications and provides training for firefighting, as well as a clearinghouse of fire-related information. The website is https://www.usfa.dhs.gov/applications/publications/ for publications. Their mission statement is to:

Promote the professional development of the fire and the emergency response community and its allied professionals. The National Fire Academy supports state and local training organizations to fulfill their obligation to the career and volunteer fire and emergency services. The National Fire Academy also develops, delivers, and manages educational and training programs having a national focus which is outside state and local training mission or exceeds state and local capabilities because of cost or audience. The programs are designed to support the DHS and FEMA goals to help state and local response agencies prevent, mitigate, prepare for, and respond to local, regional and national emergencies.

Their training has been designed to examine the local wildland/urban interface and to assist firefighting personnel in recognizing a critical hazard zone. Park managers will find it relevant to their situations. (National Fire Administration, 2010)

## Firefighting Safety

Fighting wildfire is hazardous work. In addition to a high level of fitness and rigorous training, the firefighter must be properly equipped, not only with adequate tools, but also with personal protection equipment (PPE) (Jukkala, Hensler, & Putnam, 1989).

**Personal protective equipment (PPE).** *Flame-resistant clothing.* Clothing is a key part of the PPE program. Today's yellow shirts and green pants are made from nylon-type fiber called aramid. It can withstand high temperatures, but, like most fibers, it will burn when subjected directly to flame. It stops burning when removed from flame. Rather than melting or turning to ash, the fabric forms a char that helps protect skin. However, there are constant improvements and testing of new materials by the U.S. Fire Administration Research Division (http://www.usfa.dhs.gov/fireservice/research/safety/nist9.shtm) who note:

> Firefighters' protective clothing has steadily improved over the years as new materials and improved designs have reached the market. A significant catalyst that has brought these improvements to the fire service is the National Fire Protection Association (NFPA) 1971 standard on structural firefighters' protective clothing. The fabric flammability test in this standard has resulted in the development of protective garments that resist flaming ignition. The Thermal Protective Performance (TPP) test has assisted in the development of garments that protect firefighters from short duration, high intensity, flash fire exposures. These two thermal tests methods have clearly lead to improvements in firefighter safety. However, thousands of firefighters are continuing to be seriously burned each year. Discussions with fire service personnel indicate that many of these serious burn injuries are occurring when firefighters are exposed to thermal environments that are significantly less intense than those addressed in the NFPA standard. Therefore, the National Institute of Standards and Technology (NIST) has begun the development of a method for measuring the thermal performance of firefighters' protective clothing under thermal conditions less severe than those currently specified in NFPA 1971.

*Fire shelter.* The fire shelter is the single most important component of the firefighter's PPE system. It is a pup-tent type shelter that saves lives by reflecting radiant heat away from the person inside. This leaves available a supply of breathable air inside the shelter, and the firefighter's airways and lungs are protected from flames and hot gases, the two leading killers in an entrapment. In the years since it was invented, the fire shelter has saved over 300 lives.

*Hardhat.* The next most important piece of PPE for saving lives and preventing serious injuries is the hardhat. It protects the firefighter from falling trees, limbs, and falling rocks. A cool, lightweight hardhat is recommended. For structural fires, a plastic hardhat is safer as it provides electrical hazard protection.

*Flame-resistant gloves.* Gloves are necessary to protect hands from minor burns, blisters, scratches, and small cuts. Strong, full-grained, chrome-tanned leather gloves give this level of protection as well as providing both flame and shrinkage resistance. Flame-resistant gloves are vital for firefighters seeking protection in fire shelters, because it is necessary to hold down a hot shelter being buffeted by fire-generated winds.

*Safety goggles.* Most eye injuries are caused by dust, smoke, brush, branches, and hot substances. As eye injuries account for approximately seven percent of all fire-suppression injuries, goggles have become an important safety item. These must be comfortable and not fog or scratch.

*Leather boots and wool socks.* Slips and falls account for about one-fifth of firefighting injuries. The recommended boot to serve firefighters is made of leather with at least an eighth-inch lace-up top and skid-resistant lug soles. Socks with more than 85-percent wool content not only offer thermal protection but keep feet cooler and drier, reducing the chance of blisters, a common firefighting problem.

Wildland firefighting equipment and safety is continually being researched and refined. Because materials and production technology change constantly, park managers should keep abreast of the latest in personal protective equipment. This can be done by writing the USDA Forest Service, Technology and Development Center, Missoula, MT 59801, or visiting http://www.fs.fed.us/t-d/php/tdc_search.php?category=Program&srchword=9 for publications on fire management.

## CONCLUSION

Fire is extremely useful as a management tool but presents potential hazards of which the park manager must be aware. The use of fire can minimize the need for chemical use to treat non-native species and restore ecosystem balance. Due to the nature of fire and typical perceptions attached to fire, park managers need to coordinate with surrounding and overlapping agencies to develop a comprehensive fire management plan. An important step in the plan is to divide the park into fire management units specific to the natural features of the park. This allows the park manager to respond more effectively to wildland fires. In addition, the fire management planning process provides another opportunity to develop an in depth understanding of the social and ecological environment of the park. Park employees, full-time and seasonal, need to understand their role in the fire management effort. They will be involved in preventing fires and standing ready to suppress those that might start on or near their lands.

## REFERENCES

**References Cited**

Agee, James K. (1977). "Fire Management in the National Parks," *Western Wildlands, 4*(1):79-85.

Barrows, Jack S. (1973). "Forest Fire Management: For Ecology and People," *Fire Management, 39*(3), U.S. Department of Agriculture.

Brown, Arthur A., & Davis, Kenneth P. (1973). *Forest fire: Control and use* (2nd ed.). New York: McGraw-Hill.

Despain, Don G., & Sellers, Robert E. (1977). "Natural Fire in Yellowstone National Park," *Western Wildlands, 4*(1): 20-24.

Gaylor, Harry P. (1974). *Wildfire prevention and control.* Bowie, MD: Robert J. Brady Co. of Prentice-Hall, Inc.

Gaidula, Peter. (1976). *Wildland fuel management guidelines for the California state park system.* Sacramento, CA: State of California Department of Parks and Recreation.

http://www.nwcg.gov/pms/docs/wfprevnttrat.pdf retrieved June 7, 2010

http://www.nwcg.gov/teams/ifpc/index.html retrieved June 7, 2010

http://leopold.wilderness.net/research/fire.htm, retrieved June 7, 2010.

http://www.fs.fed.us/fire/publications/index.html, retrieved June 7, 2010.

Jukkala, A., Hensler, B., & Putnam, T. (1989). "Making the Wildland Firefighter's Job Safer." *Trends*. Park Practice Program, 26(4):33-36.

Kerr, Ed. (1981). "Update: Forest Arson in the South," *American Forests, 87*(6): 30-35, 62-63.

Kilgore, Bruce M. (1975). "Restoring Fire to National Park Wilderness," *American Forests, 81*(3): 16-19, 57-59.

Kozlowski, T., & Ahlgren, C. E. (1974). *Fire and ecosystems.* New York: Academic Press.

Mutch, Robert W. (1977). "Fire Management and Land Use Planning Today: Tradition and Change in the Forest Service," *Western Wildlands, 4*(1): 37-52.

Nelson, Thomas B. (1979). "Fire Management Policy in the National Forests – A New Era," *Journal of Forestry, 77*(11): 723-725.

Northwest Interagency Fire Prevention Group. (1988). *Planning for survival. A multiple agency pamphlet.* Salem, OR: Public Affairs Office, Oregon State Department of Forestry.

Parsons, D. J., & DeBenedetti, S.H. (1979). "Impact of Fire Suppression on a Mixed-Conifer Forest," *Forest Ecology and Management, 2*(2): 21-23.

Pyne, Stephen J. (1982). *Fire in America: A cultural history of wildland and rural fire.* Princeton, NJ: Princeton University Press.

Sando, Rodney W. (1978). "Natural Fire Regimes and Fire Management – Foundations for Direction," *Western Wildlands, 4*(4): 34-44.

Stankey, George H. (1976). *Wilderness fire policy: An investigation of visitor knowledge and beliefs.* Ogden, UT: Intermt. Forest and Range Exp. Stn.

University Research Corporation. (1990). *Wildland/urban interface fire protection: A national problem with local solutions* (textbook and workbook). Emmitsburg, MD: National Fire Academy, Federal Emergency Management Agency.

Wood, Donald B. (1982). "Fuel Management's Potential for Reducing Frequency of Large Fires in the Northern Rockies," *Journal of Forestry, 80*(2): 96, 105-107.

Wright, Henry A., & Bailey, Arthur W. (1982). *Fire ecology: United States and southern Canada.* New York: Wiley.

*Chapter Sixteen*

# Interpretation

Interpretation is a critical park function and therefore falls within the purview of the park manager. Unfortunately, not all managers understand its role in park management.

Former Chief of Interpretation of the NPS Dave Dame (1985) tells us:

> The role and responsibility of interpretation in parks varies with the area's resources, the needs of its visitors and the needs of the service managing the area. This interactive threesome, park resources, park visitors, and park management, form the milieu in which park interpretation functions. They also comprise the broad categories that define the three basic areas of responsibility that can and should be addressed by any well-planned and well-managed interpretive program.

A recreation agency shows maturity and sophistication when it employs a cadre of professional interpreters with the ability to communicate and share knowledge about both natural and cultural resources.

## WHAT IS INTERPRETATION?

Visitors to parks, forests, refuges, and similar recreation areas come for relaxation and inspiration, yet many also wish to learn about natural and cultural resources. These resources include the area's geological features, animals, plants, ecological communities, and human history.

Interpretation is an educational service that explains the park's varied resources to visitors in accessible terms. In addition, sustainable park and recreation development will succeed to the degree that it anticipates and manages human experiences. Interpretation provides the best single tool for shaping experiences and sharing values. By providing an awareness of the environment, values are taught that are necessary for the protection of the environment. Sustainable design will seek to affect not only immediate behaviors but also the long-term beliefs and attitudes of the visitors (http://www.nps.gov/dsc/d_publications/d_1_gpsd.htm). Interpretation has three objectives:

1. To assist visitors in developing a keener awareness, appreciation, and understanding of the area they are visiting. Interpretation should help to make the visit a rich and enjoyable experience.
2. To accomplish management goals in two ways. First, interpretation encourages thoughtful use of the recreation resources by the visitor, helping reinforce the idea that parks are special places requiring special behavior. Second, interpretation can be used to minimize human impact on the resource.
3. To promote public understanding of an agency's goals and objectives. Well-done interpretation enhances the image of the sponsoring agency. If overdone, however, the message could be labeled propaganda rather than interpretation or public information.

Interpretation, of sorts, has been going on for centuries through writers passing their impressions of the natural environment to readers. Often the reader was removed from the resource and may have received inaccurate impressions of reality. Today those who interpret on site are usually able to work more closely with the feature itself or in direct contact with the recipient, and they have a greater variety of media to work with.

The interpretive program is the planned presentation of information about the park. In larger parks, it is usually under the direction of a permanent interpretive specialist or naturalist, directly reporting to the park manager, and usually employs other permanent and seasonal staff. In smaller parks, managers may be personally involved in the interpretive program, even though they may not be trained in this work.

Careful planning of the interpretive program is important, and there are people who specialize in this aspect of interpretation. The interpretive planner, with the assistance of other resource management specialists, follows a series of seven logical steps: determining objectives, taking inventory, analyzing the data, synthesizing alternatives, developing the plan, implementing the plan, and evaluating and revising the plan. This planning approach seeks to ensure (a) that the natural and cultural amenities important to the area's interpretive study are identified and located before any development takes place that might destroy or modify these features, and (b), that the appropriate interpretive media are used to reveal the story. The planning sequence also considers visitor needs and alternative choices of action before the final plan is selected.

Park visitors are the reason for developing the interpretive program. These visitors vary greatly in their age, education, culture, and experience. Because of this diversity, the interpretation program needs to be accessible to each person, and this presents a challenge to the person planning the presentations.

Participation in the educational interpretive program is voluntary. To hold visitor attention, an interpretive experience must be inspiring and of high quality, and it must strike the right balance between instruction and entertainment.

Seasonal interpretive employees, persons who work only during the heavy visitor-use season, do much of the day-to-day interpretation. Generally, these seasonal people form the direct link between the park and the visitor. The interpretive staff also works directly with other park personnel in matters related to park protection and maintenance as well as public relations.

## WHO USES INTERPRETATION?

Interpretation is not limited to park agencies but may be used by any organization that deals with the public. This would include public and private museums, nature centers, timber harvesting companies, public and private utilities, historical buildings and forts, wildlife refuges, fish hatcheries, restored villages and towns, and large engineering works such as hydroelectric power dams or nuclear plants. Although our main concern here is park interpretation, these other locations often have elaborate interpretive programs and are excellent areas to visit in order to obtain information and exchange ideas with the interpretive personnel working there.

## TECHNIQUES OF INTERPRETATION

A value-based visitor experience requires interpretation as an essential part of the planning and design process. Interpretive values cannot be successfully added to a development or operation as a last-minute enhancement.

The primary interpretive resources of a site must be identified early in the planning process. There can be no substitute for a scientific knowledge of the resources involved; however, interpretive opportunities can usually be identified in the planning stages of a new development by answering the following general questions:

* What is special or unusual about the site? (Consider both the natural and cultural aspects)
* What is particularly interesting, scenic, or photogenic about the site?
* What do visitors come to see?
* What is fun to do? (Answers must be resource-oriented and nonconsumptive.)
* What can be done on the site that is both environmentally sustainable and challenging?

- What resources provide particularly strong opportunities to demonstrate the underlying value system of sustainable development?
- What significant environmental controversies might be illustrated using local resources?
- What experiences are currently fashionable?
- What knowledge do visitors already have about the area?
- What knowledge and attitudes do neighboring residents have about the site and its resources?
- What messages can be offered about sustainability that visitors can use in their everyday lives?

In addition, interpretation must be reinforced in all visitor experiences and inherent in management's thinking and in the relationship of the proposed development to the larger cultural context. The value system that interpretation communicates must pervade the entire cycle of planning, design, construction, operations, and maintenance.

Once the general questions have been answered, questions that apply directly to the specific circumstances of your park should be addressed.

## About The Visitor

- Visitors need orientation either before or on arrival at your park. What medium would make them feel more welcome? What facilities does your park offer, and how can interpretive media provide answers to the visitor's questions?
- Visitors in great numbers have a certain impact on a park area. What interpretive media can lessen this impact? Visitors in unfamiliar areas need some warning of the dangers involved. What media can best inform the visitors of these dangers?
- Are many of your visitors from another language group? Do your signs and brochures speak to them too?
- Are a certain percentage of your visitors urban dwellers with little understanding of appropriate behavior in parks? How will you reach these people?

## About The Resource

- Each park has at least one interpretative theme. The essential features may be geological, ecological, or historical. Some large areas may have several themes. The inventory phase of the interpretive plan will reveal these themes.
- Some features are more vulnerable to visitor impact than others and certain media have greater resource production potential than others. On the other hand, some media have greater environmental impact than others. For instance, a conducted walk with 150 people will have greater impact than a self-guided walk over the same trail. In another example, such as fragile cave or historic building, a conducted walk with 20 people in attendance would be the wiser choice if one were to choose between it and a self-guided activity.
- Permanent facilities must be carefully planned. Even small facilities that require such developments as water, a waste disposal system, electricity, and a parking lot will have an impact on a fragile environment.

Other considerations in media selection include the cost of the original investment, maintenance and replacement costs, durability under local weather conditions, and appropriateness to an agency. Every situation presents different problems; some media, as noted, have advantages over others.

## MEDIA CHOICES

The interpretive program consists of both personal (attended) services and nonpersonal (unattended) services.

**Personal services.** In personal services, the visitor comes into direct contact with the interpretive specialist, and a two-way conversation may be entered into. The activity may be kept flexible in order to accommodate different groups. Personal contact with visitors continues to be the most important means of influencing visitor behavior.  Personal services include the following.

*Information services.* This takes place in a park entrance station, campground office, visitor center, roadside information booth, trailhead, or overlook.  Here the visitor seeks out the staffer themselves.

*Talks to groups.* In this activity, the interpreter makes a formal or informal presentation at announced times and in such places as amphitheatres, campfires, or auditoriums. The topic matter is usually related to the natural and cultural history of the local area and is often illustrated with slides. Visitors are also interested in such information as management, rescue, bear-control problems, police protection, and other behind-the-scenes activities. Poorly informed visitors may be unaware of the effects of their behavior when they deface rock art sites, carve picnic tables, damage vegetation with off-road vehicles, or release pets in the parks to survive on their own. Regulations against committing acts of vandalism, feeding wildlife, playing music loudly, allowing pets to run loose, or drinking in the park can also be dealt with during these talks.

*Conducted activities.* Here the interpreter and visitors move sequentially through a series of actual objects and views. The opportunity to ask questions and exchange ideas with a knowledgeable guide makes this medium very attractive. As we will see, it also has a certain deterrent and protective function. Conducted activities include nature walks and hikes, tours of cultural sites, automobile caravans, bus and tram tours, and various water trips.

*Living interpretation.* This is a form of historical interpretation in which some cultural activity such as carving wood, preparing food, making candles, firing old guns, making and using bows and arrows, or playing early musical instruments, is demonstrated. These activities may be a part of a vignette depicting the past. The wearing of costumes and the use of dialect are often part of the performance, which may be presented by one or more interpreters or local people familiar with the activity.

**Nonpersonal services**. Here the interpreter relies on various devices to present the interpretive story. Communication flows one way only. Although nonpersonal services are a means of expanding the interpretive program beyond the capabilities of individual interpreters, they should not totally replace personal services.

In most instances, the nonpersonal services are unscheduled and may be utilized at the convenience of the visitor.  Nonpersonal services include the following items.

*Audio services.* These machines, which utilize human voices, music, and sound effects, include tape recorders and playback units, speakers and handphones, induction loops, and radio transmitters. Audio equipment is frequently used in conjunction with other devices, such as slide programs and exhibits.

*Written material.* This encompasses signs, labels, and a variety of publications, including everything from simple checklists to elaborate books on flora, fauna, geology, and history. Publications are used where detailed presentations are needed; they also have a souvenir value that is missing in other media.

*Self-guided activities.* These include both self-guided trails (SGT) and self-guided auto tours (SGAT) and are particularly useful where visitor numbers are large and the interpretative staff is limited. Both activities are available to visitors at their convenience and at their own pace. Trails are specially built for the SGT, but existing roads are used for the SGAT.

*Exhibits.* Found both indoors and outdoors, these are a very popular medium and, if used properly, are highly effective.  The main difficulty is in poor design, with too much detail attempted.

*Visitor centers.* These usually serve as the interpretive headquarters for the park. As they are major installations, their expense is relatively high.  Such buildings are commonly equipped with an information desk, exhibit room, auditorium, staff offices and working space, restrooms, and drinking fountains.

## IMPORTANCE OF UPDATING EXHIBITS

Just as the park is not a static environment, exhibits and other interpretive interactions are not static.  Visitors can be enlisted in actively supporting the park when they find the interpretive efforts engaging. An example of methods that discover visitor expectations and the interest they may develop is that of a focus group method used to evaluate a cultural exhibit of the Nez Pierce Indians at the Nez Pierce Historical Park in Spaulding, Idaho in 2009. A series of eight focus groups examined the present exhibit and made recommendations as to what information would be most helpful. It was discovered in these sessions that people wanted more interaction and information about daily life, who the Nez Pierce were and why, and how they used the items on display. They wanted to touch and use such items themselves to place themselves in the "moccasins" of the Nez Pierce to better understand their way of life (http://psu.uidaho.edu/vsp.reports.htm)

## THE ROLE OF INTERPRETATION AS A MANAGEMENT TOOL

Traditionally, interpreters have envisioned their role as helping people enjoy the park. Certainly in the past, most naturalists or interpreters have been oriented toward natural and human history. Earlier interpreters were, for the most part, college graduates holding degrees in some aspect of natural history, and they often lacked an understanding of the fundamentals of park management. Managers look at parks from a different perspective than do interpretive specialists. The manager has a resource to guard, visitors to protect, and contending pressure groups to placate. The manager is responsible for all park activities, including administration, planning, development, protection, budget preparation, interpretation, public relations, maintenance, and operations. Interpretation can contribute to the proper functioning of the organization, and interpreters must ask themselves, "How do we fit into this organization? How do we become team members? How can we assist the manager in achieving management objectives?" If interpreters don't understand this role, it may become necessary for the manager to tactfully remind them of the park goals.

Interpreters are part of the park organization and must accept and define their role within the administrative affairs of the park. This is partly a survival action, for interpretive programs are often the first to have budgets reduced when funding is tight. To maintain their program, interpreters must prove their services are not only useful, but necessary. They cannot remain aloof from the business of park management.

Former Chief of Interpretation for the NPS William Dunmire addressed this topic:

> Interpretation should be employed by park management as a primary means of achieving all management objectives affecting the public. Interpreters should think of themselves as an integral part of the management team and should actively participate in developing and reviewing park-wide objectives and programs.

Let us briefly review the objectives of interpretation as cited earlier: (a) to assist the visitor in appreciating the area, (b) to accomplish management goals, and (c) to provide visitor understanding of the agency. The second objective is the one that we will concentrate on. How can interpretation assist the park manager in solving problems related to visitor use of an area?

Park visits increase yearly, and this higher visitation brings more vandalism, theft, fire, and safety problems. Park managers should encourage their interpretive staff to assist in reducing these problems. Here are some scenarios in which interpretation can be used.

- Suppose your park contains fragile flower meadows. The visitors are ruining these meadows with a network of impromptu "social trails."
- There is an unacceptably high injury rate among visitors and staff in your park.
- Your park has a problem of visitors collecting sea shells, arrowheads, rare plants or animals, fossils, or unusual rocks.
- You wish to close off an area or phase out a popular but damaging activity. You know there will be a public outcry, yet protection of the site is your responsibility.
- You have a poaching problem or perhaps a conflict involving visitors and park animals.

All these problems are susceptible to interpretive solutions as part of a management strategy. Let us now look at how some managers have used interpretation to assist in park management.

## APPLICATION OF INTERPRETATION TO PARK MANAGEMENT

This section examines the potential of interpretation in four distinct areas of park management: (a) natural resource management, (b) historical and cultural site management, (c) visitor protection and law enforcement, and (d) maintenance.

### Natural Resource Management

**Meadow rehabilitation.** Increased visitor use severely damaged the high mountain meadows of Mount Rainier National Park. Hikers criss-crossed the meadows with social trails, some of which ran straight up and down the slopes. The soil layer is thin, and plant regeneration is a long and laborious process. The problem: How could the meadows be saved while still providing visitor access?

Initially, "TRAIL CLOSED" signs were placed at either end of the social trails. Jute matting was laid over the trails to hold down the soil and encouraged regeneration. People continued to walk on the trails. When visitors were asked why they were not obeying the signs, they replied that they did not understand why the signs were there. Other visitors thought the jute matting was provided for better traction and was actually part of the trail system. These visitors were confused by the signs and continued to use the closed trails. Their use set an example for others, and the problem remained unresolved (Sharpe, G. & Gensler, G., 1978).

After some consideration, the signs were changed to read "CLOSED FOR MEADOW REHABILITATION." Brochures were printed to explain the delicate nature of the meadows. A self-guiding trail was constructed to simultaneously draw impact away from the meadows and educate the visitors. According to one ranger, who was with the project for six years, the new interpretive approach reduced use of the closed trails by 95 percent. The park scored several pluses by using an interpretive approach. First, the resource management problem was solved; impact on the meadows was sharply reduced. Second, the use of signs and brochures to convey the management message reduced ranger time on meadow patrol, thus freeing personnel for other duties. Finally, the friendly and explanatory tone of the outdoor exhibits and brochures gave visitors a feeling of cooperating in a joint enterprise, rather than being peremptorily ordered around on public land.

The ranger in the above Mount Rainier project believes that management should always use the "least impacting" technique. Accordingly, education and interpretation should be the first techniques used because they are the least restrictive. Interpretation means using reason rather than regulation. It tries to show relationships rather than give such orders as DO NOT or KEEP OFF, even when this is really the message (Dalle-Molle, J.,1976).

**Proper backcountry use.** A study of backcountry management at Rocky Mountain National Park demonstrated the effectiveness of using selected educational interpretive methods, combined with a permit system, to alleviate problems of improper backcountry use (Fazio, J. R., 1974). According to one reviewer, the results show that backpackers who had seen one of several interpretive exhibits or programs explaining the reasons for regulations had a significantly higher inclination to observe the rules than did those who had not been exposed to an interpretive contact before their trip. A further finding was that this group had a more positive attitude toward the park's various backcountry restrictions and had acquired a greater sensitivity to wilderness values (Dunmire, W. W., 1976).

**Littering.** State parks in northern California were having a problem with littering. It seems seasonal personnel were spending 60 percent of their time picking up after visitors. Signs and ranger contacts were not getting the message across. The solution was to start a concentrated litter-getter program in each park. An individualized award patch was created for each park, and visitors of all ages were challenged to take a stand against litter. The program has been very successful. The visitors, both young and old, have fun earning the awards, and the park managers can employ the seasonal staff in more constructive ways.

**Off-road vehicles.** Another California state park was having a problem keeping four-wheel-drive vehicles on the park roadways. Ranger conflict, enforcement, and signs did little good. The area manager, working with the interpretive specialist, tried to find some way to get the four-wheel groups to take a more positive interest in the park. The staff worked up a series of conservation projects, such as cleaning the beach, closing off short-cut roads, brushing out park roads and interpretive trails, and assisting with new signage. The program was presented to the local four-wheelers at a regular club meeting, and the membership took on all the projects. Off-road vehicle vandalism went down almost immediately, and it was found that club members who participated in a number of work projects, a certificate was prepared in addition to conservation award patch that would be worn on the club jacket.

**Fire management.** For many years, the policy of most government agencies regarding wildfire was simply to "put it out." To help gain public assistance with their program, elaborate fire prevention campaigns, including the successful Smokey Bear project, were launched.

The National Park Service and other public agencies have adopted prescribed fire to accomplish certain management objectives, such as maintaining natural conditions in wilderness areas, helping to prevent large uncontrolled fires, improving soil conditions for the entrance of desired species, and managing insect and disease problems. Not surprisingly, the National Park Service encountered considerable public resistance to its fire management policy of setting certain fires and letting some lightning fires burn. Citizens, taught for years to help prevent fires, did not understand why some fires were allowed to burn.

The park service turned to interpretation to help solve its problem. Controlled burning of 10- to 40-acre blocks of Sequoia and Kings Canyon National Parks was prescribed to rejuvenate the stagnant sequoia stands. To avoid public outcry and to sell their program, the park service developed an interpretive approach. Evening campfire talks, regular media releases, and publications described the "why" of this prescribed burning before it occurred. Interpreters were later stationed at the site of the fire to explain prescribed burning while it was occurring. As a result of this approach, the program met with a minimum of public resistance (Schlamp, P.G., 1976).

The Yellowstone fires of 1988 have focused attention on fuel buildup and its role in causing uncontrolled fires in parkland wilderness areas. The concept of "let-burn areas" is still not well understood by the general public. Interpretation has an important role in helping visitors understand what happened in the Yellowstone fires and in assessing the complexity of their aftermath.

**Fossil protection.** Visitors to Dinosaur Provincial Park in Alberta and Driftwood Canyon Provincial Park in British Columbia are encouraged to report significant sighting of fossilized materials in return for a certificate acknowledging their help. Use of the certificate has been largely responsible for altering the take-it-home tendency of earlier park visitors. The reporting also enables the park staff to systematically record and map these fossil finds (McIntyre, D., 1980).

**Wildlife protection.** In Yellowstone National Park, heavy fishing pressure at Fishing Bridge on the Yellowstone River disrupted the ecological processes of the river system. As a result, many animals dependent on the fish for their existence left the area. To make matters worse, fish catches were often discarded.

The first solution reduced the take limit. Still the problems continued. Management decided it was necessary to stop all fishing at the bridge. The bridge was closed and signed, "No Fishing From Bridge." Interpretation was chosen as the method of enforcement, and two automatic videotape machines were placed on the bridge. The taped program described the life history of the fish and their important role in the area's food chain. The hope was that visitors would comply with the closure rule if they understood the reasoning behind it. The program was successful; fishing at the bridge dropped, and no complaints were made.

At Garrison Bay on San Juan Island, Washington, visitors to the National Historical Park disrupted the ecological processes of the beach by overdigging clams. An interpretive brochure was prepared for dispersal at information stations. The brochure described the life history of the clams, identified common species, and gave tips on safety and good clamming procedures. It was low key, positive, and easy to read. In addition to the brochure, a researcher working on a scientific study of the area's clam catch made informational contacts with the visitors on the beach. The researcher was not a park service interpreter, but she did perform an interpretive contact function.

The program was successful. Once clammers became engaged in conversation with a researcher, they were cooperative. Those visitors receiving the brochure also gleaned interesting and useful information during their stay at the park (Gallucci, V.F., 1976).

Salmon poaching was becoming a problem during the early and late hours of the day in Terra Nova National Park in Newfoundland. The interpretive staff scheduled a guided walk during these same hours to watch beavers. Introducing people into the area kept poachers away.

Similarly, deer poaching was becoming a problem in Fundy National Park in New Brunswick. The problem was reduced by scheduling deer watching at the lakes frequently used by poachers. These events were held at dawn and dusk and averaged 40 people per trip.

## Cultural Site Management

Many recreation systems contain areas where the resource managed is of cultural significance. In these archaeological and historical areas, such outdoor recreation pursuits as overnight camping are usually not permitted. Those permitted may be concentrated in a small area. The problem of how best to tell the story of the site without endangering the site or structure itself must be addressed in the management objectives.

The National Park Service has long used interpretive methods to bring alive the story of its cultural history. Traditional interpretive techniques include exhibits, movies, living interpretation, and guided tours. Guided tours provide access to sensitive sites normally closed to the public (Sharpe, G.W., 1982). Living interpretation portrays the persons and events associated with the site or structure in an unforgettable way.

Living interpretation can also stimulate public interest and support for historical site preservation. This example comes from Fort Washington, a once-dilapidated National Park Service structure located on the Potomac River. A cannon-firing demonstration utilizing local volunteers was organized, and this eventually generated enough public interest, funds, and services to restore and preserve the fort (Gibbs, R. 1977).

Interpretive demonstrations can encourage protection of existing sites. At Stones River National Battlefield and Cemetery in Tennessee, the park gained local support for its presence by employing young townspeople in living interpretation demonstrations. When urban and industrial encroachment later threatened the park, the townspeople rallied to the cause and lent their support by stating, both verbally and in writing, that they were in favor of saving the park (Gibbs, R., 1977).

Interpretive techniques can be applied to specific problems of site preservation. In 1975, a large (250- to 300-unit) private recreation vehicle campground opened just outside of AnzaBorrego Desert State Park in California. In the nearby area, there were over a dozen Native American rock-art sites, many of which were within walking distance of the campground. Park personnel, fearing vandalism and souvenir taking but lacking funds for adequate physical protection of the sites, devised an exclusively interpretive method of protection.

A sign was posted inside the private campground clubhouse, where visitors would be likely to see it. Mounted on a papier-mâché mock-up of a Native American pictograph, the sign explained the sites and described the ongoing archaeological efforts to record their story. The sign enlisted visitor assistance with these efforts and directed hikers to obtain a special field brochure for use in recording their discoveries. The hope was to offer visitors an alternative to vandalism or souvenir collecting.

Unfortunately, the program had only a short test period. Nine months after its inception, the campground was destroyed by a tropical storm. Nonetheless, the program appeared successful. During this period, two-thirds of which included the primary visitor-use season, there was no vandalism at the sites (Patton, R., 1977).

Another example of cultural resource protection comes from Writing-on-Stone Provincial Park in southern Alberta. Vandalism of the native writings, for which the park was established and named, has virtually ceased since conducted walks were utilized as the sole means of visitor access (McIntyre, D., 1980).

## Visitor Protection and Law Enforcement

Visitor protection encompasses not only protection for the visitor from injury, but also protection of the park from the depreciative behavior of the visitors. Protection against bears, proper signage regarding other dangerous animals, signage for roadways and trails, and displays of safety tips are examples of the first type of protection. Apprehension of persons involved in theft, vandalism, and other unsuitable behavior, as well as prevention of this sort of conduct, are examples of the second type.

Park managers in Los Angeles's Griffith Park are trained in interpretive nature study, handling of emergencies, and public relations. These rangers combine the activities of interpreter, first aider, temporary fire fighter, and law enforcement assistant, persuading disruptive individuals or groups to cooperate in protecting the rights of all users of the park and offering guidance and help whenever sought or needed. Mounted rangers alert for safety hazards patrol the bridle trails and, by their presence, encourage proper equestrian behavior. Two-way radios allow the rangers to call for help from the city police department as they themselves carry neither guns nor batons. Widespread public acceptance of the ranger program has led to its expansion in other major Los Angeles parks.

**Bear/people management.** The deaths of several visitors caused by grizzly bear attacks have intensified concern for visitor safety at Glacier National Park in Montana. Park management has shifted personnel and dollars to the grizzly management problem at the expense of other services. The use of interpretation in solving this problem has won the support of the park superintendent. In a request for emergency funding for the bear management program, superintendent Phillip R. Iverson stated the following:

> Interpreters issued approximately 85 percent of all back-country permits through Glacier's three main visitor centers. These personal contacts were critical due to the need to better inform visitors, especially hikers and campers, about bears and safety.

Iverson requested and got increased funding to expand hours of operation of the visitor centers, to provide increased staffing of the centers, and to extend the training time of interpreters in order to add safety, bear management, and other management concerns to their program (Iverson P. R., 1976).

**Campground law enforcement.** The following example illustrates the use of interpretive techniques in solving a campground problem. Several years ago, overenthusiastic visitor use of motorbikes let to disturbances at a popular campground in Eldorado National Forest in California. Lacking enforcement surveillance, the district decided to use an interpretive approach. A short interpretive brochure with a motorbike on the cover was printed, and in plain, unofficial language it firmly stated use regulations. These were distributed to all patrol personnel, visitor centers, and administrative sites. Brochures were given to all cyclists and placed on all parked motorbikes. At the same time, campground programs began to include a message on campground behavior and proper use of motorbikes.

According to the district ranger, the change in use of the campground was startling. Once cyclists understood the rules, they complied with them. The success of Eldorado confirms the findings of a study by Ross and Moeller (1974), which suggests that campers are generally not well informed about rules. Use of brochures will increase knowledge of rules, possibly bringing a change in visitor behavior.

## Maintenance and Interpretation

Maintenance chores are an integral part of park life. Maintenance concerns include preserving roads and trails, maintaining safe and pleasant conditions within buildings, and cleaning restrooms, campgrounds, and other public-use areas. A properly maintained park offers a more enjoyable experience, contributes to good public relations, and reduces the operational costs. Prevention of vandalism avoids costly repairs as well as presenting a more serene and restful milieu. Skellinger expressed this belief as follows:

> I believe there are three areas we must explore in combating vandalism—education, maintenance, and enforcement. I cannot give priority to any one of these areas as they all must be used and are, to some extent, dependent on each other for a successful program.

Skellinger listed two pressing needs. The first was for competent public relations.

Unless we let the public know that the object was broken by vandals, visitors think that it is just poor maintenance and wonder why they are paying taxes for this type of service.

The second was for education.

…Over the period of the last ten years, I have noticed a continuing drop in the really malicious damage done in our nature centers. Another thing that I notice is that the older teenagers come to us and report acts of destruction that they observe. When this happens, they usually remark that because of the things they learn from the naturalist when they were in lower grades they want to help keep the area in good condition and don't like kids that destroy the area for others.

Public relations, education, and personalizing the park experience are jobs ideally suited to interpretation, and the foregoing has illustrated ways in which interpretation may assist the manager with ongoing problems.

The states in Australia administer many parks, and because of limited budgets, some effectively use interpretation as a management tool. In Tasmania, the park staff has developed a program they call Minimal Impact Boating. Another is Minimal Impact Bushwalking, which has as its main feature audiovisuals illustrating how to "Walk Safely and Walk Softly." In the state of Victoria, where vandalism by local youths has been a problem, the park department is attempting to develop positive attitudes and thoughtful behavior through its two environmental education programs known as Sunship Earth and Earthkeepers. Beckmann (1991) reports the programs were considered the most positive way to deal with the problem.

## CONCLUSION

The foregoing material has briefly outlined some interpretive responses to management problems. Although funds for interpretation may be difficult to obtain, the principles and techniques found in this chapter can often be put into practice with the help of interested staff, whether or not they have had interpretive training. Help is usually available from agency sources and from nearby universities or high schools. Volunteers can also recruit and organize interpretive help for your management problems.

## REFERENCES

**References Cited**

Beckmann, Elizabeth A. (1991). Environmental Interpretation for Education and Management in Australian National Parks and Other Protected Areas. Doctoral dissertation, Armidale, New South Wales, Australia: The University of New England.

Bradley, Gordon A. (1982). "The Interpretive Plan," in Grant W. Sharpe (Ed.), *Interpreting the Environment* (2nd ed.). New York: Wiley.

Dalle-Molle, John. (1976). Personal Communication. Longmire, WA: Mount Rainier National Park.

Dame, Vernon D. (1985). "Introduction: The Role and Responsibility of Interpretation as a Function in a Total Park Operation." *Trends, 22*(4): 2-7.

Dunmire, William W. (1976). "Servicewide Goals for Interpretation," *In Touch, 1*(12): 2-3.

Fazio, James R. (1974). "A Mandatory Permit System and Interpretation for Backcountry User Control in Rocky Mountain National Park: An Evaluative Study," unpublished Ph.D. thesis. Fort Collins, CO: Colorado State University.

Galluci, Vincent F. (1976). *Clams of Garrison Bay*, Pamphlet prepared for the National Park Service, Washington, D.C., and personal communication.

Gibbs, Ron. (1977). "Living History and Historic Preservation: Incompatible?" *In Touch, 1*(18):11. Washington D.C.: National Park Service.

http://www.nps.gov/dsc/d_publications/d_1_gpsd.htm, Retrieved June 10, 2010

http://psu.uidaho.edu/vsp.reports.htm, Retrieved June 10, 2010

Iverson, Phillip R. (1976). Memo from Superintendent of Glacier National Park, Montana to Regional Director of the Rocky Mountain Regional Office.

Johnson, Paul R. (1975). "Protective Interpretation," *The Interpreter, 7*(3): 17-19. Western Interpreters Association.

McIntyre, David. (1980). *Regional Annual Report.* Vulcan, Alberta: Alberta Provincial Parks.

Patton, Ray. (1977). Personal Communication. Borrego Springs, CA: Anza-Borrego Desert State Park.

Ross, Terence L., & Moeller, George H. (1974). *Communicating Rules in Recreation Areas.* USDA Forest Service Research Paper NE-297.

Schlamp. Phil G. (1976). Interpretation as a Management Tool. Presentation to Eastern Region. VIS Workshop. Milwaukee, WI: USDA Forest Service.

Sharpe, Grant W. (1982). "An Overview of Interpretation," in Grant W. Sharpe (Ed.), *Interpreting the Environment* (2nd ed.). New York: Wiley.

Sharpe, Grant W. (1982). "Selecting the Interpretive Media," in Sharpe, Grant W. (Ed.), *Interpreting the Environment* (2nd ed.). New York: Wiley.

Sharpe, Grant W., & Gensler, Gail. (1978). "Interpretation as a Management Tool," Proceedings, Association of Interpreters of Canadian Heritage, Banff, Alberta. Also *Journal of Interpretation*, November 1978, Association of Interpretive Naturalists.

Skellenger, Robert. Vandalism: What We Can Do About It. Presentation, Ann Arbor, MI: University of Michigan.

**General References**

Cornell, Joseph. (1990). *Sharing the joys of nature.* Nevada City, CA: Dawn Publications.

Freed, Mike, & Stenman, Broc. (1980). Interpretation for Resource Management, *The Interpreter, 11*(4): 27-30.

Gibson, Bob, & Moriah, Dave. (1989). Meeting the Interpretive Needs of Minorities. Proceedings. 1989 National Interpreters Workshop. St. Paul, MN.

Hooper, Jon K., & Weiss, Karen S. (1991). "Interpretation as a Management Tool: A National Study of Interpretive Professionals' Views." *Legacy, 2*(1): 10-16.

Lewis, William J. (1980). *Interpreting for park visitors.* Eastern National Park and Monument Association. Philadelphia: PA: Eastern Acorn Press.

Machlis, Gary E., & Field, Donald R. (Eds.). (1992). *On interpretation: Sociology for interpreters of natural and cultural history.* (Rev. ed.). Corvallis: Oregon State University Press.

Mills, Enos. (1990). *Adventures of a nature guide and essays in interpretation.* Friendship, WI: New Past Press.

Sharpe, Grant W. (Ed.). *Interpreting the environment* (2nd ed.). New York: Wiley.

Tildon, Freeman. (1982). *Interpreting our heritage.* Chapel Hill: The University of North Carolina Press.

VanderStoep, Gail A. (1989). "Interpretation: Benchmarking Current Status and Trends, Identifying Issues and Future Needs." Proceedings. Outdoor Recreation Benchmark 1988. National Outdoor Recreation Forum USDA Forest Service. Southeast Forest Experiment Station. General Technical Report 52. Asheville, MC.

Verveka, John A., & Poneleit, Sandra A. (1981). "Interpretation as a Management Tool for Underwater Parks." *Journal of Interpretation, 6*(2): 10-14.

Womble, Peter, Gordon Bultena, & Donald Field. 1981. "Interpretation and Backcountry Management." *Journal of Interpretation, 6*(2): 21-23.

*Chapter Seventeen*

# Visitor Services

## Visitor Characteristics

There is, of course, no average visitor. Park visitors come from all cultural backgrounds, life-styles, age classes, interests, occupations, incomes, educational levels, beliefs, mental and physical capabilities and geographical areas. There is at least one commonality, however: People seldom go to parks alone; they go in social groups, usually families or friendship groups.

Parks are places where informality prevails, and it is considered appropriate for strangers to interact with one another. This is an interesting feature of parks—the fact that although people seldom communicate with their neighbors at home, they smile and speak to strangers when in park settings, where interaction is enjoyed, and even sought.

The length of time that visitors stay in a park may be influenced by a park's size, distance from home, attractions in and near the park, kinds of facilities and accommodations, interpretive and interactive opportunities, location in reference to major travel routes, length-of-stay policy, and cost of overnight fees.

## Visitor Expectations

Visitors are usually looking for a particular experience when they arrive at a park. These anticipations are influenced by their background, previous experience with parks, and motivations for visiting a park. The name of the park arouses certain expectations. For example, the words "fort," "village," or "homestead" indicate the possibility of it being a culturally oriented park. A park with the words "recreation area" may be seen as simply a place to have fun. One named after a person doesn't give any clues, but one with the name of a lake, mountain, wilderness, or other natural feature or incorporating an agency designation, gives a hint of what to expect.

Not every activity can or should be provided in each park. Certain parks can better offer specific activities than other parks. It must be made clear to potential visitors which parks offer which activities and where in the park they are available. There are various ways to accomplish this, including off-site presentations, radio, TV, newspapers, agency maps or brochures, and centralized phone information systems providing pre-arrival information. Many of these methods are being superseded by instant information available through the internet. Cell phones and associated technology can provide maps and other information including reservations and amenities and even driving directions to attractions.

### Pre-arrival Information

This is not a static body of information; some changes occur seasonally and some from day to day; for example, a popular park camping area may be filled to capacity by noon on the Thursday preceding a long holiday weekend, whereas in early autumn, camping sites in the same park will be available all weekend. Agencies generally endorse dissemination of pre-arrival information because the users who plan ahead are more likely to have an enjoyable experience.

Response to this need, while possible on an individual park basis, really requires a central and widely available information center to fully serve the public. Such a center needs to include a means of receiving and dispensing information, information that may change rapidly. It also needs a means of storing statistical data concerning a large variety of recreational activities and facilities that might only occasionally be sought by patrons, but that, when sought, are needed quickly.

One tool of a central information center is the toll-free telephone line. This system, which must not be confused with the reservation system discussed earlier nor the on-site information that follows, provides toll-free access to information specialists or trained volunteers. If personnel costs exceed budget resources, the same lines can be answered by a recording device, which allows the calling party to leave a message in the case of specific information requests, and provides for a menu of frequently asked questions which have standard responses. A staff person can respond to those questions not covered in the menu on a regular basis. It is important that this telephone number be widely publicized both in printed material and on the internet so the public is aware of the service.

In the United States, any state-owned recreational land is a park in the minds of most patrons. Many generalize even further and believe that any recreational area in a given state is a state park even if it is part of the National Park Service or the U.S. Forest Service or is a county or city park. Some patrons additionally lump all private resorts and recreational areas into their definition of a state park. Whatever the reason for this lack of discrimination on the part of users, there is a need for coordinated information dispersal from all agencies involved. An effort to establish a moderately comprehensive data system is sometimes undertaken at the state or provincial levels. In local jurisdictions, such as the regional, county, municipal, or city level, the job is less imposing. Basic contact lists for current information about related facilities can be maintained. Updates can be made on a periodic basis through the use of mailed questionnaires and electronic communication. Public agencies can be requested to volunteer information on changes for which they are responsible, and most of them will cooperate.

## REGULATING NUMBERS

Regulating the number and placement of visitors is becoming more common. Regrettable though the necessity of interference might be, it protects a finite resource. The number of people using parks needs to be controlled as well as limited in certain time periods and situations.

### How Many?

In the chapters on facilities and environmental impact, the subject of use limits has been discussed. Most agencies establish a capacity limit and require managers to enforce it by refusing admittance to the park once that capacity has been reached. In situations where this has not been done, issues of fairness and the maintenance of good order necessitate the agency's formal adoption of a capacity policy; the authority to administer this policy should be vested in the head of the agency. It is also important for the agency head to provide the park manager with the needed authority and flexibility to determine when the park should be open and when it must be closed because of overcrowding.

A park currently maintaining its optimum capacity might be in trouble if visitation should dramatically increase for some reason. An improved road system leading to the park, a local population increase due to a contract awarded to a manufacturer, close proximity to a population center during economic downturns resulting in visitation closer to home or even a natural catastrophe, such as a huge rock slide, a snow slide, or the eruption of a volcano may cause visitation to increase suddenly.

Once it has been established that use limits are necessary, it is important that notice be posted at each park so that visitors are aware of the rules and reasons for limitations. It is also important for the park manager to have the posting as evidence of a rule violation if it is needed in a dispute or arrest.

## Permits

There will be many circumstances in which the agency will want to control the place of use, the amount of use, and the time of use. These controls will seek to protect people, areas, and facilities. The issuance of special permits is the usual method of control. The following are some common examples: climbing permits to regulate the number of climbers on a mountain face and the hours when the climb may be undertaken; trail permits to regulate the number of people on trails, usually to control erosion; backcountry permits to disperse use, to ensure safety, and to register people so they can be traced should they not reach their destination on time; fire permits for campfires out of designated fire pits; facility permits to ensure the availability of ball fields, or kitchen shelters for family outings and to control group use; and research permits for the collecting of specimens or the recording and monitoring of authorized archaeological digs. Permits can be awarded on several criteria. Some are awarded by lottery in the case of extremely popular activities such as floating the Grand Canyon of the Colorado river, while others in less well known areas can be awarded on a first come, first served basis, with online reservation of the permit. The Bureau of Land Management provides permits for several such locations. Westwater Canyon of the Colorado river, a popular boating destination, has such a permit system for private party boaters at http://www.blm.gov/ut/st/en/fo/moab/recreation/river_recreation/how_to_obtain_a_private.html

## Reservation Systems

The major factor in the establishment of reservation systems has been that of rapidly increasing park use particularly within the strictures of increasing energy costs. This use is often focused on a relatively small number of parks within a given state or province during peak usage periods, such as summer months (June through September), weekends (Friday through Sunday), and holidays. At these parks, prospective campers are turned away in large numbers, often after a long delay caused by traffic buildup on park entrance roads. The resulting complaints have encouraged park officials to institute reservation systems. Some popular state and national parks in the United States have had to go to a computerized or write-in reservation system because campgrounds in these parks are often filled to capacity throughout the summer. Oregon State Parks has contracted with a private company which provides reservations and availability information up to nine months in advance for popular sites http://www.oregon.gov/OPRD/PARKS/reserve.shtml. The commercial organization, ReserveAmerica, has contracted with a number of states to manage such reservations.

A related problem is the overuse of certain parks that are well known coupled with the under-utilization of others. An important asset of a reservation system is the inventory of currently available sites that allows campers to switch from one park to another thus aiding the distribution of use among all areas.

There are four basic reasons for reservation systems: (a) to alleviate park overuse by redistribution of campers, (b) to reduce campers' anxiety and frustration by assuring them a place to sleep that night, (c) to reduce fuel consumption and costs by allowing campers to proceed directly to an assured campsite, and (d) to assist management and planners in serving the users.

As the irritations and consequences of reservation systems fall rather directly on managers, it is worthwhile for them to understand the ramifications of trying to set up such a system. If and when a decision is made to develop and implement a reservation system within an agency, the following questions must be considered.

- Should the reservation system be centralized or decentralized at individual parks? (Centralized control is essential if the system is to have the ability to redistribute campers to other parks.)
- Should the reservation system be a manual or a computerized system? For a state-generated system, the initial cost and annual personnel cost for operations and equipment must be carefully calculated, although one can assume the computer costs and telephone charges that will far exceed projections.

- What percentage of the sites in each park or in the total system should be reserved? To allow for possible error and to consider special circumstances, a small number of sites—two to six—should be withheld from inventory to act as a cushion.
- Should the sites be assigned by drawing lots or on a first-come, first-serve basis?
- Should the system be self-supporting (fee charged pays for cost of system) or subsidized?
- Should campsites be assigned by specific site number before campers arrive in a park or after they arrive?
- Should there be year-round or just busy-season reservation coverage?
- Should there be a toll-free or a toll telephone system?
- Should payment be required in advance or on the campers' arrival at the park? If there is a mail-in reservation deposit, should all, or part, or any of it apply toward the camping fee?
- If a camper cancels, does the camper get a refund, a rain check, or nothing?
- Would commercial reservation organizations provide a more cost-effective method of administering such a system?

For the season or two after converting to a reservation system, park personnel must be prepared for confusion and resentment among visitors who, despite notice by media and signs, arrive without reservations.

## Camper Registration

The primary purpose of camper registration is to have an acceptable means of accounting for the fees charged for an overnight stay. This is done through camper registration forms that provide a triplicate accounting of the transaction, one copy going to the agency fiscal officer in charge of fees, one copy remaining with the park, and the third going to the user. There are other benefits or opportunities inherent in registration, but all are secondary to the fiscal aspect. The additional benefits include a means for campers to prove a given site is theirs by right of payment, a way to locate a visitor if the need arises, and provision of statistical data for agency or other use. Increasingly these forms are generated on site by electronic means.

**Self-registration.** An alternative method, self-registration, has been used by some agencies for many years. Policy on this matter changes as availability of personnel and other factors influence decisions. The overnight self-registration system is used in the province of British Columbia for both auto campgrounds and marine parks.

Newcastle Island, a marine park near Nanaimo, British Columbia, can be reached only by private boat and foot-passenger ferry. There is a resident manager, but the island is large, and the workload requires that visitors register themselves. On arrival by private boat or ferry, the visitor is notified of the self-registration system by a sign on the dock. On walking ashore, the visitor is greeted by a second and more conspicuous entrance sign. Just beyond this, adjacent to the footpath, is the self-registration fee station, designed in this instance for both boaters and walk-in campers. The station includes two signs, a small registration box containing fee envelopes, and a locked deposit vault. The two panels are brown-painted marine plywood. White silk-screen lettering is used for all signage information except the fee amount, for which press-on plastic material is used so it can be changed if the fee changes. The envelope containing the fee and registration information is slipped through a slot into the double-locked deposit vault.

With minor adjustment to the wording, either of these signs could be used for vehicle registration in other types of parks. Neither vandalism nor theft has been a problem here yet, perhaps in part because the self-registration station is within easy view of the manager's residence.

It is still necessary to visit each campsite and moorage slip to see whether a registration stub is displayed. If the ranger or park aide carried the forms, people would not bother to register but would wait for the park employee to arrive. This must be avoided, so delinquent users should be asked to go to the box to register. Of course, it is possible to cheat under this system. Some areas state a fine will be levied or campers will be evicted if self-registration is not properly carried out.

Workload on those staffing the parks is such that electronic tracking of campsite assignments and placement will become far more prevalent in popular or remote locations. The ubiquitous barcode can track not only if the fees have been paid but who to contact if there is damage or vandalism to the site.

## ACCOMMODATION OF GROUPS

The basic camping unit used to be the family; however, camping today is frequently a group activity.  There are several ways to provide for people who wish to camp as a group.

### Group Camping Areas

These are in the park apart from the regularly designated overnight family-camping area.  Such areas may or may not have full restroom facilities, but they should at least have pit toilets and water.

A group can be any formal organization, such as scouts, trailer clubs, special interest clubs, church members, or school groups, or it can be an organized collection of families who wish to camp together.  The group must have identifiable leadership, such as a president, chairman, wagon master; or in the case of a youth group, at least one adult who is responsible for the minors.

### Groups in Regularly Designated Areas

Areas used by individual families may also be used for groups, provided regulations about the number of campers per site are enforced. There are campground designs suitable for groups that avoid undue burden on facilities or inconvenience for other campers. Considerations should include adaptability for smaller groups, the ability to mix both larger and smaller groups, common areas, noise isolation, continued access to and use of sanitary facilities, and the option to rest and rehabilitate particular campsites on a regular basis.

### Reservations for Groups

Advance notice of group camping is usually encouraged so that group campers can be separated from regular campers if possible.  Reservations are usually taken by the park manager rather than through a central office.

### Group Fees

Those groups camping in regular camp areas and sites used by individual campers should pay the regular fee charged the individual family unit. Those groups using designated group-camping areas should also pay a fee, but it should be a lesser one computed on a different basis. This is usually computed as a fee per person, and the minimum and maximum limit is based on the services and facilities provided.  The purpose of this system is to encourage groups to reserve and use these areas by offering privacy and group rates while also discouraging use by one or two people rather than an actual group.  Consideration should also be given to a per-car charge as an incentive for fuel conservation and air-quality concerns.

## SPECIAL USAGE

### Environmental Learning Camps

In many states and provinces, there are special camps, either strategically located within a given park or composing a total park themselves, devoted to environmental learning.  These camps contain sleeping and living quarters for enrollees and staff, a nurse's station, food preparation and dining areas, environmental education facilities, and recreational facilities. They are often called ELCs (Environmental Learning Camps or Centers).

The objective of ELCs is to provide an opportunity for groups to participate in educational, social, intellectual, spiritual, and physical development programs in a group living situation in an outdoor environment. These resident camping facilities are made available to school and other interested groups. The agency provides the facilities and the environment. Programs can be proved either by the agency or the users. It is the combination of facilities, environment, and specific learning programs that make a complete ELC.

## Hostels

Hostelling is a very old, time-tested method of providing safe, pleasant accommodations for an overnight stay. Hostelling, which started in Germany, has not been as common in the United States as in Europe or Canada. Agencies engaged in hostelling try to provide a structure where the traveling public (usually youths hiking, biking, or hitchhiking) can stay overnight at minimal cost. The structure will contain basic sleeping and cooking accommodations and have a person or couple to serve as house parents. The formal hostelling program is a network of similar facilities under one organizational umbrella. Membership in the organization provide accommodation opportunities around the world.

Park managers interested in providing this sort of opportunity should determine whether there are suitable unused facilities available. Those facilities might include bunkers, barracks, lighthouses, Civilian Conservation Corps building, construction camps, surplus trailers or purpose constructed facilities. Many parks now provide yurts as part of the accommodation mix. Hostels should be located away from the park campground or heavy-use areas if possible. More information on hostelling is available at several sites online. One such site is http://www.hihostels.com.

## Elderhostel Programs

One of the fastest growing group activities in North America is Elderhostel, Inc., an organized catering to people in their later years who wish to keep learning about a wide variety of subjects. This program, which began in 1975 as a Monday-through-Friday summer activity on college campuses, now has over 1,800 different programs to offer. Programs are now housed in hotels, motels, conference centers, forestry camps, park lodges, and training centers, ships, and recreation vehicles in addition to college dormitories. Some programs feature camping in parks and include study of the area's natural and human history. In 2009, this organization became Road Scholar. Parks and park institutes often sponsor programs for participants. For information, visit the website at http://www.roadscholar.org.

## Group Use of Day-Use Areas

Frequently park managers will be asked to provide a picnic shelter or some other place in the day-use area for groups to gather for reunions, annual picnics, or farewell parties. Meeting these requests may cause scheduling problems and increased costs. There will be a need for additional cleanup, and these groups may annoy or inconvenience families using the facilities. Conspicuous consumption of alcohol, whether tolerated or not, sometimes complicates the situation. For these reasons, the park manager may want to develop a group-use policy and also use a permit process. These steps, plus providing a separate area where possible, should help meet the needs of such users with minimum disruption.

## PROVIDING FOR NEEDS

The visitors have arrived. They are in campsites, on diving boards, schussing the slopes, exploring caves, climbing mountains, and snowmobiling in the woods. They also are hungry and thirsty and having emergencies: losing kids, getting hurt, awaiting an important phone call, getting bitten by animals, or becoming lost or stranded. Let's look at how managers can handle these emergencies and perhaps even prevent some of them.

## Safety

Each park organization has responsibility for the safety of park visitors and park personnel. Every reasonable precaution should be taken to reduce or eliminate existing and potentially hazardous or defective conditions that might be sources of injury to persons and property. Operating procedures should provide for the detection and reduction of these conditions through an adequate program of inspection (see chapter 7, Maintenance and Safety). When accidents or disturbances do occur, the manager must be ready.

## First Aid

First aid, now sometimes called "first responder," is the immediate and temporary care given a victim of an accident or sudden illness until the services of a physician can be obtained. Wilderness medicine is defined as care provided when access to definitive care (hospitals, clinics) is more than an hour away. In park areas, this usually includes transport to a distant facility. The level of care a park is able to provide will vary from state to state. Some have a sophisticated emergency medical services (EMS) system with training available at community colleges for the different levels of competency. Other states do not yet have such a system in place. The National Park Service has its own EMS program. Park managers must acquaint themselves with the state and local situation and have a plan and supplies ready for emergency response. Trained personnel should be available, especially during the high-use season. Private companies such as the Wilderness Medicine Institute of the National Outdoor Leadership School (www.nols.edu/wmi/) provide training for wilderness first-aid situations.

Injuries to park visitors must be reported. It is important that the necessary information on the injury be obtained as soon as possible after the treatment so that the data are accurate. Accurate information is also needed about any treatment so managers will be able to properly represent the agency or themselves in a lawsuit. The park employee must not prescribe treatment or medicine unless trained to do so, and a physician should not be recommended. The victim or relatives should be provided with a list of local doctors and allowed to make the choice. Regular review and training should take place in all rescue and treatment procedures, and equipment and procedures should be state of the art if at all possible.

## Public Telephone Usage

Park visitors often need to make phone calls during their stay to check on family or friends left behind, to see whether there are any messages waiting at home, to conduct business, or to make plans for the rest of the trip. Cellular service is often nonexistent in remote locations, so traditional landline service is the only viable option. Phones should be outside, lighted, sheltered, and available 24 hours a day.

Phone books and coin boxes, as well as the booth and phone itself, are frequently targets of vandals, so booths should be placed in an area where surveillance is possible and should be frequently checked to make sure they are in working order, to remove graffiti, and to repair minor damage. Some people seem susceptible to suggestion, so upkeep may reduce these problems.

## Emergencies

Regardless of how well the park is planned, constructed, and operated, there are certain situations that cannot be circumvented. Emergencies by their very nature are unexpected, but can be anticipated. They demand an immediate coordinated response on the part of park personnel. These emergencies include fires, accidents, lost persons, group disturbances, and evacuation in the event of a fire, flood, severe storm threat, or other catastrophe. Emergency routes should be clearly identified and kept clear of obstacles.

**Procedures.** Whatever the emergency, there are five basic rules to follow:

1. Get complete information.
2. Think it through. Plan first, then act. Don't turn an emergency into a disaster by precipitous action.
3. Act in ways that prevent compounding the emergency.
4. Ask for assistance. Better too much than too little.
5. Alert supervisors.

Inherent in any emergency is the need to act quickly. Preparation and training are critical to successful outcomes. Many organizations, such as law enforcement, EMS services, fire departments, and volunteer search and rescue teams provide both expertise and training for park staff and others. They have extensive experience and can direct almost any rescue or emergency operation.

Emergency plans and training are available through these organizations. An example of emergency response plan available for the Santa Cruz County, Arizona area includes an interagency coordination plan, with each agency providing skills and equipment not generally found in other agencies. This example is found at http://www.co.santa-cruz.az.us/es/oem/ERPlan/ESF%2016. pdf. Since many emergencies require resources outside of those available to most parks, such coordination and cooperation is desirable, and should be fostered in each immediate and extended state park area. The wise manager will promote such training and cooperation well before it is needed.

## Controlling Unruly Groups

Control and containment of unruly groups is one of the most difficult jobs a park manager has. Protection of life, property, and individual rights must be balanced with maintaining organizational credibility and goodwill.

Disturbances come from a variety of sources and manifest themselves in many ways. In some instances, the people involved are simply young people out for a good time. However, it could be people who are drunk or on drugs and people who have knives and guns. Some of these people care what others will think, while others have no regard for their reputations. Some will respond to the warden's or ranger's warning promptly, almost with appreciation for being stopped before they make fools of themselves. Others will challenge authority instantly, perhaps viciously. The appearance on the scene of vehicles marked with identifying authority and uniformed personnel with badges in evidence will sometimes be sufficient to control such situations, and these should be used before more severe measures are contemplated.

Generally speaking, the role of the park ranger will be one of planning and education. When expectations of appropriate conduct in parks is clearly outlined to visitors, the park staff then maintains order by observing, collecting data, reporting, coordinating, and helping local law enforcement officials rather than actually quelling the disturbance with physical force.

## Groups with Special Needs

All people, no matter their specific disability, deserve to enjoy parks and the benefits that can be secured there. The range of abilities, disabilities, needs, and desires of individuals is wide. Managers should cultivate an awareness of these differences. Beechel's *Handbook* (1975), is useful in this respect. The facility and service needs of the disabled and elderly must be considered in the planning process. This is a legal responsibility in most instances where federal, state, or provincial funds are used for public buildings. The Americans with Disabilities Act mandates accommodation for those who have differing physical abilities.

Another good reason for accepting the responsibility lies in the fact that senior citizens constitute an ever-increasing percentage of the population. In 1990 in the United States, people over 65 made up 12.7 percent of the population. By 2030, they will represent 17 percent. The number of people with disabilities venturing out to public recreation areas is increasing. Planning construction and access of facilities and programs with these people in mind is far less expensive than changing the facilities after the fact. Retrofitting existing facilities to appropriate standards for barrier-free access is an ongoing problem. Consideration should be made for blind, deaf, and the physically challenged when providing signage, interpretation, and access to such simple things as restrooms or pavilions.

The growth of the retired population presents both problems and opportunity. Many of these individuals spend much time in the parks, and many become campground hosts and otherwise contribute to operations and maintenance as volunteers. Programs developed for their interests, varied as any program for a younger population, can be very successful. Several federal and state programs provide access at reduced rates to senior citizens. The Golden Age Passport in the United States has been superseded by the Senior Pass, which gives lifetime access to parks to anyone over the age of 62 for a one-time fee of $10. Other passes are available on a yearly basis, or as a result of volunteer hours, or as a result of disabilities (http://www.nps.gov/fees_passes.htm).

## Basic Amenities

Food, water toilets, and fuel are basic amenities to a park experience. Many people who are prepared will bring sufficient supplies of these necessities. If there are food concessions close by, the park itself will not have to provide them. Concessionaires often supply the most cost-effective approach to such amenities and can provide a profit center for the park though a lease or a percentage of sales.

Clean, potable water is a most precious but frequently taken-for-granted commodity. Any failure of responsibility in this matter might lead to serious consequences. Drinking from remote mountain streams was once considered safe, but as park use has increased, most water sources should be considered contaminated. Hikers and backpackers must be warned to boil or filter their water. The disease *Giardia lamblia* results from a protozoan parasite that causes stomach pains and diarrhea.

Where there is a scarcity of water, not only must the public be warned of that scarcity in advance, but they should also be informed as to why there is a lack of water. The need for water conservation should be emphasized, and water use should be regulated.

## Toilet Facilities

One of the most crucial services in any park is the provision of toilet facilities. Managers should give careful attention to maintenance of the floor, mirrors, waste paper receptacles, toilets, and urinals and should be sure adequate supplies are available. Out-of-order or vandalized facilities must be repaired as soon as possible, both for the visitors' convenience and to prevent further damage. Visitors notice this one aspect of parks more than any other. Chapter 11 covers this topic in more detail.

## Firewood

A supply of wood should reduce the impact on the forest floor near campgrounds, and certainly it is good for public relations. Parks where wood is not provided are often compared unfavorably to parks where wood is available. What isn't mentioned is the tendency of campers to build larger-than-necessary fires when the supply is free, to carry wood off with them when they leave in case the next park doesn't supply it, or as noted, to take it home. Local people also may drive into the park and load up the trunks of their cars with firewood. In spite of these problems, some parks supply wood for their campers, especially if a good supply is conveniently located.

In heavily used campgrounds where the demand is great enough, firewood may be sold either by the park staff or the park concessionaire. Two advantages stem from this practice: Campers conserve wood and keep fires smaller, and if they haul wood away with them, they paid for it. It is also possible that a modest profit may be made in the transaction. Agency policy may allow these monies to be used within the park.

# INFORMATION

After visitors have arrived in a chosen park, the need for information does not lessen. It changes, however. It will be more detailed and site specific, but wide ranging, as these visitors seek to satisfy individual needs and interests.

## Outside the Park

Because parks and other recreational lands are prime tourist attractions, entities other than the land-managing agencies themselves may well have information available. The local merchants have a vested interest in the park's success and promote attractions. Some of the merchants may include service stations, grocery stores, libraries, museums with local historical or cultural exhibits, retail outdoor stores, restaurants, and stores which sell fishing and hunting licenses. Many of these local establishments act as a clearinghouse for services directly related to the park and the features inside it, such as guide and outfitter services. Hotels and motels many times provide housing to those visiting the park and compile such information.

Managers should be aware of these sources and provide them with accurate information and regulatory data, promoting not only the park but the success of the local economy in a friendly and cooperative spirit. Certainly these local entrepreneurs will appreciate knowing about any important changes in regulations or other pertinent matters such as road conditions, hazards, or campground closures. If there is no time to maintain such a liaison, volunteers might be found who would handle this for the park.

With the advent of the Internet, those who are tech savvy are learning about projected park visits through many websites. The National Park Service promotes parks and activities at a wide range of its locations through a website at http://www.nps.gov/index.htm, while the Forest Service does the same at http://www.fs.fed.us/, and the Bureau of Land Management provides information at http://www.blm.gov/wo/st/en.html with links to specific states. Outside the United States, Costa Rica, an ecotourism destination, also provide information about parks at http://www.centralamerica.com/cr/parks/index.htm. Other nations are developing websites that promote parks in their own countries. A browser search on the internet will provide information from around the world on parks and progress in administration of those parks. A web presence is necessary to provide information for potential visitors.

## Within the Park

Once visitors reach the park, everyone with whom they speak should be able to supply information. The front-line person is the one who gives visitors a lasting impression of the park. It is important that front-line people know as much as possible and can communicate it.

**Interpretive services.** Increasing visitors' enjoyment of the park, contributing to resource protection, and forwarding understanding of the managing agency's objectives are the goals of interpretive services. In chapter 16, the many personal and nonpersonal approaches to interpretation available to park managers are discussed. Four of these are also mentioned here because of their roles in information dispersal.

**Information duty.** In larger parks, certain people are employed specifically to answer visitors' questions. Often they are located at an entrance station or a visitor center. They may, however, be placed on roving or point duty in order to cover areas of visitor concentration more effectively.

The person on information duty not only greets and informs the new arrivals, but also is a tangible representative of the agency. As such, he or she is performing in the area of public relations perhaps more definitively than anyone else the visitor will meet during the park stay. Appearance and politeness must be stressed. A pleasant, mature personality is indispensable, as the information post will also be a magnet for complaints. Another useful adjunct to information services is a list of nearby services and supplies.

**Publications.** Some areas have a map and informational handout to give to visitors when they enter the park or make contact at an information station. This may be as elaborate as a broadside with color or as simple as a single-folded sheet. It can carry informational, educational, and regulatory messages and will help orient and direct the visitors both geographically and behaviorally.

**Limited-range broadcasting.** Limited-range broadcasting is a means of transmitting information that might be available to managers of certain areas. Visitors can be advised by roadside signs to tune in to a certain frequency to obtain park information. In Canada's Rocky Mountain national parks, limited-range broadcasts are used to warn of avalanche danger as well as to provide information and interpretation.

**Bulletin boards.** Nearly every park unit has a bulletin board that serves as an information center 24 hours a day. Display of park information should be given careful thought. It must be kept to an essential minimum and must look fresh to be accepted as up to date. Regulatory messages are often found here, as is an orientation map.

Bulletin board location is important. Those situated near restrooms get the most attention and, short of ranger or host contact, are probably the prime means of information dispersal in parks and other recreation areas. Bulletin boards present an image of the park and of management style, so it is well worth the time required to keep them in good order.

**Appropriate signage.** Signs have many purposes. They can direct people to sights, facilities, or just to the right campsite. They can warn them of danger, instruct them on sanitation, regulate speed or behavior, educate them on history, geology, culture, and acknowledge founders, donations, or benefactors. Effective signage can reduce the workload of staff by giving answers to those frequently asked questions. Placement and care of all types of signs set an example of respect, or lack of it, for park visitors to observe.

## GETTING FEEDBACK

The park manager, after his or her best efforts, still must wonder how all of these efforts to care for visitors are being received. What does the visitor really think of the experience?

British Columbia's provincial parks have what is called a quality service guarantee. The agency is willing to ask for comments and suggestions about their service. A simple comment card is available to all park visitors. It gives the visitor a chance to complain or compliment, thus providing feedback to the park manager.

### Research the Visitor

Park managers who know something about the makeup of their visitor population and what they do while in the park can better serve visitors' needs. Yet it is important to remember that there is no average visitor. While it may seem obvious to some, different parks have different visitors with different interests. Historical parks may require much more interpretation for the visitor, while parks dependent on natural resources may require more amenities for recreation. Each park and each visitor is unique, and research in one park may not easily transfer to another. It is important to carefully research the characteristics of visitors to meet their needs.

## CONCLUSION

The composite annual total of visitor days to federal, state, provincial, and local park areas in North America is in the billions. During whatever time of the 24-hour period these visitors are in the parks, their care is of prime concern to the park staff.

All too frequently, park professionals secretly or openly express the sentiment that visitors are a necessary evil and the land itself is all important. This attitude must be replaced with one of balanced concern: care for the visitors and care for the resource. The main reason a park agency exists is to provide places where the visitors can recreate. Preservation is paramount and conservation is crucial, but both are for naught if we do not care for our visitor-guests in such a way that they enjoy and appreciate their park.

# REFERENCES

## References Cited

http://www.blm.gov/ut/st/en/fo/moab/recreation/river_recreation/how_to_obtain_a_private.html, Retrieved June 8, 2010

http://www.blm.gov/wo/st/en.html, Retrieved June 8, 2010

http://www.centralamerica.com/cr/parks/index.htm, Retrieved June 8, 2010

http://www.co.santa-cruz.az.us/es/oem/ERPlan/ESF%2016.pdf, Retrieved June 8, 2010

http://www.exploritas.org/, Retrieved June 8, 2010

http://www.fs.fed.us/, Retrieved June 8, 2010

http://www.hiho/stels.com, Retrieved June 8, 2010

http://www.nols.edu/wmi/, Retrieved June 8, 2010

http://www.nps.gov/fees_passes.htm, Retrieved June 8, 2010

http://www.nps.gov/index.htm, Retrieved June 8, 2010

http://www.oregon.gov/OPRD/PARKS/reserve.shtml, Retrieved June 8, 2010

## General References

Architectural and Transportation Barriers Compliance Board. (1985). *Uniform Federal Accessibility Standards.* Washington, D.C.: U.S. Government Printing Office.

Beechel, Jacque. (1975). *Interpretation for handicapped persons: A handbook for outdoor recreational personnel.* National Park Service, Cooperative Park Studies Unit. Seattle, WA: College of Forest Resources, University of Washington.

Geiger, Jr., Roy A., Ellis, W. Kay, & Cromlish, Suzanne. (1989). "Making Your Facilities and Programs Accessible to Disabled Visitors." Proceedings, 1989 National Interpreters Workshop, St. Paul, MN.

Machlis, Gary, & Machlis, Sally. (1974). *Creative design for bulletin boards.* National Park Service. Seattle, WA: Cooperative Park Studies Unit, College of Forest Resources, University of Washington.

National Park Foundation. (1990). *Access to parks and recreation: Disabled people speak out.* Washington D.C.

Park, D.C., Ross, W. M., & Ellis, W. K. (1986). *Interpretation for disabled visitors in the national park system.* Washington D.C.: U.S. Department of the Interior.

Robinette, Gary O. (Ed.). (1985). *Barrier-free exterior design: Anyone can go anywhere.* New York: Van Nostrand Reinhold.

Voorhis, Ken. (1989). "The what, how, and why of elderhostels." Proceedings, 1989 National Interpreters Workshop, St. Paul, MN.

*Chapter Eighteen*

# Sustainability

The concept of sustainable development is still ambiguous even in definition. The 1987 report of the United Nations World Commission on the Environment and Development popularized the term "sustainable development." The report "Our Common Future," also known as "The Brundtlund Report," broadly defined sustainable development as "development that meets the needs of the present without compromising the ability of future generations to meet their own needs" (United Nations, 1987). Discussion following the Brundtlund Report focussed on definition. Miller (1990) offered three definitions culled from 20 sources representing the main thrust in the literature. The first was the definition from the Brundtlund Report. The second defined sustainability as "leaving the same or an improved resource endowment as a bequest to the future." The third definition suggested what the concept of sustainable development does not include and contends that preserving the current stock of natural resources does not define sustainability, because the resource base changes as development proceeds. In this definition, preservation applies only to certain assets. This definition differentiates between economic and noneconomic assets, natural or transformed, recognizes those natural resources that cannot be remedied by some technological process such as the ozone layer, and recognizes that change is an ongoing process.

We, as a global community, continue to debate sustainable development. The debate addresses whether technology can solve the ecological crises we have created and the degree to which we need to restructure belief systems of prosperity, health, and well-being. Global warming, ozone depletion, toxic waste disposal, deforestation, and the loss of biodiversity in flora and fauna all have global significance—a significance about which society is aware, but to which it has failed to respond. Increasingly, organizations representing a variety of disciplines are attempting to include sustainable practices in their operations. However, at both a personal level and organizational level, the problem is perpetuated by our inability to significantly change lifestyles that degrade the long-term livability and sustainability of our communities.

This chapter presents some basic information on sustainability and sustainable policy and practices for federal, state, and local park management agencies, the U.S. National Park Service, U.S. Forest Services, and other organizations. The chapter concludes with visitor and park management frameworks such as LAC and VERP. These frameworks should be viewed as management tools to implement, in part, sustainability concepts. Figure 18.1 presents the relationships, the challenges, and the tools by which parks are managed today. Importantly, one can note the tripartite components of citizen participation, the economic frameworks, and the governmental frameworks. In support of these frameworks, we have environmental management and planning to address the impacts and land stewardship mechanism. Adding pressure to the framework of park management, we can see the political, economic, and public (visitors, extraction interests, etc.). The model suggests that parks can be managed to address impacts associated with overuse and competing interests. The requirement for a park manager is to recognize the complexity and use planning frameworks that provide for effective management of our parks.

## Figure 18.1. The Participants and Pressures on Park Systems and Sustainable Management

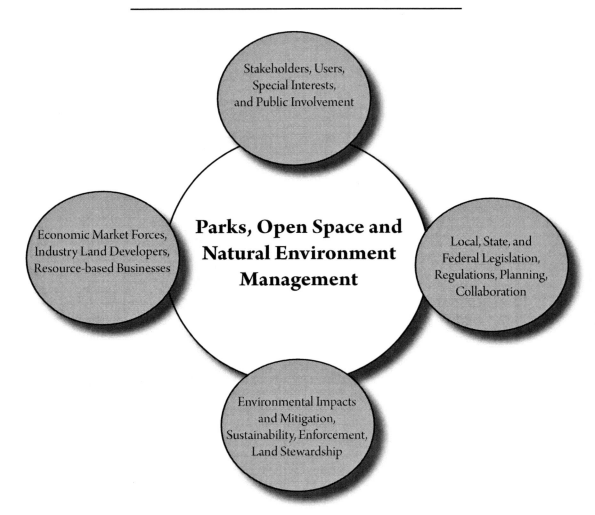

## SUSTAINABLE DEVELOPMENT POLICY AND PRACTICE

Recreation and park organizations have an advantage over many organizations because the core of their mission includes principles of sustainability to maintain, improve, and guide the long-term health and well-being of the entire community and the elements on which they rely—the people, flora and fauna of earth, water, air. These fundamental principles allow us to question the range of user needs and demands. Ecosystem management can be seen as a means rather than an end to provide an avenue for land management agencies to work with an array of constituencies and operationalize the concept of sustainable development. The basic goal of sustainability aligns well with the mission of the National Park Service:

> . . . which purpose is to conserve the scenery and natural and historic objects and the wildlife therein, and to provide for the enjoyment of the same in such manner and by such means as will leave them unimpaired for the enjoyment of future generations (Organic Act, 1916).

In addition, the National Park Service has more recently developed a specific definition in relation to its facility design and operation:

> ... [Sustainability] is a concept that recognizes that human civilization is an integral part of the natural world and that nature must be preserved and perpetuated if the human community is to sustain itself indefinitely. Sustainable design is the philosophy that human development should exemplify the principles of conservation and encourage the application of those principles in our daily lives (NPS, 1993).

An interesting timeline of Zion National Park's history of sustainability follows. One can see the progression and advancement within a short time frame (National Park Service, 2010).

**1995**
- Zion begins working with the Gateway community of Springdale on addressing the issue of an overabundance of motorized vehicles in Springdale and the park.

**1996**
- The Zion National Park Comprehensive Plan addresses sustainable design for transportation and buildings.
- Zion receives "Partnership Leadership for Beyond Park Boundaries" Award from the National Park Foundation. (many more awards would follow).

**2000**
- Opening of the new Zion Canyon Visitor Center
- Running the new Zion Canyon/Springdale propane powered shuttle buses
- New interpretive materials/programs produced on shuttle and visitor center
- Recycling program in cooperation with park concessionaire Xanterra
- Landscaping utilizing native, water efficient, wildlife friendly plants

**2001**
- "Environmental Management System" is mandated in the NPS, requiring purchasing environmentally friendly (green) products, establishing a "green team," green design, recycling, along with other management and policy change.

**2002**
- Zion's general management plan includes a section on "Sustainability." View at http://www.nps.gov/zion/parkmgmt/upload/zion_gmp.pdf

**2003**
- New Emergency Operations Center, a LEED-certified building opens

**2004**
- Zion hosts a "Climate Friendly Parks" workshop with EPA and NPS national office.
- Zion hosts a workshop on "Collaborative Problem Solving" on building partnerships with neighboring public lands managers.

**2005**
- "Environmental Management System" draft report on Zion managing release of green house gas emissions
- Cooperating with Environmental Protection Agency and Utah Dept. of Transportation, Zion instituted a van pool operation to serve employees.
- Purchased Honda Civic Hybrid

**2006**
- Additional interpretive materials prepared, park website pages produced on sustainability in the park and beyond.

**2007**
- Purchased Toyota Prius hybrid
- Continued development of interpretive materials and further development of website
- Formation of "green team" to institutionalize sustainability in the park and beyond
- Developed orientation materials for seasonals and new hires on sustainability in Zion

According to the National Park Service, two events in particular were instrumental in the adoption of the National Park Service's Sustainable Design Initiative. The first was the National Park Service Vail Symposium. In October 1991, five working groups studied "the state of the parks" as part of the organizational renewal activities associated with the 75th anniversary of the National Park Service. They found that National Park Service is being stressed by a variety of factors: population increases; park visitation increases; demographic changes; increased numbers and types of sites to manage; environmental degradation; lack of capable leadership; and the need to protect whole ecosystems.

The concept of sustainable design was mentioned frequently, as it covers a wide range of topics. It integrates principles that enable humans to live in harmony with the rest of the natural world, protecting biodiversity and sharing habitats with other species.

Secondly, in November 1991, the Sustainable Development Initiative was officially launched with a workshop in Maho Bay for the Virgin Islands National Park. This partnership forum included participants from the American Institute of Architects (AIA), American Society of Landscape Architects (ASLA), the Ecotourism Society, National Parks and Conservation Association, National Oceanic and Atmospheric Administration (NOAA), Greenpeace, local representatives from the Virgin Islands, private architectural and engineering (A/E) firms, and ecotourism resort operators. Representatives from various NPS offices included professionals and managers from parks, regional offices, Washington office, and the Denver Service Center.

The participants brought diverse perspectives and ideas to the workshop and subsequently produced the following guiding principles for the application of sustainability to the management of natural and cultural resource-sensitive areas. These efforts resulted in the development of *Guiding Principles of Sustainable Design* design and planning manual in 1993. The manual provides guidelines for interpretation, natural and cultural resources, site and building design, energy management, water supply and waste prevention, and facility maintenance and operations. See http://www.nps.gov/dsc/d_publications/d_1_gpsd_1_ch1.htm for details and guidelines.

The National Park Service has also applied sustainable practices to cultural and historical sites. Figure 18.2 is from the Fort Vancouver National Historic Site (http://www.nps.gov/sustain/spop/ftvan.htm#Bench). One can view the phases—site visit and interviews to review sustainability components, strategy formulation to include best practices as applied to the current situation, and implementation.

## Figure 18.2. Sustainable Practices and Opportunities Plan

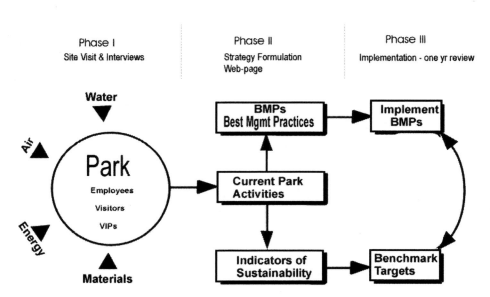

From http://www.nps.gov/sustain/spop/ftvan.htm#Bench, 1998. Reprinted with permission.

The SPOP team at Fort Vancouver developed nine sets of benchmarks and performance targets for areas of improvement based on relevant policies. These benchmarks and performance targets are intended to provide long-term management objectives for improving the sustainability of the park. Table 18.1 is a summary of the nine benchmarks that have been developed for the park.

## Table 18.1. Summary of Sustainability Benchmarks

| Indicator | Current | Benchmark | % Improvement |
|---|---|---|---|
| **Energy** | | | |
| Electrical energy consumption/cost | 288,000 kWh | 175,000 kWh | 40% |
| Fuel energy consumption/cost | 315,000 kWh | 220,000 kWh | 30% |
| Total energy consumption/cost | 603,000 kWh | 425,000 kWh | 30% |
| **Water** | | | |
| Water consumption/cost | 890 HCF | 630 HCF | 30% |
| **Air Quality** | | | |
| Vehicle miles traveled | 125,000 VMT | 87,500 VMT | 20% |
| Emissions generated | N/A | N/A | 30% |
| **Materials** | | | |
| Solid Waste | 33,000 lbs. | 31,000 lbs. | 5% |
| Recycling and Composting | 10,000 lbs. | 14,000 lbs. | 40% |
| Recycled Products | $2,250 | $5,000 | 220% |

From http://www.nps.gov/sustain/spop/ftvan.htm#Bench, 1998.

Oregon Parks and Recreation Department ("State Parks"), according to the Oregon State Parks Trust (http://oregonstateparkstrust.org/OurWork/CentralOR/tumalosp), is continually working to develop model sustainable parks that use sustainable practices that can be monitored, evaluated and replicated in other state parks. These sustainable practices include efforts to reduce waste, eliminate hazardous substances, achieve climate neutrality, enhance ecosystem function and share information with all stakeholders. The State of Oregon State Parks and Recreation Department has developed a sustainability plan. In the section of "What Will Sustainability Look Like? 2014 Objectives" numerous tasks and benchmarks have been listed. These examples below illustrate objectives for the park managers to address waste elimination, hazardous materials reduction and best energy practices.

## Waste elimination examples
- Adaptive reuse of buildings and structures
- Deconstruction to extract high-value materials
- Look to Ft. Stevens as a model recycling program
- Composting is widely used for turf in parks leaving cuttings on lawn when frequently cut or bagged and composted as a future topdressing
- Waterless urinals
- Composting or gray water toilets (Lobby DEQ)
- Low flow and timed metered faucets and shower heads

- Irrigate with gray water when possible (Lobby DEQ)
- Reuse high-value materials
- Extend existing building life, by using long life expectancy building materials
- Audit/maintain water system integrity
- Zero leakage, long life expectancy water and wastewater systems design

## Sample hazardous substance elimination techniques
- No toxic release inventory chemicals
- Use citric acid based disinfectants
- Eliminate use of products in aerosol cans
- Buy cleaning products in bulk and reuse containers
- Paint will meet or exceed California VOC regulations with prevalent use of recycled paint
- Cleaning of spraying equipment does not drain to waterways
- Mow-strips under fence lines and around fixed site furniture to eliminate the need for herbicides
- Only non-toxic wood preservatives

## Some energy best practices
### *Buildings:*
- Day lighting
- Passive cooling
- Fully insulated
- Efficient lighting and appliances
- Occupancy sensors
- On demand hot water
- High-efficiency heating only as needed when heating required

### *Energy Source:*
- 100% renewable
- Generated on site where feasible
- Wind at the coast and gorge
- Solar east of Cascades
- Geothermal (wherever feasible)
- Non-dam small hydro (wherever feasible)

### *Visitor Transportation:*
- Partner with local transit districts to reduce vehicle impact
- Weight fees toward vehicles, not visitors

The Oregon Parks and Recreation Department ("state parks"), according to the Oregon State Parks Trust (http://oregonstateparkstrust.org/OurWork/CentralOR/tumalosp) is continually working to develop model sustainable parks that use sustainable practices that can be monitored, evaluated, and replicated in other state parks. These sustainable practices include efforts to reduce waste, eliminate hazardous substances, achieve climate neutrality, enhance ecosystem function and share information with all stakeholders. The State of Oregon State Parks and Recreation Department has developed a sustainability plan. In the section of "What Will Sustainability Look Like? 2014 Objectives" numerous tasks and benchmarks have been listed. These examples below illustrate objectives for the park managers to address waste elimination, hazardous materials reduction and best energy practices.

The Regional Parks Department in Vancouver British Columbia has initiated an effort to identify policy and practices to effectively advance the economic, environmental and social objectives of a sustainable parks system within greater Vancouver. (http://www.vcn.bc.ca/parkptnr/pdfs/Review_Sustainability_Initiatives.pdf) Results of the effort summarized 12 parks sustainability stories, a list of project and program ideas suggested by staff to advance sustainability and a series of recommendations for how the parks department might effectively support sustainability in the future. Future project and program ideas were identified by staff follow. The ideas are categorized according to general park functions. Many of the ideas could involve members of the Greater Vancouver Regional Development (GVRD) organization who have relevant expertise to contribute. These ideas have been italicized.

## Administration/office
- *Pursue more strategies for paper reduction such as:*
  *—Procedure manuals and training re: printing fewer emails, minimizing paper drafts and soon;*
  *—Purchase digital copiers; and*
  *—Purchase duplex printers to reuse used paper.*
- *Revisit composting at area offices.*
- *Conduct energy audits at area offices.*
- Explore feasibility of workspace swap to reduce commuting.
- *Complete personal waste audits as an educational exercise.*

## Engineering
- Establish CMMS computer system to enhance consistency of preventative maintenance.
- Assign engineering staff smaller cars with trucks accessible on site.
- *Change to "life-cycle-cost" purchasing policy.*
- Expand use of alternate products such as recycled plastic wood.
- *Enhance job site recycling in connection with corporate initiative.*
- An up-to-date map outlining recycling facilities would be a good first step.

## Energy
- *Conduct energy audits on structures to discover efficiency options.*
- *Employ green building standards for the design of the Kanaka Creek Hatchery and the redevelopment of Brae Island and Fort Camping.*
- Consider Minnekhada as a possible pilot of alternate energy and water treatment.

## Water
- Explore the use of electronic sensor flush units for water pumps.
- Emphasize water reduction first.
- Review pumping of lowlands at Colony Farm before replacement. Explore other options for power source such as wind.

## Interpretation/visitor services
- Explore feasibility of expanding interpretation messages to include more urban environmental issues such as invasive species.
- Consider partnering with Naturescape British Columbia to run programs for park neighbours concerning encroachment and habitat enhancement.
- Consider cultural events at outdoor amphitheatres, which work very well in European countries.
- Make sustainability visible. If a pilot project is pursued, make sure that it's visible through the use of signs, announcements, and so on.
- Consider a Sustainability Center, which would highlight Lower Mainland initiatives, including all elements of GVRD functions such as bio-solids, watershed planning and so on.

## Operations
- Investigate smaller and/or alternate fuel trucks where appropriate. Market the trucks with a sticker saying, "I Manage GVRD Parks."
- Compost green materials and explore possibility of selling or taking to charitable facility.
- Revisit seed capital for continued use of HRDC crews.
- Consider recycling of grass clippings.
- Provide additional recycling stations at parks and for housing tenants.

- Continue change from hog fuel to gravel trails.
- Continue exploring pilot ideas such as 4-cycle weed whackers.
- Explore using energy alternatives in parks equipment and operations such as propane, wind, solar and geothermal.

## Park management
- Investigate feasibility of dog feces composting stations at one or more busy off-leash areas.
- Consider greater focus on protecting environmental aspect of parks in the face of growing Lower Mainland population and increased emphasis on revenue generation activities.
- Place additional emphasis on "carrying capacity" research and policy.
- Establish management zones within parks.

## Parks partnership initiative
- Clarify roles through shared decision-making group in order to move toward collaboration with accountability.
- Consider building greater depth of Park Association Boards so that leadership base and number of volunteers can be expanded.
- Provide enhanced support/training for staff to work productively with partner groups and park associations. For example, engage staff as teams together with community development coordinators.

## Revenue generation
- Develop natural heritage guidelines for filming. Possibly give up some revenue in order to uphold conservation values.
- Explore methods to determine "cost of doing business" in order to understand profits versus revenue.
- Explore mechanisms to return profits directly back into parks programs.
- Take forward a key project or two to demonstrate that it's possible to integrate revenue generation with environmental and social park functions.
- Consider cultural events at outdoor amphitheatres in GVRD Parks, which work well in European settings.
- Implement pay parking.
- Utilize Widgeon Marsh to generate revenue by charging for access and ecotours and requiring groups to pay for attendant at company picnics.

## Stewardship and habitat protection
- Expand collection of accurate baseline information and consistently bring results into decision making.
- Afford greater opportunity to monitor and review stewardship actions.
- Create policies for best management practices for all park activities—vegetation management, invasive species management, mountain bike parks, and so on.
- Consider allowing natural succession in some parks as an alternative to active management.
- Pursue further field management programs at Colony Farm and Minnekhada.
- Enhance the ecological contributions of greenways. Conduct research to determine options for integrating ecological values with recreation and alternate transportation.

## Sustainability
- Develop statement of sustainability principles for programs and projects.
- Consider policy direction of "doing less with the same" versus "doing more with less" in order to sustain existing parks and implement sustainability.
- Develop analytical framework to monitor and evaluate sustainability progress. Foster open discussion to review strengths and weakness.
- Develop systems to measure longer-term impacts and intangibles.

## Transportation
- Encourage transit access to regional parks in partnership with TransLink.
- Develop trail from Sperling Skytrain Station to Burnaby Lake.

- Investigate enhanced carpooling between parks and other departments and consider buying vehicles that are smaller and/or utilize alternate fuels.
- Explore implementing public pay parking in order to generate revenue and encourage car pooling and use of transit.

## VISITOR MANAGEMENT FRAMEWORKS

Park planners and managers need processes and methodologies to establish the research and planning documentation to create sustainable places. The following section provides a brief review of some of these frameworks. These frameworks were not developed to support sustainable practices per se, but can be used with sustainability as a goal.

The National Park Service is required by law to address user capacity in planning for parks. Relevant legislation and guidelines include the National Parks and Recreation Act, the Wild and Scenic Rivers Act, and the 1982 Wild and Scenic Rivers Guidelines. These are briefly summarized below.

**1978 National Parks and Recreation Act (Public Law 95-625).** Requires each park's general management plan to include "identification of and implementation commitments for visitor carrying capacities for all areas of the [park]."

**Wild and Scenic Rivers Act, §10(a).** "Each component of the National Wild and Scenic Rivers System shall be administered in such a manner as to protect and enhance the values which cause it to be included in said system without, insofar as is consistent therewith, limiting other uses that do not substantially interfere with public use and enjoyment of these values. In such administration, primary emphasis shall be given to protecting its aesthetic, scenic, historic, archeologic, and scientific features. Management plans for any such component may establish varying degrees of intensity for its protection and development of the special attributes of the area."

**Wild and Scenic Rivers Act, §3(d)(1).** "The [comprehensive management plan] shall address resource protection, development of lands and facilities, user capacities, and other management practices necessary or desirable to achieve the purpose of this act."

**1982 Interagency Guidelines on the Wild and Scenic Rivers Act.** Defines user capacity as: "the quantity of recreation use which an area can sustain without adverse impact on the Outstandingly Remarkable Values and free-flowing character of the river area, the quality of recreation experience, and public health and safety."

The following section is based upon a presentation by Haider (2004) that summarizes the management frameworks used in park and wildland recreation management.

**1979—ROS (Recreation Opportunity Spectrum).** ROS acknowledges the diversity of recreation opportunities and classes. The three key components of recreation management are: (a) setting (opportunity), (b) activity, and (c) experience. There are six land classes, comprised of primitive, semi-primitive (non-motorized and motorized), semi-developed and developed natural, and highly developed. ROS is a tool for landscape/regional recreation planning and zoning of uses. Figure 18.3 depicts these classes and management factors.

**1985—LAC (Limits of Acceptable Change).** There are nine steps in establishing a limits of acceptable change plan. These are: (a) identify areas of concern and issues; (b) define and describe management objectives; (c) select indicators of resource and social conditions such as soil compaction, soil erosion, loss of species, number of encounters etc.; (d) inventory resource and social conditions; (e) specify standards for resource and social conditions that address each indicator chosen, such as no more than x number of encounters with another party per day, no more that x number of trampled plants within a campsite etc.; (f) specify alternatives; (g) identify management actions for each alternative; (h) evaluate and select an alternative; and (i) implement actions and monitor conditions.

**1990—VIM (Visitor Impact Management) which appears to be very similar to LAC—** built specifically for the U.S. Parks Service. It is a prescriptive management approach that utilizes a standardized catalogue of impacts and a list of monitoring tools. This system was replaced by the VERP process, which is listed below.

## Figure 18.3. Example ROS Framework

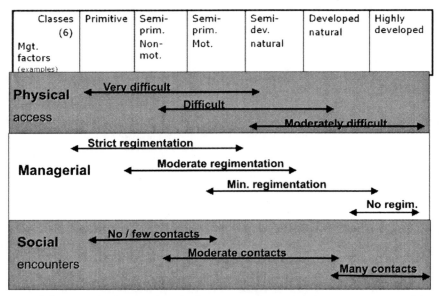

From Clark, R. N., & Stankey, G. H. (1979). *The Recreation Opportunity Spectrum: A Framework for Planning, Management and Research.* U.S. Department of Agriculture Forest Service Pacific Northwest Forest and Range Experiment Station. General Technical Report PNW-98 December. Reprinted with permission.

**1993—VERP (Visitor Experience Resource Protection).** In the VERP framework, user capacity is defined as: "The type and level of visitor use that can be accommodated while sustaining the desired resource and social conditions that complement the purposes of the park units and their management objectives." VERP addresses user capacity by prescribing desired conditions, not by prescribing maximum visitor use (e.g., numbers of people). Monitoring of the desired conditions replaces the monitoring of maximum visitor use. Based on the desired conditions, VERP will identify the types and levels of visitor use that are appropriate, with particular focus on the protection of outstanding and remarkable values. (Yosemite National Park Merced River Plan, retrieved June 7, 2010). Figure 18.4 depicts the VERP process for the Merced River Plan. One can see the progression of tasks—establishing desired outcome, setting indicators and standards to monitor the environment, conducting research and monitoring resources to identify if standards are being met and to determine if visitors are inducing the change or if it is natural.

Table 18.2 from the Yosemite National Park Merced River Plan presents example indicators and standards for the Outstanding Remarkable Values as used in the VERP process. One gains the ability to quantify the changes in order for management to take appropriate action when change occurs.

## CONCLUSION

Issues of sustainability permeate how an organization operates from supporting alternative transportation for employees or members to asset management and investment, from establishing hours of operation to purchasing practices, from defining marketing efforts to physical structure design, from developing a fire management plan to developing a visitor education and interpretation plan. It is easy for one facet of an organization to work in opposition to another facet unless principles of sustainability permeate the organization. Adopting sustainable principles comprehensively is often extremely difficult because an organization relies on established systems that are not sustainable perpetuating the problem.

## Figure 18.4. Example of VERP Framework

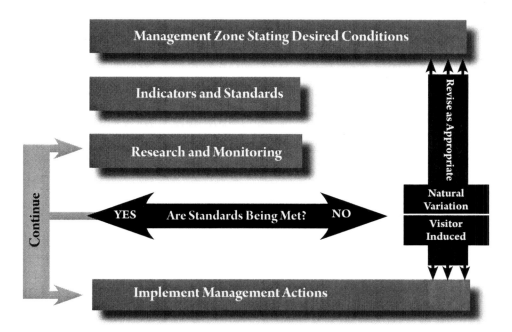

From *Yosemite National Park Merced River Plan, 2000.* Reprinted with permission.

To embrace sustainable development, park managers must look to local resources both within the organization and the region. Local resources often generate local solutions or responses that fit or are specific to that region. Adopting practices from another region does not guarantee fit and can result in importing another set of problems.

Dimensions of sustainability include but are not limited to: (a) energy, (b) wildlife habitat, (c) transportation, (d) education, (e) economy, and (f) citizen participation. These dimensions can help form the basis of park planning and management process. However a thorough understanding of sustainable development and management can not replace an intimate understanding of the place itself.

## Table 18.2. Example Indicators and Standards

**Sample Hydrologic Process Outstandingly Remarkable Value Indicators and Standards**

Indicator:       Fecal coliform bacteria (pristine water quality, Outstandingly Remarkable Value)
Standard:       Fecal coliform bacteria should not exceed a geometric mean of 100/100 ml based on five samples for any 30-day period.

Indicator:       Dissolved oxygen content (pristine water quality Outstandingly Remarkable Value)
Standard:       The dissolved oxygen concentrations should not be reduced below 5.0 mg/l for waters designated as warm waters nor 7.0 mg/l for waters designated cold waters or spawning waters.

Indicator:       Water/stream turbidity (pristine water quality Outstandingly Remarkable Value)
Standard:       Where natural turbidity is between 0 and 5 Nephelometric Turbidity Units (NTUs) increases shall not exceed 1 NTU; where natural turbidity is between 5 and 50 NTUs increases shall not exceed 20%; where natural turbidity is between 50 and 100 NTUs, increases shall not exceed 10 NTUs; where natural turbidity is over 100 NTUs, increases shall not exceed 10%.

**Sample Biological Resource Outstandingly Remarkable Value Indicators and Standards**

Indicator:       The amount of bare ground or exposed roots within riverine habitats (generic biological resource Outstandingly Remarkable Value)
Standard:       No more than 10% of a 100-square-foot-use area shall be composed of bare ground or exposed roots as compared to a similar natural area

**Sample Cultural Resource Outstandingly Remarkable Value Indicators and Standards**

Indicator:       The amount of soil compaction or soil loss (generic cultural resource Outstandingly Remarkable Value)
Standard:       No more than 5% soil loss within a 100-square-foot-use area as compared to a similar natural area

**Sample Recreation Outstandingly Remarkable Value Indicators and Standards**

Indicator:       The number of visitors encountered upon a trail in a specified period of time (generic recreation Outstandingly Remarkable Value)
Standard:       The number of encounters is at a level visitors would find desirable (e.g., an average of no more than five groups within sight and sound along the trail at any given time)

Indicator:       The number of people at one time at a park feature (e.g., the lower Yosemite Fall Bridge), (generic recreation Outstandingly Remarkable Value)
Standard:       The number of people is within a level that visitors would find tolerable (e.g., an average of no more than 25 groups at a park feature at any one time

Indicator:       The number of people encountered while floating on the river during a specific period of time (generic recreation Outstandingly Remarkable Value)
Standard:       The number of encounters is at a level visitors would find acceptable (an average of no more than 10 groups are encountered at any given time)

# REFERENCES

## References Cited

Bower, C. (1992). The Conservative Misinterpretation of the Education and Ecological Crisis, *Environmental Ethics, 14*.

Capra, Fritz. (1975). *The tao of physics: An exploration of the parallels between modern physics and eastern mysticism.* Berkeley: Shambala.

Capra, Fritz. (1982). *The turning point: Science, society, and the rising culture.* New York: Simon and Schuster.

Driver, B. L., Brown, P. J., Stankey, G. H., & Gregoire, T. G. (1987). The ROS Planning System: Evolution, Basic Concepts and Research Needed. *Leisure Sciences, 9*, pp. 201-212.

Haider, W. (2004). Forests for Recreation and Nature Tourism (FORREC). 2nd Management Committee meeting + WGs meeting + Workshop in Edinburgh, Scotland 31 Oct. – 2 Nov., 2004

Kant, I. (1959). *Foundations of the metaphysics of morals.* New York: Library of Liberal Arts Press.

Kuhn, Thomas. (1962). *The structure of scientific revolutions.* Chicago: University of Chicago Press.

Knowles-Lankford, J., & Lankford, S. (1995). Sustainable Practices: Implications for Tourism and Recreation Development. In McCool, S. & Watson, A. (Eds.), *Linking tourism, the environment, and sustainability.* Topical Volume of compiled papers from a special session of the annual meeting of the National Recreation and Park Association. 1994 October 12-14; Minneapolis, MN. Gen. Tech. Rep. INT-GTR-323. Ogden, UT: U.S. Department of Agriculture; Forest Service; Intermountain Research Station.

Nash, Roderick F. (1989). *The rights of nature.* Madison: University of Wisconsin Press.

National Park Service. (1993). Guiding Principles of Sustainable Design, http://www.nps.gov/dsc/d_publications/d_1_gpsd.htm, retrieved June 8, 2010

National Park Service. (1998). Fort Vancouver National Historic Site, Sustainable Practices and Opportunities Plan (SPOP), Phase 1 Report, http://www.nps.gov/sustain/spop/ftvan.htm#Bench, retrieved June 8, 2010

National Park Service. (2010). The Emerging Culture of Sustainability. http://www.nps.gov/zion/historyculture/the-emerging-culture-of-sustainability.htm, retrieved June 8, 2010

Oregon Parks and Recreation Department. (2002), Framework for a Sustainable Future, http://www.oregonstateparks.org/images/pdf/sustainability.pdf

Orr, David W. (1992a). Education and the ecological design arts. *Conservation Biology 6*(2):162-164.

Orr, David W. (1992b). *Ecological literacy.* Albany: State University of New York Press.

Orr, David W. (1993). The problem of disciplines/the discipline of problems. *Conservation Biology 7*(1):10-12.

Peterson, Brenda. (1993). We must control ourselves, not wolves. *Seattle Times*, January 27.

Randolf, J. (2004). *Environmental land use planning and management.* Washington, D.C.: Island Press.

Starkey, E., & Tappeiner, J. C. (1992). *Recovery plan for the northern spotted owl: Draft.* U.S. Department of the Interior, Washington, D.C.

Taylor, P. (1981). The ethics of respect for nature. *Environmental Ethics 3*(Fall):197-218.

van Hagen, B., Kellogg, E., & Frerichs, E. (2003). *Rebuilt green.* Portland, OR: Ecotrust.

Yosemite National Park Merced River Plan, Retrieved from http://www.nps.gov/archive/yose/planning/mrp/2000/final_mpr/html/mrpverp.htm, June 6, 2010.

# Index

## *About the Authors*

**SAM LANKFORD** holds a Ph.D. in leisure studies and services (with a specialization in planning) and a master's degree in urban planning from the University of Oregon, as well as a MA in recreation and park planning and a BA in community planning from California State University, Chico. He has been a practicing planner in both staff and consulting roles in California, Oregon, Washington, Hawaii, and Iowa. He has conducted numerous studies, plans, and training programs in those states and other countries such as The Netherlands, Greece, Canada, Vietnam, Taiwan, Korea, Japan, and Thailand.

**JILL LANKFORD** is the director of the University of Northern Iowa's Recreation Research and Service. She holds a master's degree in urban planning and a master's degree in landscape architecture from the University of Oregon. She received her BA in recreation administration from California State University at Chico. Jill has been a director of recreation and recreation and park consultant for a number of communities. She has conducted numerous studies and park development plans in California, Oregon, Hawaii, and Iowa. She has conducted training programs in South Africa, Bolivia, and Vietnam, as well as in the United States.

**DANIEL A. WHEELER** holds an Ed.D. in leisure services from the University of Northern Iowa, and is ABD from the University of Oregon. He holds an MA from Brigham Young University in recreation management, outdoor education, and a BA from Brigham Young University in youth leadership. Dan has extensive experience in outdoor recreation leading groups in adventure recreation and has consulted for a number of organizations in parks and recreation. He has led training sessions and presented in Canada, Korea, Japan, and the United States.